You're So Cool

vol. 4

YoungHee Lee

Yen Press

THE STORY SO FAR...

WITH TOP-NOTCH LOOKS, THE BEST GRADES, AND THE MOST SHINING DISPOSITION, SEUNG-HA RYU WAS 100% PRINCE QUALITY, NO MATTER HOW YOU LOOKED AT IT. BUT NAN-WOO HAD NO IDEA THAT FALLING IN LOVE WITH THIS PRINCE AMONG PRINCES MEANT FALLING INTO THE PITS OF HELL. WITHOUT KNOWING WHY SEUNG-HA AGREED TO GO OUT WITH HER IN THE FIRST PLACE, NAN-WOO QUICKLY DISCOVERED THAT HER PRINCE WAS A TWO-FACED JERK LEADING A DOUBLE LIFE! BUT AS THE TWO CONTINUED TO CHASE AFTER ONE ANOTHER IN THEIR CHAOTIC RELATIONSHIP, THEIR FEELINGS FOR EACH OTHER GREW. AND FOR NOW, NAN-WOO'S DREAM OF HAVING A HOT BOYFRIEND HAS COME TRUE. AFTER MEETING NAN-WOO'S UNIQUE FAMILY AT HER BIRTHDAY PARTY, EVEN THE COLD-HEARTED SEUNG-HA BEGAN TO MELT A BIT FROM THEIR WARMTH . . . BUT SEUNG-HA, WHY ARE THERE STILL SOME SHADOWS LURKING ON YOUR FACE?! NAN-WOO, GO FORTH AND CONQUER!

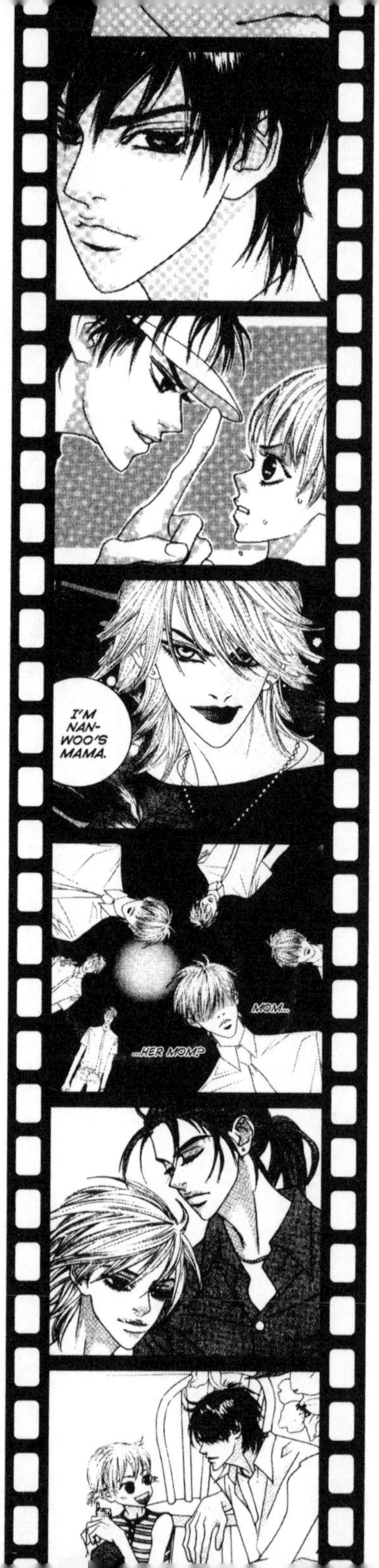
I'M NAN-WOO'S MAMA.
MOM...
...HER MOM?

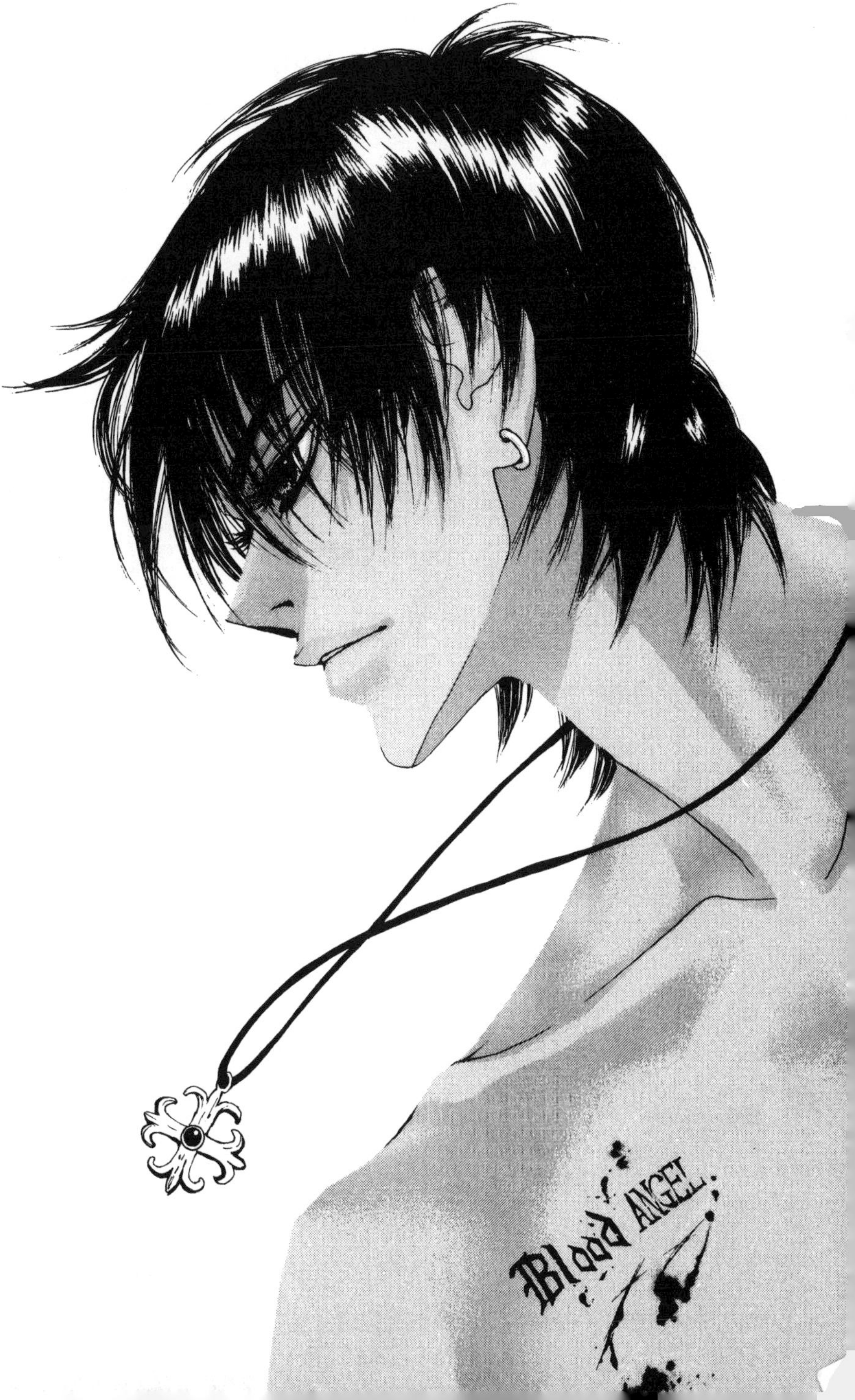
Blood ANGEL.

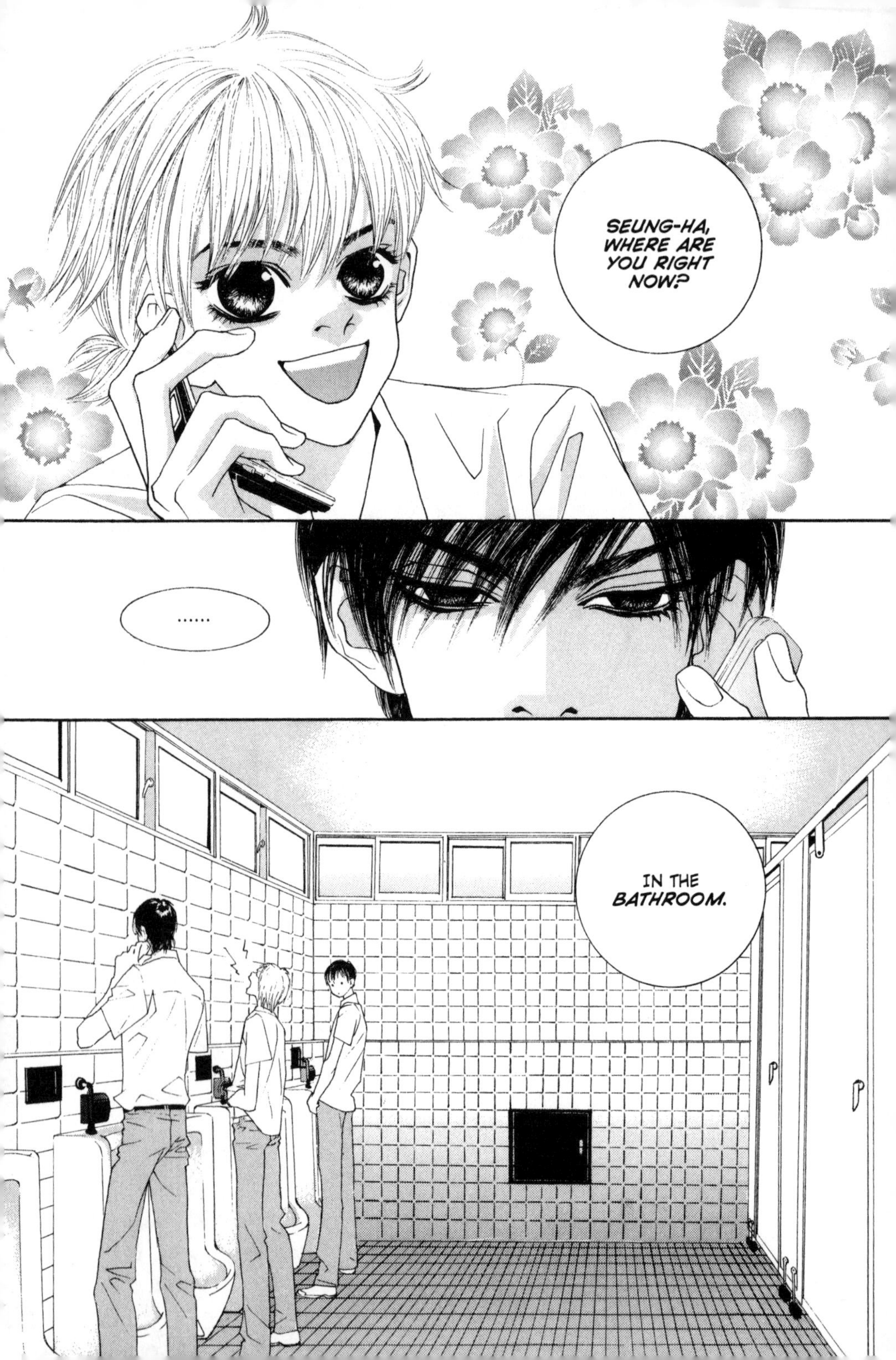
SEUNG-HA, WHERE ARE YOU RIGHT NOW?
......
IN THE BATHROOM.

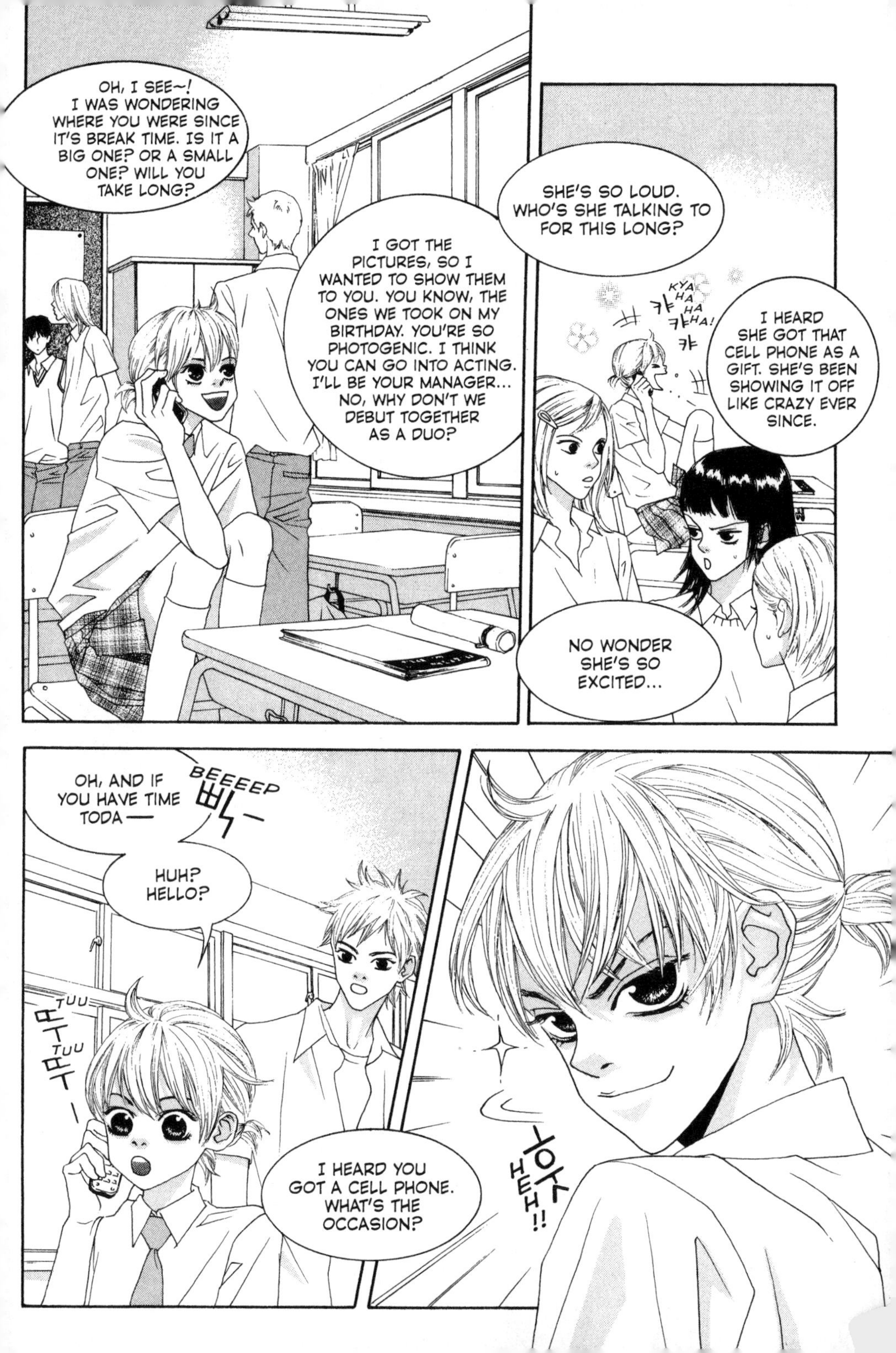
OH, I SEE~! I WAS WONDERING WHERE YOU WERE SINCE IT'S BREAK TIME. IS IT A BIG ONE? OR A SMALL ONE? WILL YOU TAKE LONG?
I GOT THE PICTURES, SO I WANTED TO SHOW THEM TO YOU. YOU KNOW, THE ONES WE TOOK ON MY BIRTHDAY. YOU'RE SO PHOTOGENIC. I THINK YOU CAN GO INTO ACTING. I'LL BE YOUR MANAGER... NO, WHY DON'T WE DEBUT TOGETHER AS A DUO?
SHE'S SO LOUD. WHO'S SHE TALKING TO FOR THIS LONG?
캬 캬 캬 캬
KYA HA HA HA!
I HEARD SHE GOT THAT CELL PHONE AS A GIFT. SHE'S BEEN SHOWING IT OFF LIKE CRAZY EVER SINCE.
NO WONDER SHE'S SO EXCITED...
OH, AND IF YOU HAVE TIME TODA—
삐-
BEEEEP
HUH? HELLO?
뚜 뚜
TUU TUU
I HEARD YOU GOT A CELL PHONE. WHAT'S THE OCCASION?
HEH!!

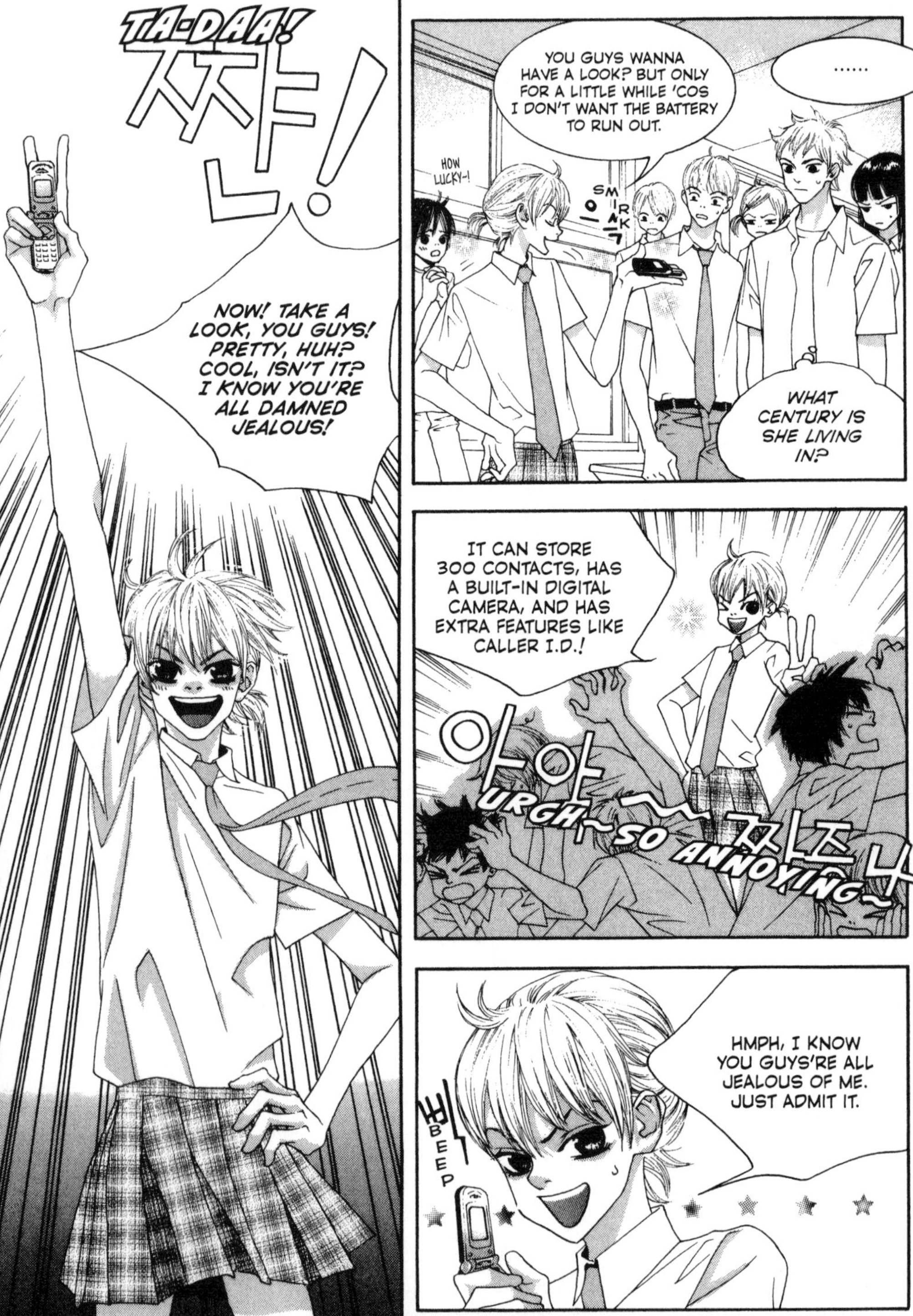
TA-DAA!
짜잔!
NOW! TAKE A LOOK, YOU GUYS! PRETTY, HUH? COOL, ISN'T IT? I KNOW YOU'RE ALL DAMNED JEALOUS!
YOU GUYS WANNA HAVE A LOOK? BUT ONLY FOR A LITTLE WHILE 'COS I DON'T WANT THE BATTERY TO RUN OUT.
......
HOW LUCKY~!
SMIRK
WHAT CENTURY IS SHE LIVING IN?
IT CAN STORE 300 CONTACTS, HAS A BUILT-IN DIGITAL CAMERA, AND HAS EXTRA FEATURES LIKE CALLER I.D.!
URGH~SO ANNOYING~
HMPH, I KNOW YOU GUYS'RE ALL JEALOUS OF ME. JUST ADMIT IT.
BEEP

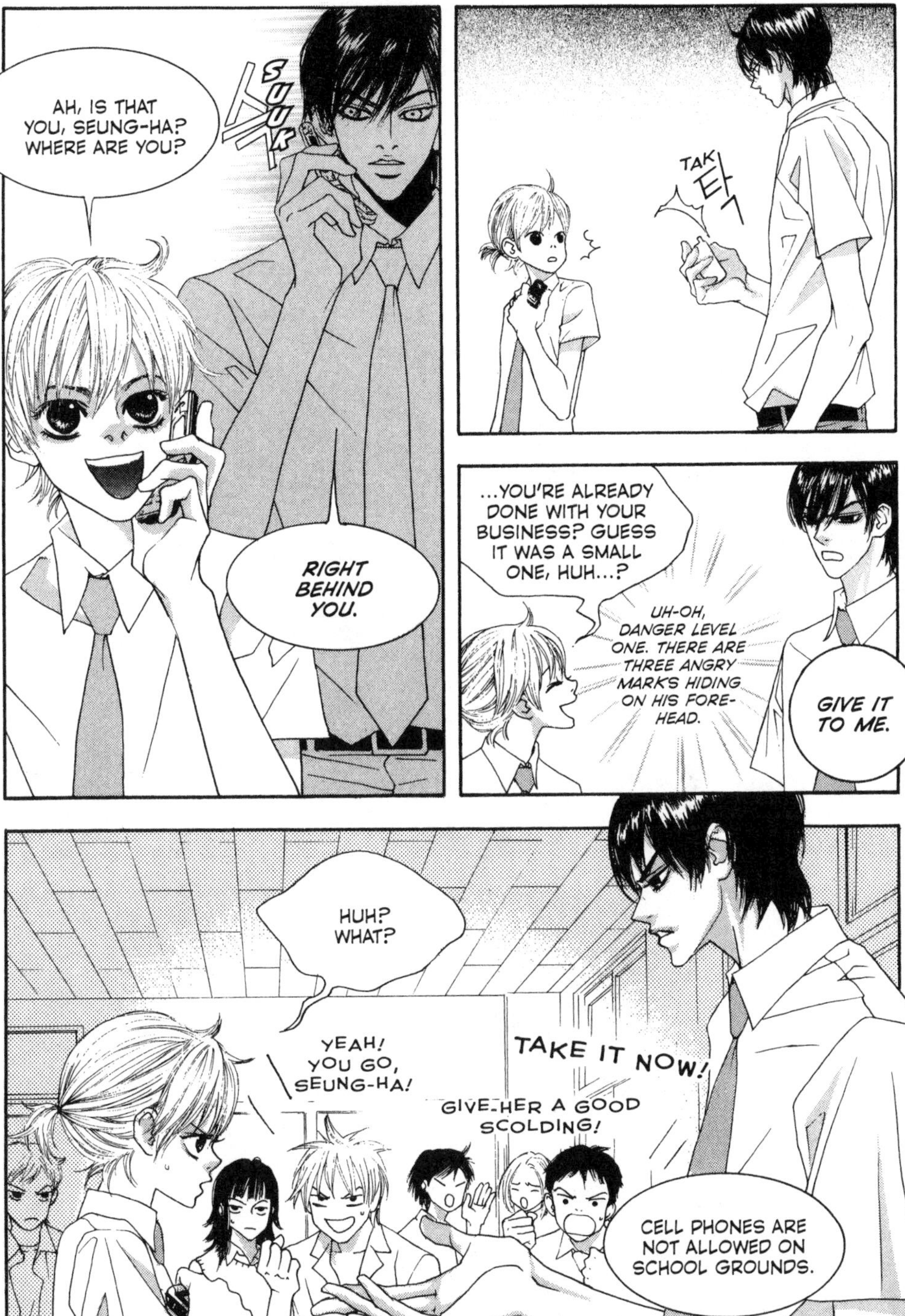
AH, IS THAT YOU, SEUNG-HA? WHERE ARE YOU?
SUUK
RIGHT BEHIND YOU.
TAK
탁
...YOU'RE ALREADY DONE WITH YOUR BUSINESS? GUESS IT WAS A SMALL ONE, HUH...?
UH-OH, DANGER LEVEL ONE. THERE ARE THREE ANGRY MARKS HIDING ON HIS FORE-HEAD.
GIVE IT TO ME.
HUH? WHAT?
YEAH! YOU GO, SEUNG-HA!
TAKE IT NOW!
GIVE HER A GOOD SCOLDING!
CELL PHONES ARE NOT ALLOWED ON SCHOOL GROUNDS.

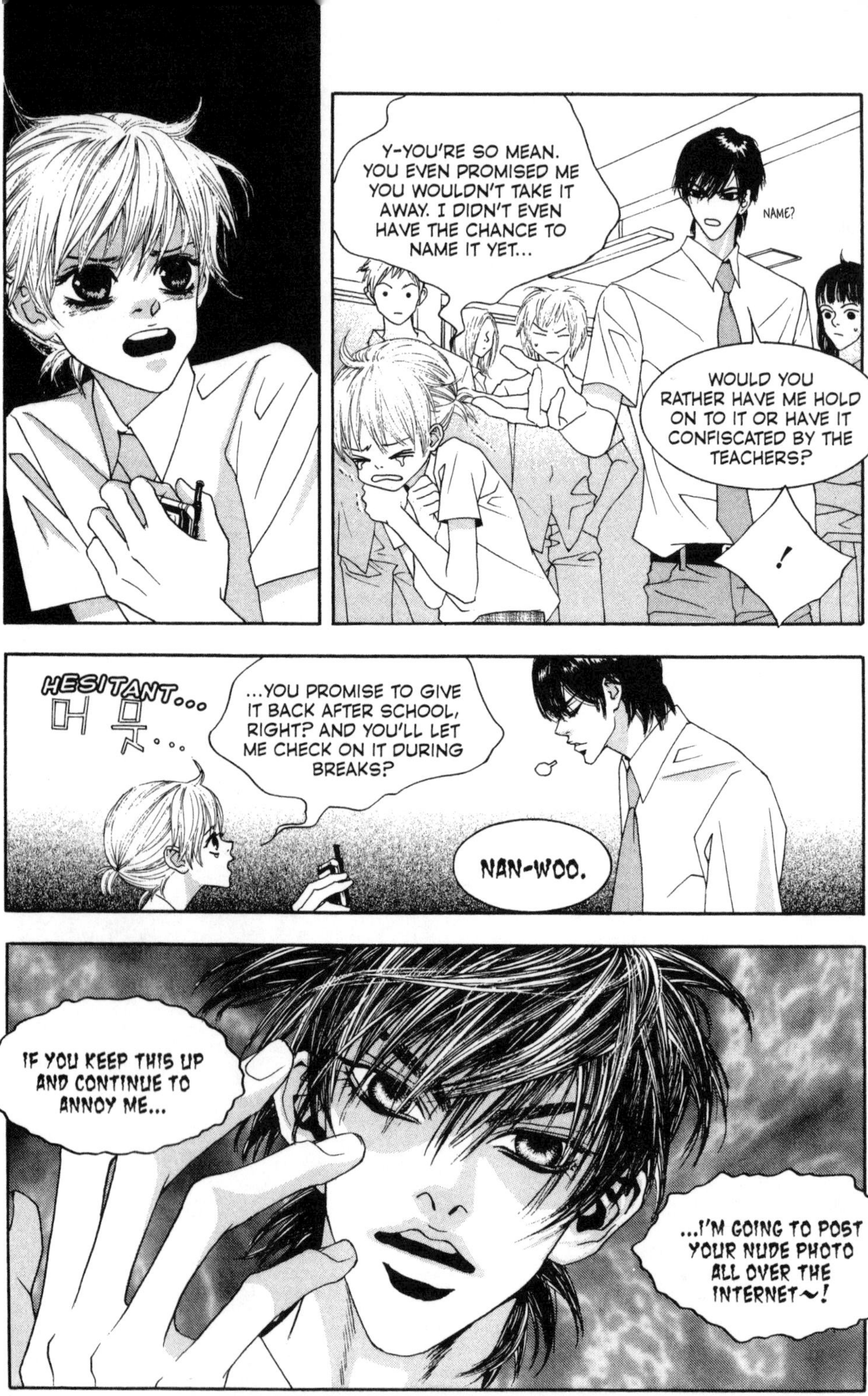
Y-YOU'RE SO MEAN. YOU EVEN PROMISED ME YOU WOULDN'T TAKE IT AWAY. I DIDN'T EVEN HAVE THE CHANCE TO NAME IT YET...
NAME?
WOULD YOU RATHER HAVE ME HOLD ON TO IT OR HAVE IT CONFISCATED BY THE TEACHERS?
!
HESITANT...
머뭇...
...YOU PROMISE TO GIVE IT BACK AFTER SCHOOL, RIGHT? AND YOU'LL LET ME CHECK ON IT DURING BREAKS?
NAN-WOO.
IF YOU KEEP THIS UP AND CONTINUE TO ANNOY ME...
...I'M GOING TO POST YOUR NUDE PHOTO ALL OVER THE INTERNET~!

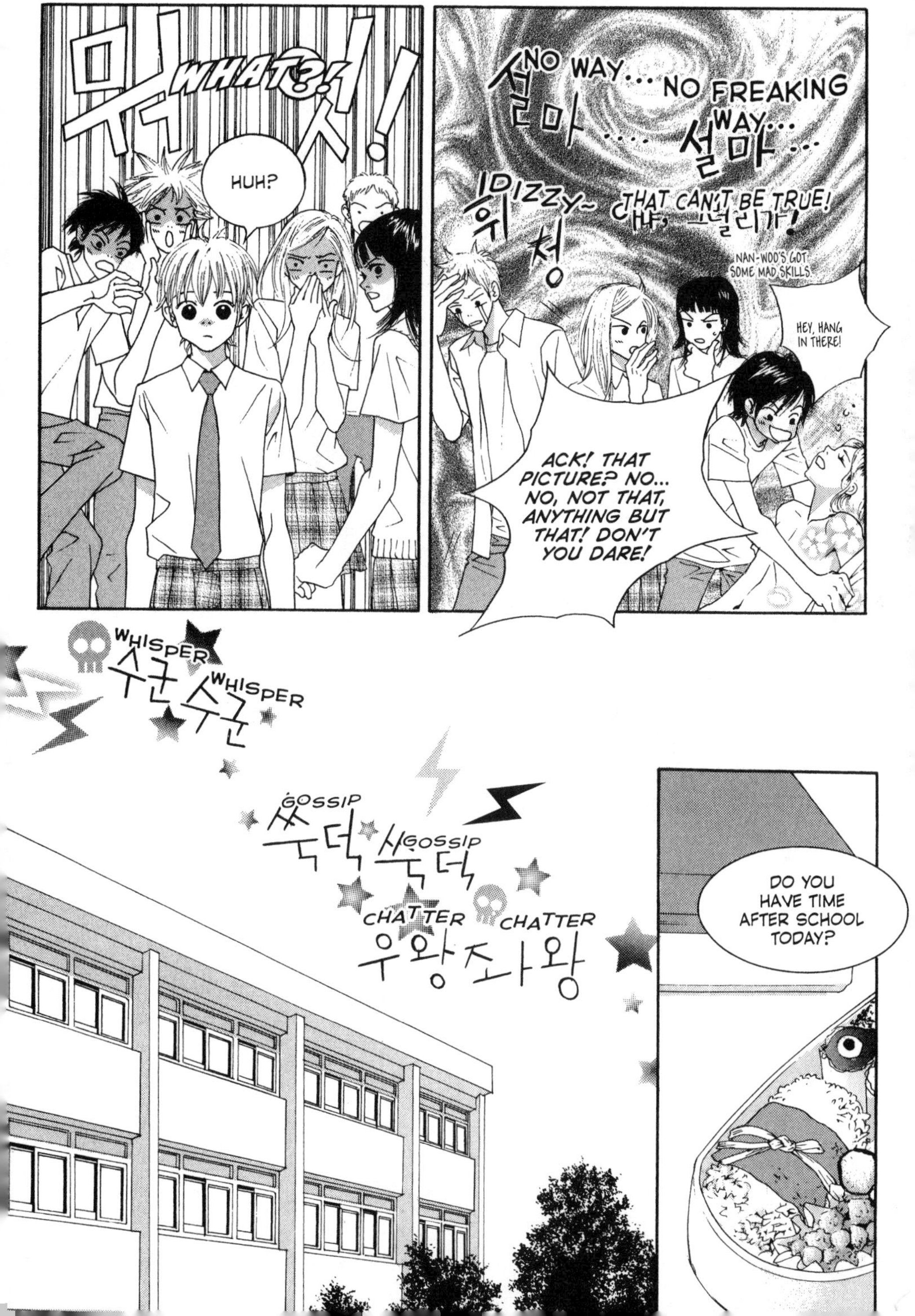

WHAT?!
HUH?
NO WAY... NO FREAKING WAY...
설마 ..... 설마 ...
DIZZY~
휘청
THAT CAN'T BE TRUE!
NAN-WOO'S GOT SOME MAD SKILLS.
HEY, HANG IN THERE!
ACK! THAT PICTURE? NO... NO, NOT THAT, ANYTHING BUT THAT! DON'T YOU DARE!
WHISPER WHISPER
수군수군
GOSSIP GOSSIP
쑥덕쑥덕
CHATTER CHATTER
우왕좌왕
DO YOU HAVE TIME AFTER SCHOOL TODAY?

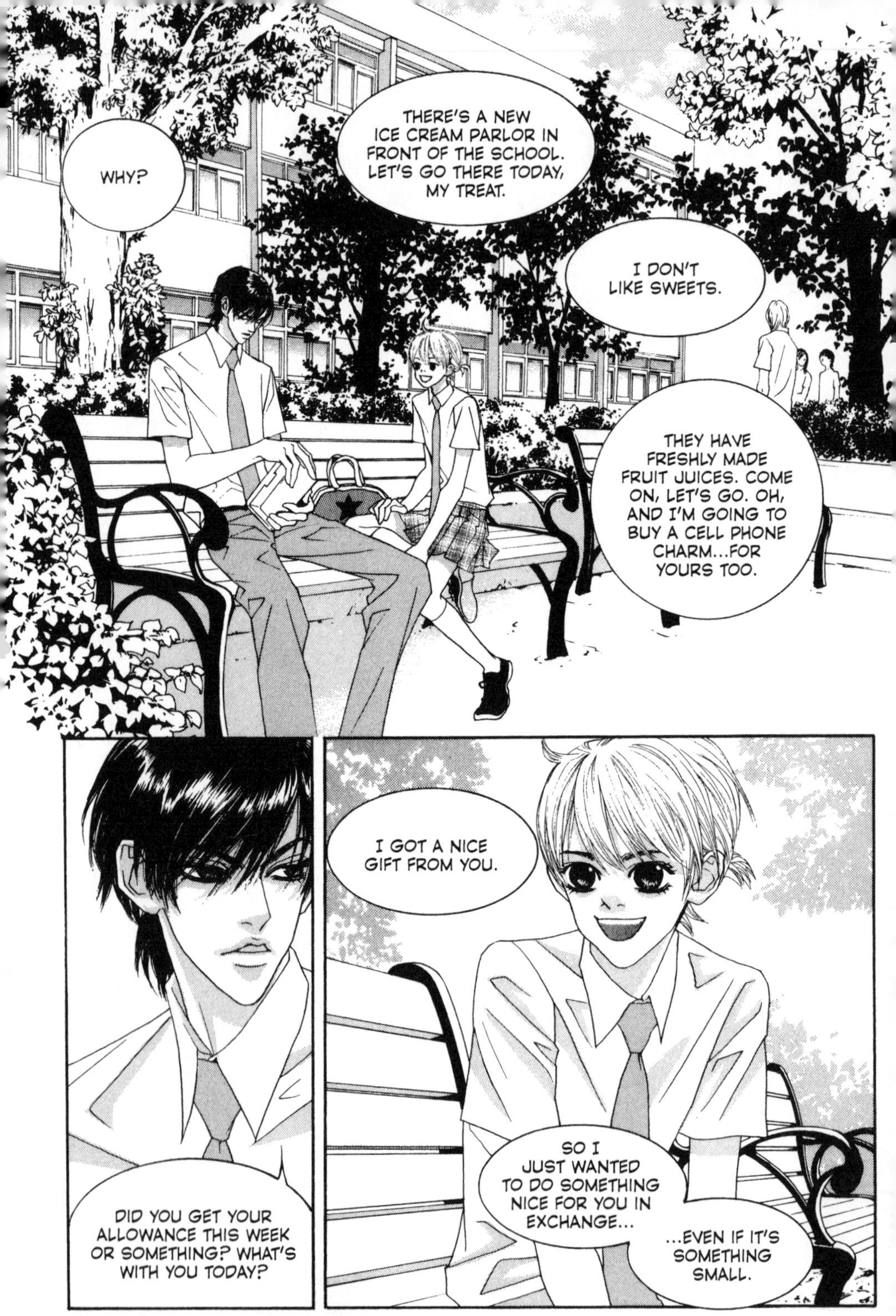
WHY?
THERE'S A NEW ICE CREAM PARLOR IN FRONT OF THE SCHOOL. LET'S GO THERE TODAY, MY TREAT.
I DON'T LIKE SWEETS.
THEY HAVE FRESHLY MADE FRUIT JUICES. COME ON, LET'S GO. OH, AND I'M GOING TO BUY A CELL PHONE CHARM...FOR YOURS TOO.
DID YOU GET YOUR ALLOWANCE THIS WEEK OR SOMETHING? WHAT'S WITH YOU TODAY?
I GOT A NICE GIFT FROM YOU.
SO I JUST WANTED TO DO SOMETHING NICE FOR YOU IN EXCHANGE...
...EVEN IF IT'S SOMETHING SMALL.

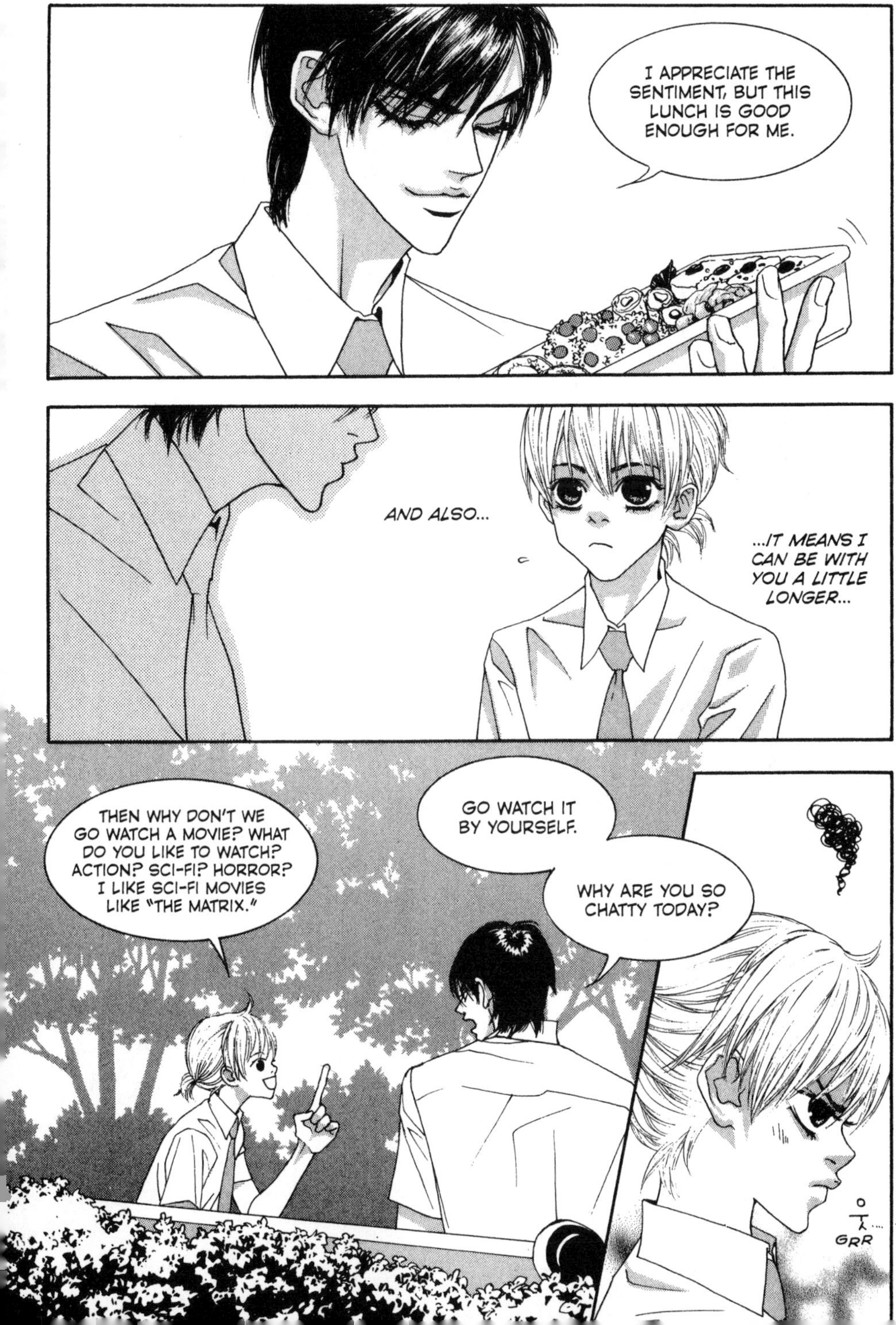
I APPRECIATE THE SENTIMENT, BUT THIS LUNCH IS GOOD ENOUGH FOR ME.
AND ALSO...
...IT MEANS I CAN BE WITH YOU A LITTLE LONGER...
THEN WHY DON'T WE GO WATCH A MOVIE? WHAT DO YOU LIKE TO WATCH? ACTION? SCI-FI? HORROR? I LIKE SCI-FI MOVIES LIKE "THE MATRIX."
GO WATCH IT BY YOURSELF.
WHY ARE YOU SO CHATTY TODAY?
GRR

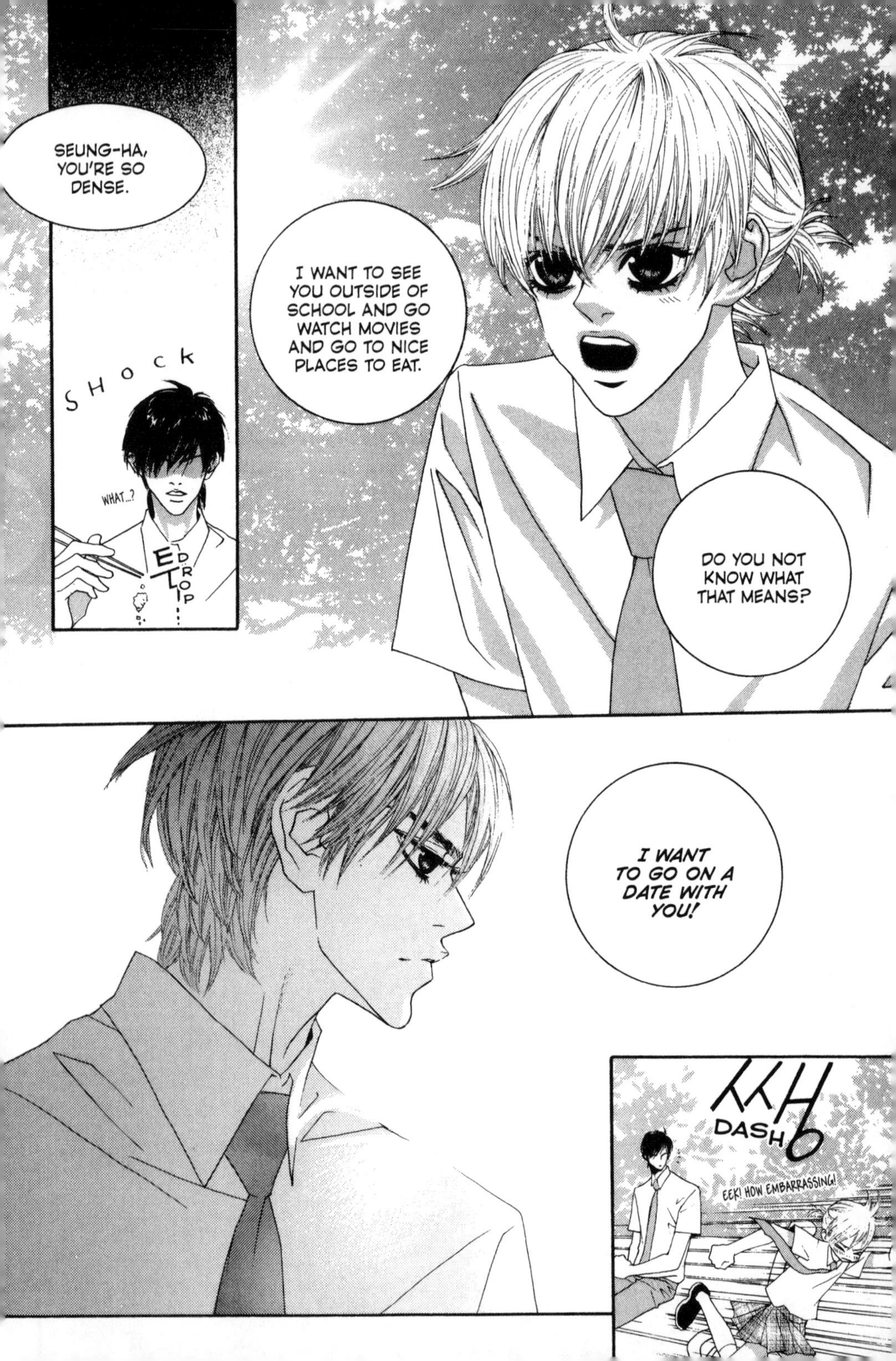
SEUNG-HA, YOU'RE SO DENSE.
SHOCK
WHAT...?
DROP
I WANT TO SEE YOU OUTSIDE OF SCHOOL AND GO WATCH MOVIES AND GO TO NICE PLACES TO EAT.
DO YOU NOT KNOW WHAT THAT MEANS?
I WANT TO GO ON A DATE WITH YOU!
DASH
EEK! HOW EMBARRASSING!

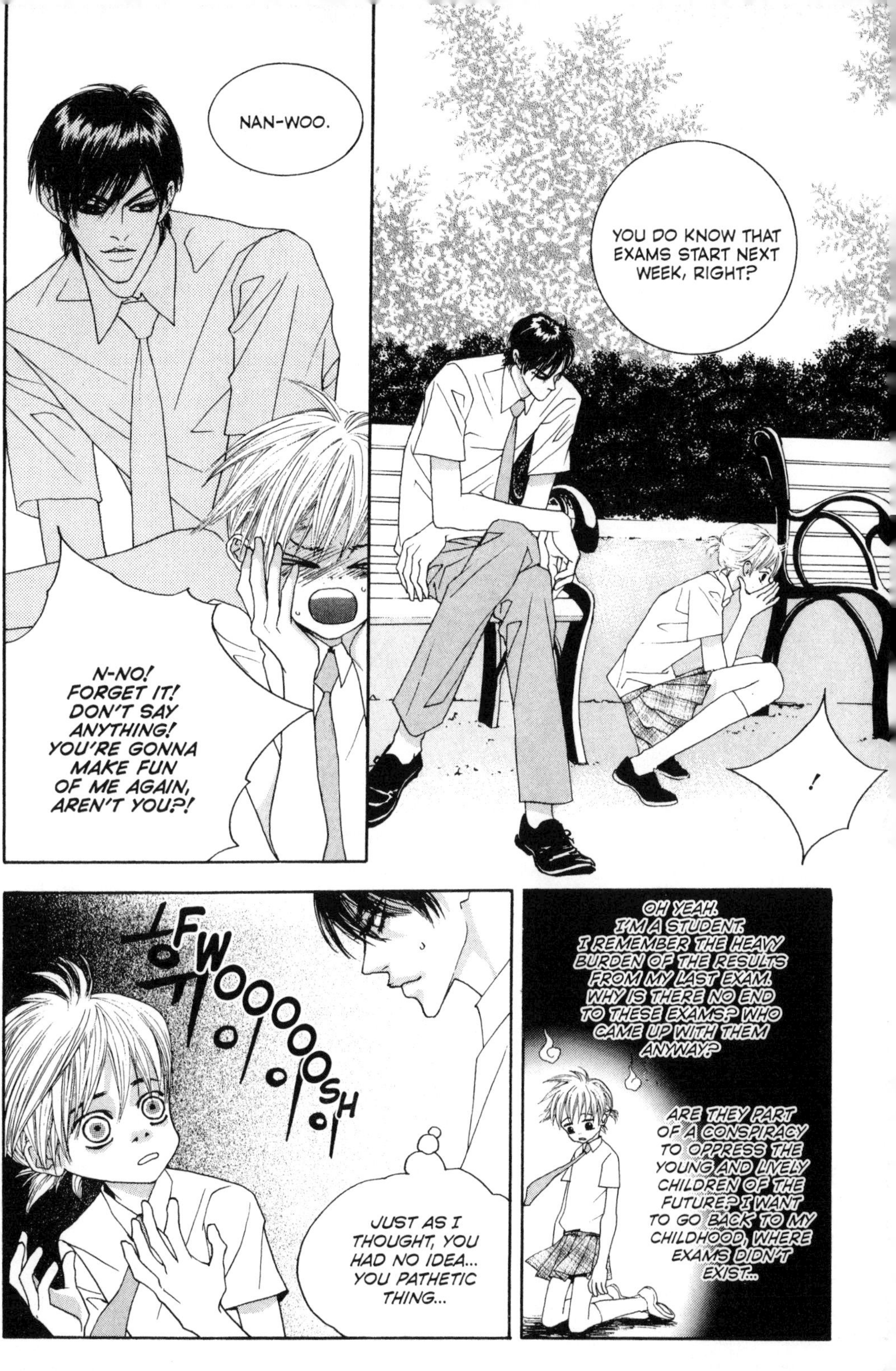
NAN-WOO.
N-NO! FORGET IT! DON'T SAY ANYTHING! YOU'RE GONNA MAKE FUN OF ME AGAIN, AREN'T YOU?!
YOU DO KNOW THAT EXAMS START NEXT WEEK, RIGHT?
!
FWOOOOOOSH
JUST AS I THOUGHT, YOU HAD NO IDEA... YOU PATHETIC THING...
OH YEAH. I'M A STUDENT. I REMEMBER THE HEAVY BURDEN OF THE RESULTS FROM MY LAST EXAM. WHY IS THERE NO END TO THESE EXAMS? WHO CAME UP WITH THEM ANYWAY?
ARE THEY PART OF A CONSPIRACY TO OPPRESS THE YOUNG AND LIVELY CHILDREN OF THE FUTURE? I WANT TO GO BACK TO MY CHILDHOOD, WHERE EXAMS DIDN'T EXIST...

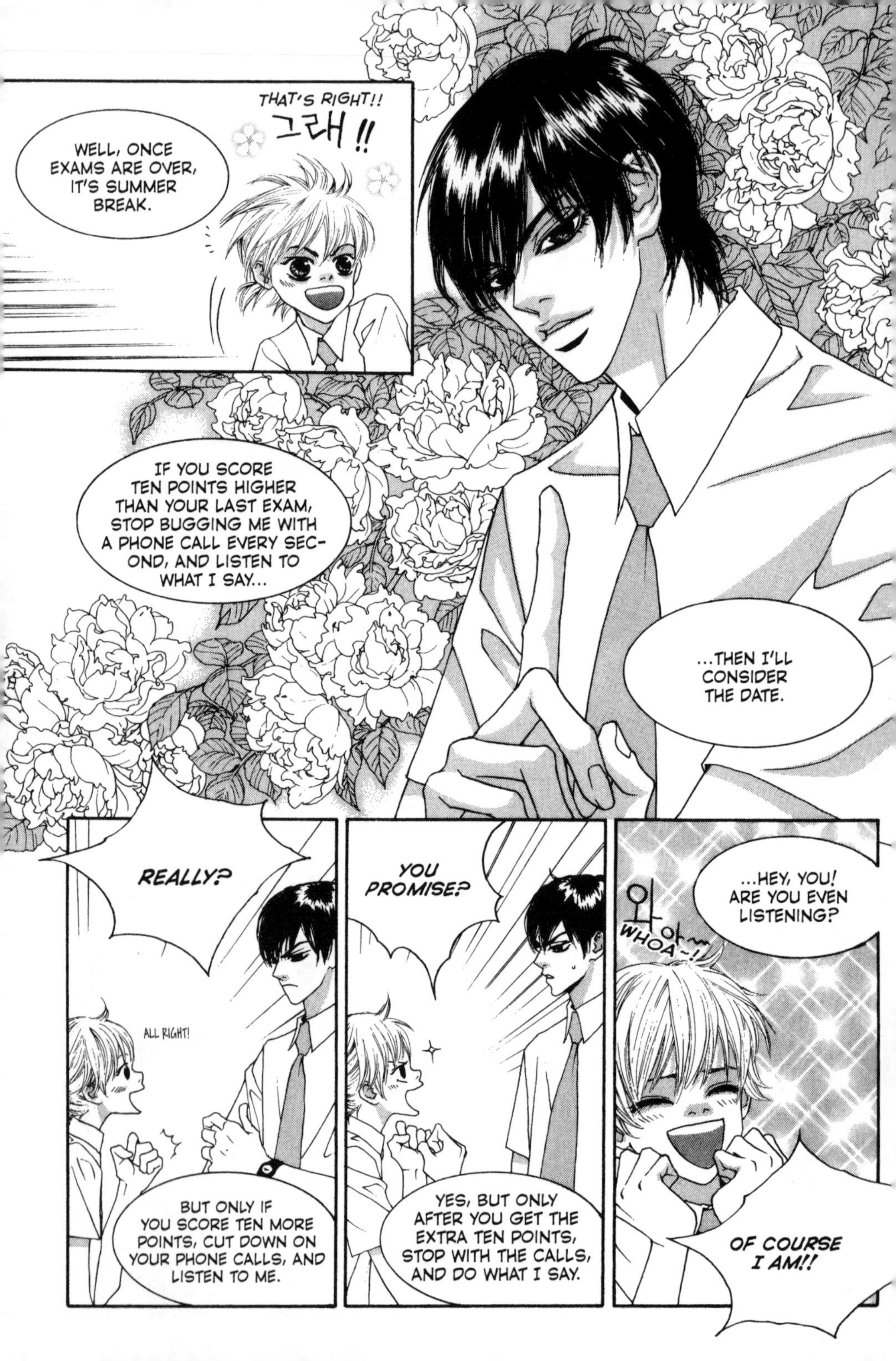

WELL, ONCE EXAMS ARE OVER, IT'S SUMMER BREAK.
THAT'S RIGHT!!
그래 !!
IF YOU SCORE TEN POINTS HIGHER THAN YOUR LAST EXAM, STOP BUGGING ME WITH A PHONE CALL EVERY SEC-OND, AND LISTEN TO WHAT I SAY...
...THEN I'LL CONSIDER THE DATE.
REALLY?
ALL RIGHT!
BUT ONLY IF YOU SCORE TEN MORE POINTS, CUT DOWN ON YOUR PHONE CALLS, AND LISTEN TO ME.
YOU PROMISE?
YES, BUT ONLY AFTER YOU GET THE EXTRA TEN POINTS, STOP WITH THE CALLS, AND DO WHAT I SAY.
와아~
WHOA~!!
...HEY, YOU! ARE YOU EVEN LISTENING?
OF COURSE I AM!!

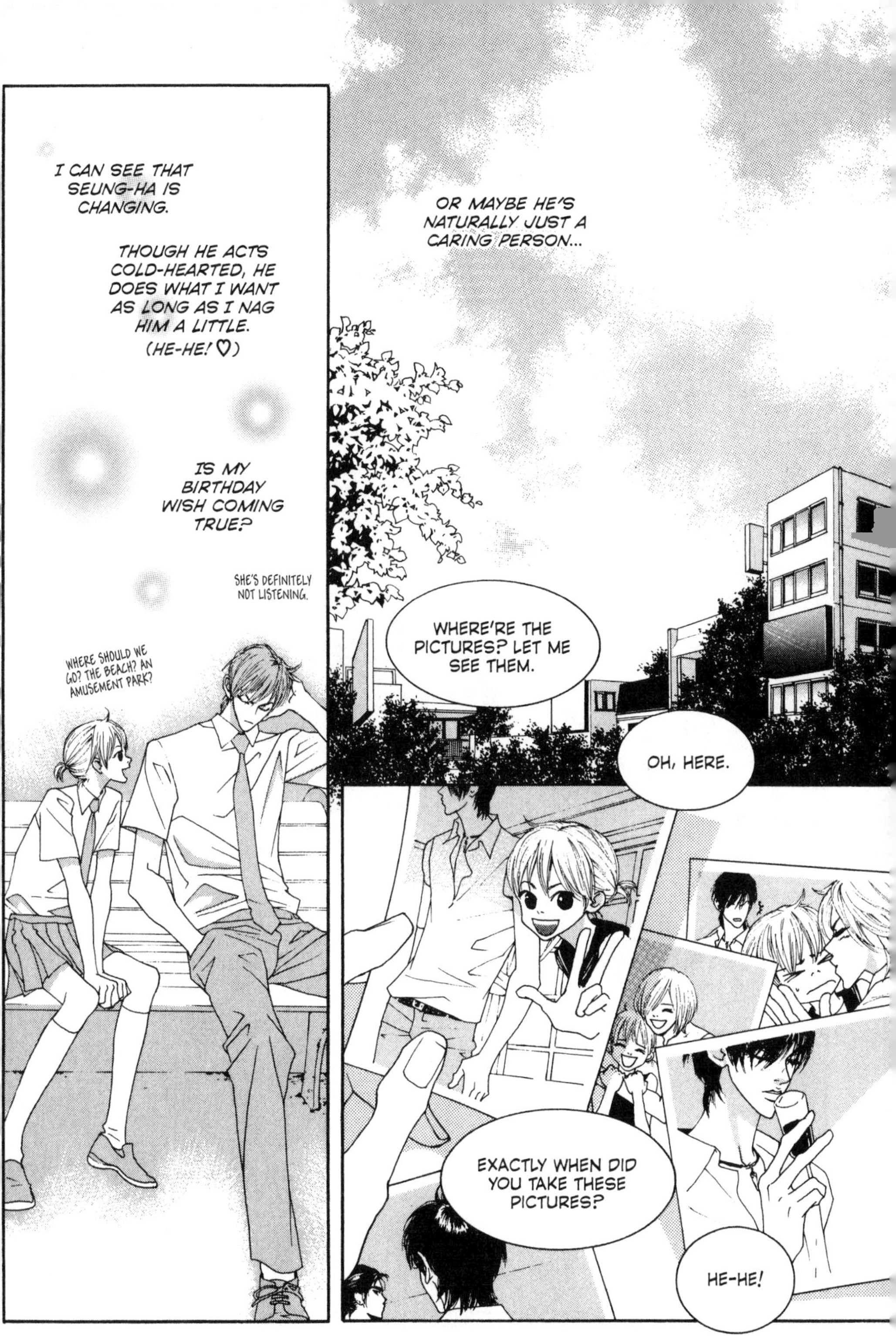
I CAN SEE THAT SEUNG-HA IS CHANGING.
THOUGH HE ACTS COLD-HEARTED, HE DOES WHAT I WANT AS LONG AS I NAG HIM A LITTLE.
(HE-HE! ♡)
IS MY BIRTHDAY WISH COMING TRUE?
SHE'S DEFINITELY NOT LISTENING.
WHERE SHOULD WE GO? THE BEACH? AN AMUSEMENT PARK?
OR MAYBE HE'S NATURALLY JUST A CARING PERSON...
WHERE'RE THE PICTURES? LET ME SEE THEM.
OH, HERE.
EXACTLY WHEN DID YOU TAKE THESE PICTURES?
HE-HE!

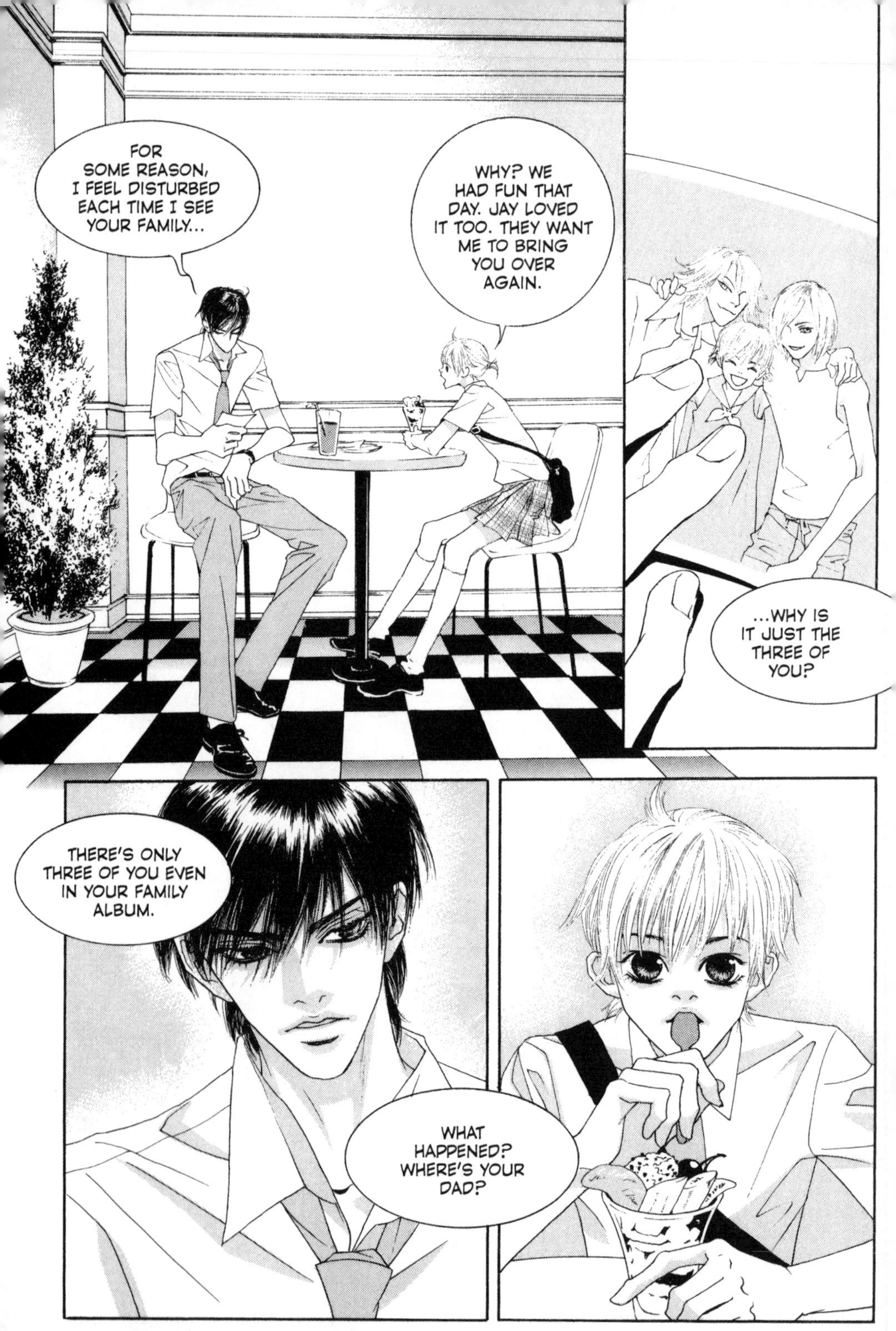
FOR SOME REASON, I FEEL DISTURBED EACH TIME I SEE YOUR FAMILY...
WHY? WE HAD FUN THAT DAY. JAY LOVED IT TOO. THEY WANT ME TO BRING YOU OVER AGAIN.
...WHY IS IT JUST THE THREE OF YOU?
THERE'S ONLY THREE OF YOU EVEN IN YOUR FAMILY ALBUM.
WHAT HAPPENED? WHERE'S YOUR DAD?

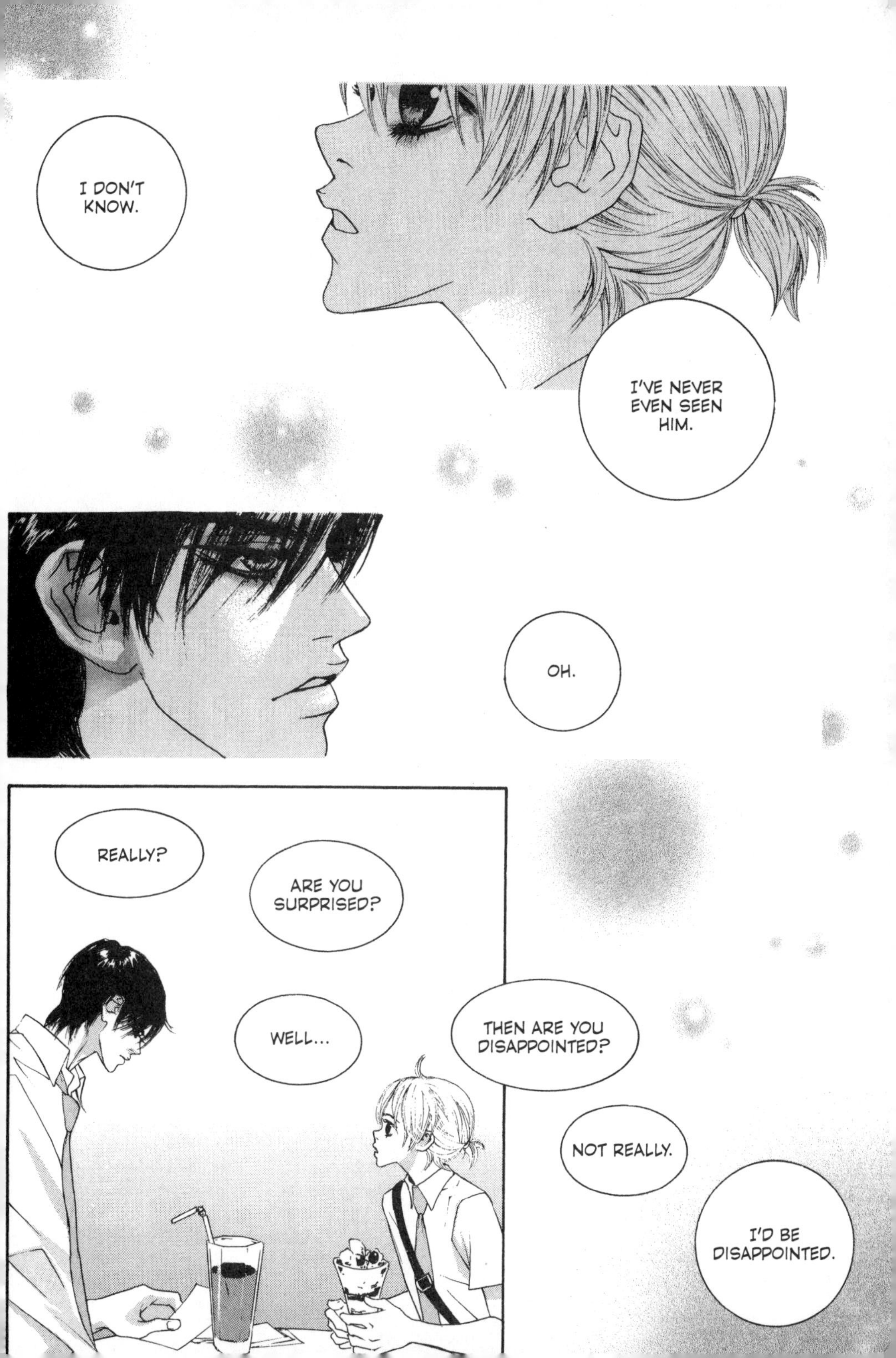
I DON'T KNOW.
I'VE NEVER EVEN SEEN HIM.
OH.
REALLY?
ARE YOU SURPRISED?
WELL...
THEN ARE YOU DISAPPOINTED?
NOT REALLY.
I'D BE DISAPPOINTED.

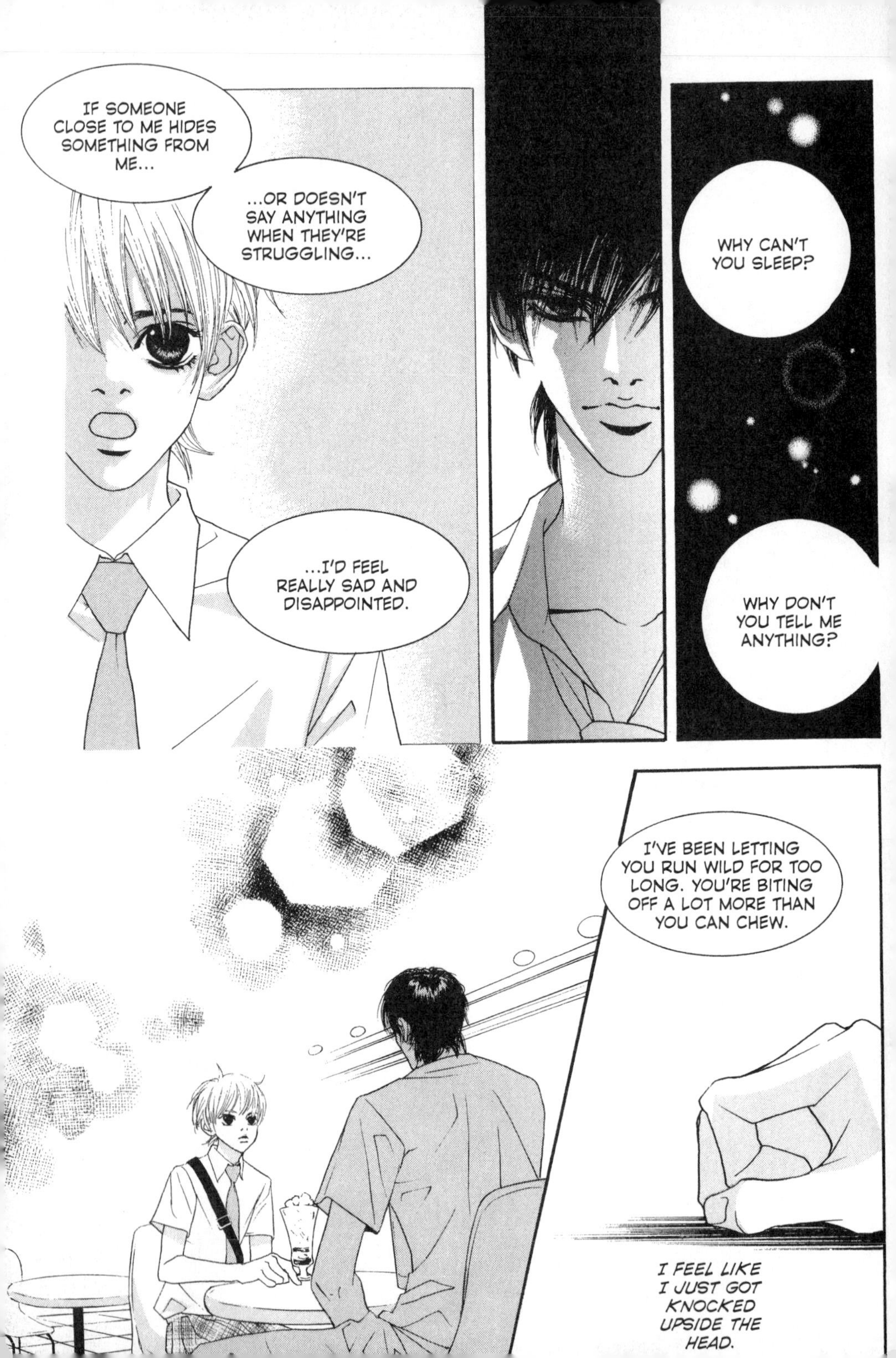
IF SOMEONE CLOSE TO ME HIDES SOMETHING FROM ME...
...OR DOESN'T SAY ANYTHING WHEN THEY'RE STRUGGLING...
...I'D FEEL REALLY SAD AND DISAPPOINTED.
WHY CAN'T YOU SLEEP?
WHY DON'T YOU TELL ME ANYTHING?
I'VE BEEN LETTING YOU RUN WILD FOR TOO LONG. YOU'RE BITING OFF A LOT MORE THAN YOU CAN CHEW.
I FEEL LIKE I JUST GOT KNOCKED UPSIDE THE HEAD.

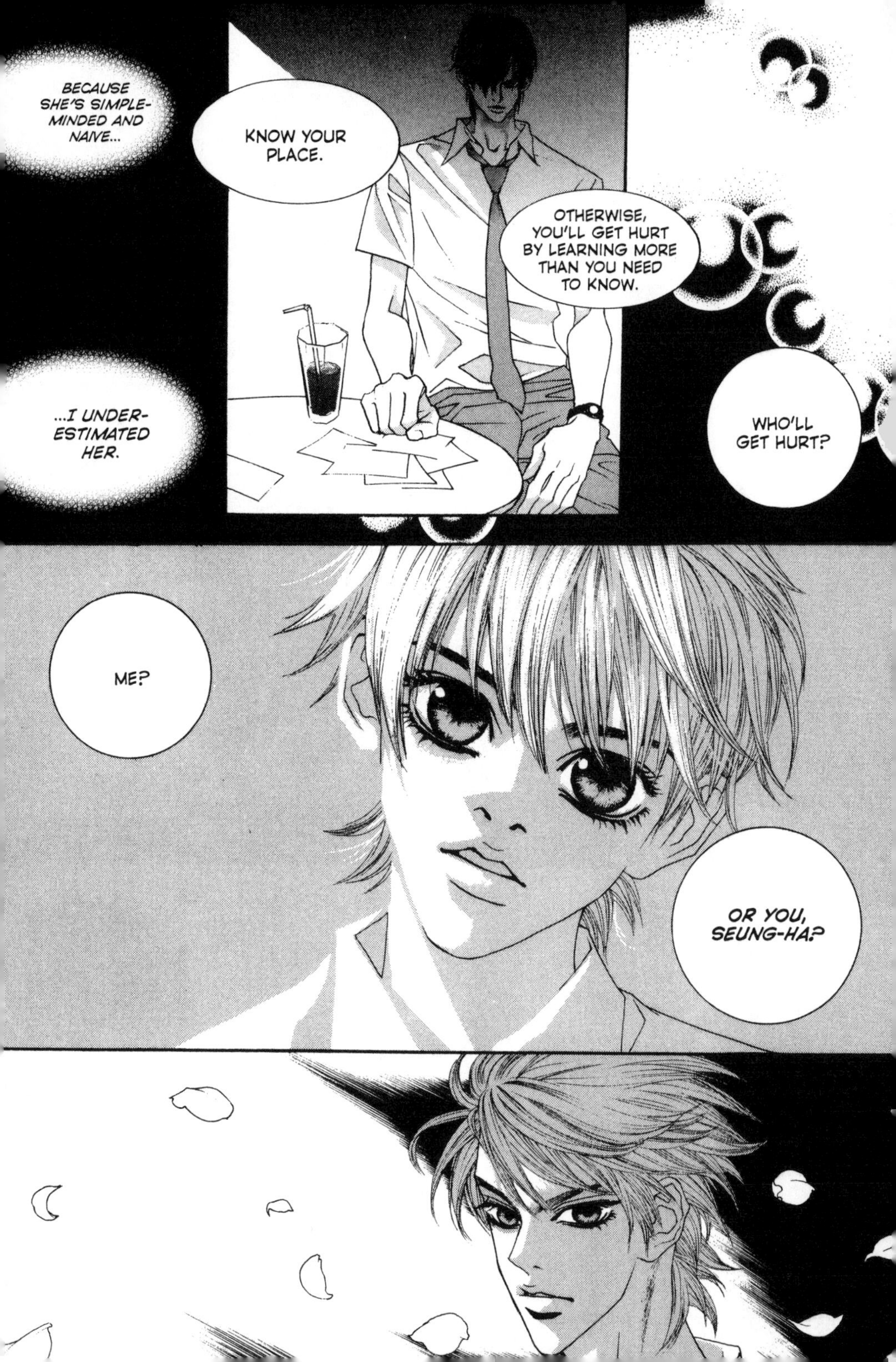
BECAUSE SHE'S SIMPLE-MINDED AND NAIVE...
KNOW YOUR PLACE.
OTHERWISE, YOU'LL GET HURT BY LEARNING MORE THAN YOU NEED TO KNOW.
...I UNDER-ESTIMATED HER.
WHO'LL GET HURT?
ME?
OR YOU, SEUNG-HA?

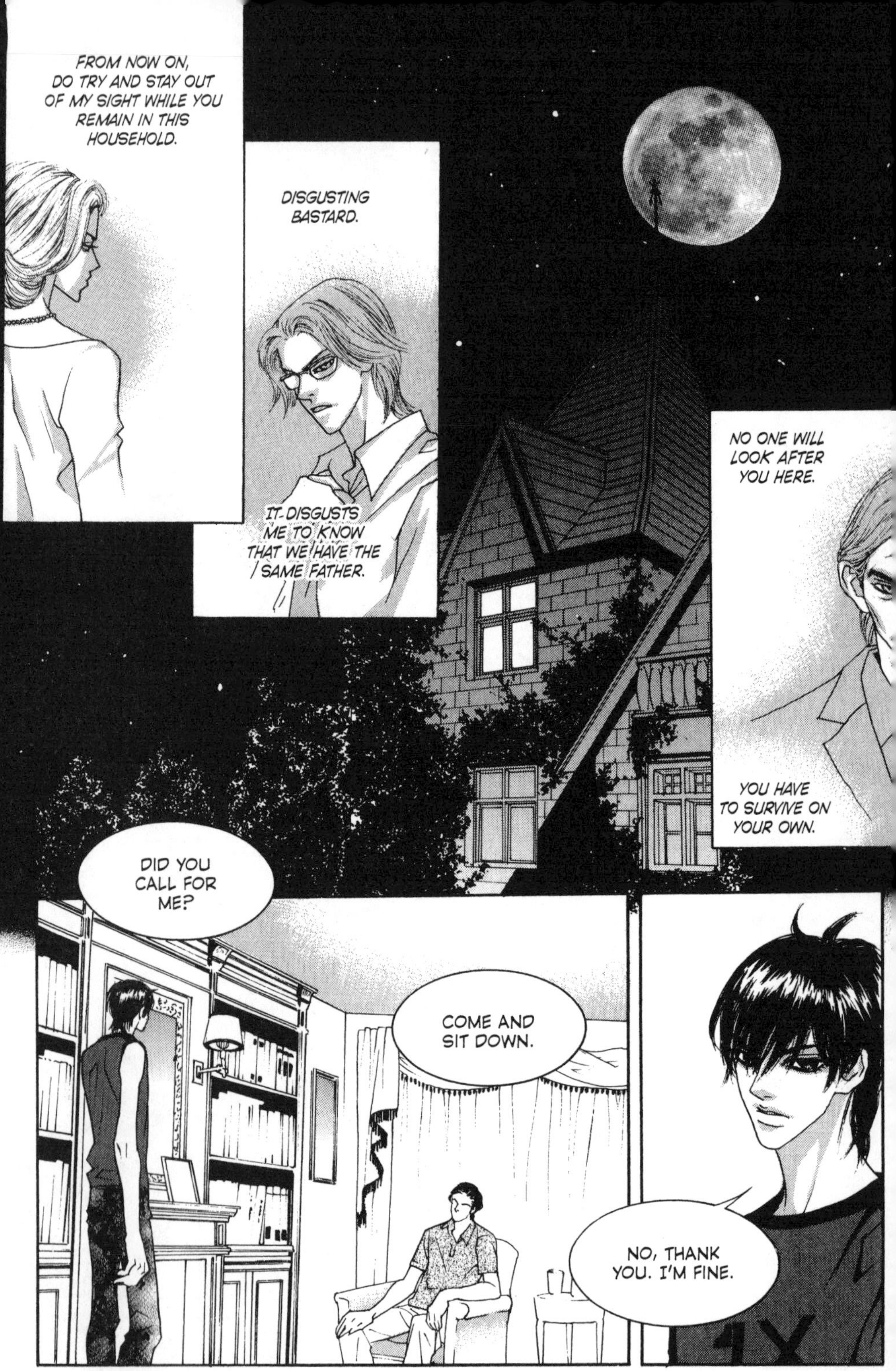
FROM NOW ON, DO TRY AND STAY OUT OF MY SIGHT WHILE YOU REMAIN IN THIS HOUSEHOLD.
DISGUSTING BASTARD.
IT DISGUSTS ME TO KNOW THAT WE HAVE THE SAME FATHER.
NO ONE WILL LOOK AFTER YOU HERE.
YOU HAVE TO SURVIVE ON YOUR OWN.
DID YOU CALL FOR ME?
COME AND SIT DOWN.
NO, THANK YOU. I'M FINE.

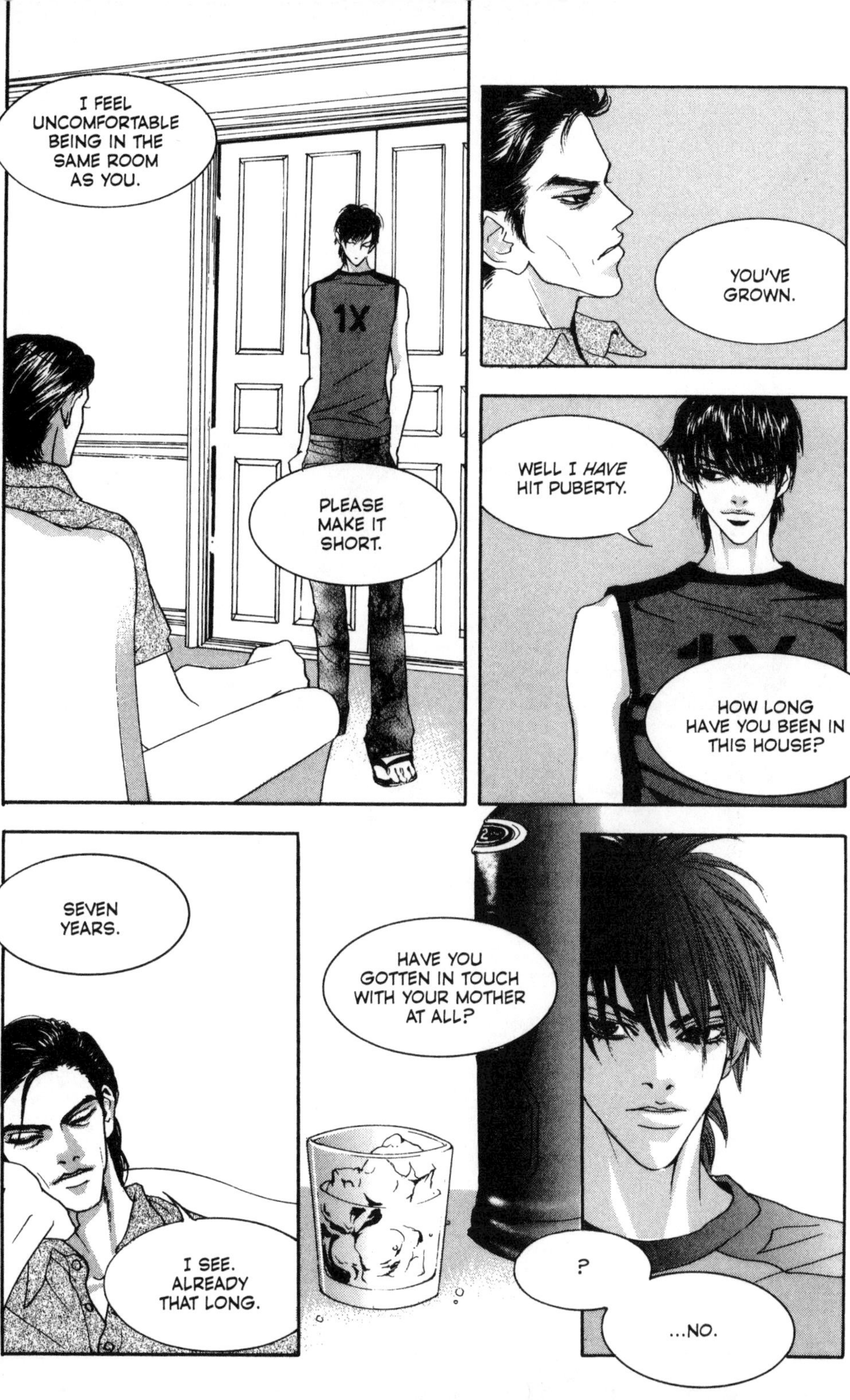
I FEEL UNCOMFORTABLE BEING IN THE SAME ROOM AS YOU.
1X
PLEASE MAKE IT SHORT.
YOU'VE GROWN.
WELL I *HAVE* HIT PUBERTY.
HOW LONG HAVE YOU BEEN IN THIS HOUSE?
SEVEN YEARS.
I SEE. ALREADY THAT LONG.
HAVE YOU GOTTEN IN TOUCH WITH YOUR MOTHER AT ALL?
?
...NO.

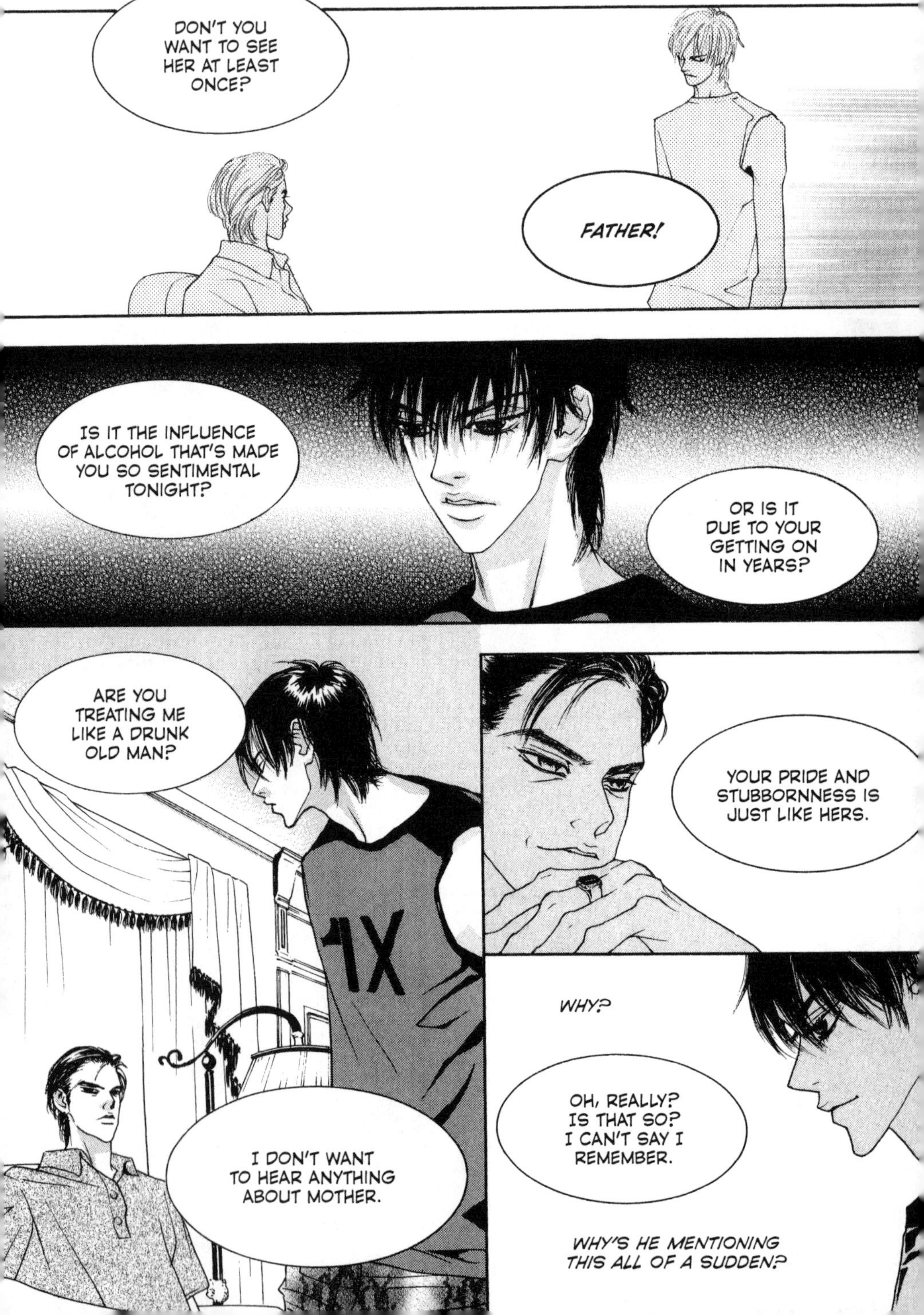
DON'T YOU WANT TO SEE HER AT LEAST ONCE?
FATHER!
IS IT THE INFLUENCE OF ALCOHOL THAT'S MADE YOU SO SENTIMENTAL TONIGHT?
OR IS IT DUE TO YOUR GETTING ON IN YEARS?
ARE YOU TREATING ME LIKE A DRUNK OLD MAN?
I DON'T WANT TO HEAR ANYTHING ABOUT MOTHER.
YOUR PRIDE AND STUBBORNNESS IS JUST LIKE HERS.
WHY?
OH, REALLY? IS THAT SO? I CAN'T SAY I REMEMBER.
WHY'S HE MENTIONING THIS ALL OF A SUDDEN?

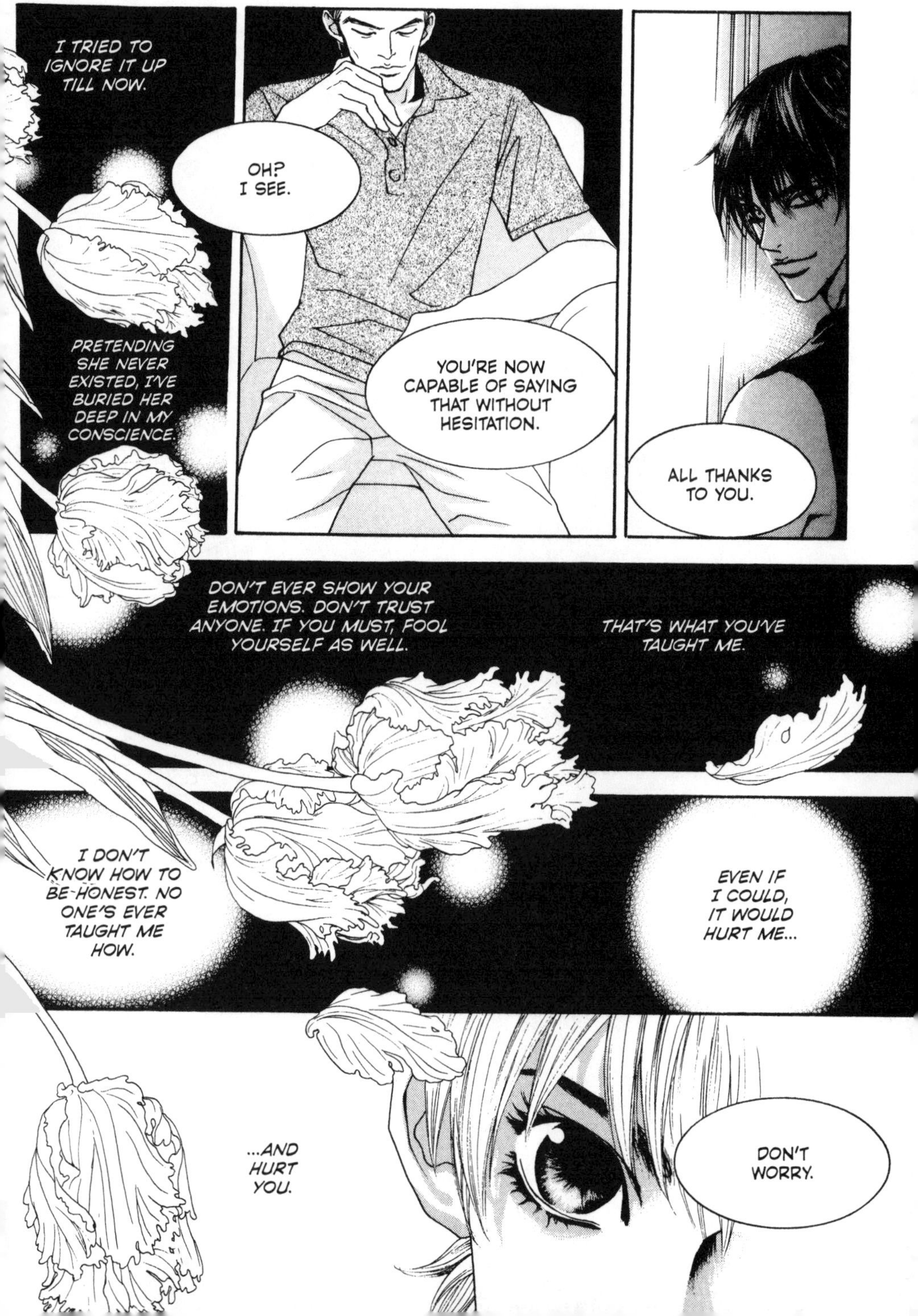
I TRIED TO IGNORE IT UP TILL NOW.
PRETENDING SHE NEVER EXISTED, I'VE BURIED HER DEEP IN MY CONSCIENCE.
OH? I SEE.
YOU'RE NOW CAPABLE OF SAYING THAT WITHOUT HESITATION.
ALL THANKS TO YOU.
DON'T EVER SHOW YOUR EMOTIONS. DON'T TRUST ANYONE. IF YOU MUST, FOOL YOURSELF AS WELL.
THAT'S WHAT YOU'VE TAUGHT ME.
I DON'T KNOW HOW TO BE HONEST. NO ONE'S EVER TAUGHT ME HOW.
EVEN IF I COULD, IT WOULD HURT ME...
...AND HURT YOU.
DON'T WORRY.

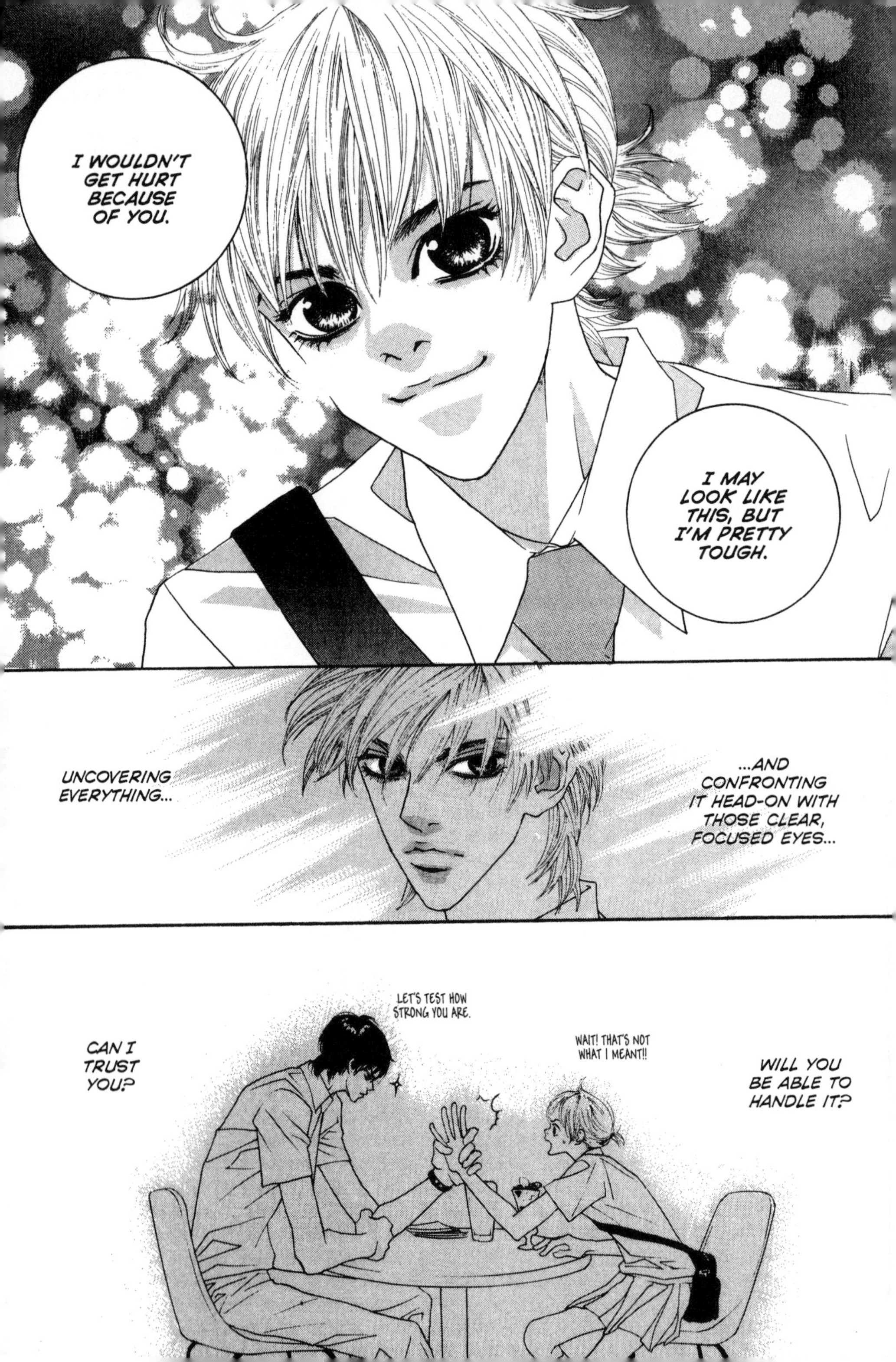
I WOULDN'T GET HURT BECAUSE OF YOU.
I MAY LOOK LIKE THIS, BUT I'M PRETTY TOUGH.
UNCOVERING EVERYTHING...
...AND CONFRONTING IT HEAD-ON WITH THOSE CLEAR, FOCUSED EYES...
CAN I TRUST YOU?
LET'S TEST HOW STRONG YOU ARE.
WAIT! THAT'S NOT WHAT I MEANT!!
WILL YOU BE ABLE TO HANDLE IT?

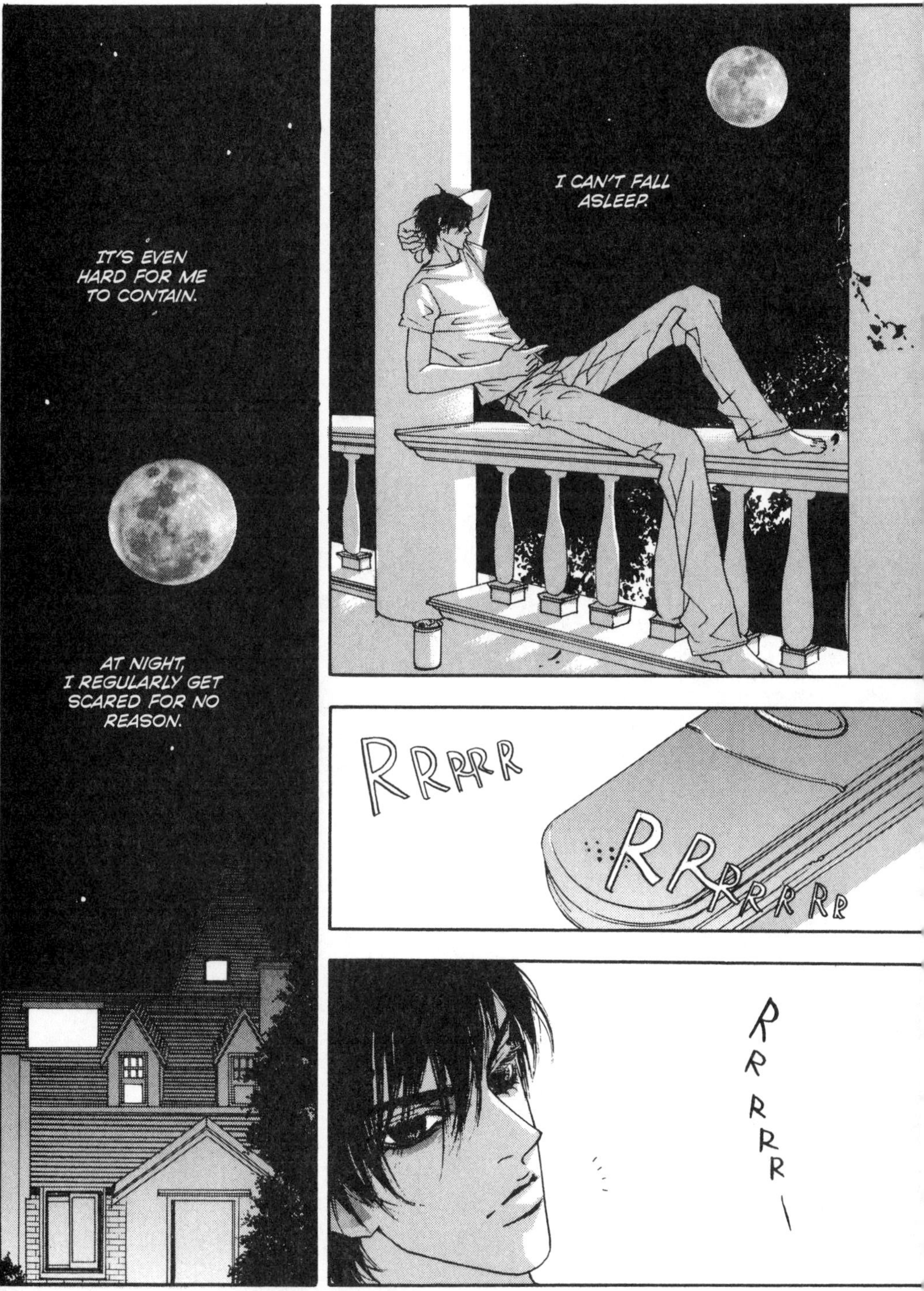
IT'S EVEN HARD FOR ME TO CONTAIN.
AT NIGHT, I REGULARLY GET SCARED FOR NO REASON.
I CAN'T FALL ASLEEP.
RRRRR
RRRRRRRR
RRRRR

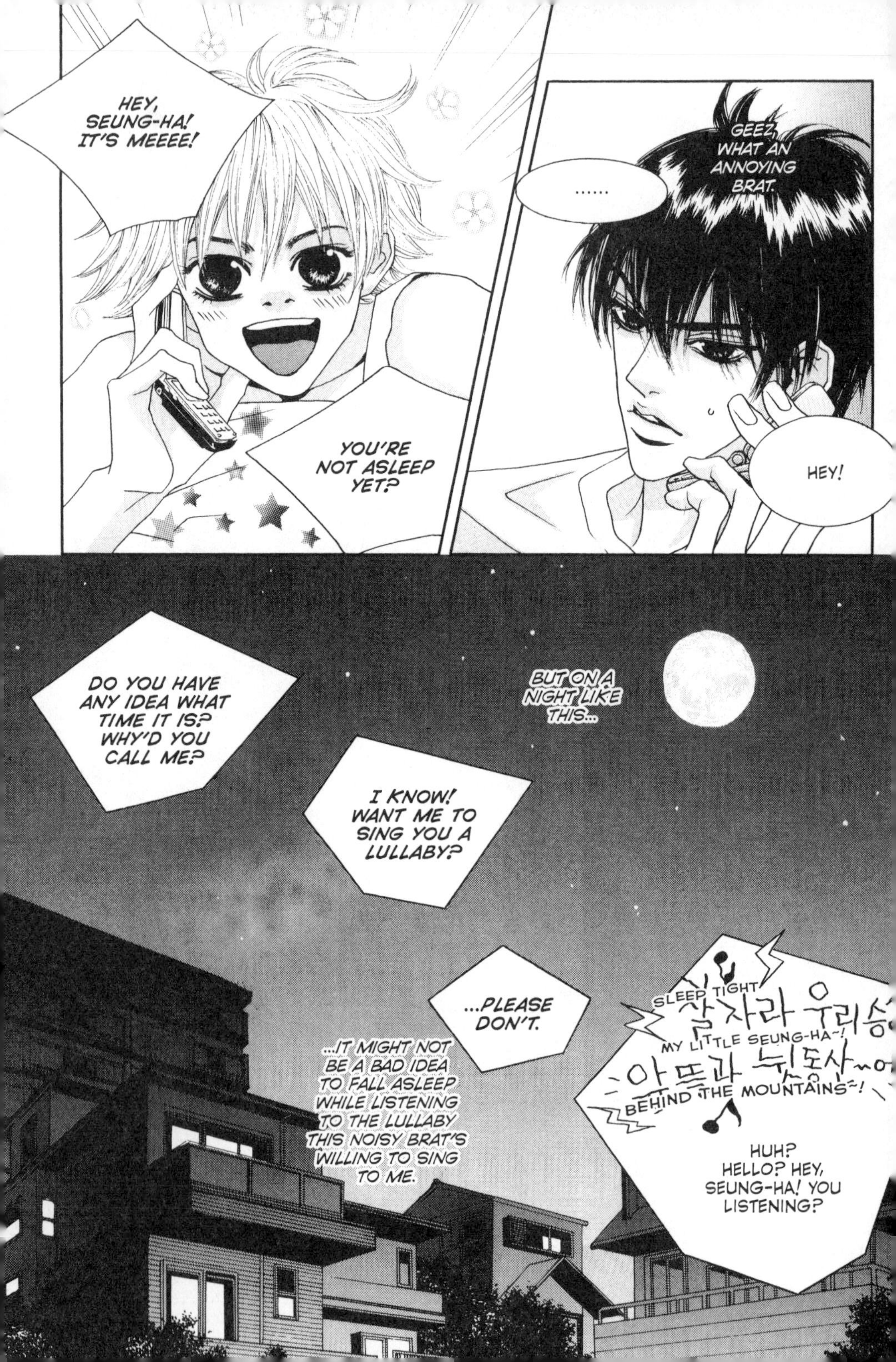
HEY, SEUNG-HA! IT'S MEEEE!
YOU'RE NOT ASLEEP YET?
......
GEEZ, WHAT AN ANNOYING BRAT.
HEY!
DO YOU HAVE ANY IDEA WHAT TIME IT IS? WHY'D YOU CALL ME?
I KNOW! WANT ME TO SING YOU A LULLABY?
BUT ON A NIGHT LIKE THIS...
...PLEASE DON'T.
...IT MIGHT NOT BE A BAD IDEA TO FALL ASLEEP WHILE LISTENING TO THE LULLABY THIS NOISY BRAT'S WILLING TO SING TO ME.
SLEEP TIGHT MY LITTLE SEUNG-HA~! BEHIND THE MOUNTAINS~!
HUH? HELLO? HEY, SEUNG-HA! YOU LISTENING?

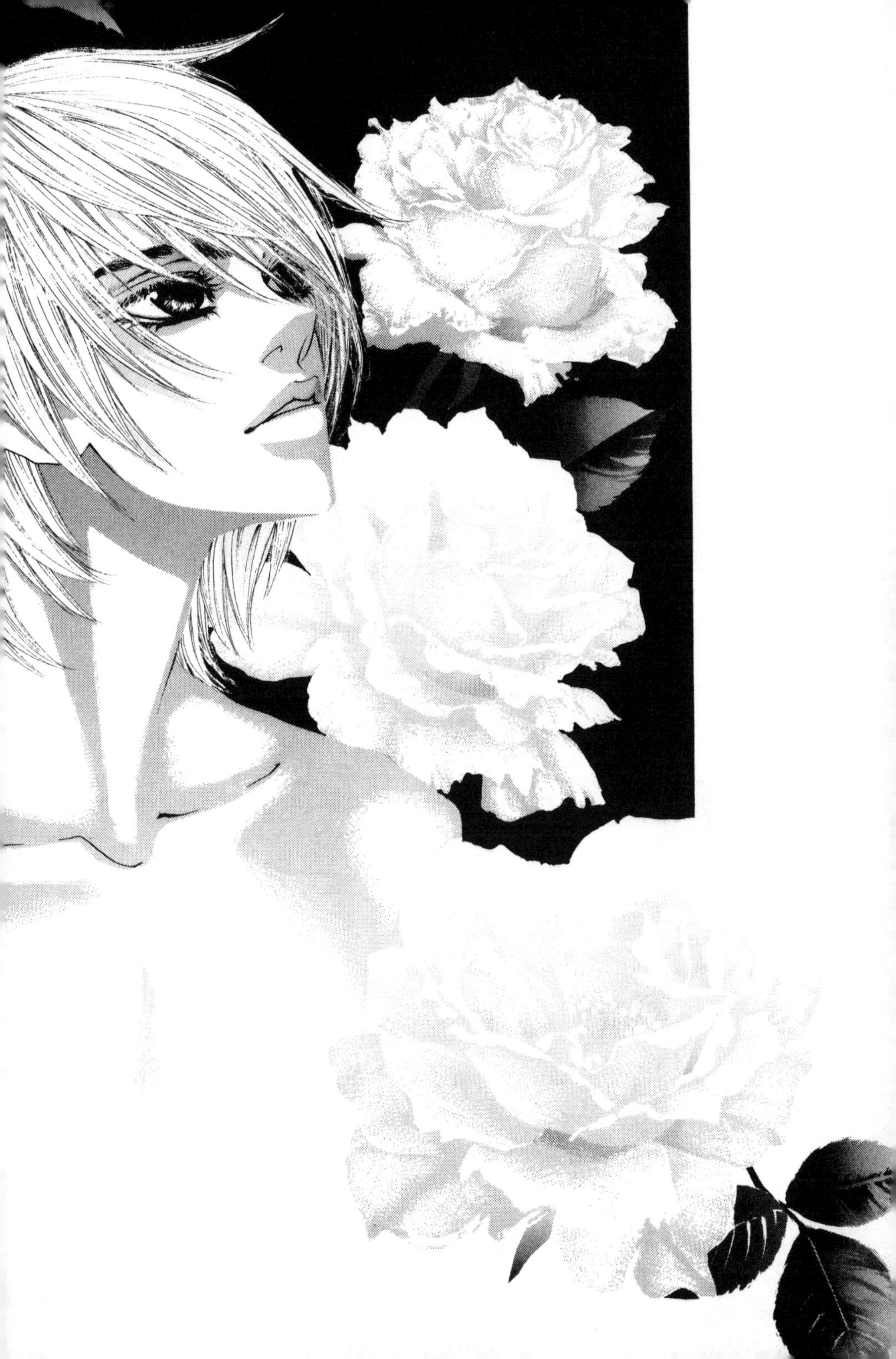

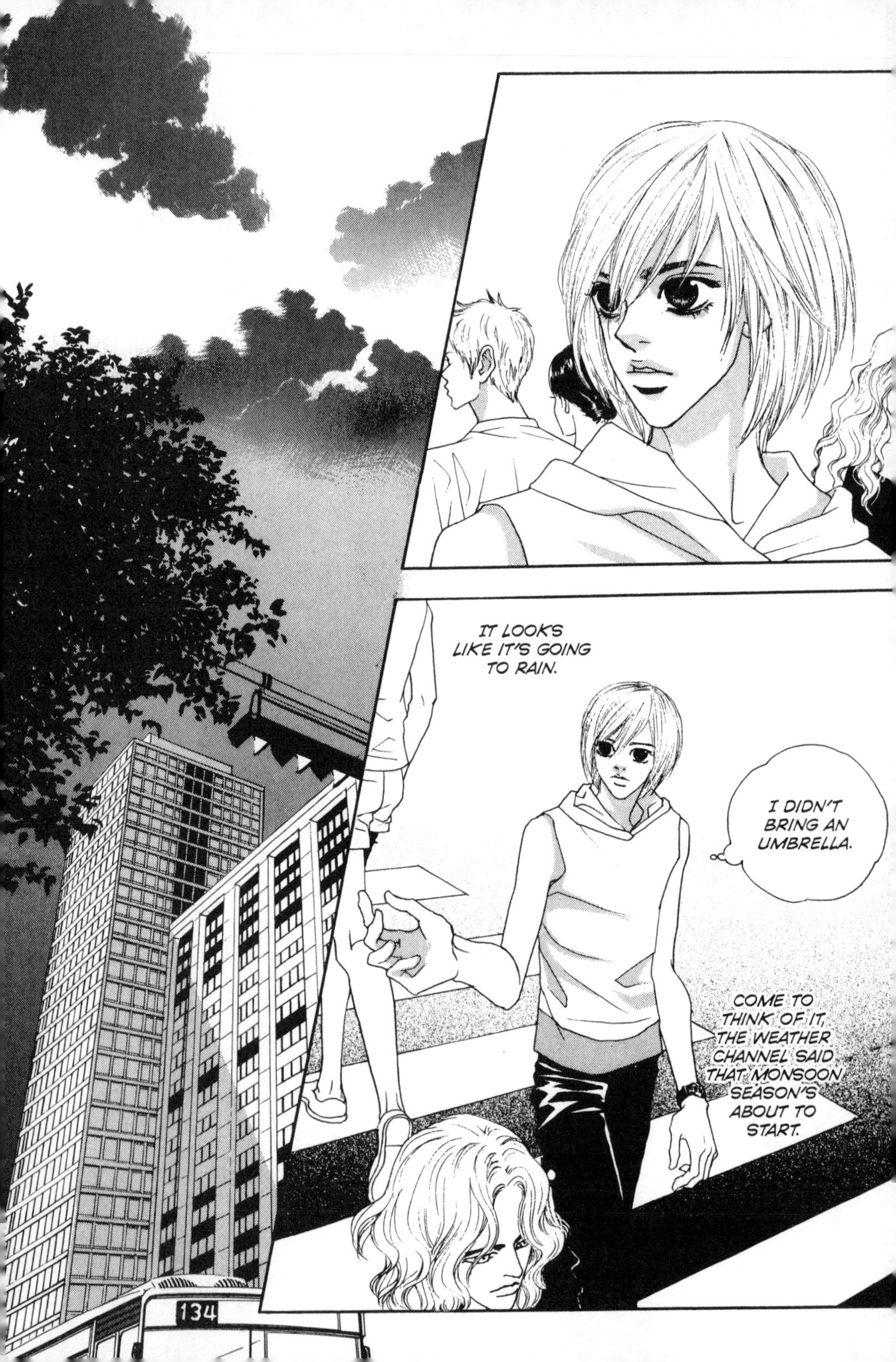
IT LOOKS LIKE IT'S GOING TO RAIN.
I DIDN'T BRING AN UMBRELLA.
COME TO THINK OF IT, THE WEATHER CHANNEL SAID THAT MONSOON SEASON'S ABOUT TO START.
134

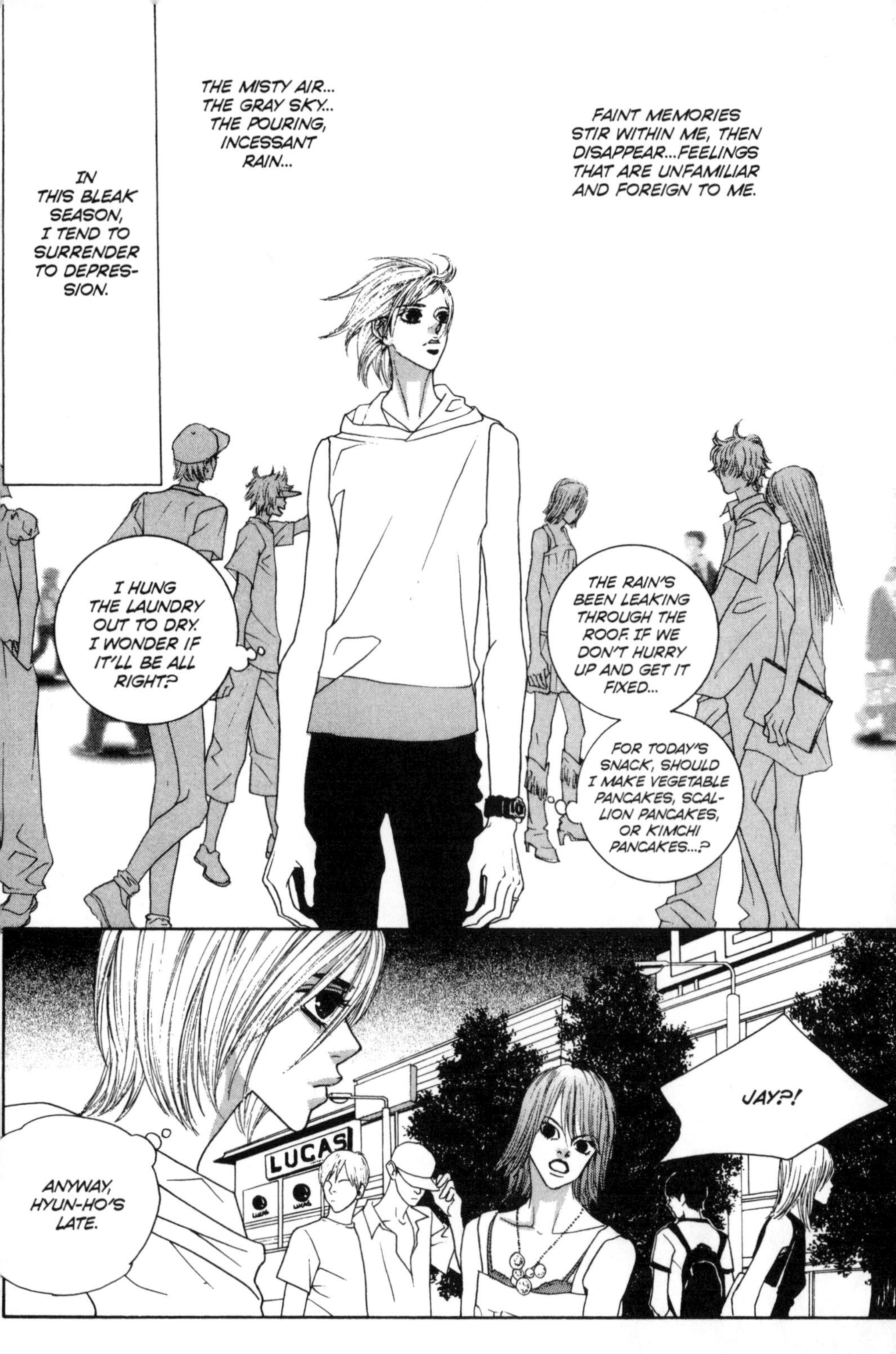
IN THIS BLEAK SEASON, I TEND TO SURRENDER TO DEPRESSION.
THE MISTY AIR... THE GRAY SKY... THE POURING, INCESSANT RAIN...
FAINT MEMORIES STIR WITHIN ME, THEN DISAPPEAR...FEELINGS THAT ARE UNFAMILIAR AND FOREIGN TO ME.
I HUNG THE LAUNDRY OUT TO DRY. I WONDER IF IT'LL BE ALL RIGHT?
THE RAIN'S BEEN LEAKING THROUGH THE ROOF. IF WE DON'T HURRY UP AND GET IT FIXED...
FOR TODAY'S SNACK, SHOULD I MAKE VEGETABLE PANCAKES, SCALLION PANCAKES, OR KIMCHI PANCAKES...?
ANYWAY, HYUN-HO'S LATE.
LUCAS
JAY?!

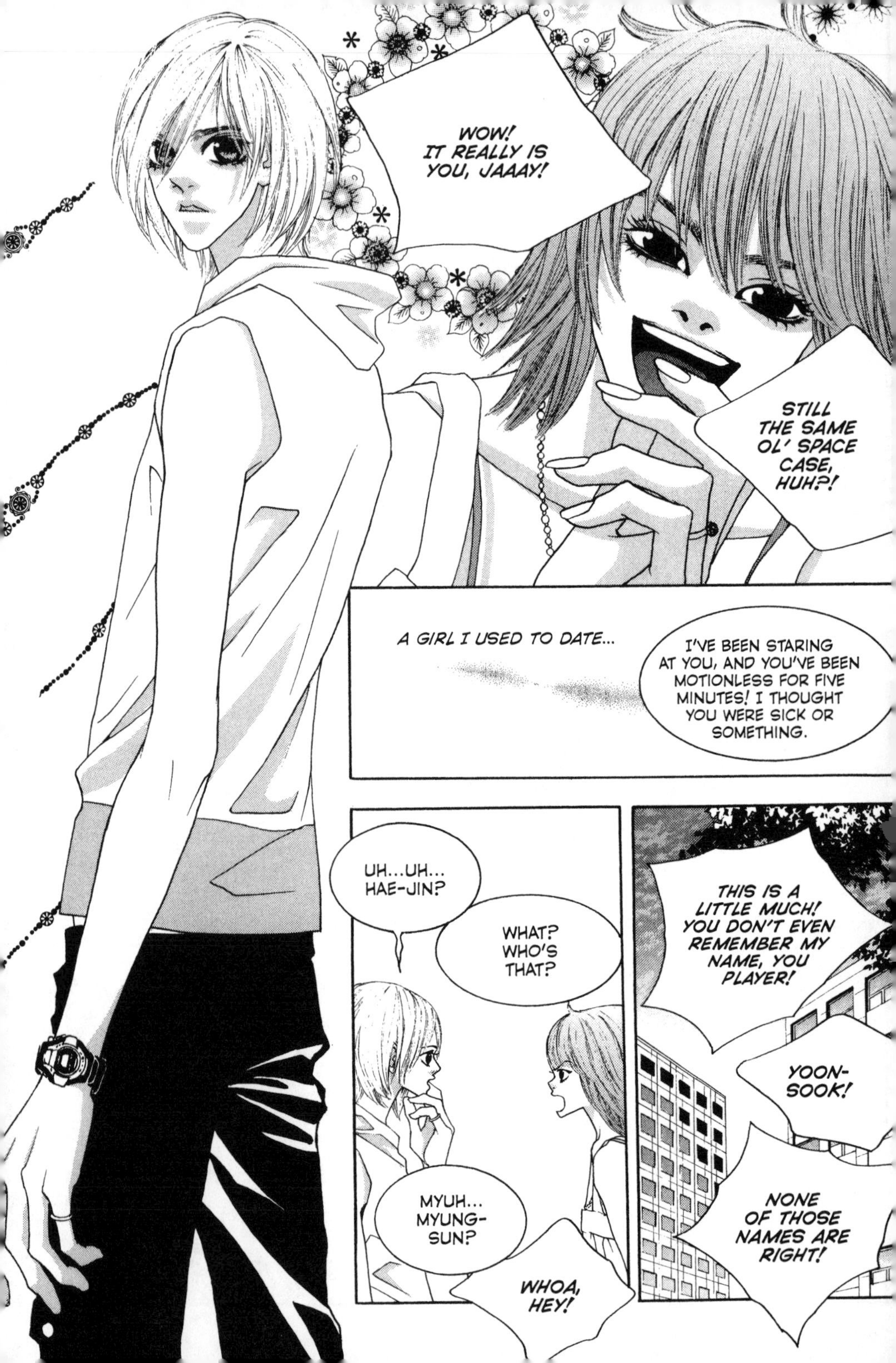

WOW! IT REALLY IS YOU, JAAAY!
STILL THE SAME OL' SPACE CASE, HUH?!
A GIRL I USED TO DATE...
I'VE BEEN STARING AT YOU, AND YOU'VE BEEN MOTIONLESS FOR FIVE MINUTES! I THOUGHT YOU WERE SICK OR SOMETHING.
UH...UH... HAE-JIN?
WHAT? WHO'S THAT?
MYUH... MYUNG-SUN?
WHOA, HEY!
THIS IS A LITTLE MUCH! YOU DON'T EVEN REMEMBER MY NAME, YOU PLAYER!
YOON-SOOK!
NONE OF THOSE NAMES ARE RIGHT!

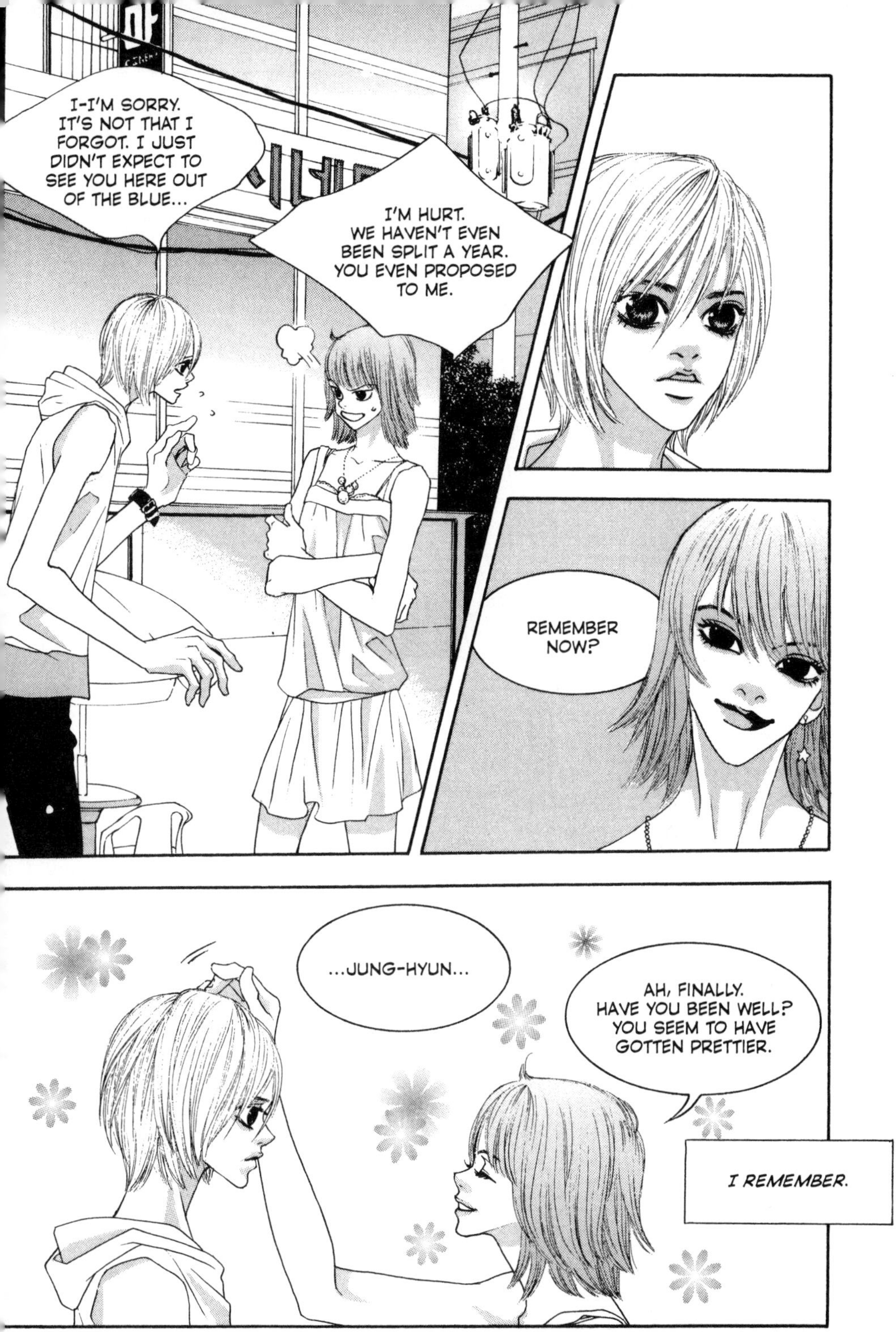
I-I'M SORRY. IT'S NOT THAT I FORGOT. I JUST DIDN'T EXPECT TO SEE YOU HERE OUT OF THE BLUE...
I'M HURT. WE HAVEN'T EVEN BEEN SPLIT A YEAR. YOU EVEN PROPOSED TO ME.
REMEMBER NOW?
...JUNG-HYUN...
AH, FINALLY. HAVE YOU BEEN WELL? YOU SEEM TO HAVE GOTTEN PRETTIER.
I REMEMBER.

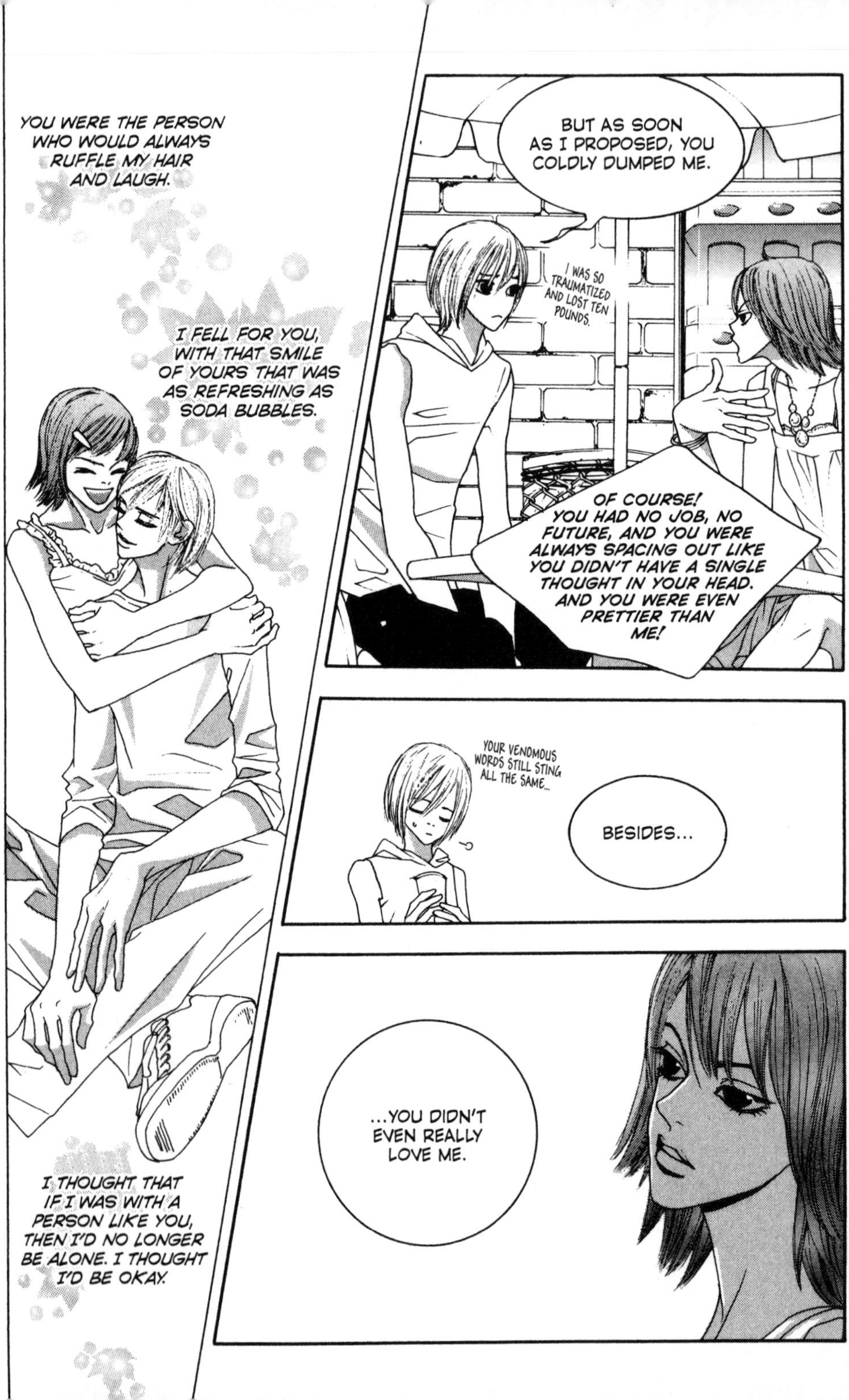
YOU WERE THE PERSON WHO WOULD ALWAYS RUFFLE MY HAIR AND LAUGH.
I FELL FOR YOU, WITH THAT SMILE OF YOURS THAT WAS AS REFRESHING AS SODA BUBBLES.
I THOUGHT THAT IF I WAS WITH A PERSON LIKE YOU, THEN I'D NO LONGER BE ALONE. I THOUGHT I'D BE OKAY.
BUT AS SOON AS I PROPOSED, YOU COLDLY DUMPED ME.
I WAS SO TRAUMATIZED AND LOST TEN POUNDS.
OF COURSE! YOU HAD NO JOB, NO FUTURE, AND YOU WERE ALWAYS SPACING OUT LIKE YOU DIDN'T HAVE A SINGLE THOUGHT IN YOUR HEAD. AND YOU WERE EVEN PRETTIER THAN ME!
YOUR VENOMOUS WORDS STILL STING ALL THE SAME...
BESIDES...
...YOU DIDN'T EVEN REALLY LOVE ME.

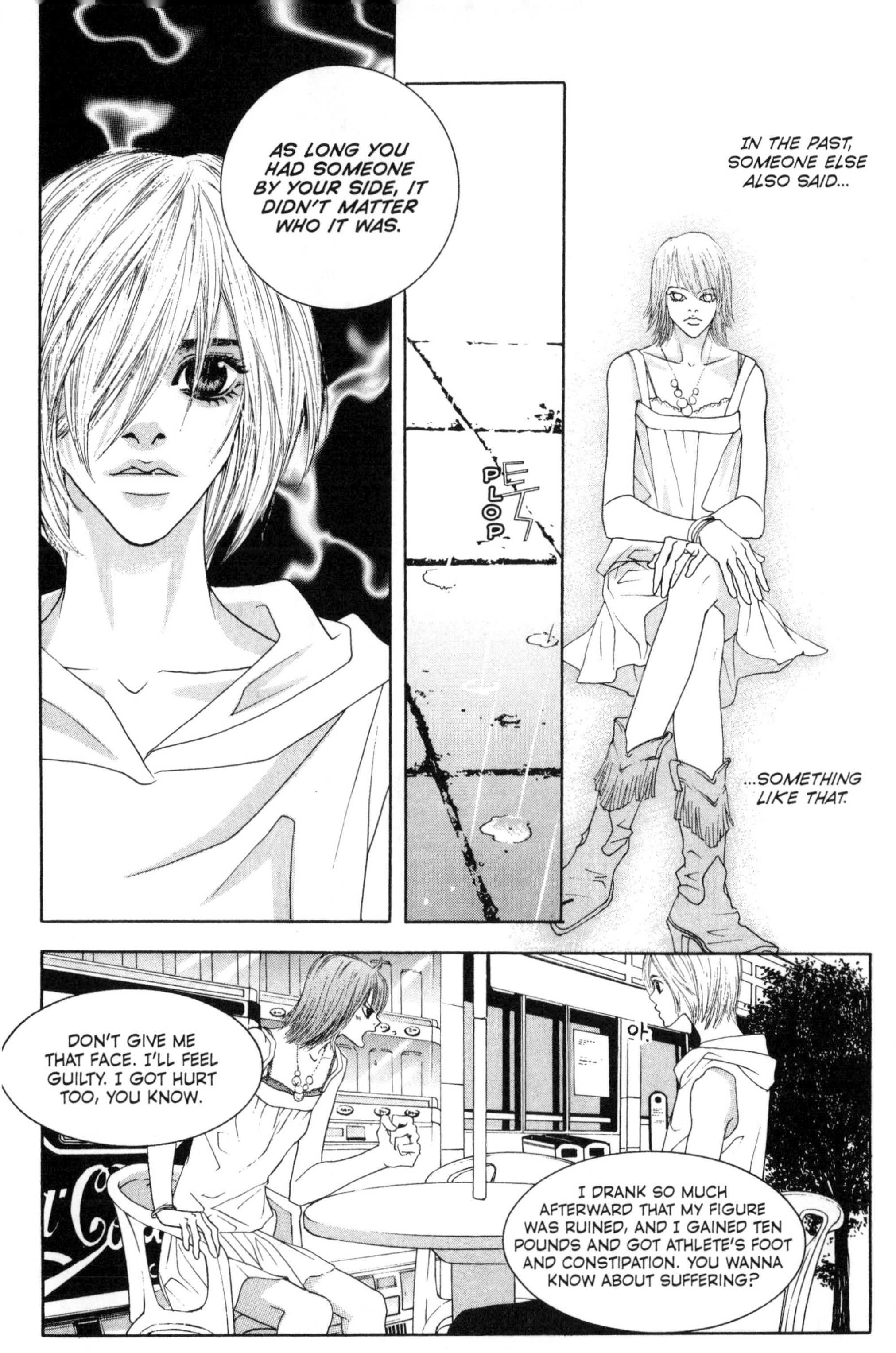

AS LONG YOU HAD SOMEONE BY YOUR SIDE, IT DIDN'T MATTER WHO IT WAS.
PLOP
IN THE PAST, SOMEONE ELSE ALSO SAID...
...SOMETHING LIKE THAT.
DON'T GIVE ME THAT FACE. I'LL FEEL GUILTY. I GOT HURT TOO, YOU KNOW.
I DRANK SO MUCH AFTERWARD THAT MY FIGURE WAS RUINED, AND I GAINED TEN POUNDS AND GOT ATHLETE'S FOOT AND CONSTIPATION. YOU WANNA KNOW ABOUT SUFFERING?

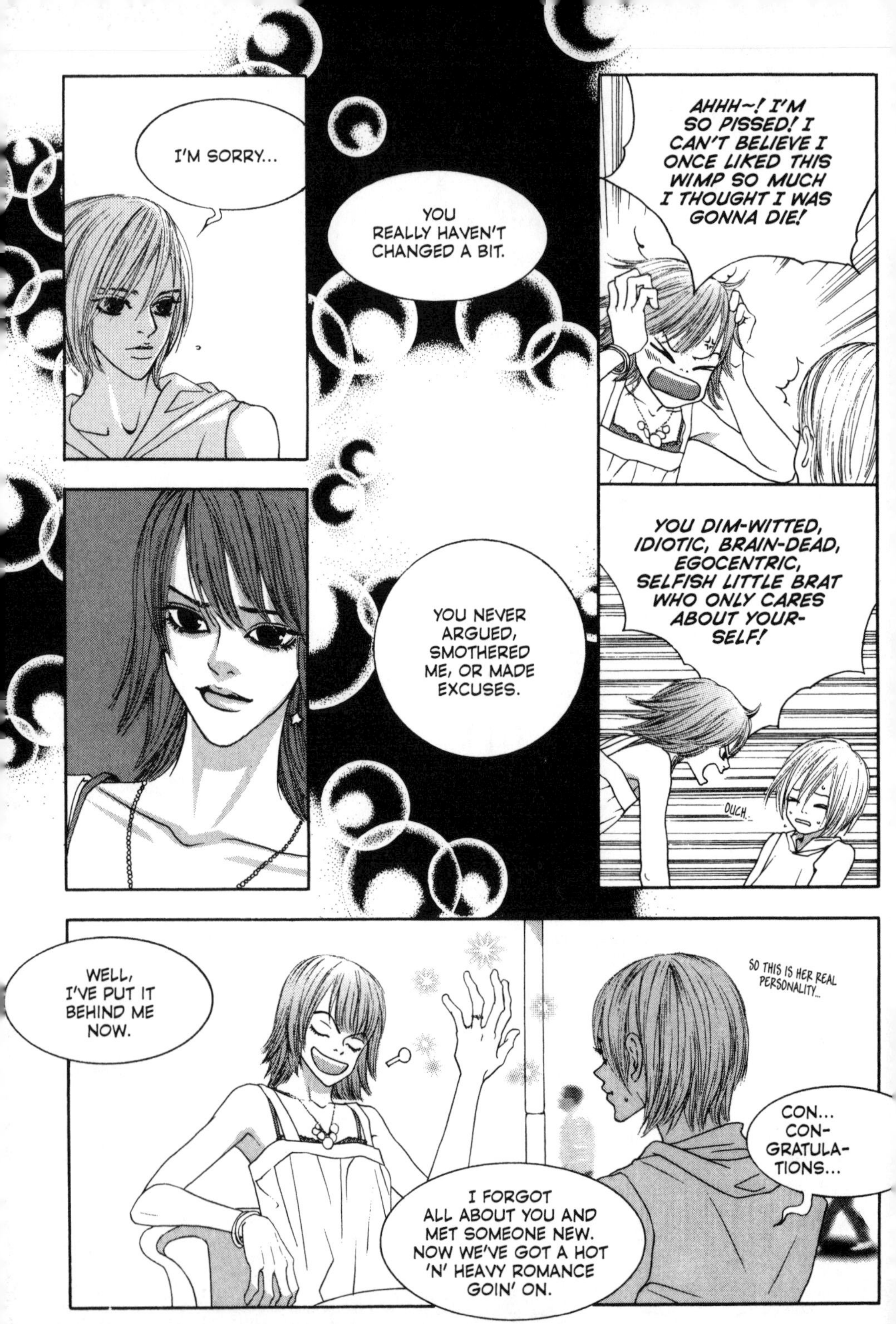
I'M SORRY...
YOU REALLY HAVEN'T CHANGED A BIT.
AHHH~! I'M SO PISSED! I CAN'T BELIEVE I ONCE LIKED THIS WIMP SO MUCH I THOUGHT I WAS GONNA DIE!
YOU NEVER ARGUED, SMOTHERED ME, OR MADE EXCUSES.
YOU DIM-WITTED, IDIOTIC, BRAIN-DEAD, EGOCENTRIC, SELFISH LITTLE BRAT WHO ONLY CARES ABOUT YOUR-SELF!
OUCH.
WELL, I'VE PUT IT BEHIND ME NOW.
I FORGOT ALL ABOUT YOU AND MET SOMEONE NEW. NOW WE'VE GOT A HOT 'N' HEAVY ROMANCE GOIN' ON.
SO THIS IS HER REAL PERSONALITY...
CON... CON-GRATULA-TIONS...

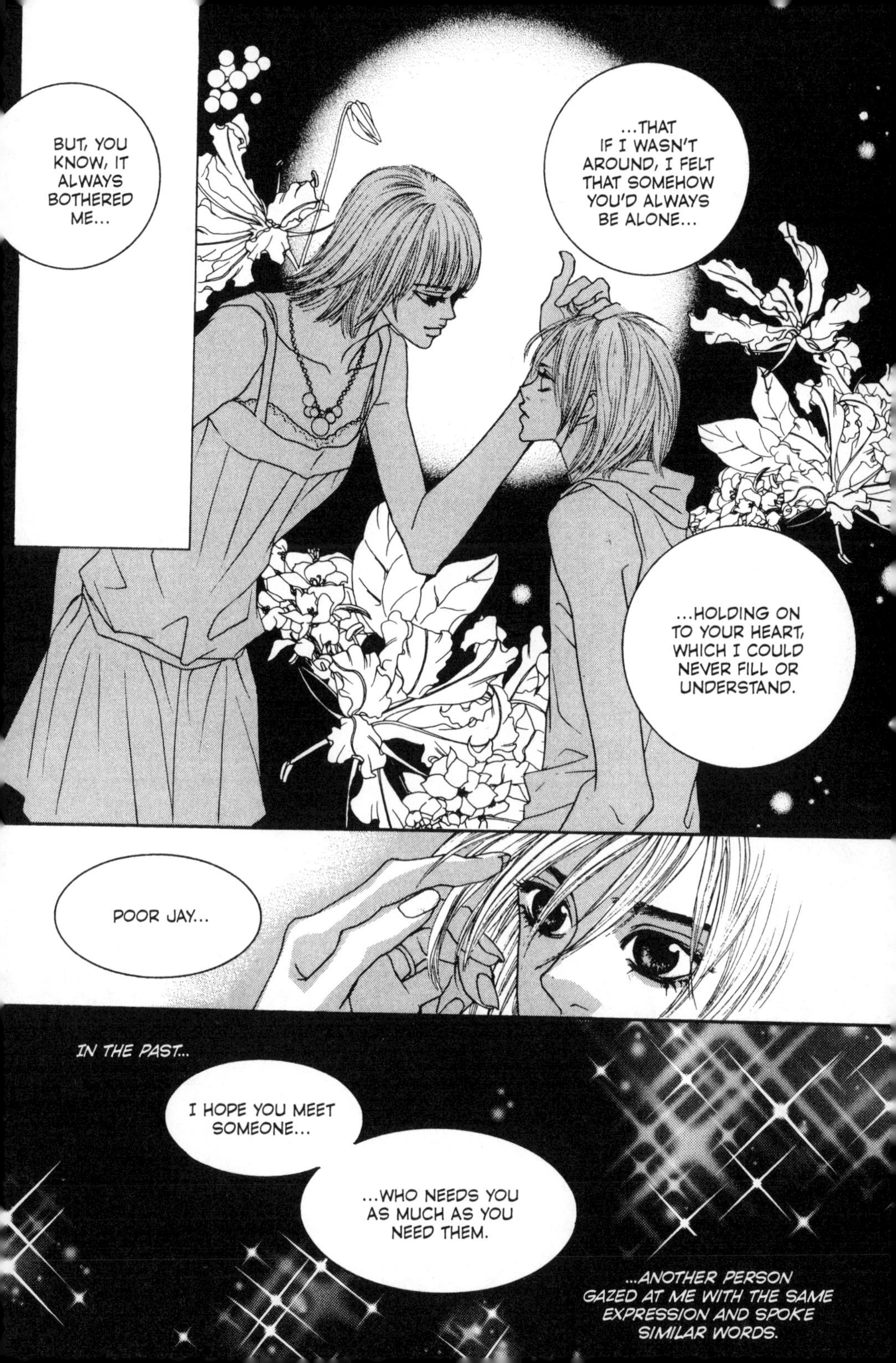
BUT, YOU KNOW, IT ALWAYS BOTHERED ME...
...THAT IF I WASN'T AROUND, I FELT THAT SOMEHOW YOU'D ALWAYS BE ALONE...
...HOLDING ON TO YOUR HEART, WHICH I COULD NEVER FILL OR UNDERSTAND.
POOR JAY...
IN THE PAST...
I HOPE YOU MEET SOMEONE...
...WHO NEEDS YOU AS MUCH AS YOU NEED THEM.
...ANOTHER PERSON GAZED AT ME WITH THE SAME EXPRESSION AND SPOKE SIMILAR WORDS.

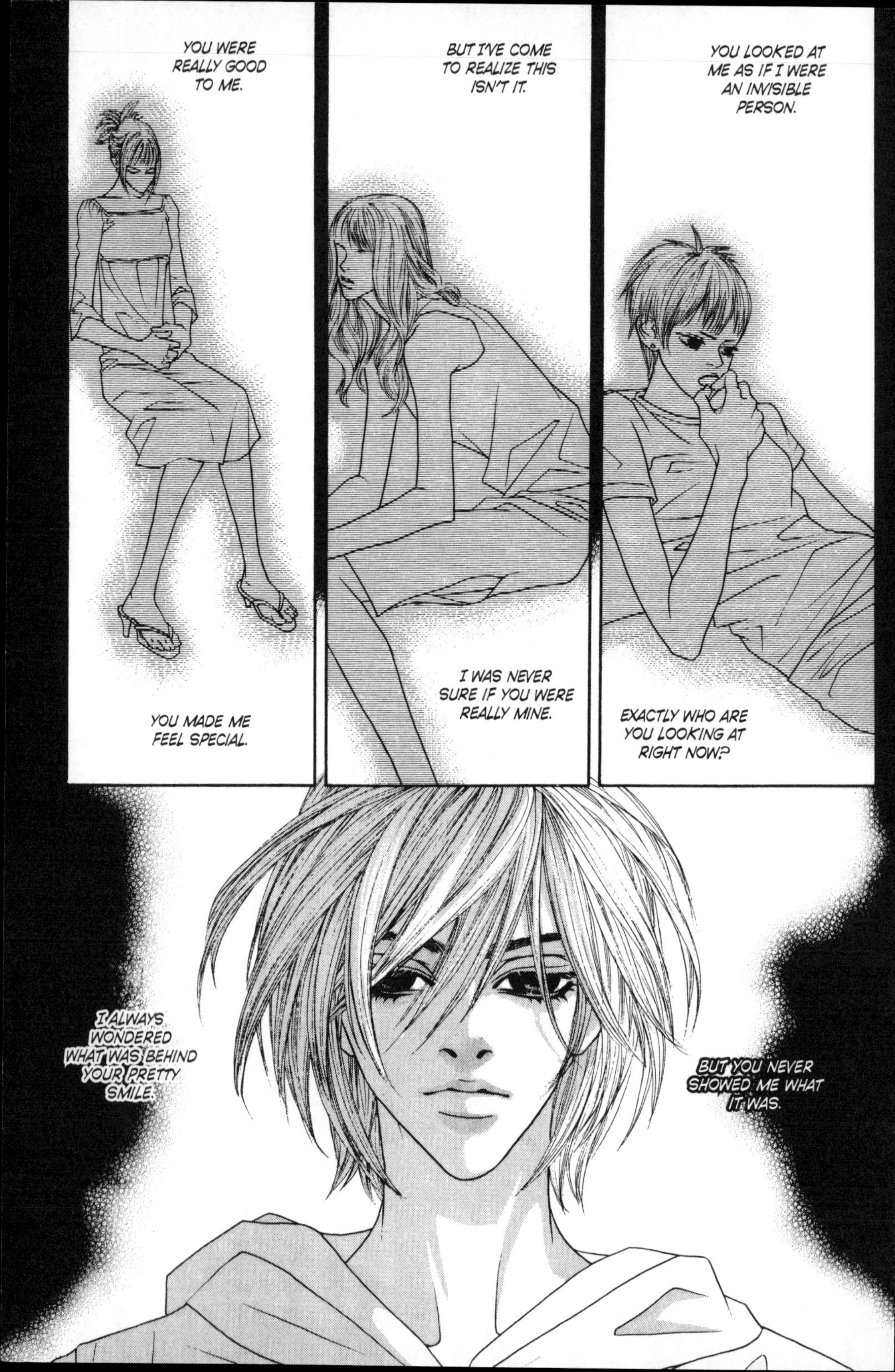
YOU WERE REALLY GOOD TO ME.
YOU MADE ME FEEL SPECIAL.
BUT I'VE COME TO REALIZE THIS ISN'T IT.
I WAS NEVER SURE IF YOU WERE REALLY MINE.
YOU LOOKED AT ME AS IF I WERE AN INVISIBLE PERSON.
EXACTLY WHO ARE YOU LOOKING AT RIGHT NOW?
I ALWAYS WONDERED WHAT WAS BEHIND YOUR PRETTY SMILE.
BUT YOU NEVER SHOWED ME WHAT IT WAS.

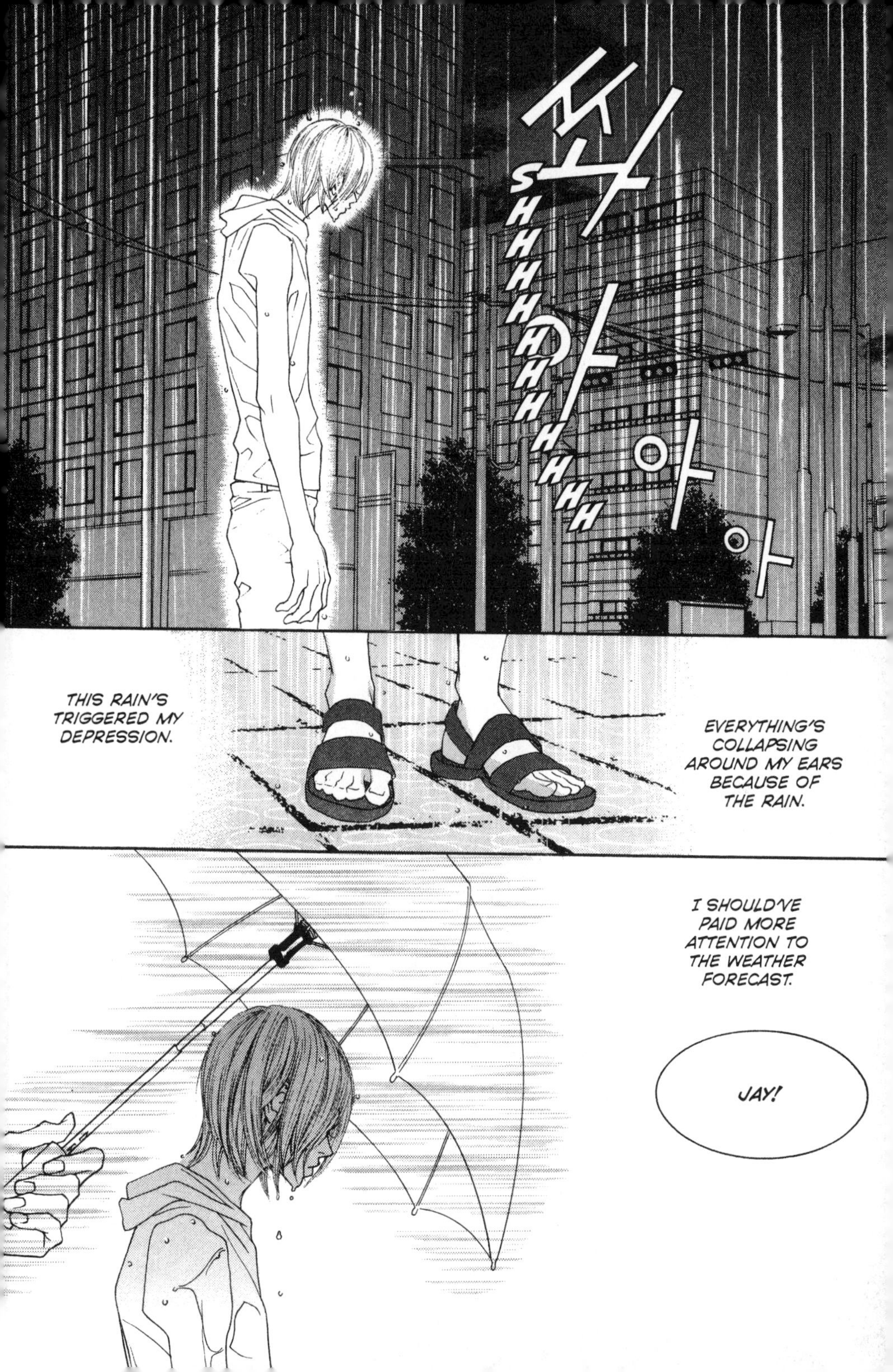
쏴아아아
SHHHHHHHHHHHH
THIS RAIN'S TRIGGERED MY DEPRESSION.
EVERYTHING'S COLLAPSING AROUND MY EARS BECAUSE OF THE RAIN.
I SHOULD'VE PAID MORE ATTENTION TO THE WEATHER FORECAST.
JAY!

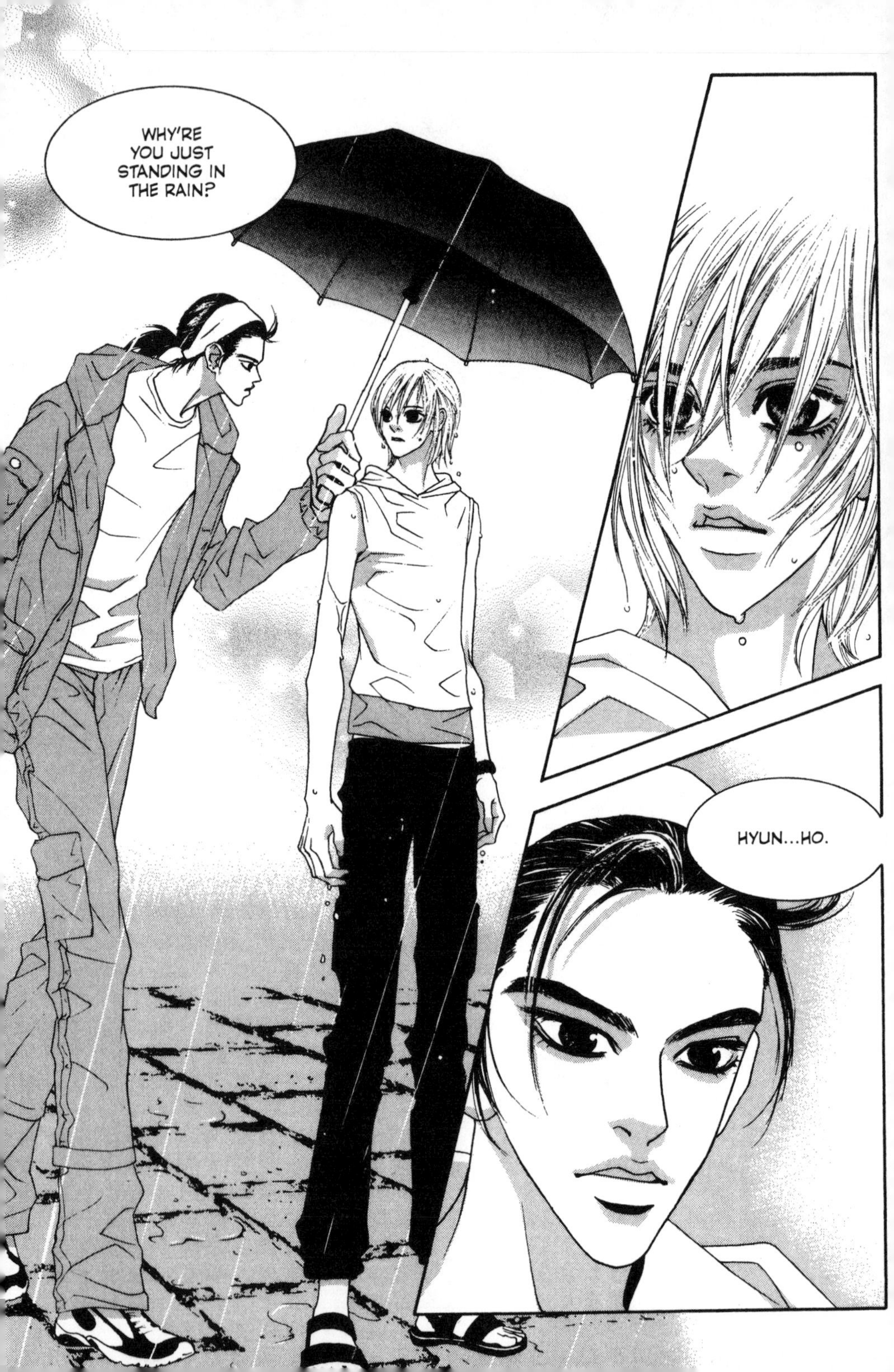
WHY'RE YOU JUST STANDING IN THE RAIN?
HYUN...HO.

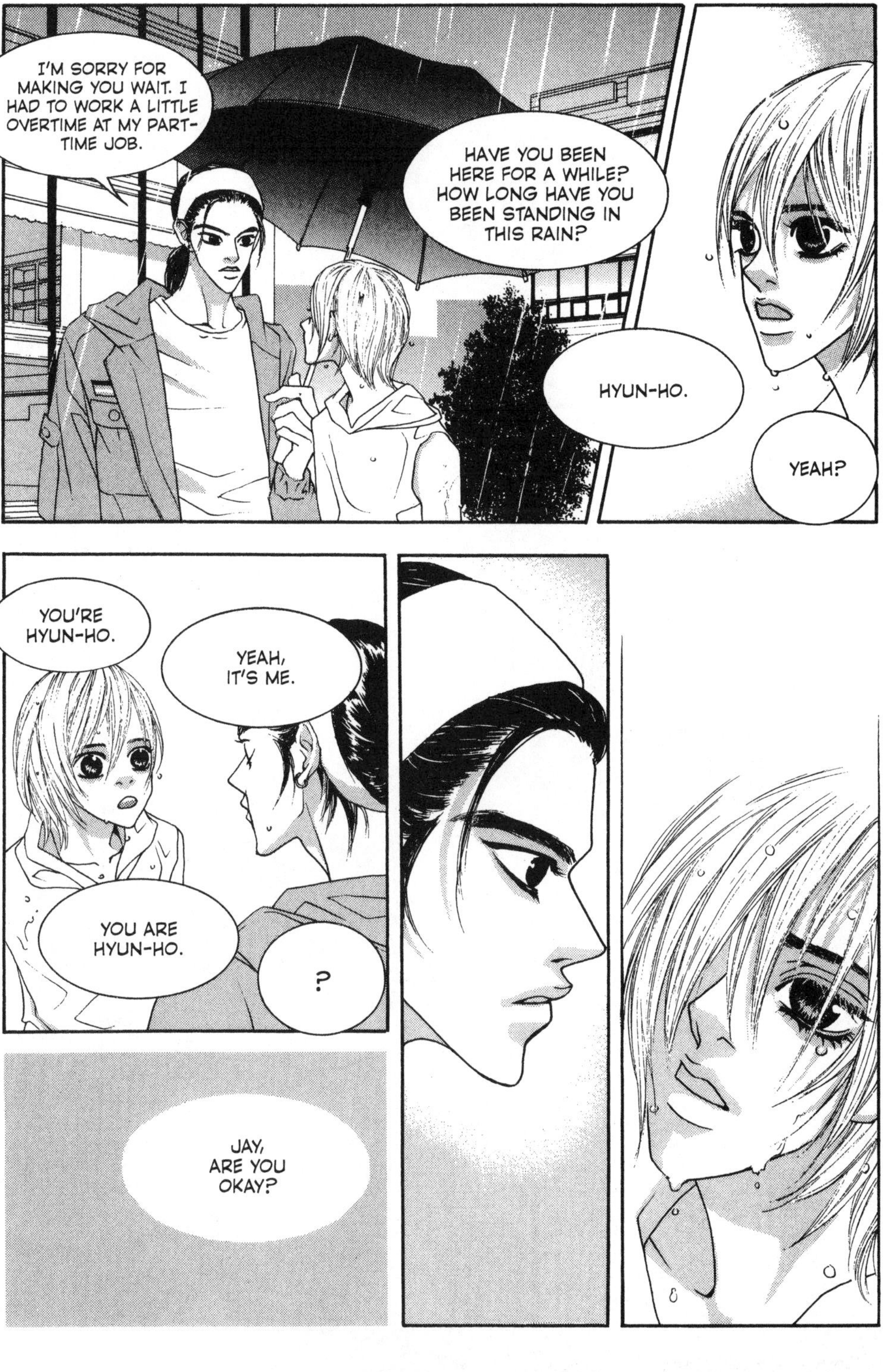
I'M SORRY FOR MAKING YOU WAIT. I HAD TO WORK A LITTLE OVERTIME AT MY PART-TIME JOB.
HAVE YOU BEEN HERE FOR A WHILE? HOW LONG HAVE YOU BEEN STANDING IN THIS RAIN?
HYUN-HO.
YEAH?
YOU'RE HYUN-HO.
YEAH, IT'S ME.
YOU ARE HYUN-HO.
?
JAY, ARE YOU OKAY?

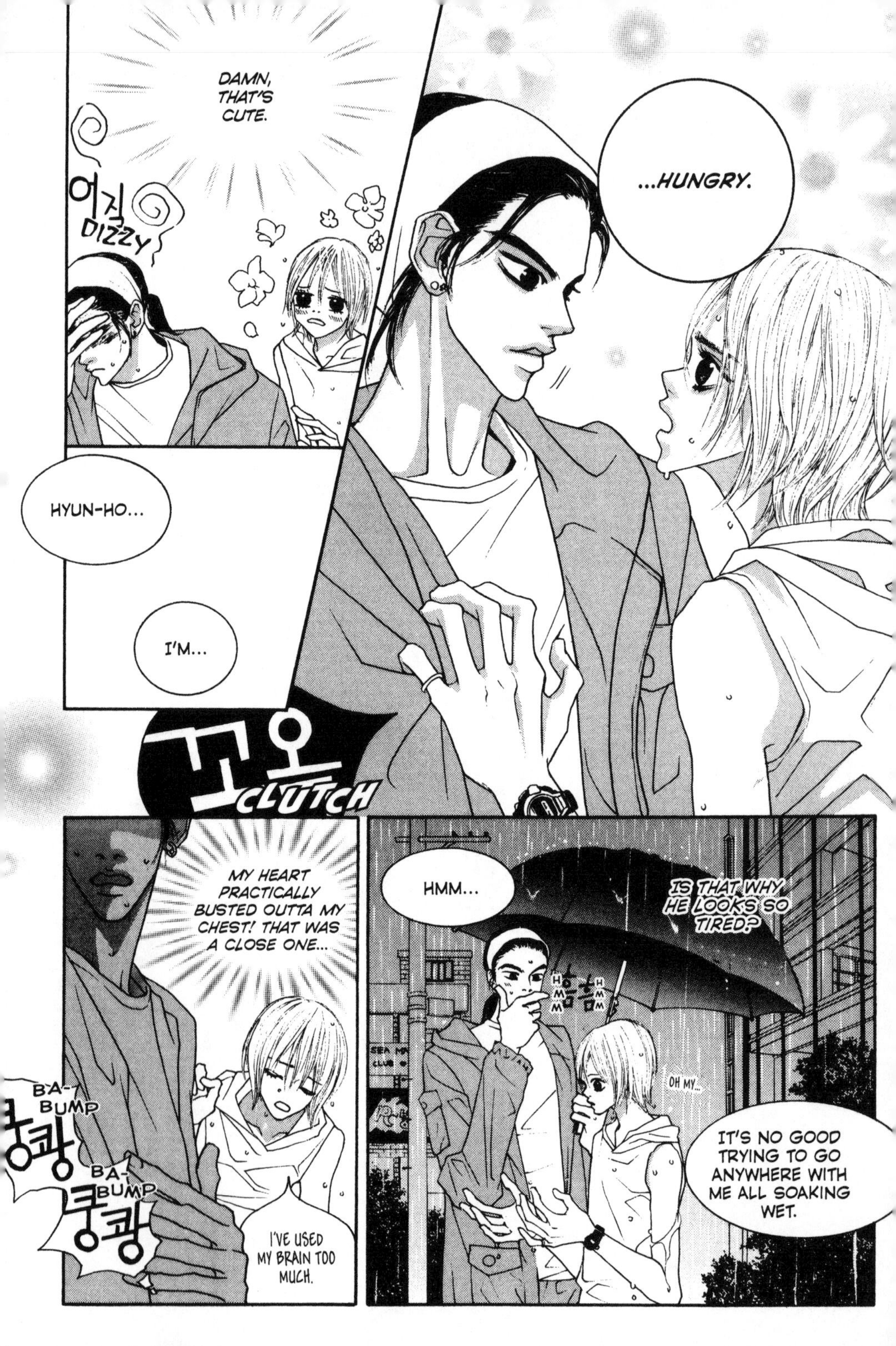

DAMN, THAT'S CUTE.
어질
DIZZY
HYUN-HO...
I'M...
...HUNGRY.
CLUTCH
MY HEART PRACTICALLY BUSTED OUTTA MY CHEST! THAT WAS A CLOSE ONE...
BA-BUMP
쿵쾅
BA-BUMP
쿵쾅
I'VE USED MY BRAIN TOO MUCH.
HMM...
IS THAT WHY HE LOOKS SO TIRED?
HMM
HMM
OH MY...
IT'S NO GOOD TRYING TO GO ANYWHERE WITH ME ALL SOAKING WET.

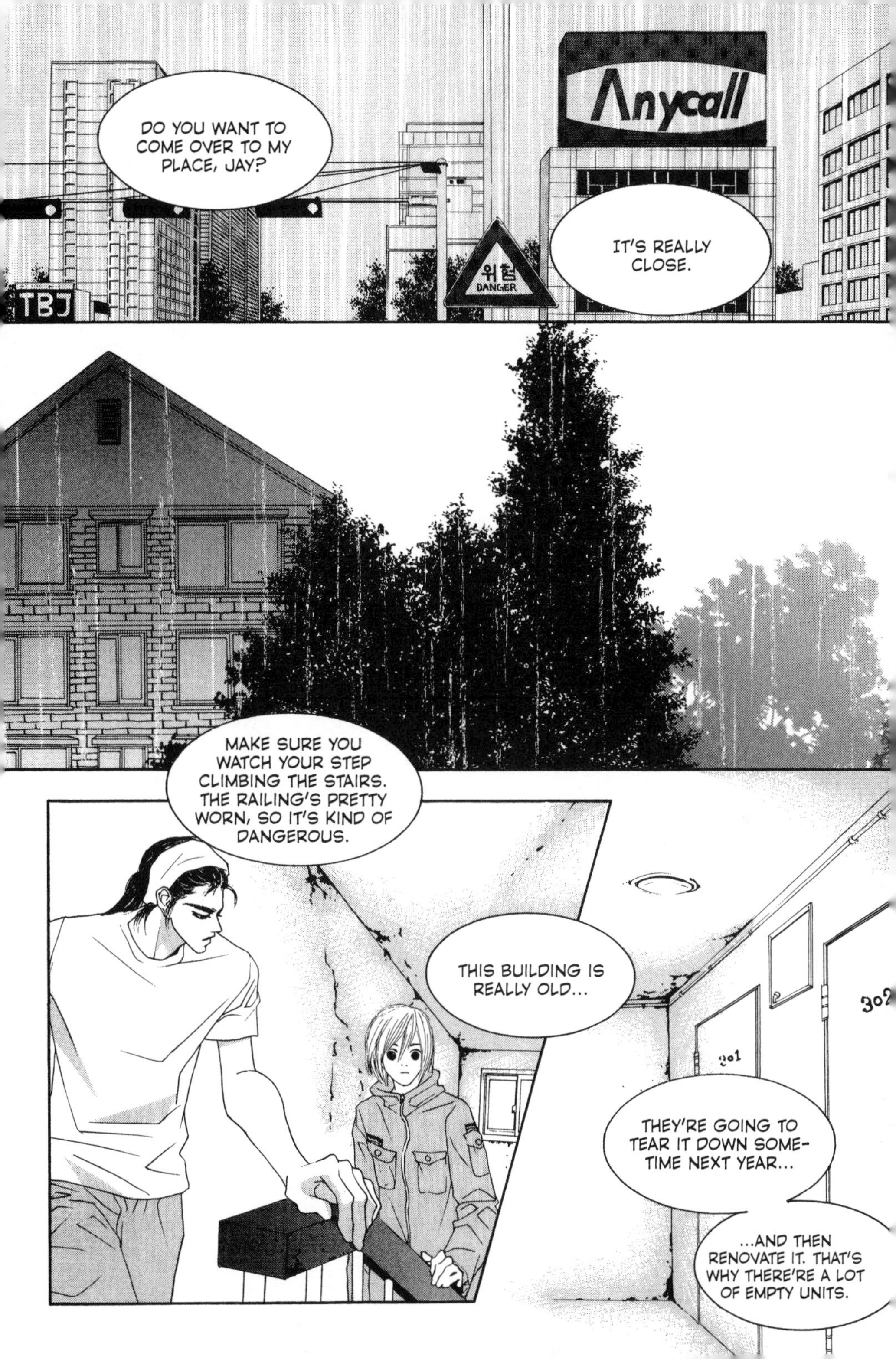
DO YOU WANT TO COME OVER TO MY PLACE, JAY?
Anycall
TBJ
위험
DANGER
IT'S REALLY CLOSE.
MAKE SURE YOU WATCH YOUR STEP CLIMBING THE STAIRS. THE RAILING'S PRETTY WORN, SO IT'S KIND OF DANGEROUS.
THIS BUILDING IS REALLY OLD...
301
302
THEY'RE GOING TO TEAR IT DOWN SOME-TIME NEXT YEAR...
...AND THEN RENOVATE IT. THAT'S WHY THERE'RE A LOT OF EMPTY UNITS.

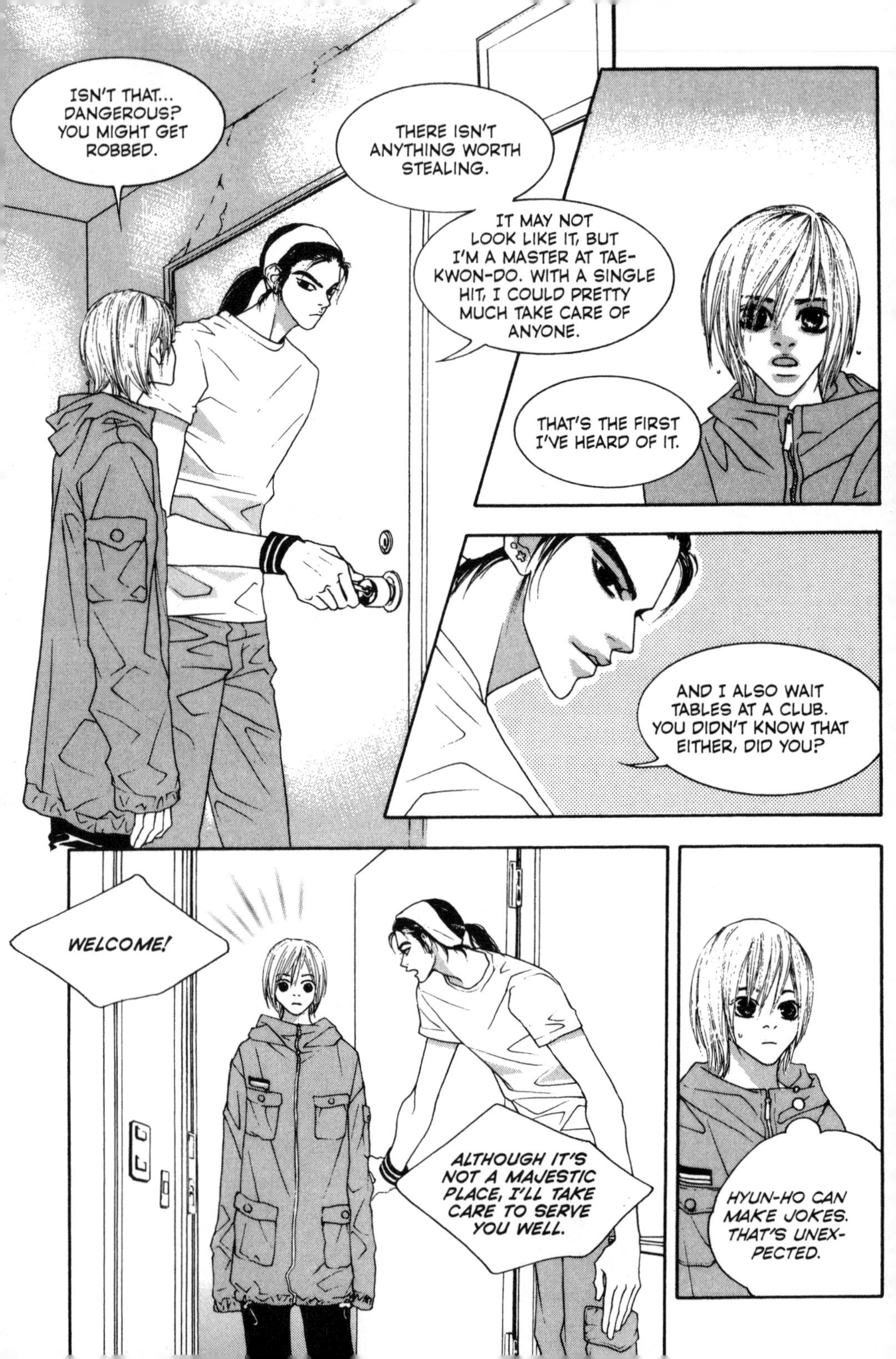
ISN'T THAT... DANGEROUS? YOU MIGHT GET ROBBED.
THERE ISN'T ANYTHING WORTH STEALING.
IT MAY NOT LOOK LIKE IT, BUT I'M A MASTER AT TAE-KWON-DO. WITH A SINGLE HIT, I COULD PRETTY MUCH TAKE CARE OF ANYONE.
THAT'S THE FIRST I'VE HEARD OF IT.
AND I ALSO WAIT TABLES AT A CLUB. YOU DIDN'T KNOW THAT EITHER, DID YOU?
WELCOME!
ALTHOUGH IT'S NOT A MAJESTIC PLACE, I'LL TAKE CARE TO SERVE YOU WELL.
HYUN-HO CAN MAKE JOKES. THAT'S UNEX-PECTED.

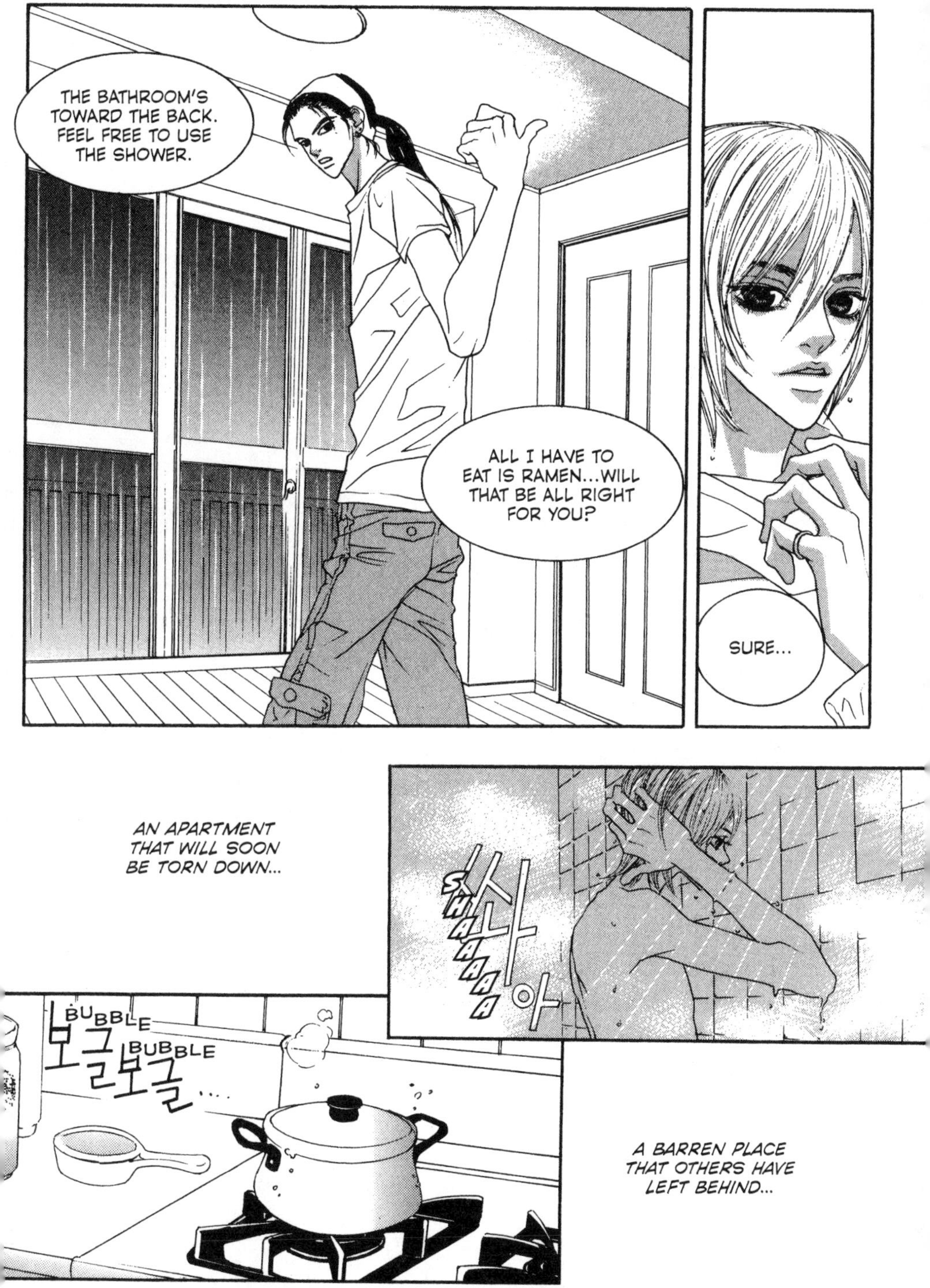
THE BATHROOM'S TOWARD THE BACK. FEEL FREE TO USE THE SHOWER.
ALL I HAVE TO EAT IS RAMEN...WILL THAT BE ALL RIGHT FOR YOU?
SURE...
AN APARTMENT THAT WILL SOON BE TORN DOWN...
샤아
SHAAAAAA
보글보글...
BUBBLE BUBBLE
A BARREN PLACE THAT OTHERS HAVE LEFT BEHIND...

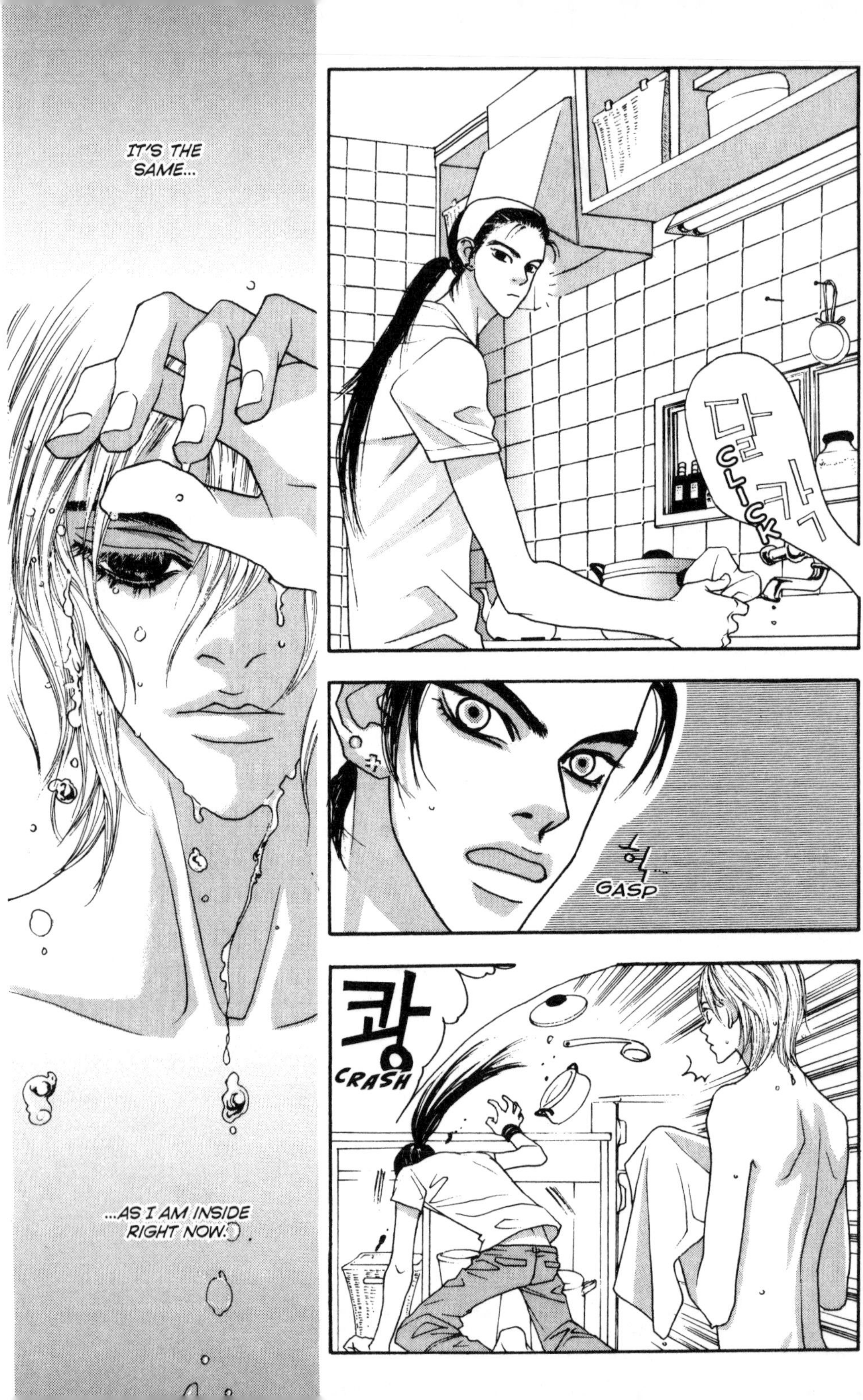
IT'S THE SAME...
...AS I AM INSIDE RIGHT NOW.
달칵
CLICK
헉...
GASP
쾅
CRASH

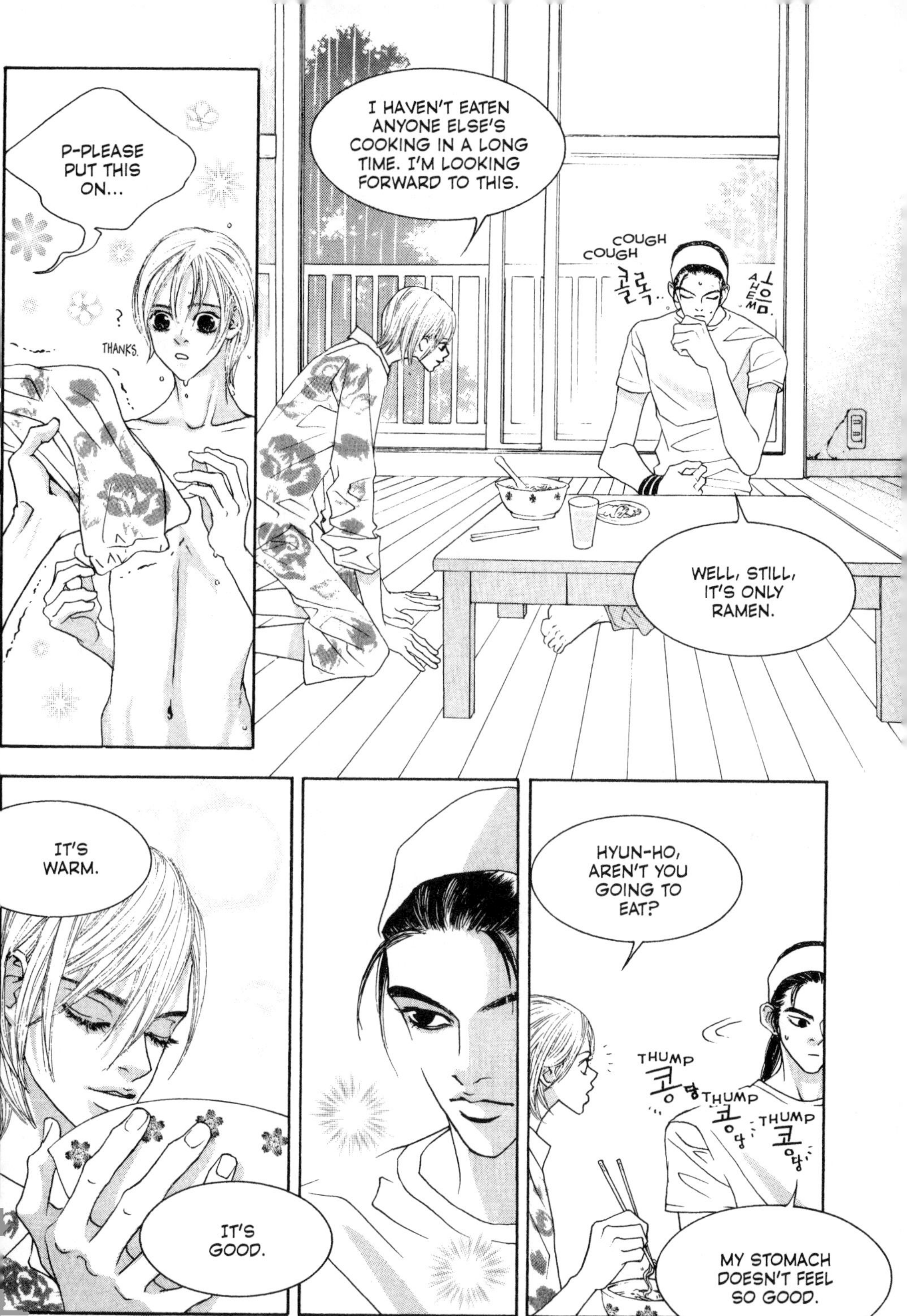

P-PLEASE PUT THIS ON...
?
THANKS.
I HAVEN'T EATEN ANYONE ELSE'S COOKING IN A LONG TIME. I'M LOOKING FORWARD TO THIS.
COUGH COUGH
콜록..
AHEM
흠.
WELL, STILL, IT'S ONLY RAMEN.
IT'S WARM.
IT'S GOOD.
HYUN-HO, AREN'T YOU GOING TO EAT?
THUMP
콩닥
THUMP
콩닥
THUMP
콩닥
MY STOMACH DOESN'T FEEL SO GOOD.

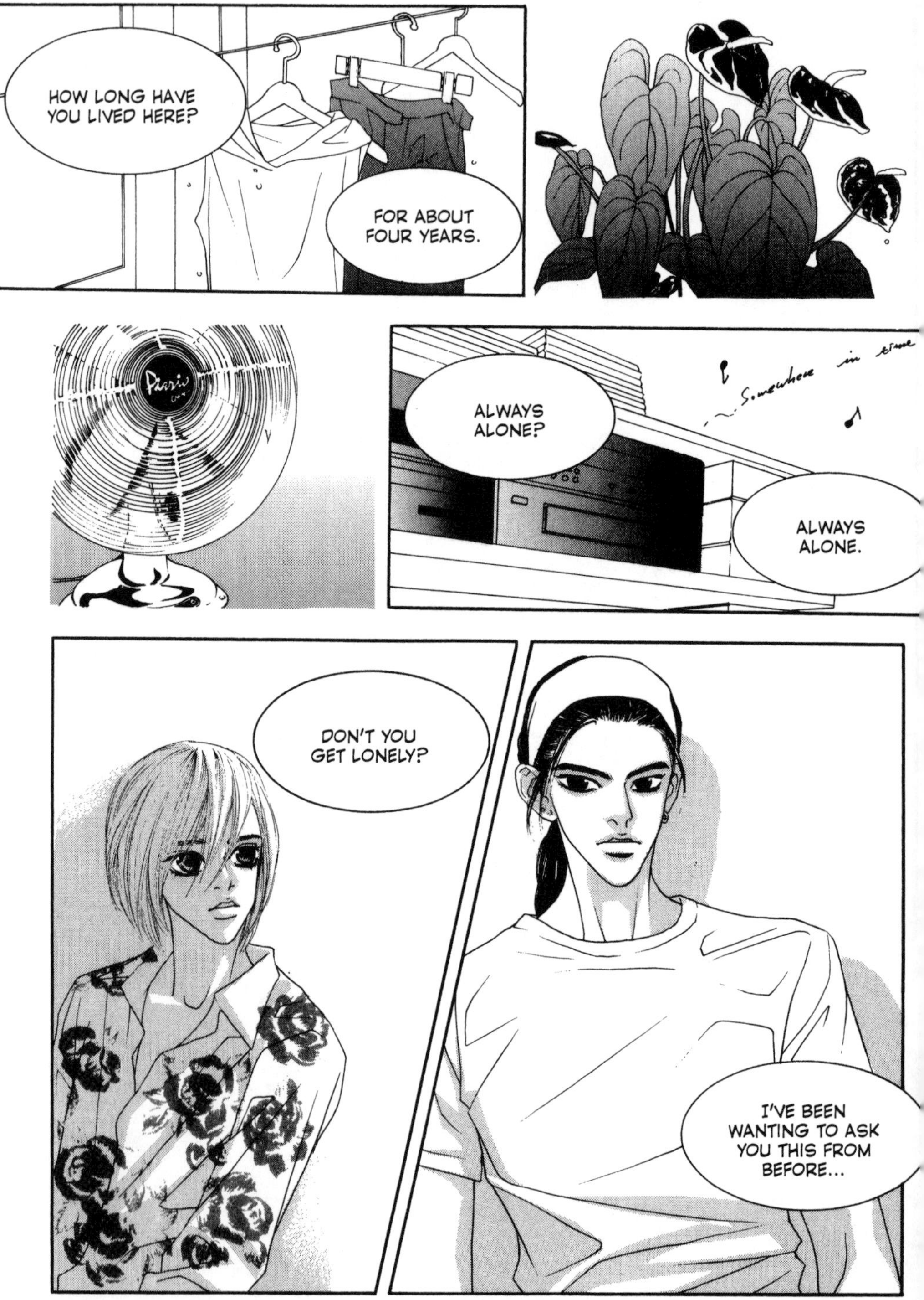
HOW LONG HAVE YOU LIVED HERE?
FOR ABOUT FOUR YEARS.
ALWAYS ALONE?
Somewhere in time
ALWAYS ALONE.
DON'T YOU GET LONELY?
I'VE BEEN WANTING TO ASK YOU THIS FROM BEFORE...

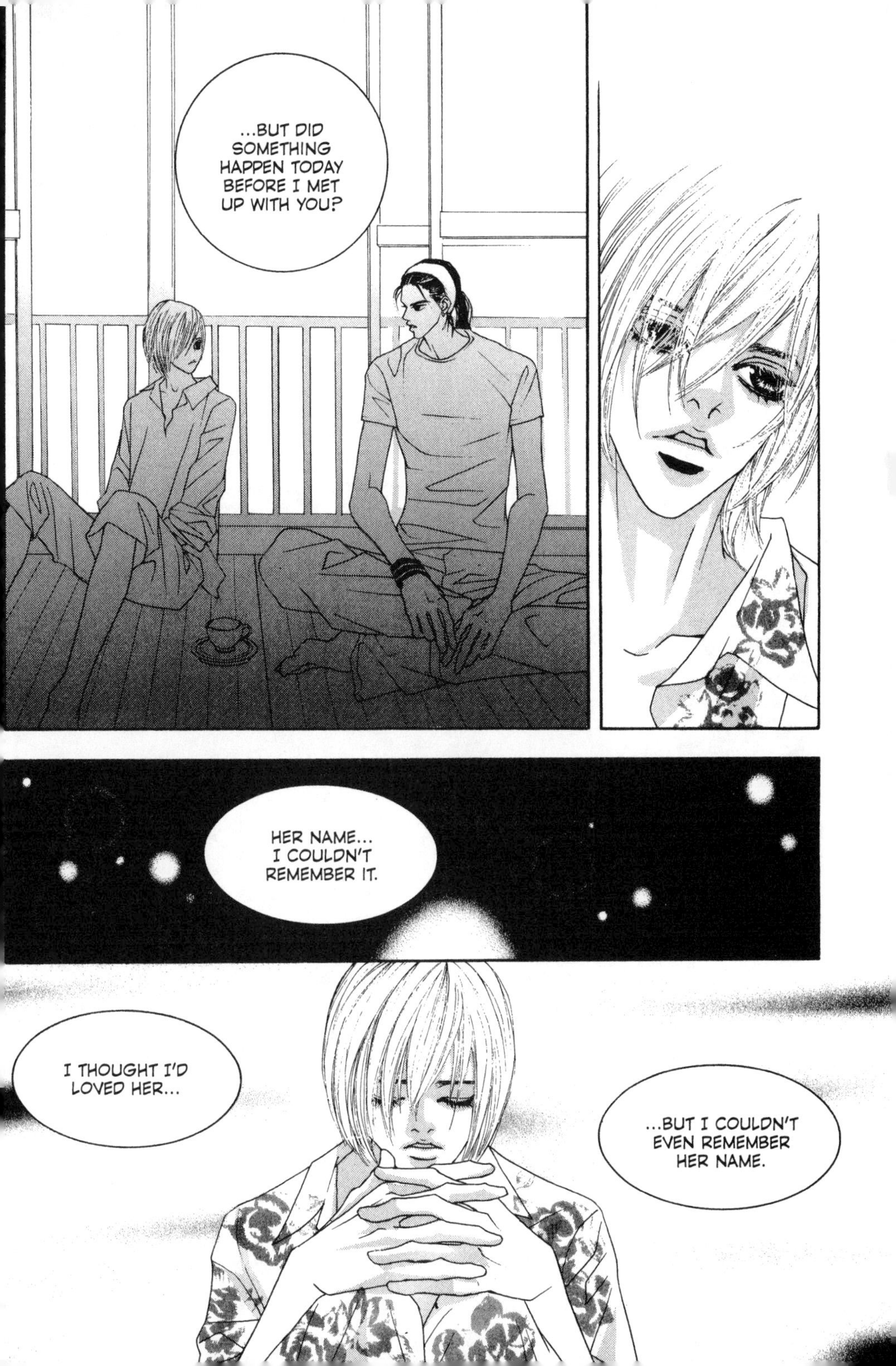
...BUT DID SOMETHING HAPPEN TODAY BEFORE I MET UP WITH YOU?
HER NAME... I COULDN'T REMEMBER IT.
I THOUGHT I'D LOVED HER...
...BUT I COULDN'T EVEN REMEMBER HER NAME.

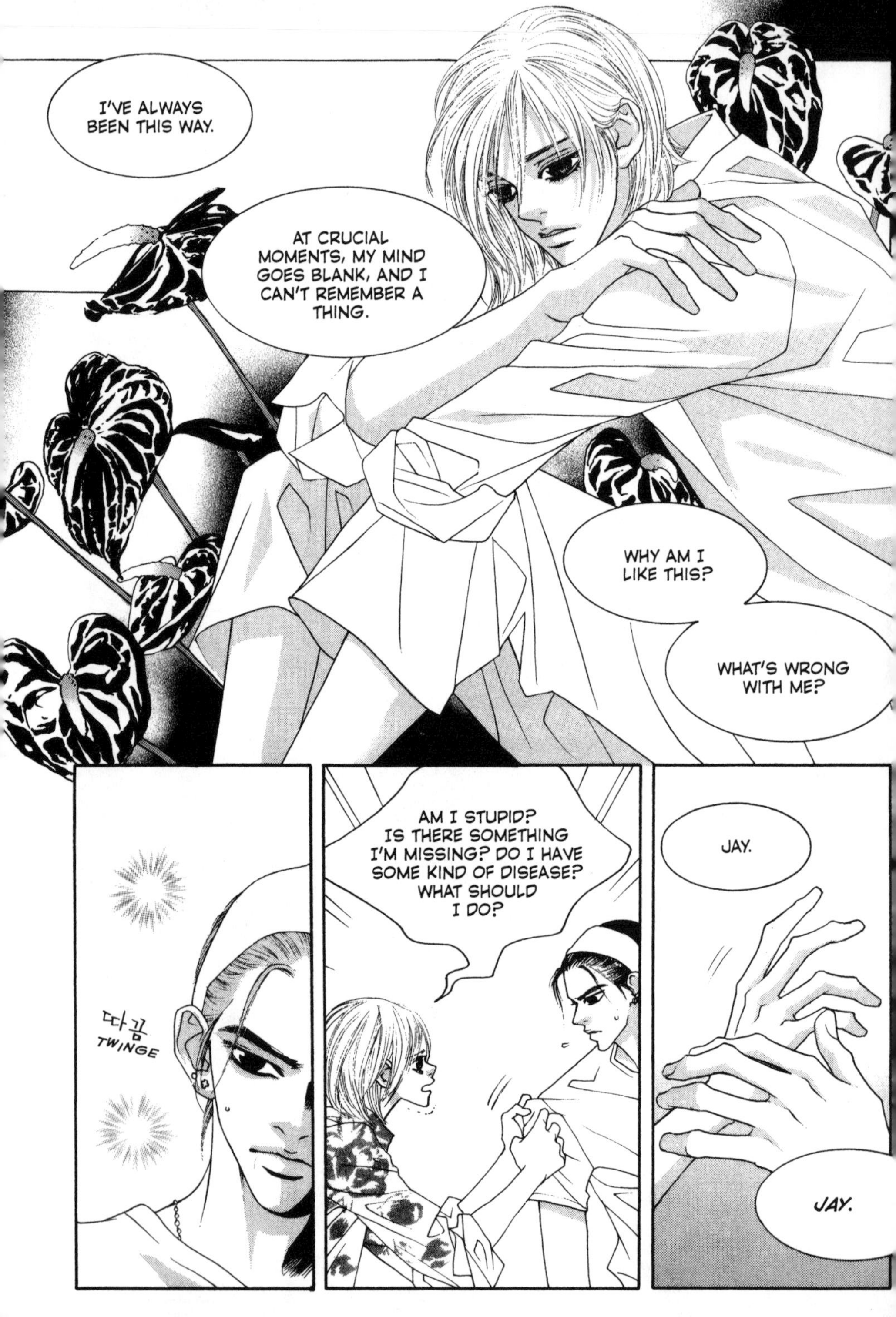
I'VE ALWAYS BEEN THIS WAY.
AT CRUCIAL MOMENTS, MY MIND GOES BLANK, AND I CAN'T REMEMBER A THING.
WHY AM I LIKE THIS?
WHAT'S WRONG WITH ME?
따끔
TWINGE
AM I STUPID? IS THERE SOMETHING I'M MISSING? DO I HAVE SOME KIND OF DISEASE? WHAT SHOULD I DO?
JAY.
JAY.

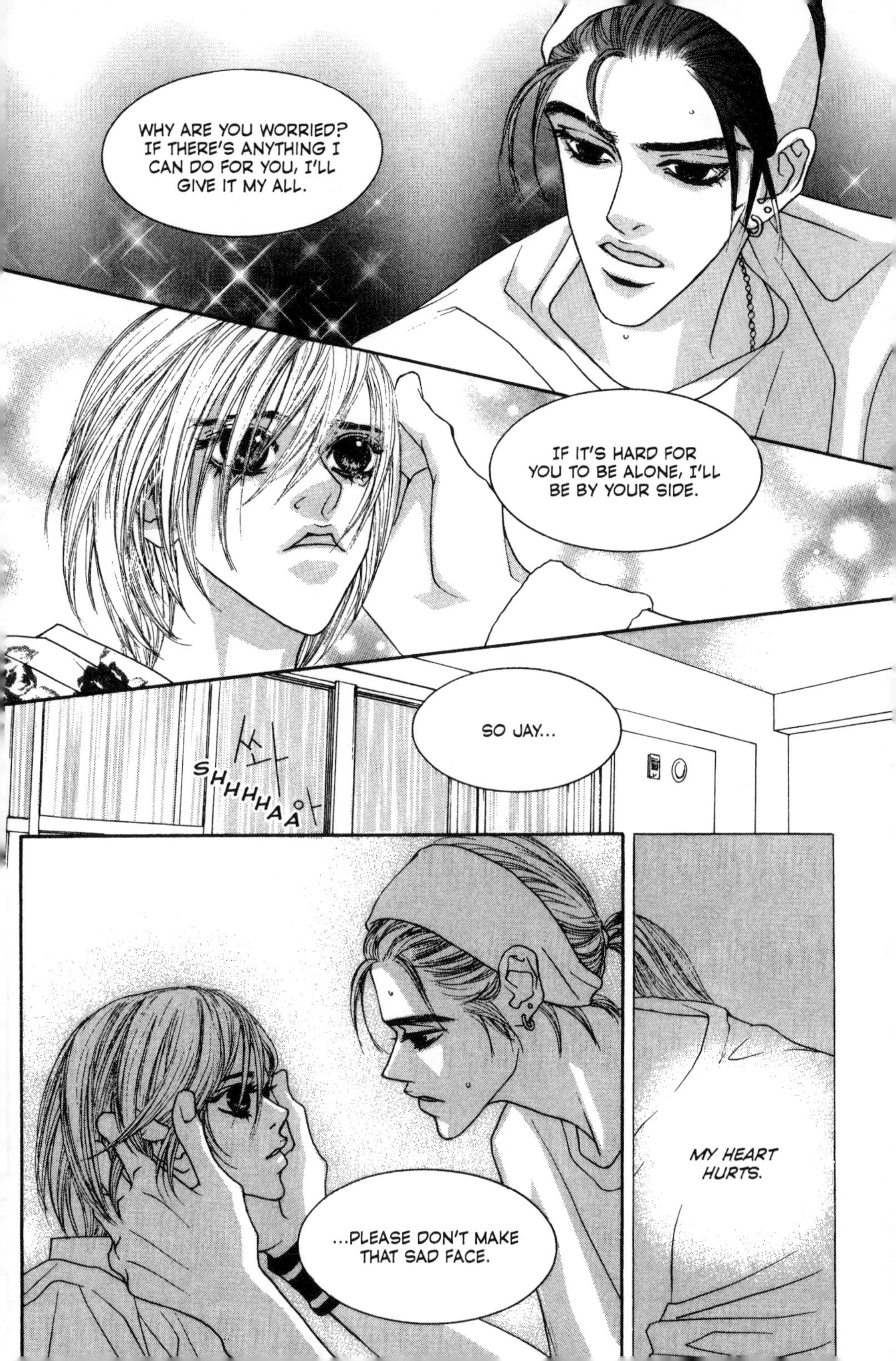
WHY ARE YOU WORRIED? IF THERE'S ANYTHING I CAN DO FOR YOU, I'LL GIVE IT MY ALL.
IF IT'S HARD FOR YOU TO BE ALONE, I'LL BE BY YOUR SIDE.
SHHHHAAA
SO JAY...
...PLEASE DON'T MAKE THAT SAD FACE.
MY HEART HURTS.

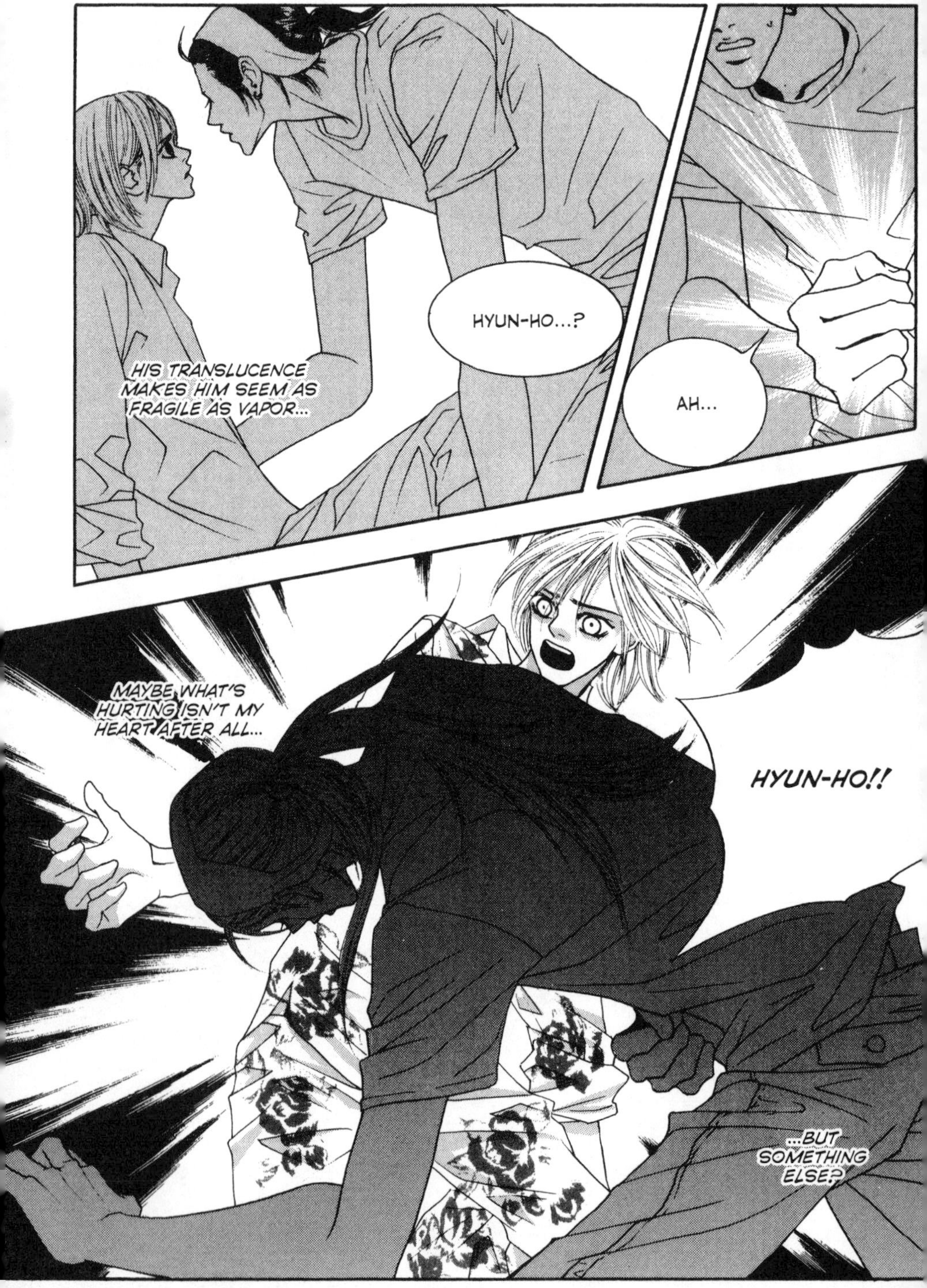

HIS TRANSLUCENCE MAKES HIM SEEM AS FRAGILE AS VAPOR...
HYUN-HO...?
AH...
MAYBE WHAT'S HURTING ISN'T MY HEART AFTER ALL...
HYUN-HO!!
...BUT SOMETHING ELSE?

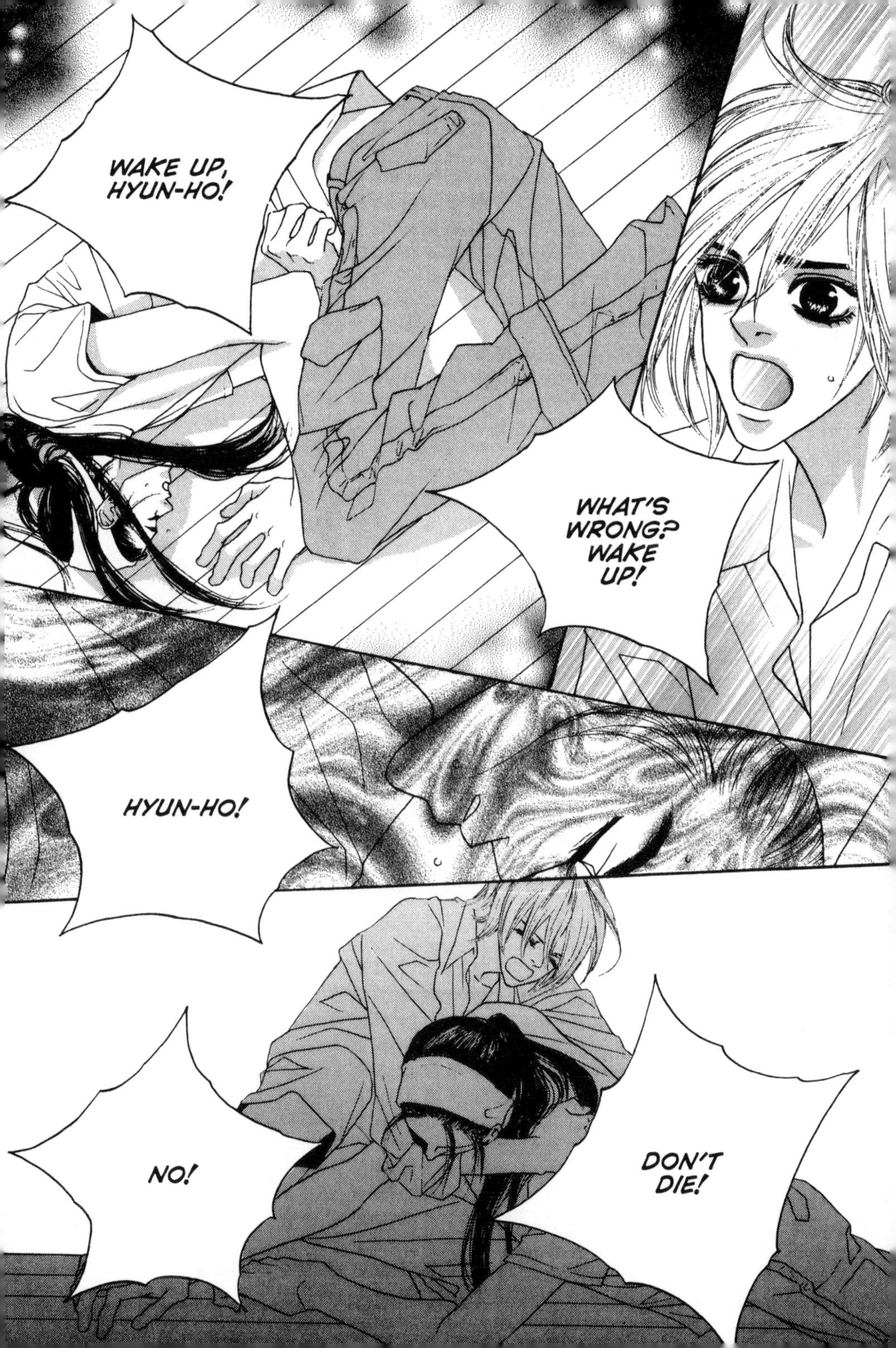
WAKE UP, HYUN-HO!
WHAT'S WRONG? WAKE UP!
HYUN-HO!
NO!
DON'T DIE!

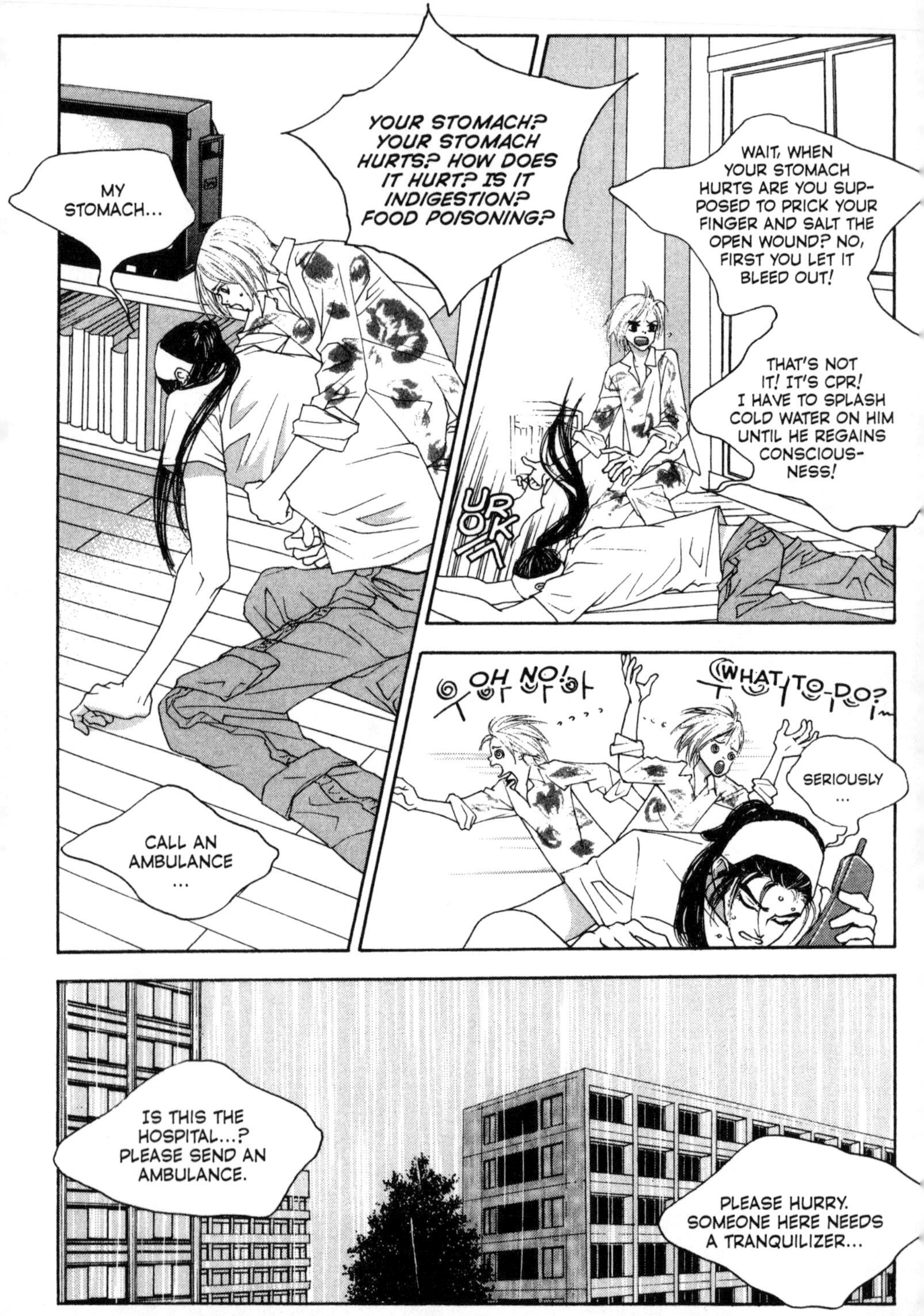
MY STOMACH...
YOUR STOMACH? YOUR STOMACH HURTS? HOW DOES IT HURT? IS IT INDIGESTION? FOOD POISONING?
CALL AN AMBULANCE ...
WAIT, WHEN YOUR STOMACH HURTS ARE YOU SUPPOSED TO PRICK YOUR FINGER AND SALT THE OPEN WOUND? NO, FIRST YOU LET IT BLEED OUT!
THAT'S NOT IT! IT'S CPR! I HAVE TO SPLASH COLD WATER ON HIM UNTIL HE REGAINS CONSCIOUSNESS!
UROK
OH NO!
WHAT TO DO?
SERIOUSLY ...
IS THIS THE HOSPITAL...? PLEASE SEND AN AMBULANCE.
PLEASE HURRY. SOMEONE HERE NEEDS A TRANQUILIZER...

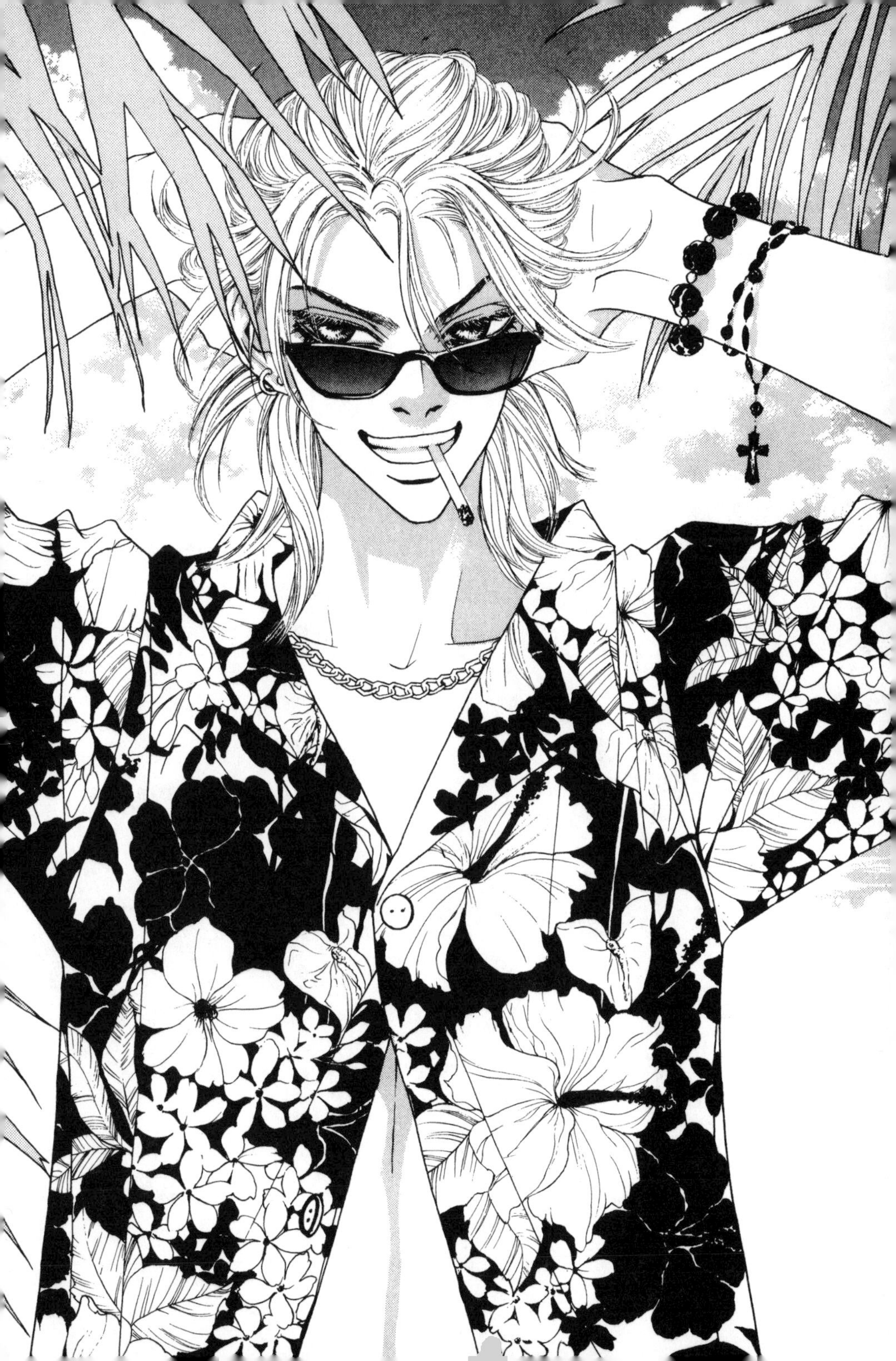

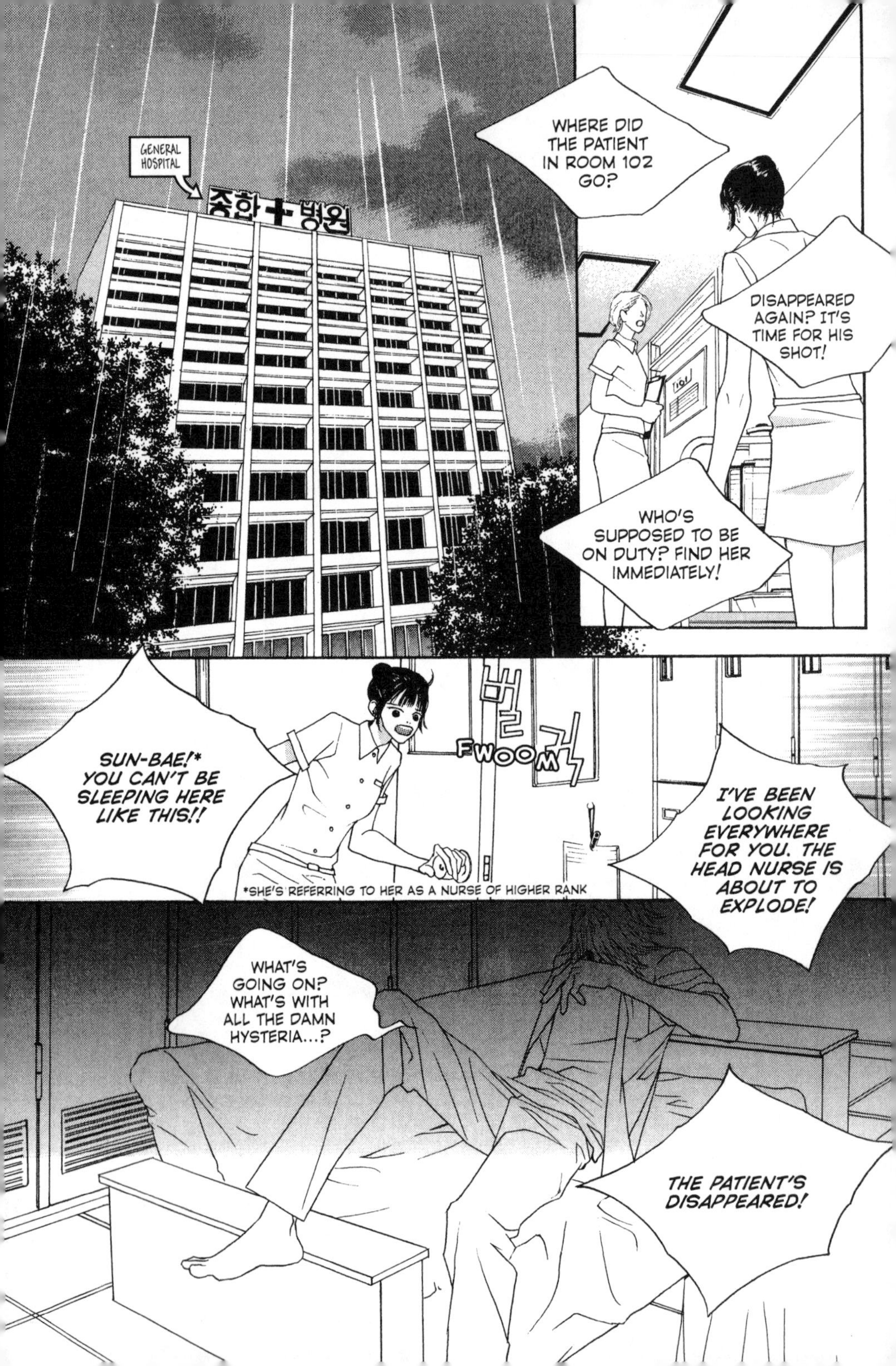
GENERAL HOSPITAL
종합 병원
WHERE DID THE PATIENT IN ROOM 102 GO?
DISAPPEARED AGAIN? IT'S TIME FOR HIS SHOT!
WHO'S SUPPOSED TO BE ON DUTY? FIND HER IMMEDIATELY!
SUN-BAE!* YOU CAN'T BE SLEEPING HERE LIKE THIS!!
벌컥
FWOOM
I'VE BEEN LOOKING EVERYWHERE FOR YOU. THE HEAD NURSE IS ABOUT TO EXPLODE!
*SHE'S REFERRING TO HER AS A NURSE OF HIGHER RANK
WHAT'S GOING ON? WHAT'S WITH ALL THE DAMN HYSTERIA...?
THE PATIENT'S DISAPPEARED!

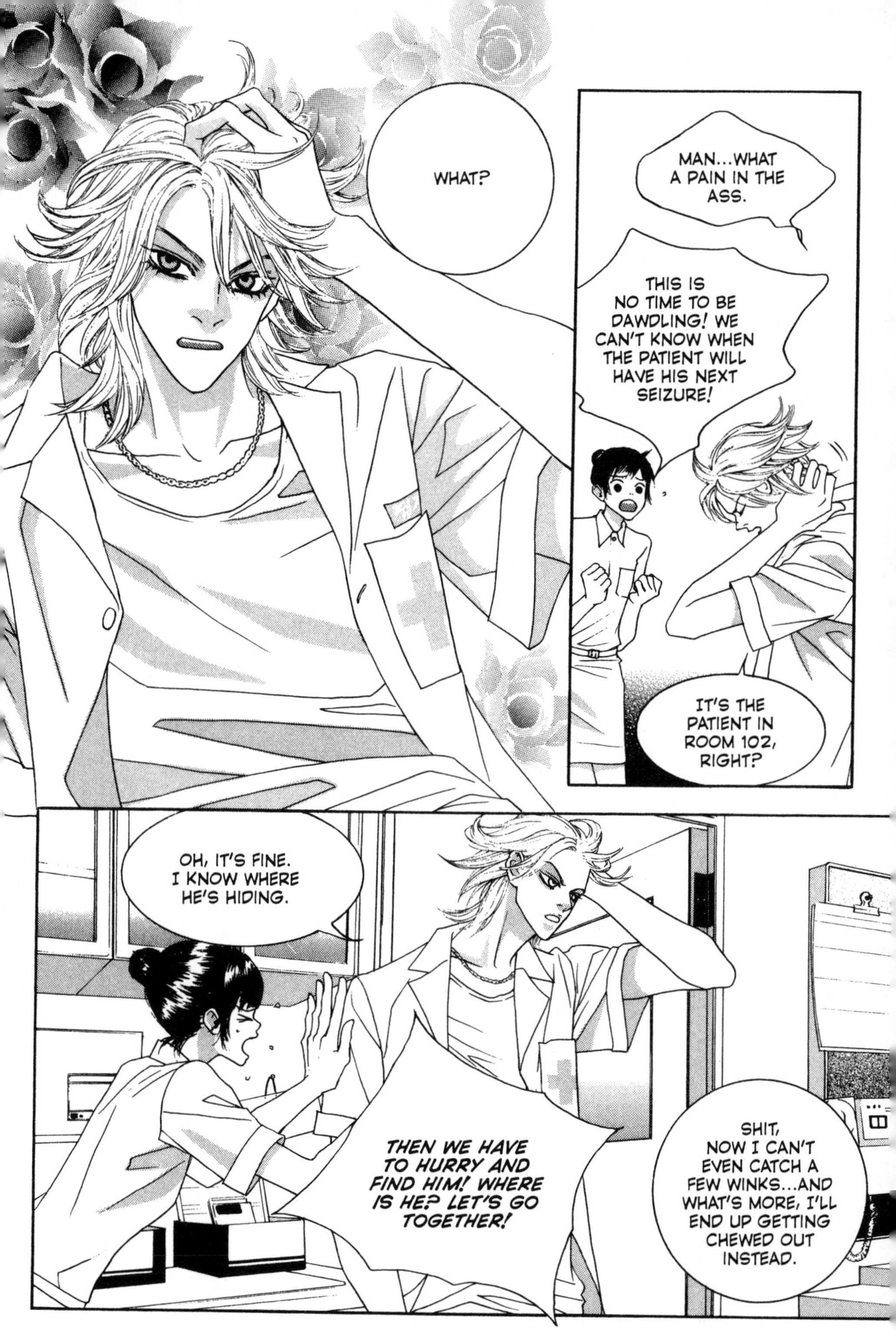

WHAT?
MAN...WHAT A PAIN IN THE ASS.
THIS IS NO TIME TO BE DAWDLING! WE CAN'T KNOW WHEN THE PATIENT WILL HAVE HIS NEXT SEIZURE!
IT'S THE PATIENT IN ROOM 102, RIGHT?
OH, IT'S FINE. I KNOW WHERE HE'S HIDING.
THEN WE HAVE TO HURRY AND FIND HIM! WHERE IS HE? LET'S GO TOGETHER!
SHIT, NOW I CAN'T EVEN CATCH A FEW WINKS...AND WHAT'S MORE, I'LL END UP GETTING CHEWED OUT INSTEAD.

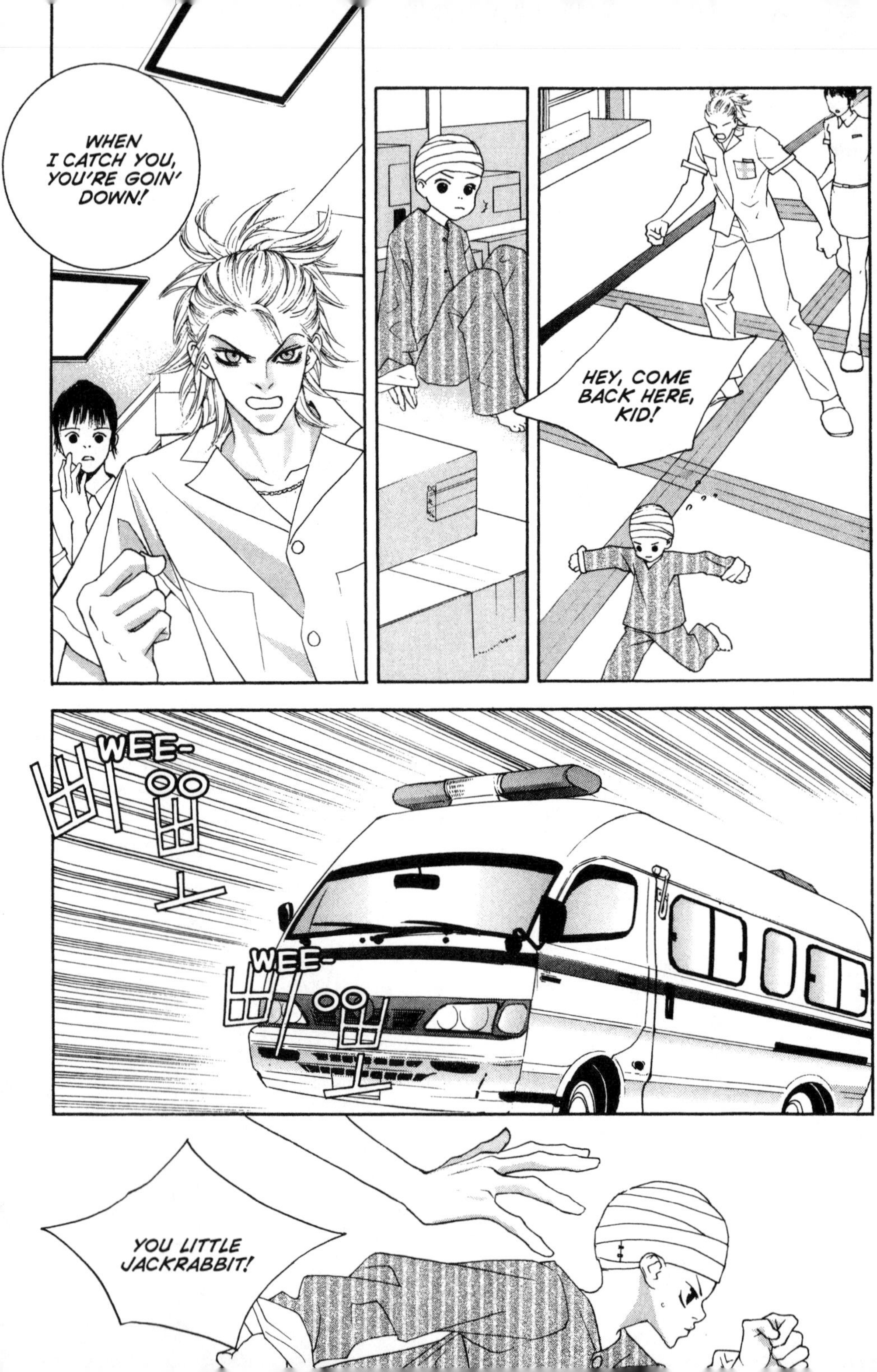
WHEN I CATCH YOU, YOU'RE GOIN' DOWN!
HEY, COME BACK HERE, KID!
WEE-
OO
WEE-
OO
YOU LITTLE JACKRABBIT!

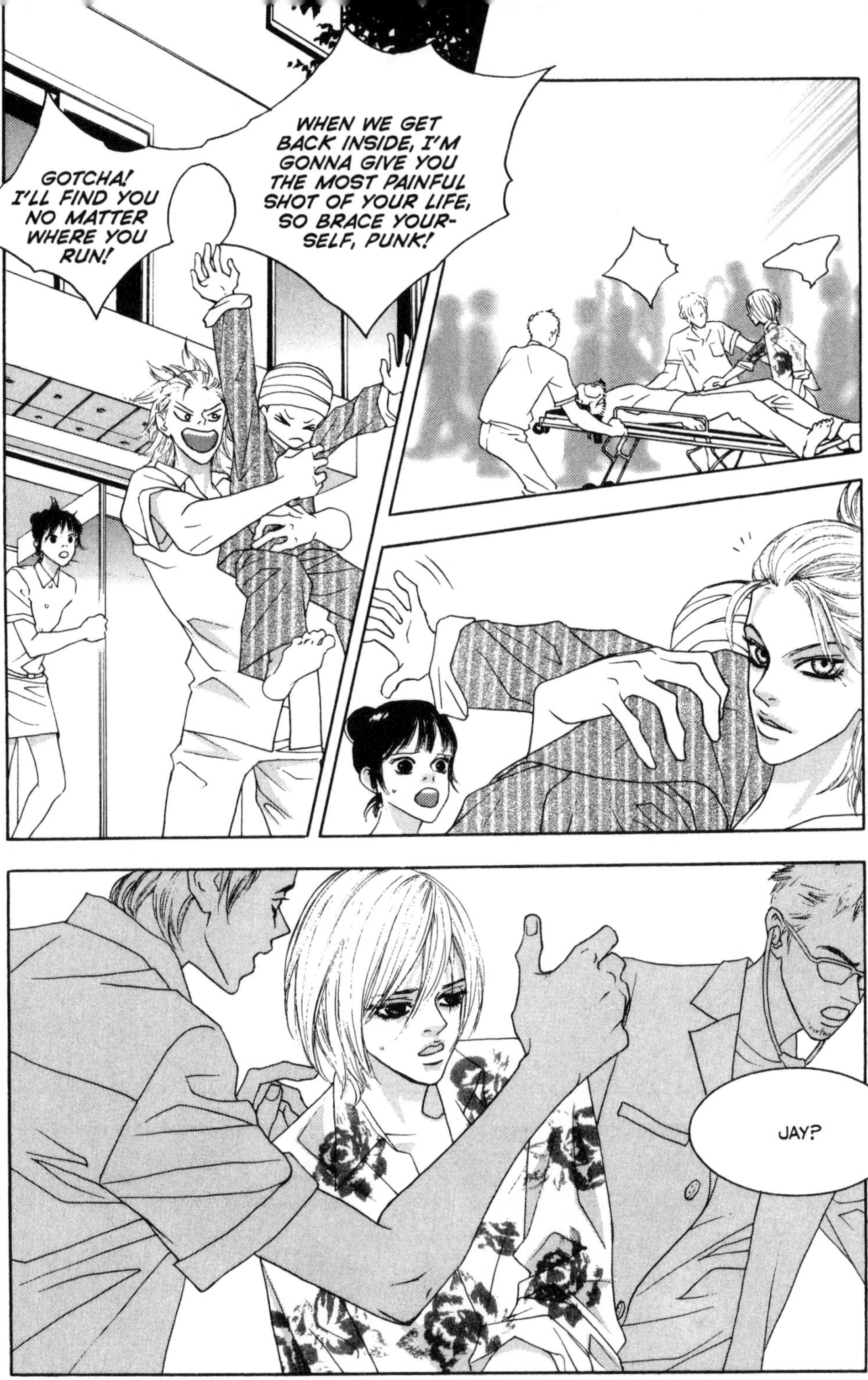
GOTCHA! I'LL FIND YOU NO MATTER WHERE YOU RUN!
WHEN WE GET BACK INSIDE, I'M GONNA GIVE YOU THE MOST PAINFUL SHOT OF YOUR LIFE, SO BRACE YOURSELF, PUNK!
JAY?

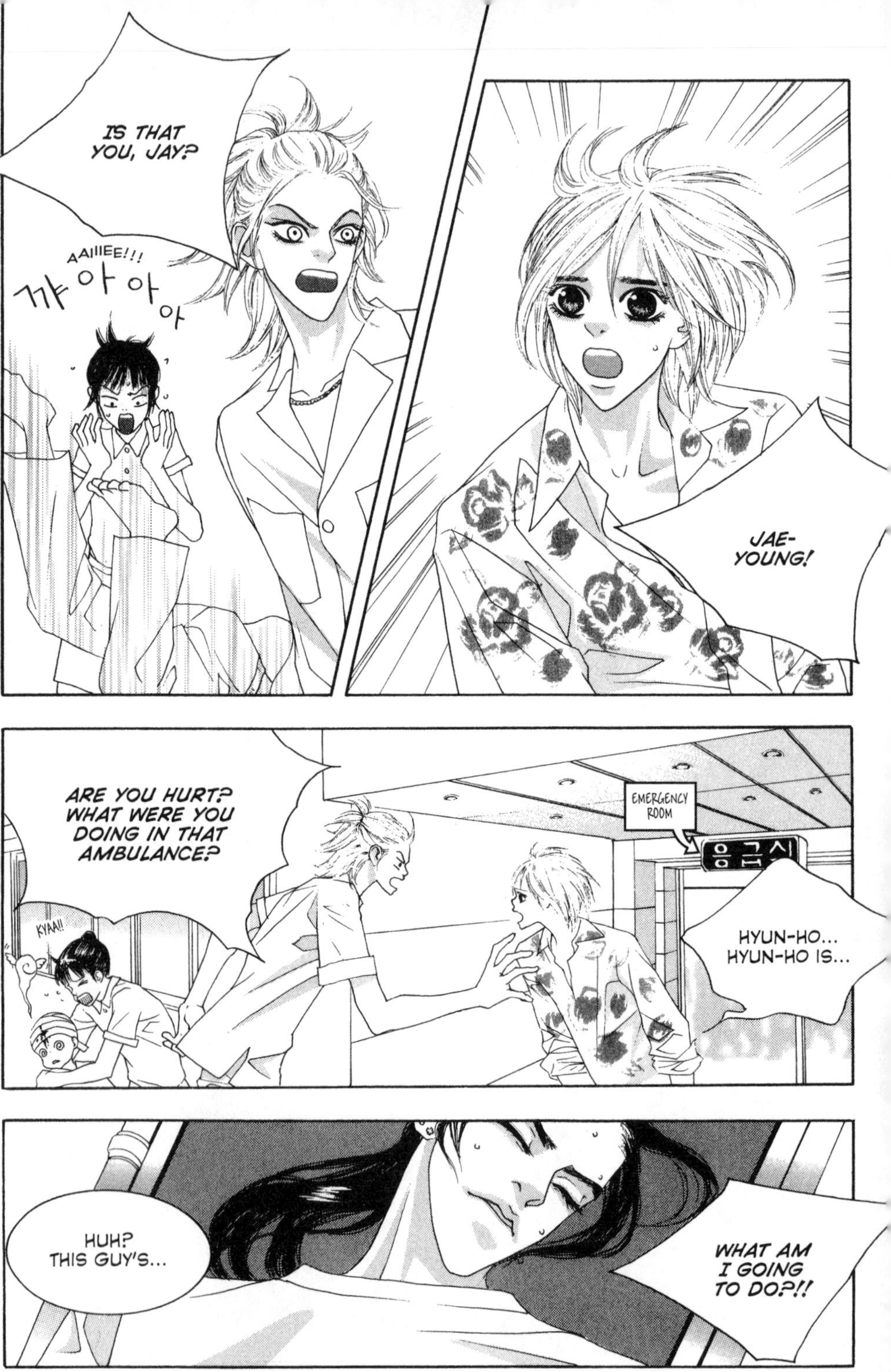
IS THAT YOU, JAY?
AAIIIEE!!!
갸아아아
JAE-YOUNG!
ARE YOU HURT? WHAT WERE YOU DOING IN THAT AMBULANCE?
KYAA!!
EMERGENCY ROOM
HYUN-HO... HYUN-HO IS...
HUH? THIS GUY'S...
WHAT AM I GOING TO DO?!!

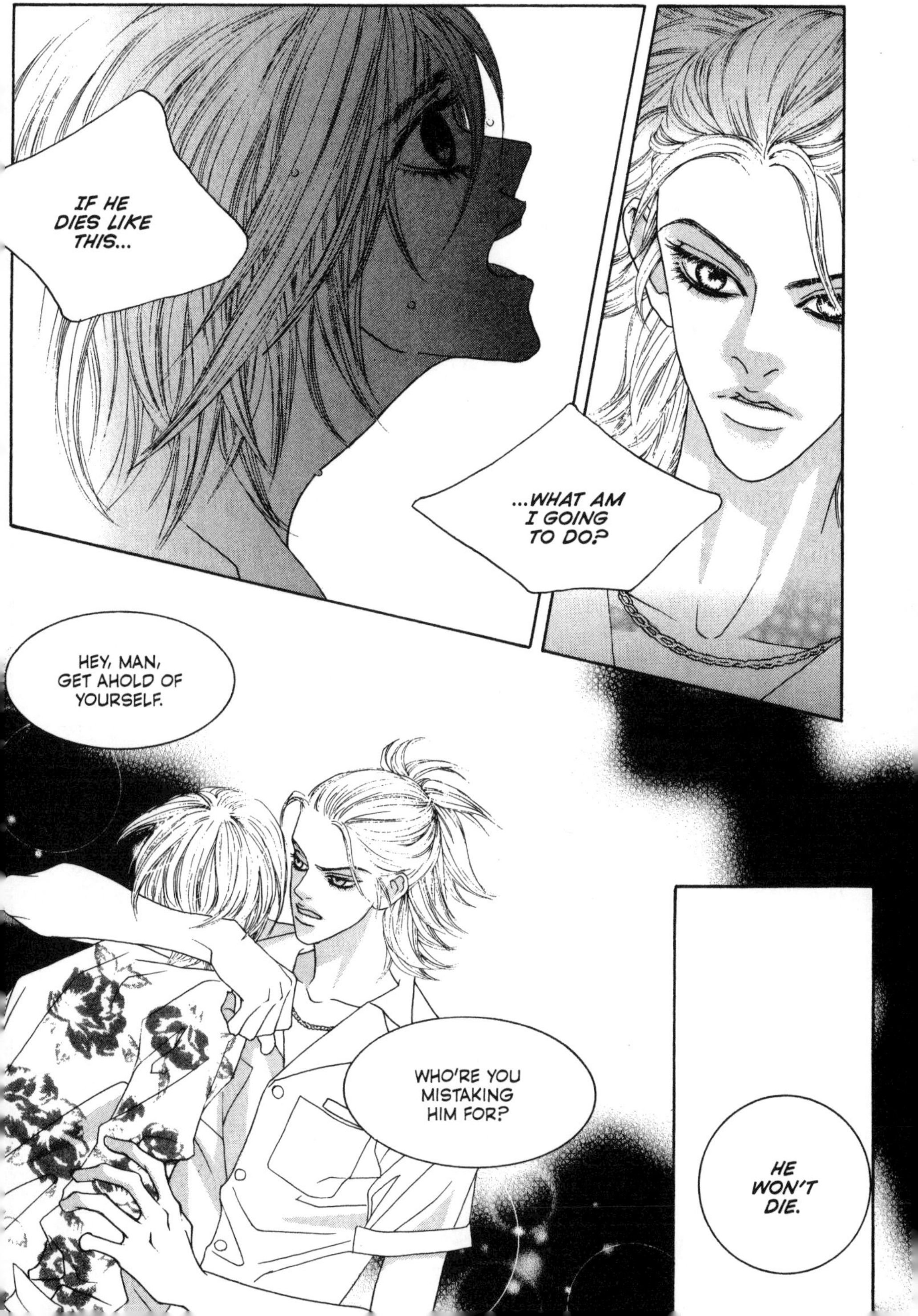
IF HE DIES LIKE THIS...
...WHAT AM I GOING TO DO?
HEY, MAN, GET AHOLD OF YOURSELF.
WHO'RE YOU MISTAKING HIM FOR?
HE WON'T DIE.

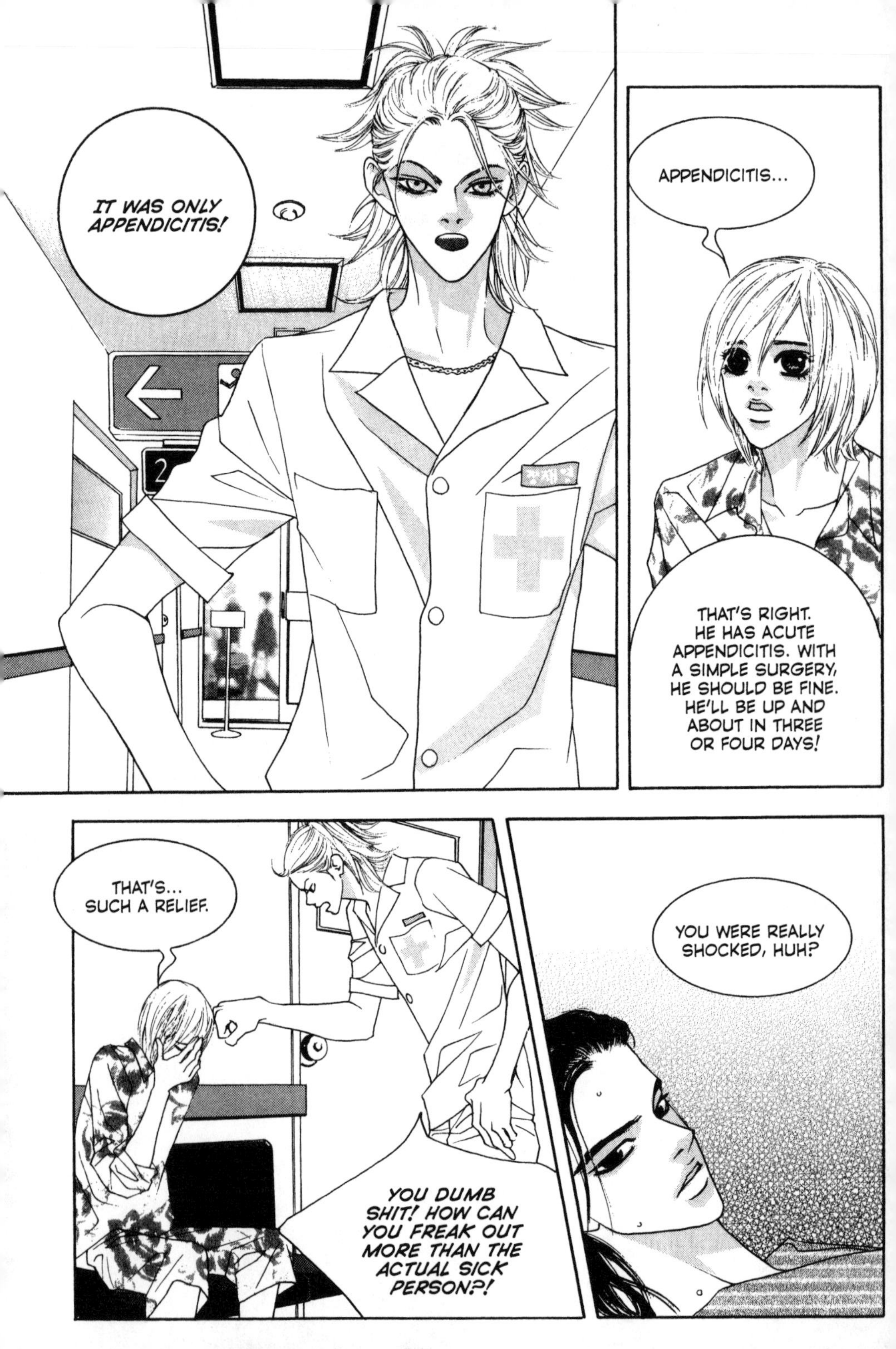
IT WAS ONLY APPENDICITIS!
APPENDICITIS...
THAT'S RIGHT. HE HAS ACUTE APPENDICITIS. WITH A SIMPLE SURGERY, HE SHOULD BE FINE. HE'LL BE UP AND ABOUT IN THREE OR FOUR DAYS!
THAT'S... SUCH A RELIEF.
YOU DUMB SHIT! HOW CAN YOU FREAK OUT MORE THAN THE ACTUAL SICK PERSON?!
YOU WERE REALLY SHOCKED, HUH?

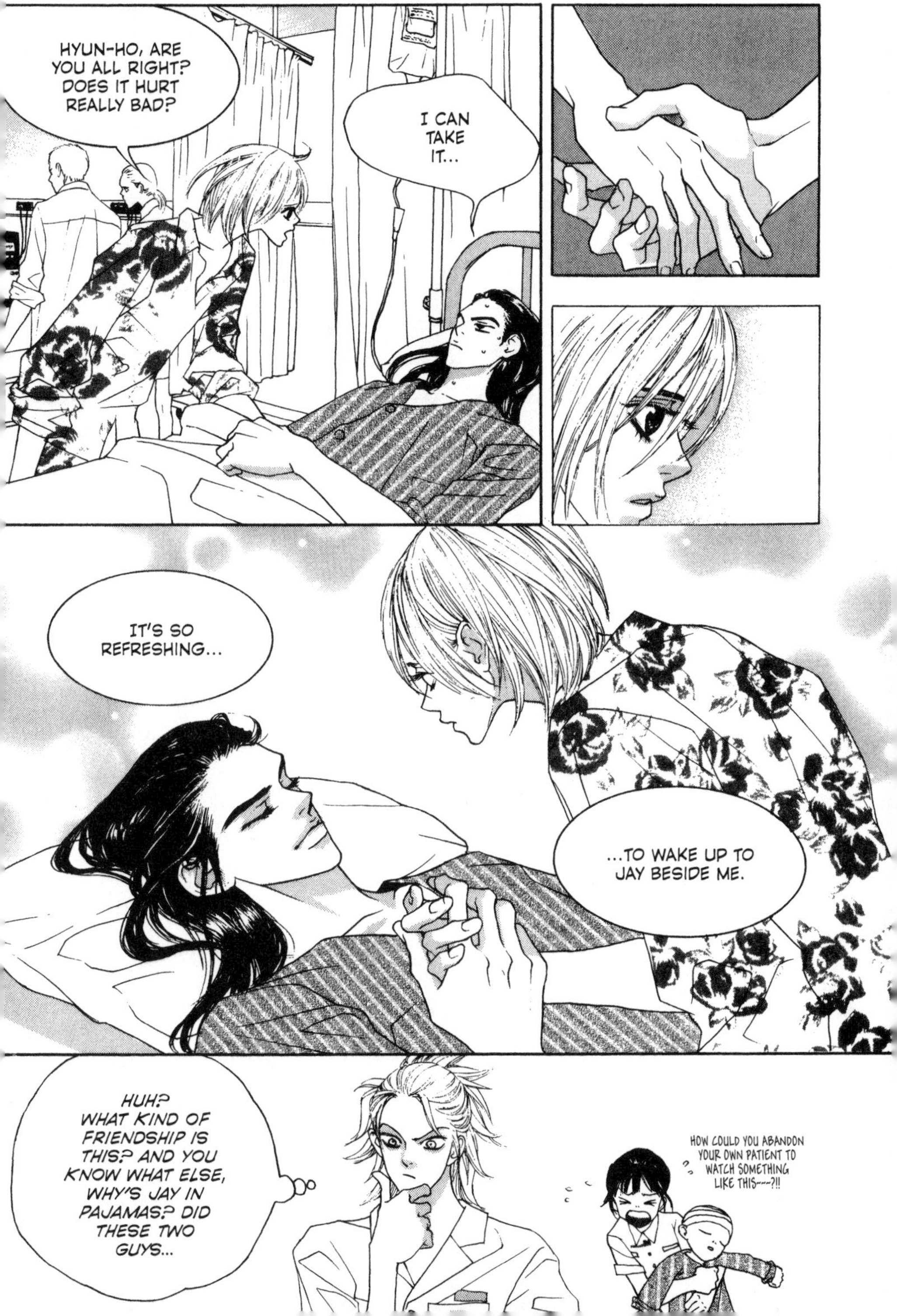
HYUN-HO, ARE YOU ALL RIGHT? DOES IT HURT REALLY BAD?
I CAN TAKE IT...
IT'S SO REFRESHING...
...TO WAKE UP TO JAY BESIDE ME.
HUH? WHAT KIND OF FRIENDSHIP IS THIS? AND YOU KNOW WHAT ELSE, WHY'S JAY IN PAJAMAS? DID THESE TWO GUYS...
HOW COULD YOU ABANDON YOUR OWN PATIENT TO WATCH SOMETHING LIKE THIS~~~?!!

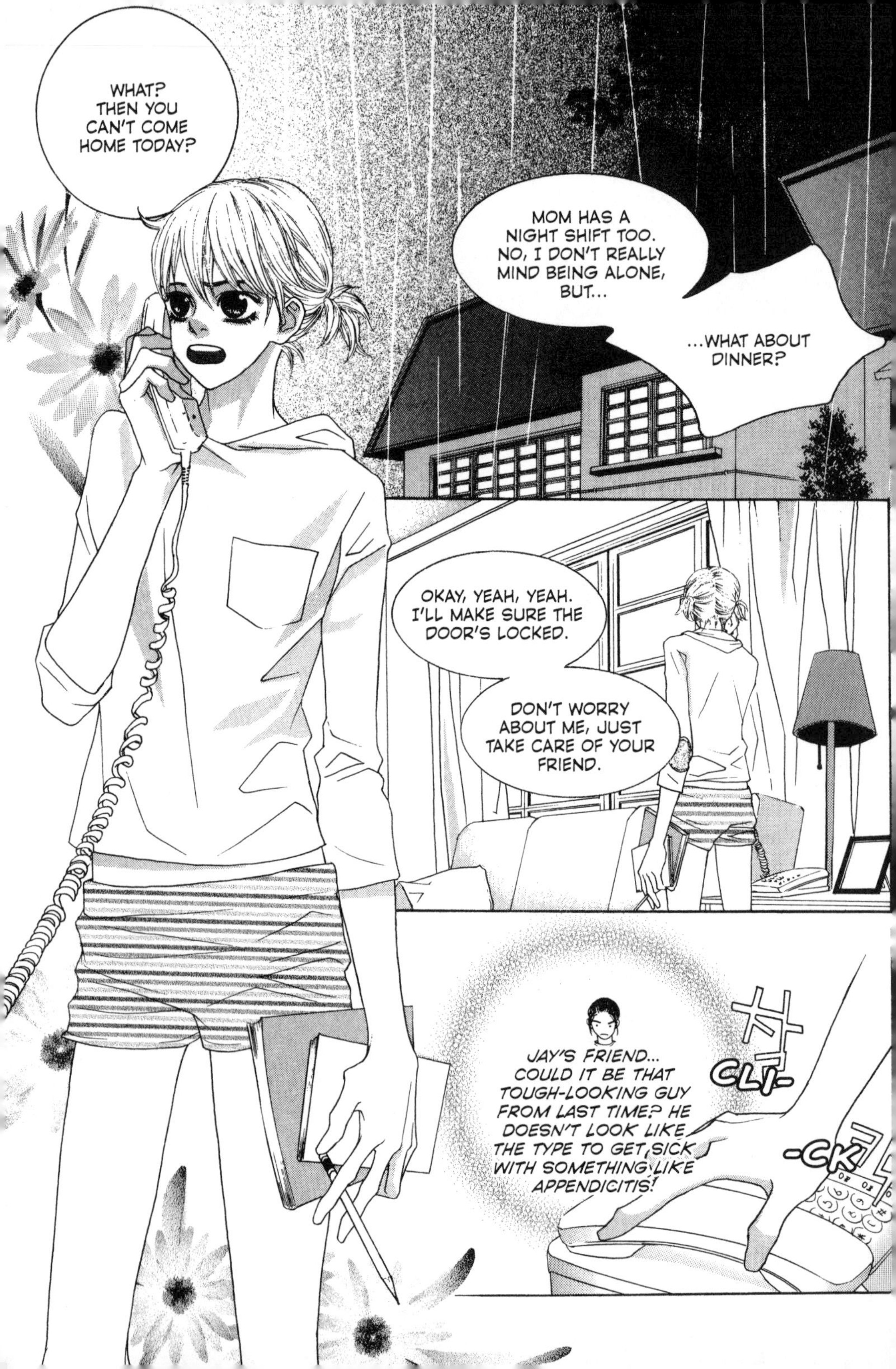
WHAT? THEN YOU CAN'T COME HOME TODAY?
MOM HAS A NIGHT SHIFT TOO. NO, I DON'T REALLY MIND BEING ALONE, BUT...
...WHAT ABOUT DINNER?
OKAY, YEAH, YEAH. I'LL MAKE SURE THE DOOR'S LOCKED.
DON'T WORRY ABOUT ME, JUST TAKE CARE OF YOUR FRIEND.
JAY'S FRIEND... COULD IT BE THAT TOUGH-LOOKING GUY FROM LAST TIME? HE DOESN'T LOOK LIKE THE TYPE TO GET SICK WITH SOMETHING LIKE APPENDICITIS!
CLI-
-CK

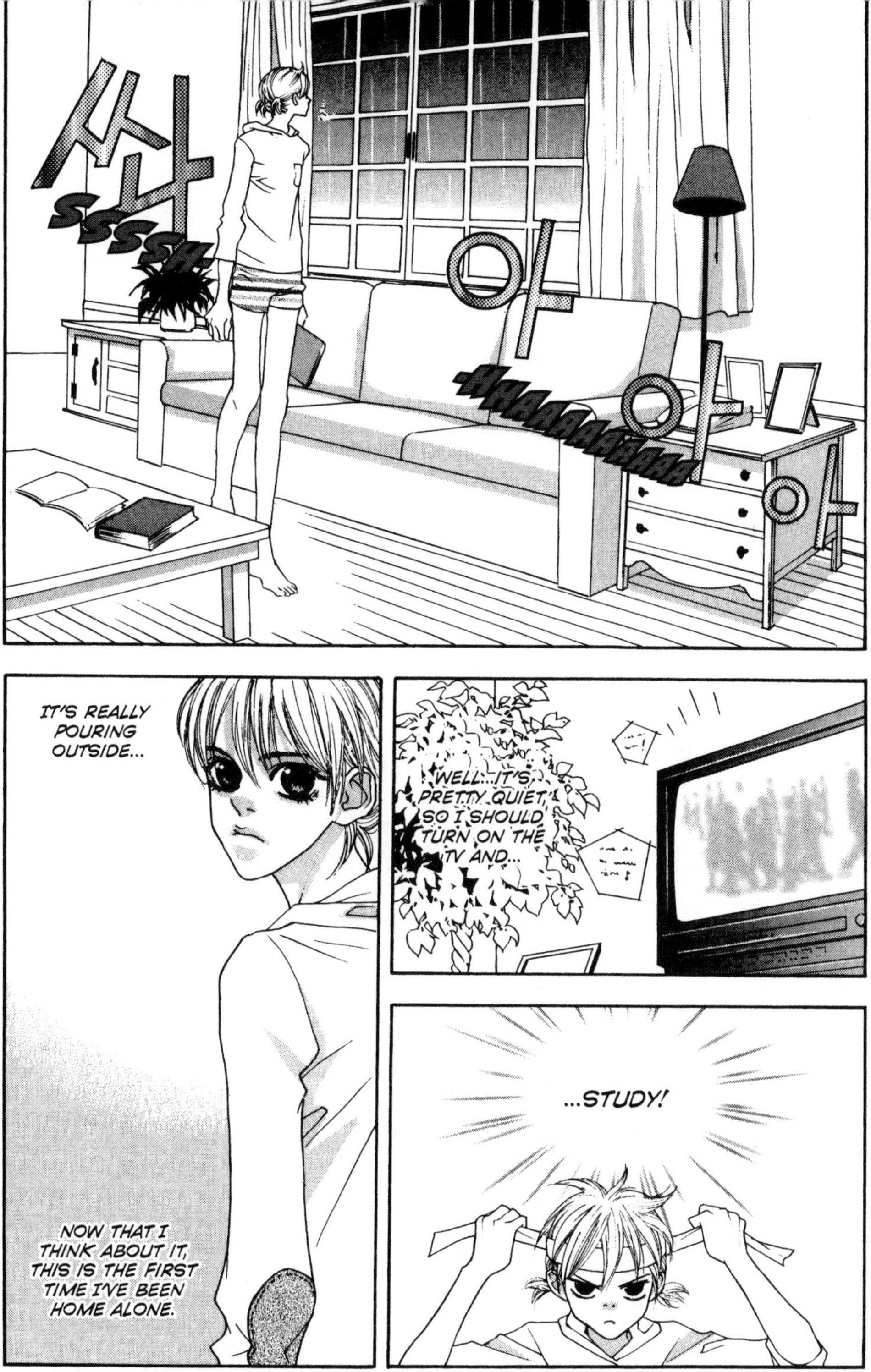
쏴
SSSSH-
아
아
아
-HAAAAAAAAA
IT'S REALLY POURING OUTSIDE...
NOW THAT I THINK ABOUT IT, THIS IS THE FIRST TIME I'VE BEEN HOME ALONE.
WELL...IT'S PRETTY QUIET, SO I SHOULD TURN ON THE TV AND...
...STUDY!

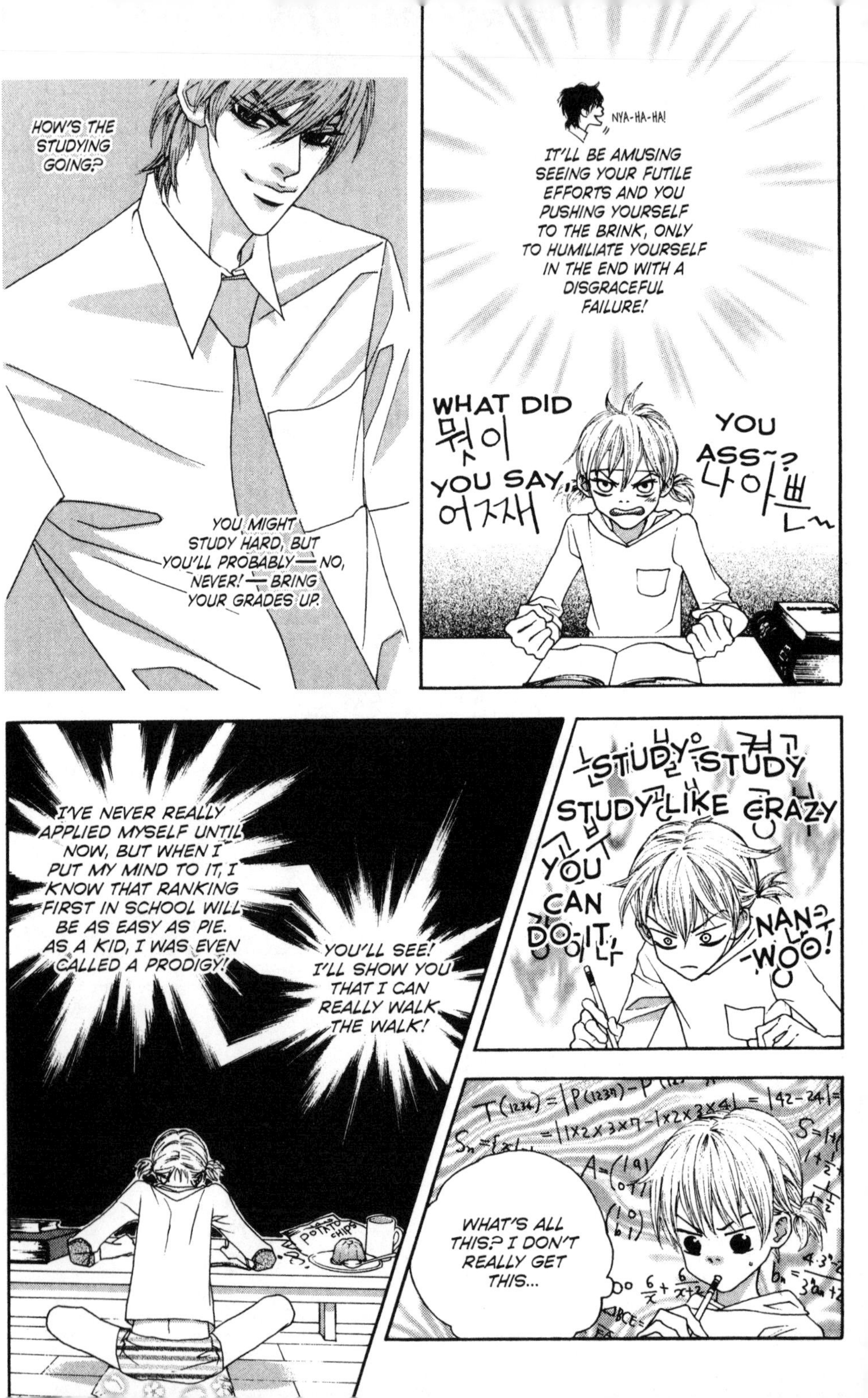
HOW'S THE STUDYING GOING?
YOU MIGHT STUDY HARD, BUT YOU'LL PROBABLY — NO, NEVER! — BRING YOUR GRADES UP.
NYA-HA-HA!
IT'LL BE AMUSING SEEING YOUR FUTILE EFFORTS AND YOU PUSHING YOURSELF TO THE BRINK, ONLY TO HUMILIATE YOURSELF IN THE END WITH A DISGRACEFUL FAILURE!
WHAT DID YOU SAY,
YOU ASS~?
I'VE NEVER REALLY APPLIED MYSELF UNTIL NOW, BUT WHEN I PUT MY MIND TO IT, I KNOW THAT RANKING FIRST IN SCHOOL WILL BE AS EASY AS PIE. AS A KID, I WAS EVEN CALLED A PRODIGY!
YOU'LL SEE! I'LL SHOW YOU THAT I CAN REALLY WALK THE WALK!
POTATO CHIPS
STUDY STUDY STUDY LIKE CRAZY
YOU CAN DO IT,
NAN-WOO!
WHAT'S ALL THIS? I DON'T REALLY GET THIS...

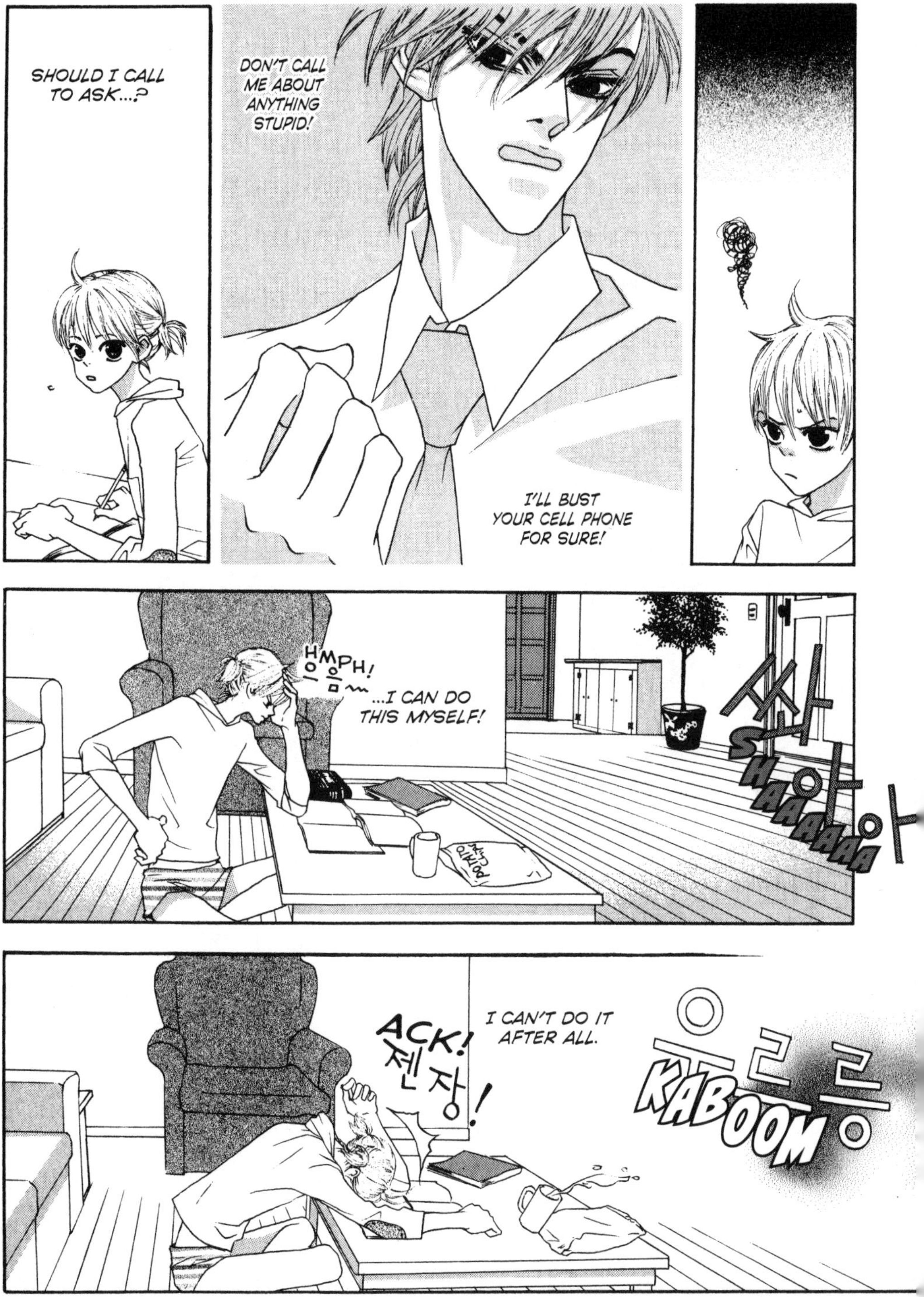
SHOULD I CALL TO ASK...?
DON'T CALL ME ABOUT ANYTHING STUPID!
I'LL BUST YOUR CELL PHONE FOR SURE!
HMPH!
으음~
...I CAN DO THIS MYSELF!
쏴아아
SHAAAAAA
ACK!
젠장!
I CAN'T DO IT AFTER ALL.
우르릉
KABOOM

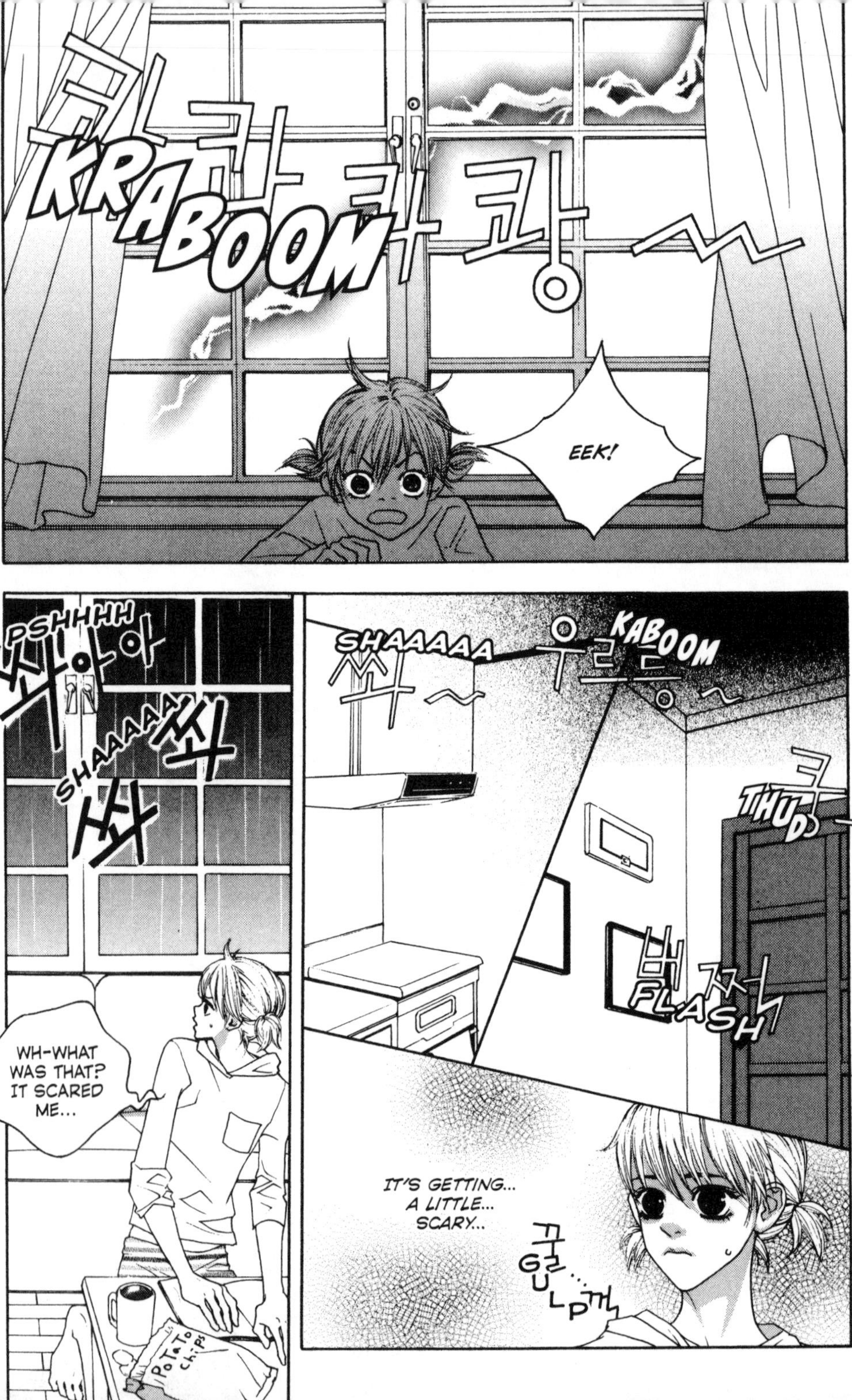
KRABOOM
EEK!
PSHHHH
SHAAAAA
WH-WHAT WAS THAT? IT SCARED ME...
POTATO chips
SHAAAAAA
KABOOM
THUD
FLASH
IT'S GETTING... A LITTLE... SCARY...
GULP

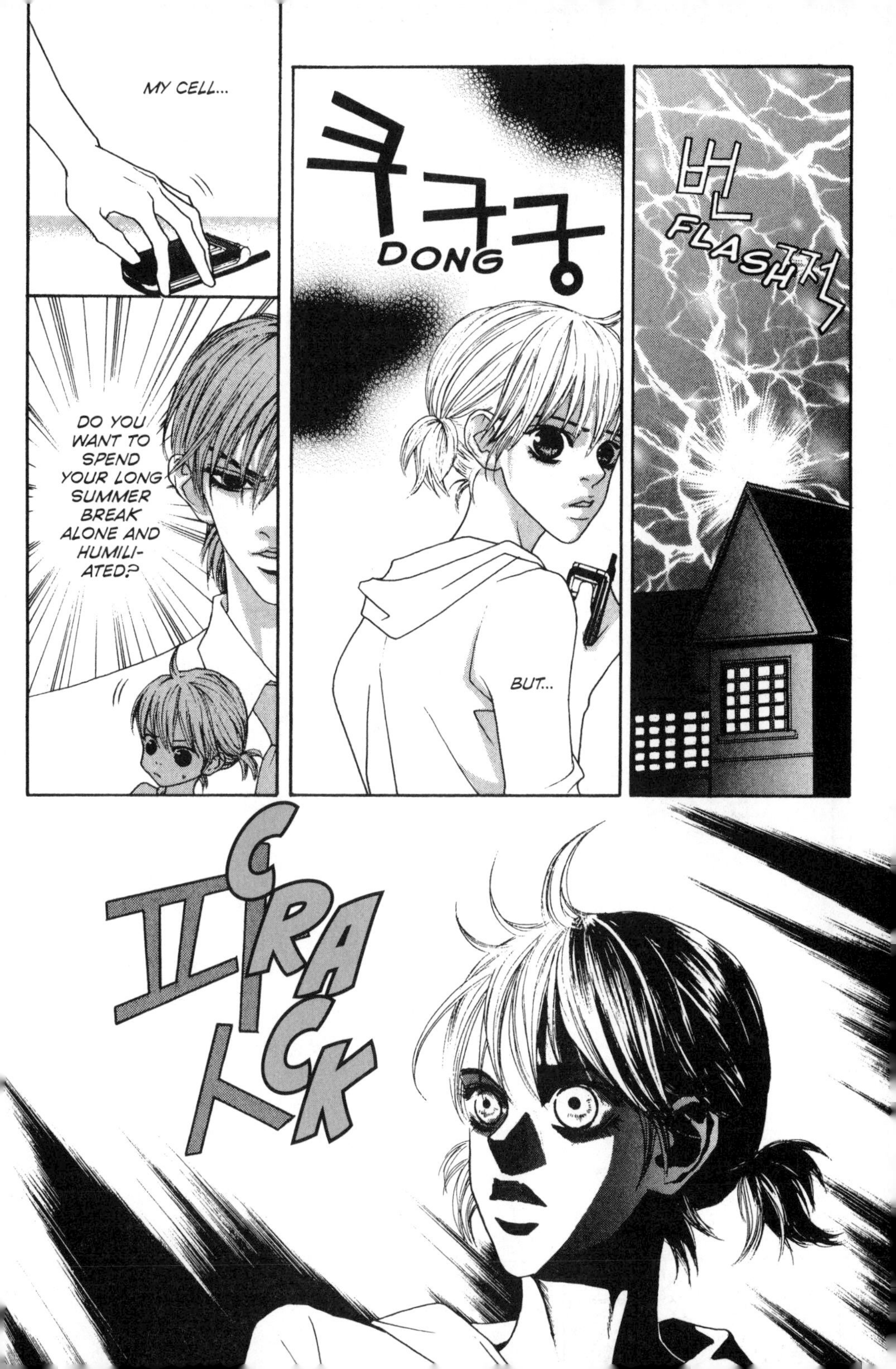

MY CELL...
DO YOU WANT TO SPEND YOUR LONG SUMMER BREAK ALONE AND HUMILI-ATED?
쿠구궁
DONG
BUT...
번쩍
FLASH
CRACK

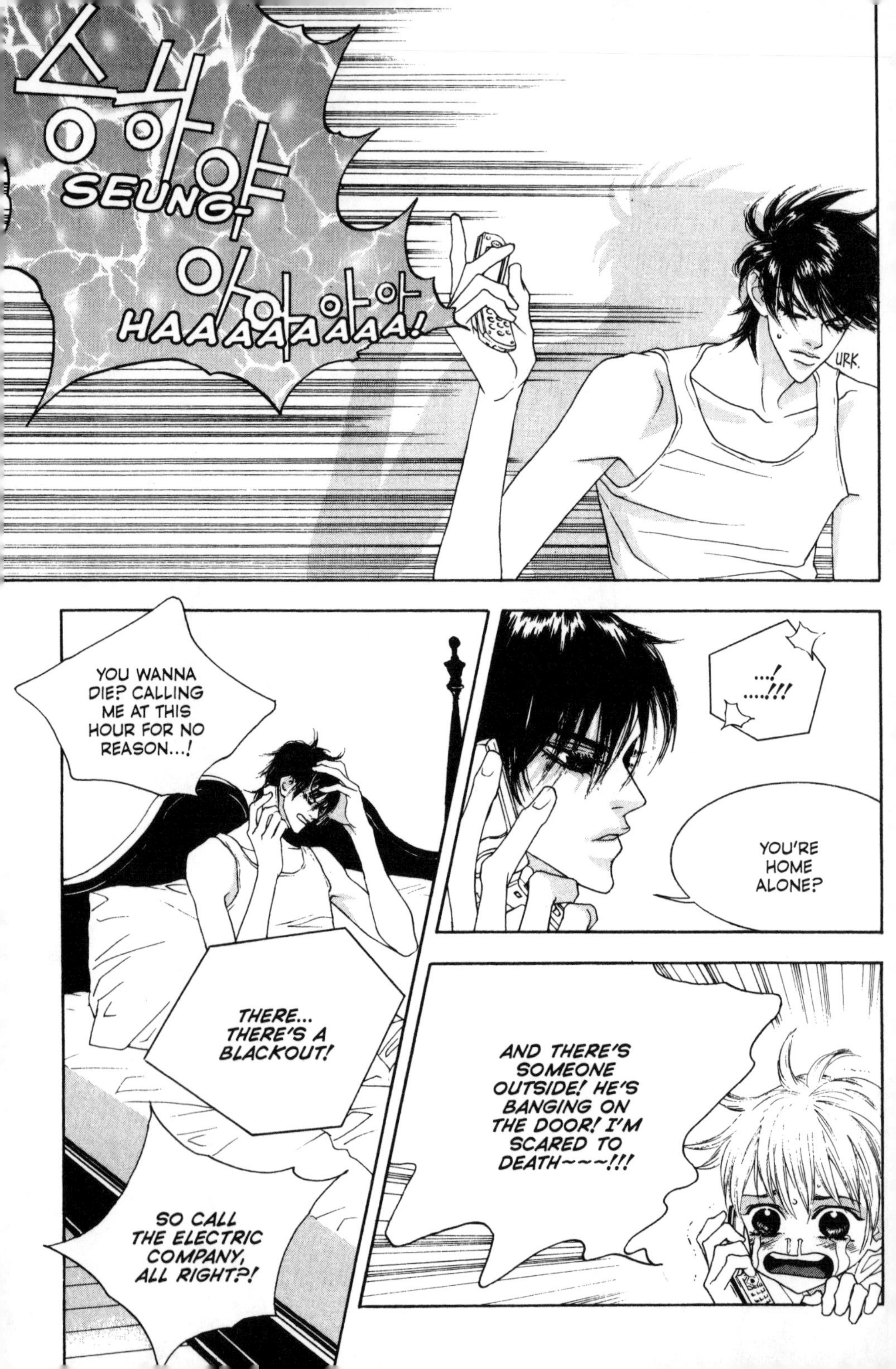
SEUNG-HAAAAAAAA!
URK.
YOU WANNA DIE? CALLING ME AT THIS HOUR FOR NO REASON...!
THERE... THERE'S A BLACKOUT!
SO CALL THE ELECTRIC COMPANY, ALL RIGHT?!
...! ....!!!
YOU'RE HOME ALONE?
AND THERE'S SOMEONE OUTSIDE! HE'S BANGING ON THE DOOR! I'M SCARED TO DEATH~~~!!!

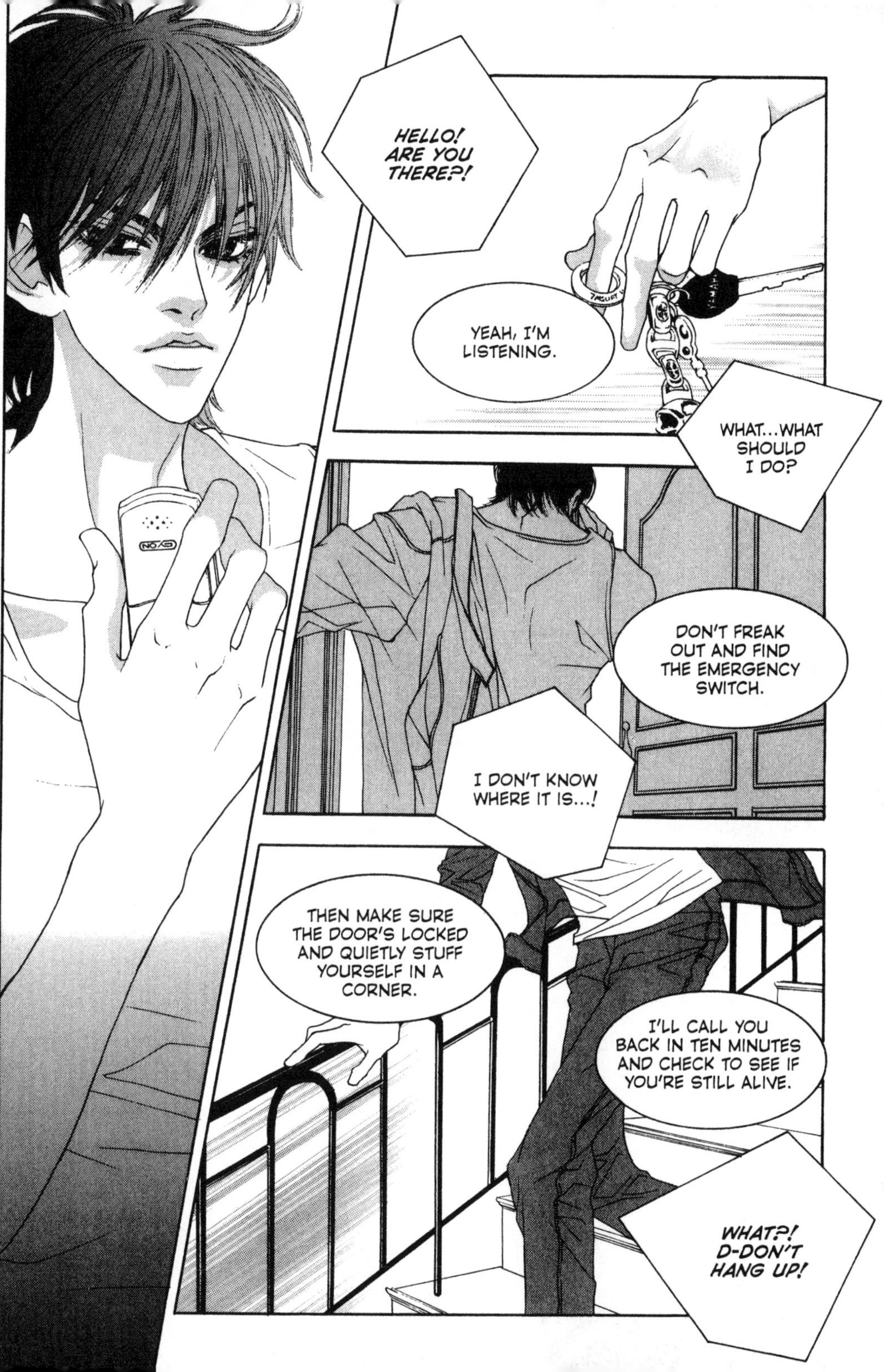
HELLO! ARE YOU THERE?!
YEAH, I'M LISTENING.
WHAT...WHAT SHOULD I DO?
DON'T FREAK OUT AND FIND THE EMERGENCY SWITCH.
I DON'T KNOW WHERE IT IS...!
THEN MAKE SURE THE DOOR'S LOCKED AND QUIETLY STUFF YOURSELF IN A CORNER.
I'LL CALL YOU BACK IN TEN MINUTES AND CHECK TO SEE IF YOU'RE STILL ALIVE.
WHAT?! D-DON'T HANG UP!

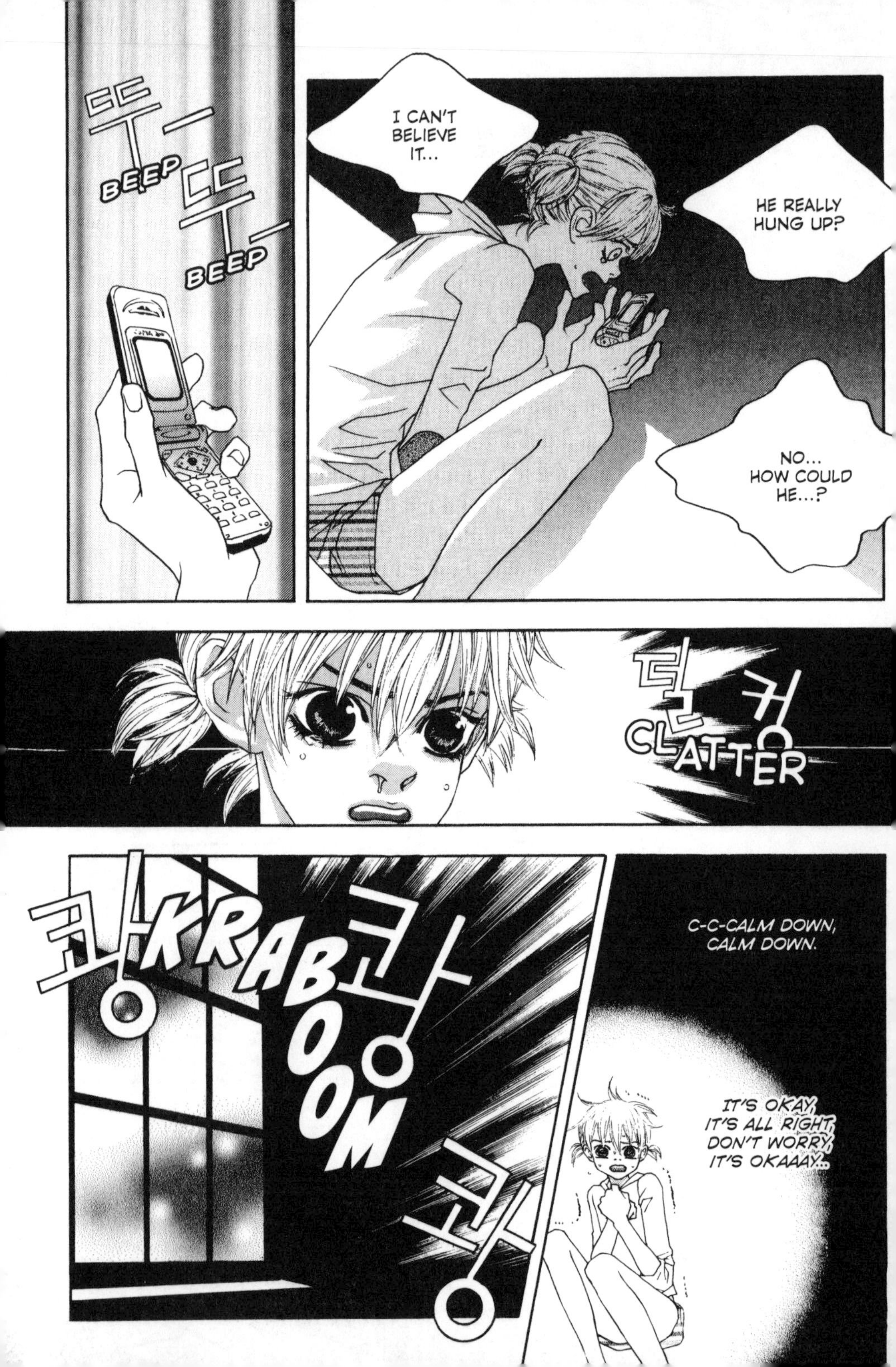
뚜ㅡ
BEEP
뚜ㅡ
BEEP
I CAN'T BELIEVE IT...
HE REALLY HUNG UP?
NO... HOW COULD HE...?
털컹
CLATTER
쾅
KRABOOM
쾅
쾅
C-C-CALM DOWN, CALM DOWN.
IT'S OKAY, IT'S ALL RIGHT, DON'T WORRY, IT'S OKAAAY...

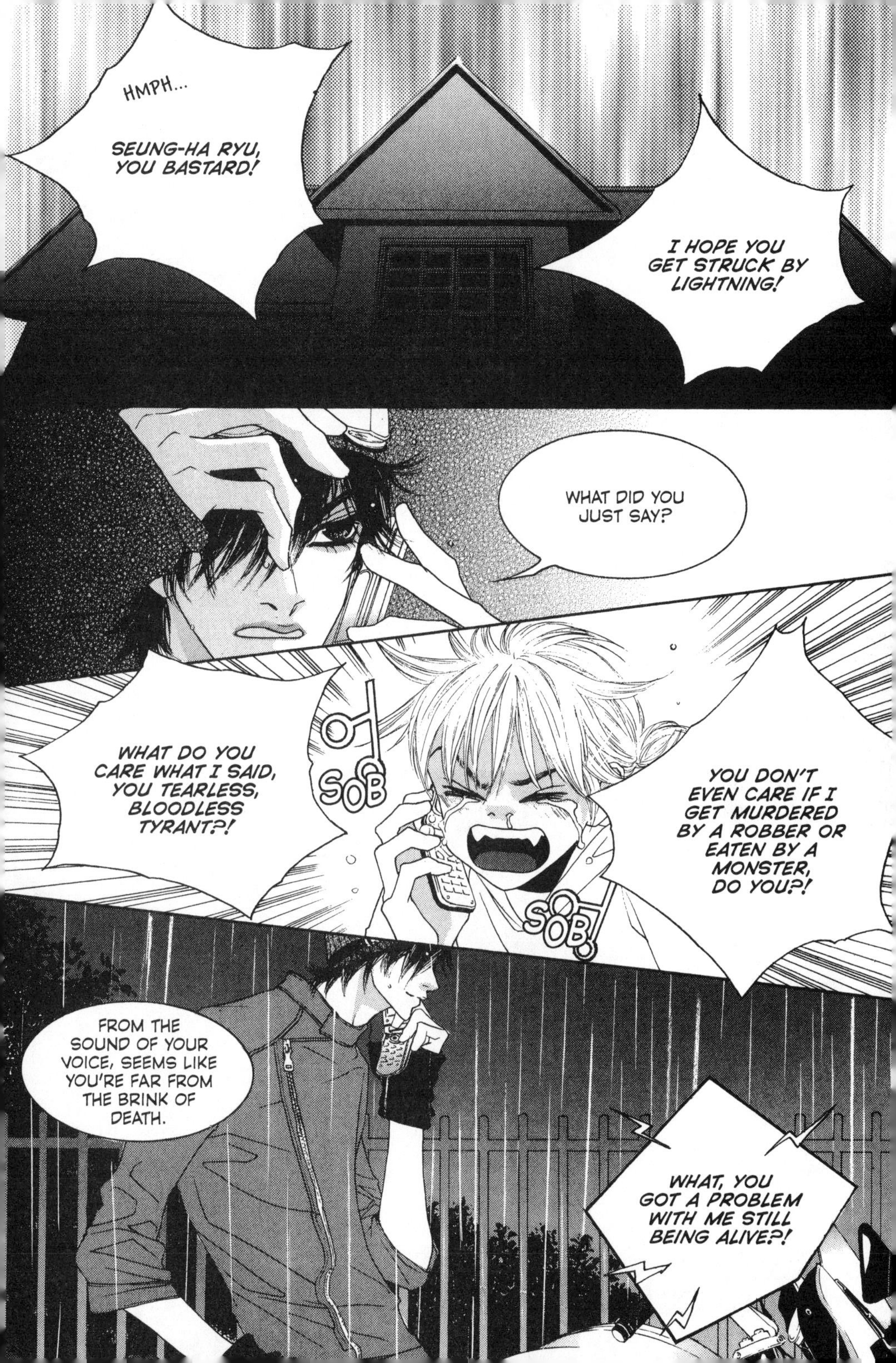
HMPH...
SEUNG-HA RYU, YOU BASTARD!
I HOPE YOU GET STRUCK BY LIGHTNING!
WHAT DID YOU JUST SAY?
WHAT DO YOU CARE WHAT I SAID, YOU TEARLESS, BLOODLESS TYRANT?!
SOB
YOU DON'T EVEN CARE IF I GET MURDERED BY A ROBBER OR EATEN BY A MONSTER, DO YOU?!
SOB
FROM THE SOUND OF YOUR VOICE, SEEMS LIKE YOU'RE FAR FROM THE BRINK OF DEATH.
WHAT, YOU GOT A PROBLEM WITH ME STILL BEING ALIVE?!

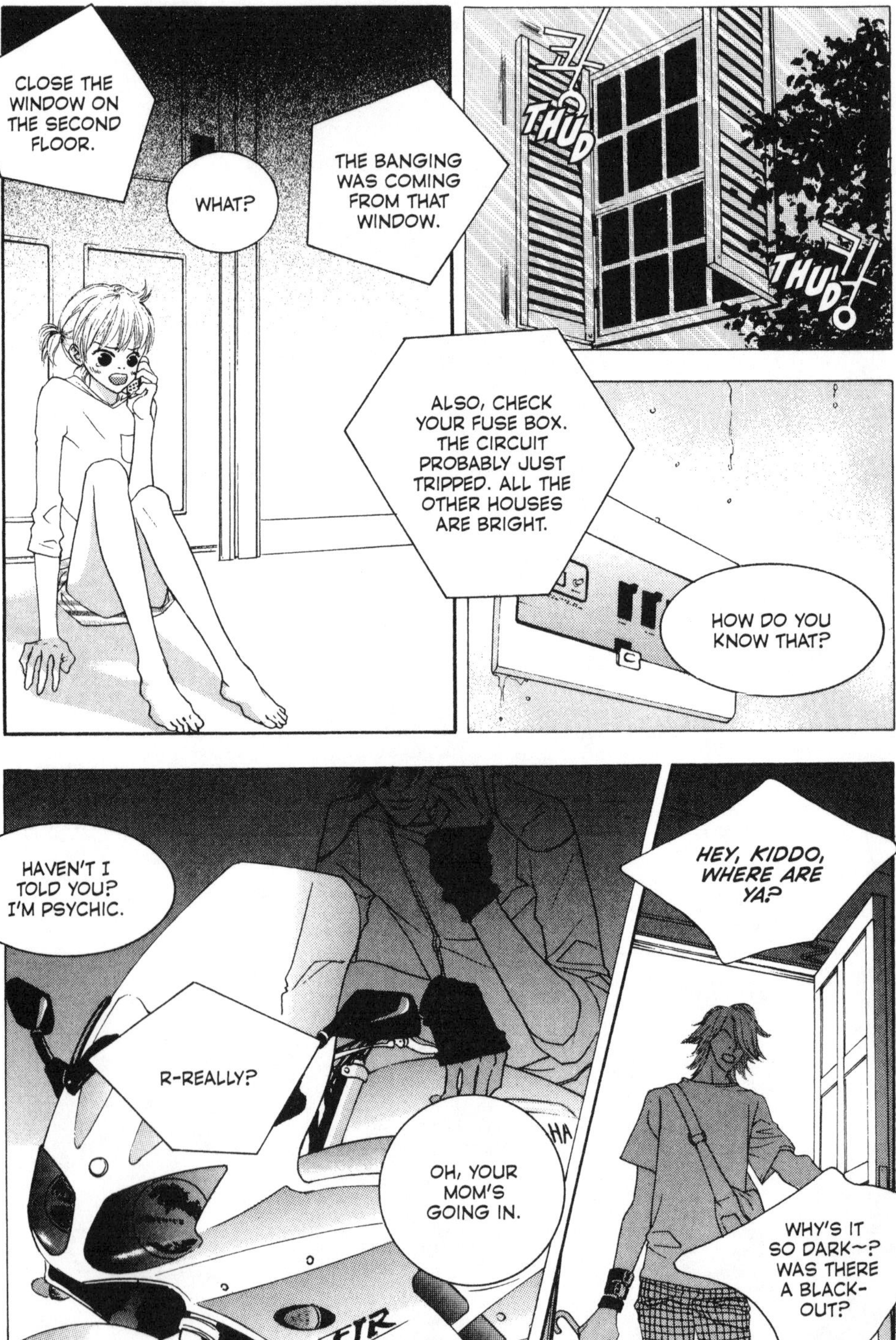
CLOSE THE WINDOW ON THE SECOND FLOOR.
WHAT?
THE BANGING WAS COMING FROM THAT WINDOW.
THUD
THUD
ALSO, CHECK YOUR FUSE BOX. THE CIRCUIT PROBABLY JUST TRIPPED. ALL THE OTHER HOUSES ARE BRIGHT.
HOW DO YOU KNOW THAT?
HAVEN'T I TOLD YOU? I'M PSYCHIC.
R-REALLY?
HA
OH, YOUR MOM'S GOING IN.
FJR
HEY, KIDDO, WHERE ARE YA?
WHY'S IT SO DARK~? WAS THERE A BLACK-OUT?

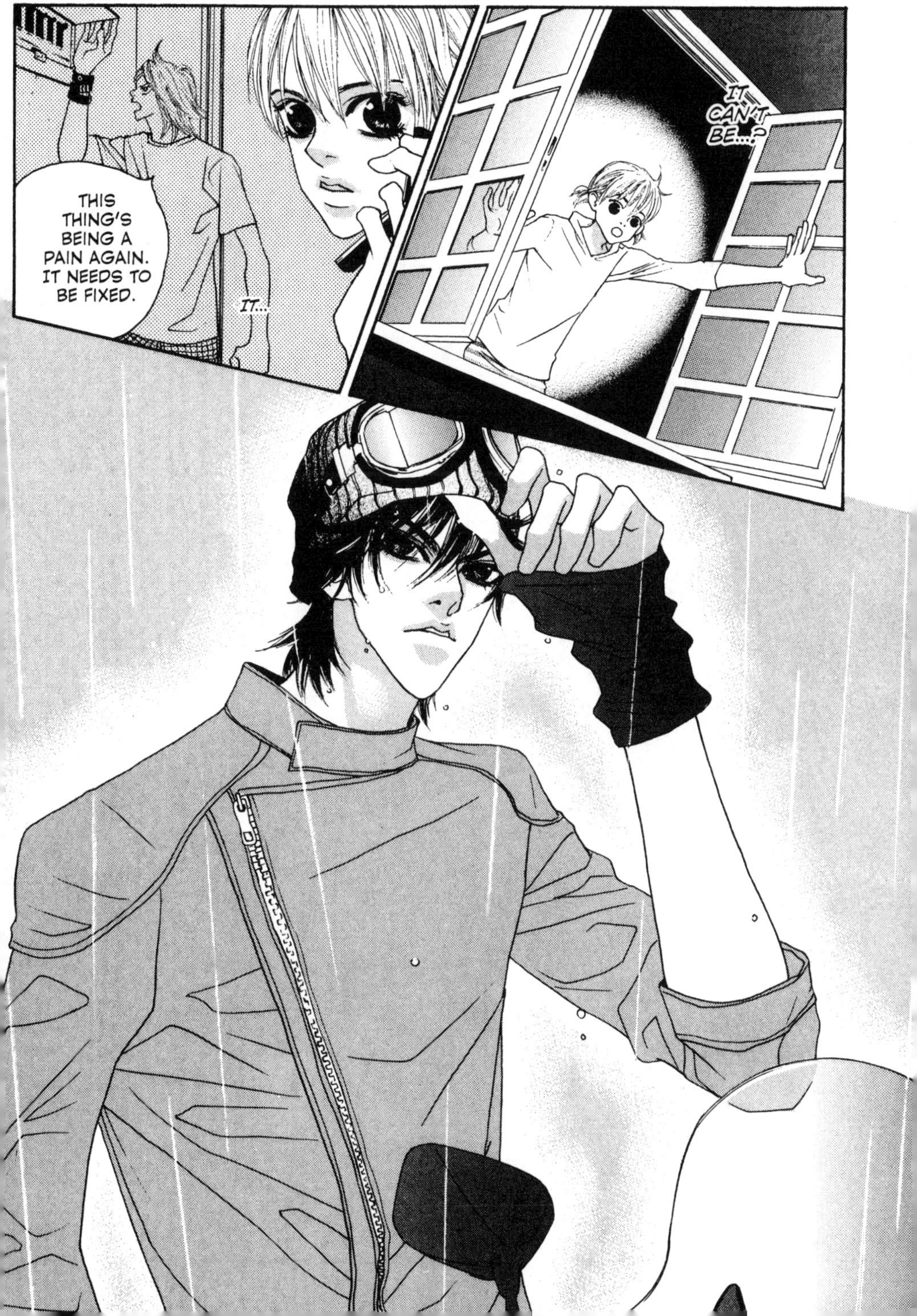
THIS THING'S BEING A PAIN AGAIN. IT NEEDS TO BE FIXED.
IT...
IT CAN'T BE...?

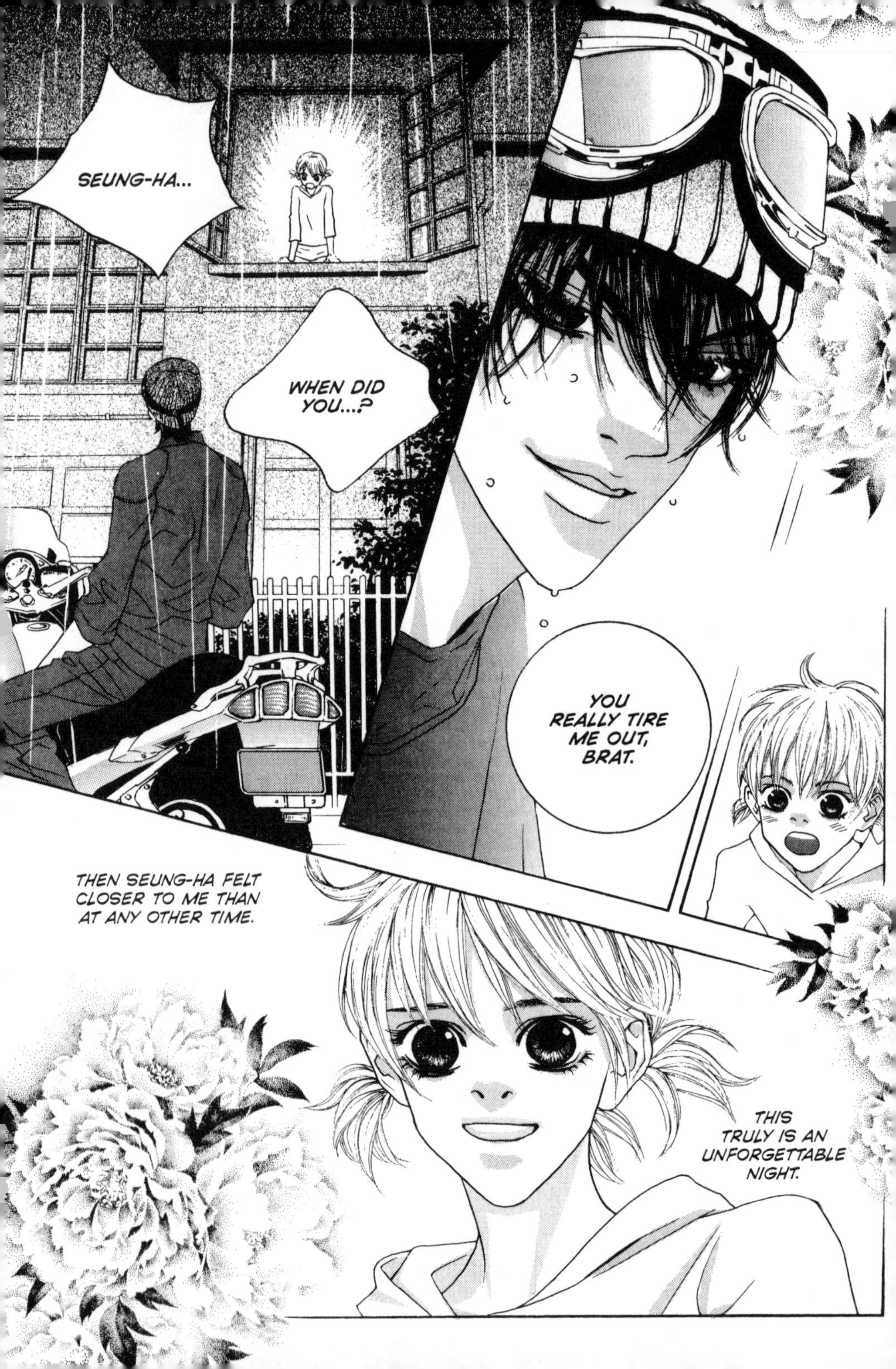
SEUNG-HA...
WHEN DID YOU...?
YOU REALLY TIRE ME OUT, BRAT.
THEN SEUNG-HA FELT CLOSER TO ME THAN AT ANY OTHER TIME.
THIS TRULY IS AN UNFORGETTABLE NIGHT.

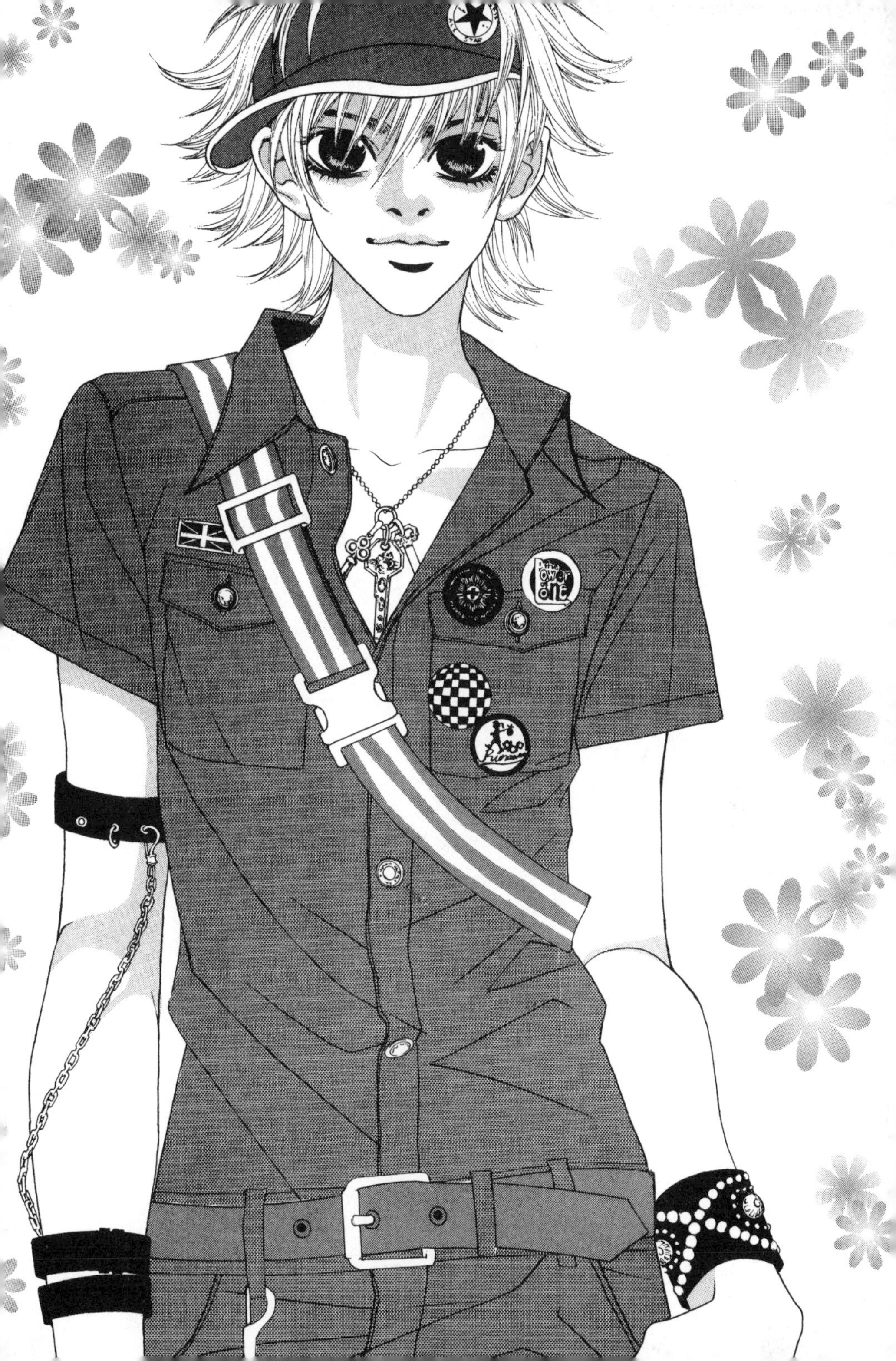

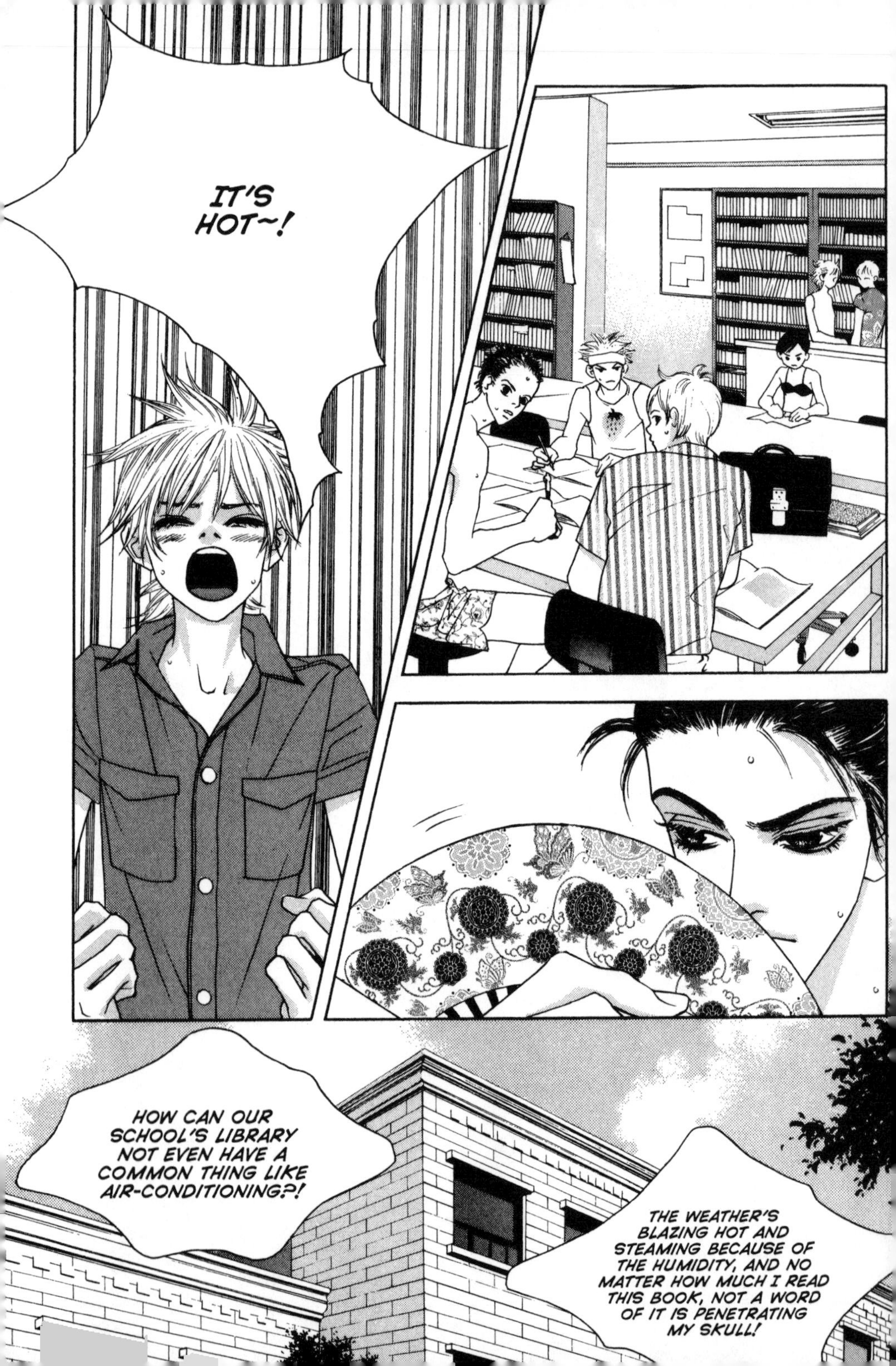
IT'S HOT~!
HOW CAN OUR SCHOOL'S LIBRARY NOT EVEN HAVE A COMMON THING LIKE AIR-CONDITIONING?!
THE WEATHER'S BLAZING HOT AND STEAMING BECAUSE OF THE HUMIDITY, AND NO MATTER HOW MUCH I READ THIS BOOK, NOT A WORD OF IT IS PENETRATING MY SKULL!

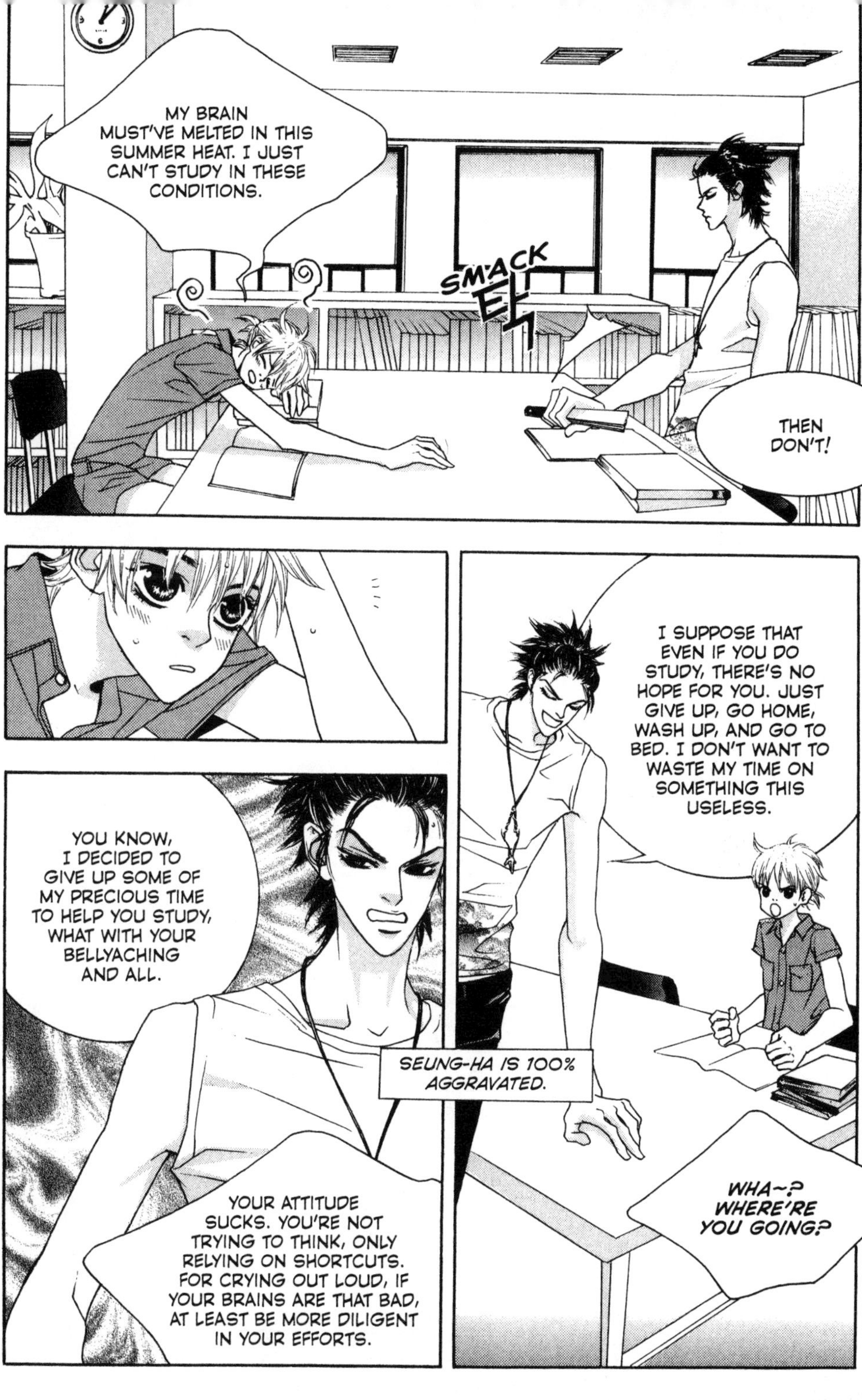
MY BRAIN MUST'VE MELTED IN THIS SUMMER HEAT. I JUST CAN'T STUDY IN THESE CONDITIONS.
SMACK
THEN DON'T!
I SUPPOSE THAT EVEN IF YOU DO STUDY, THERE'S NO HOPE FOR YOU. JUST GIVE UP, GO HOME, WASH UP, AND GO TO BED. I DON'T WANT TO WASTE MY TIME ON SOMETHING THIS USELESS.
YOU KNOW, I DECIDED TO GIVE UP SOME OF MY PRECIOUS TIME TO HELP YOU STUDY, WHAT WITH YOUR BELLYACHING AND ALL.
SEUNG-HA IS 100% AGGRAVATED.
YOUR ATTITUDE SUCKS. YOU'RE NOT TRYING TO THINK, ONLY RELYING ON SHORTCUTS. FOR CRYING OUT LOUD, IF YOUR BRAINS ARE THAT BAD, AT LEAST BE MORE DILIGENT IN YOUR EFFORTS.
WHA~? WHERE'RE YOU GOING?

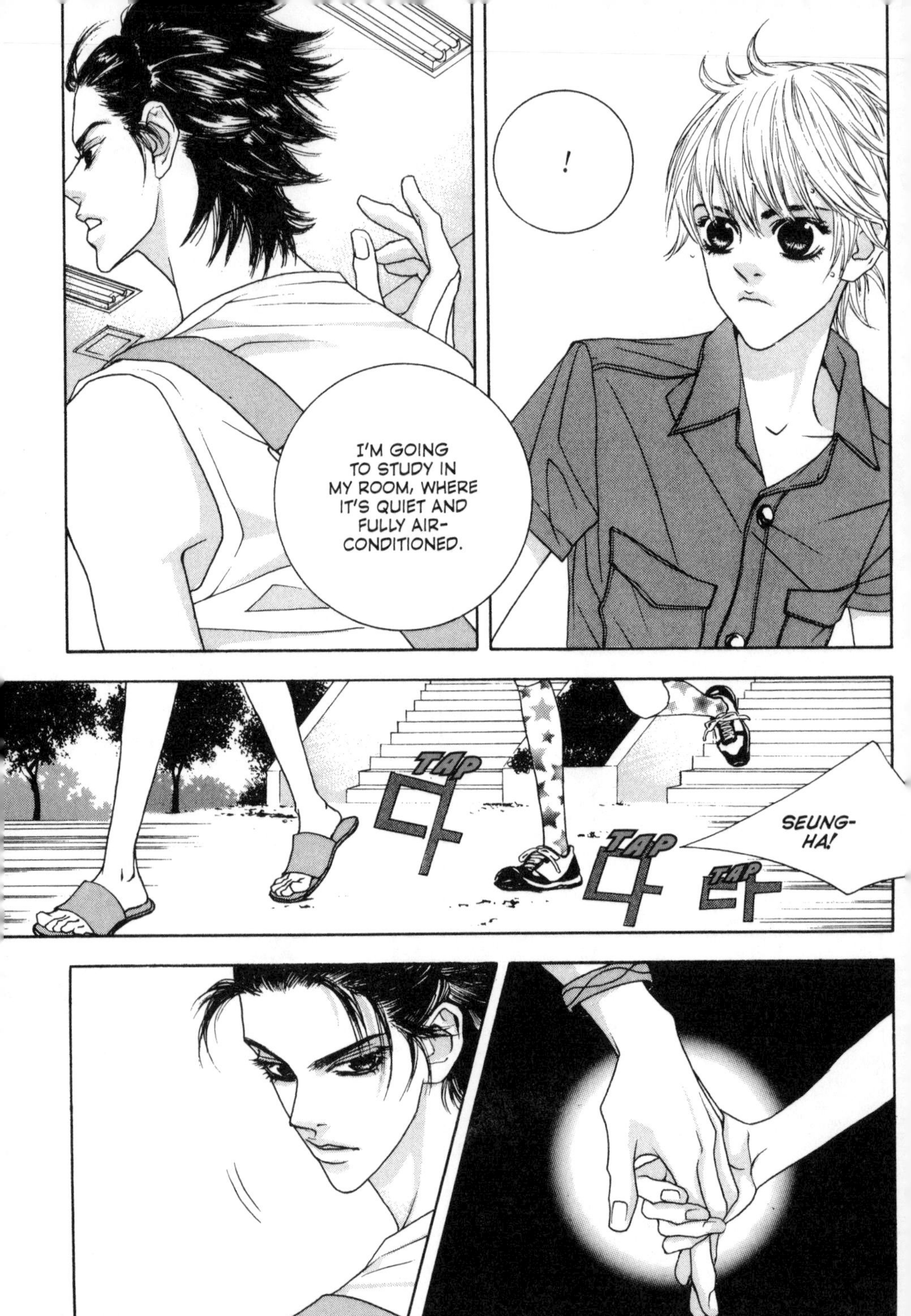

I'M GOING TO STUDY IN MY ROOM, WHERE IT'S QUIET AND FULLY AIR-CONDITIONED.
!
TAP
TAP
TAP
SEUNG-HA!

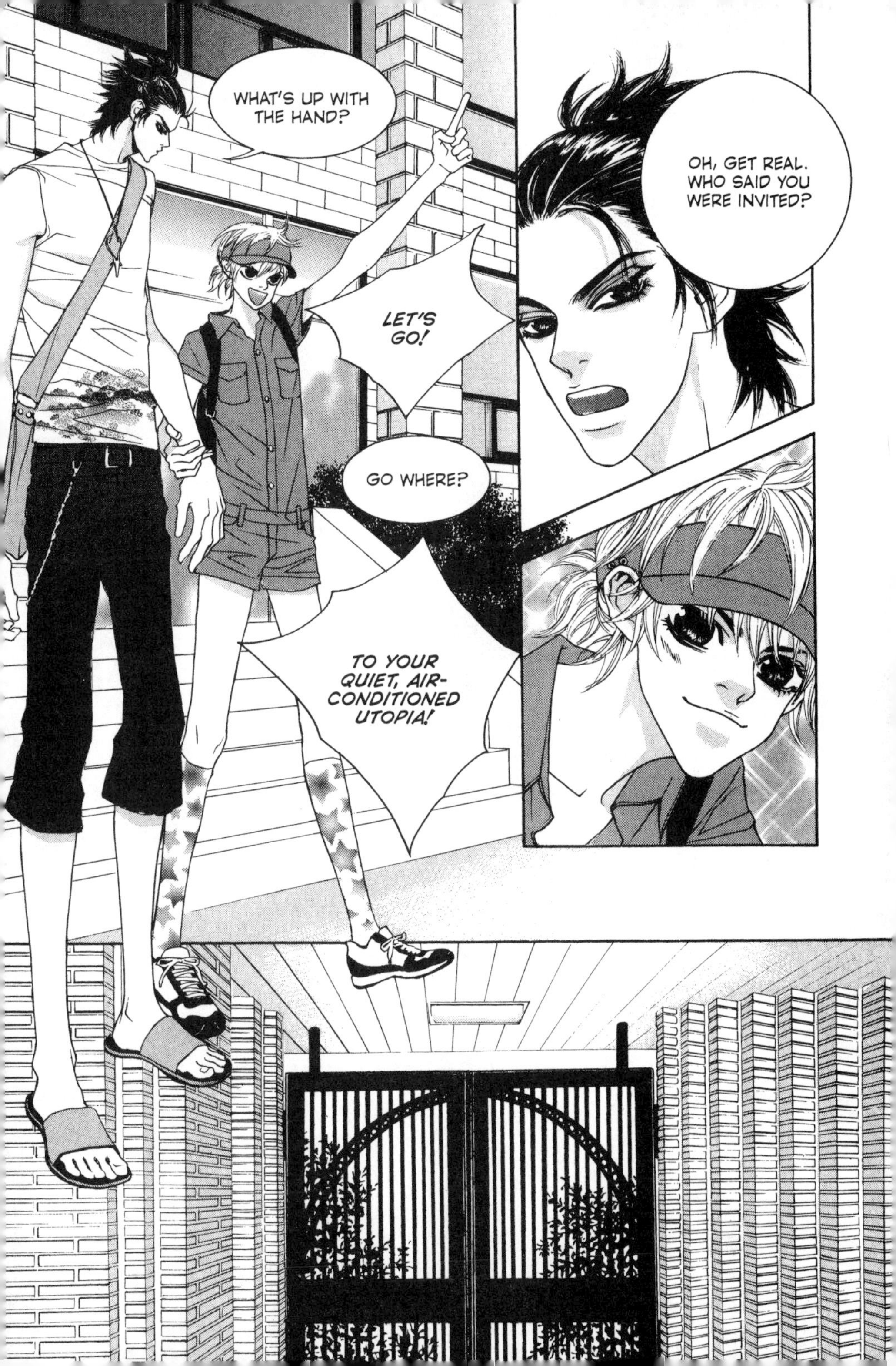

WHAT'S UP WITH THE HAND?
LET'S GO!
GO WHERE?
TO YOUR QUIET, AIR-CONDITIONED UTOPIA!
OH, GET REAL. WHO SAID YOU WERE INVITED?

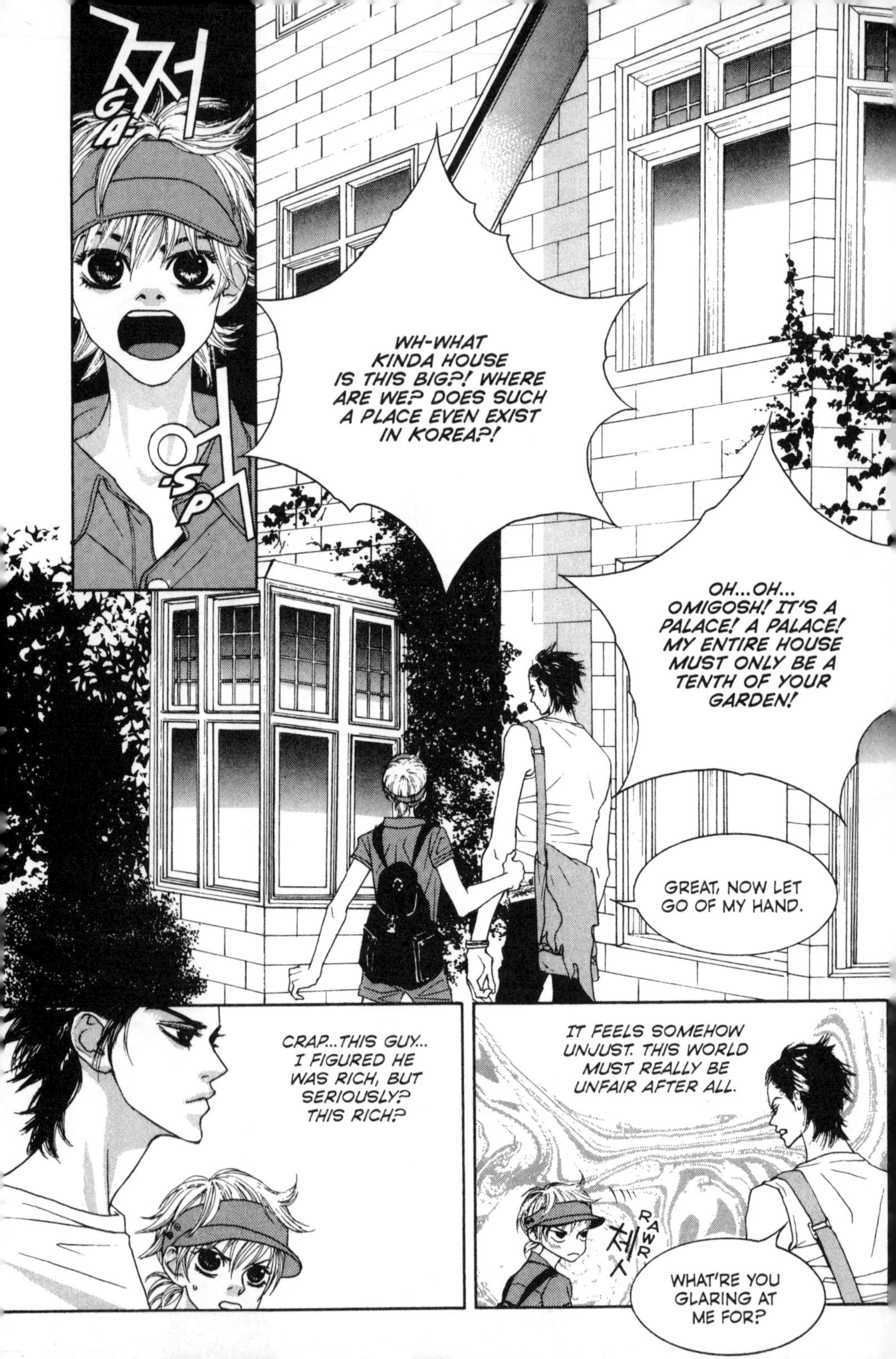
GA-
-SP
WH-WHAT KINDA HOUSE IS THIS BIG?! WHERE ARE WE? DOES SUCH A PLACE EVEN EXIST IN KOREA?!
OH...OH... OMIGOSH! IT'S A PALACE! A PALACE! MY ENTIRE HOUSE MUST ONLY BE A TENTH OF YOUR GARDEN!
GREAT, NOW LET GO OF MY HAND.
CRAP...THIS GUY... I FIGURED HE WAS RICH, BUT SERIOUSLY? THIS RICH?
IT FEELS SOMEHOW UNJUST. THIS WORLD MUST REALLY BE UNFAIR AFTER ALL.
RAWR
WHAT'RE YOU GLARING AT ME FOR?

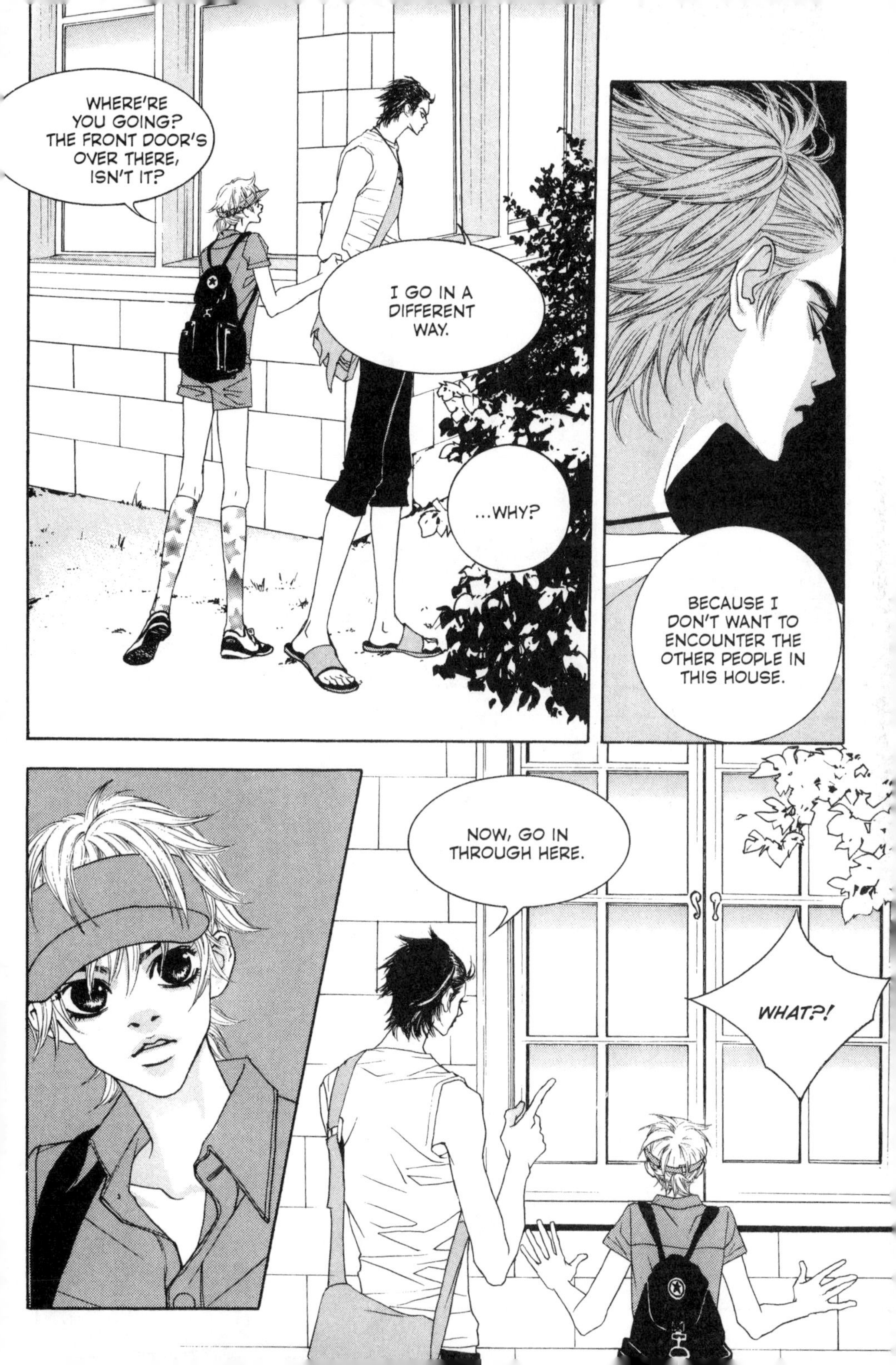
WHERE'RE YOU GOING? THE FRONT DOOR'S OVER THERE, ISN'T IT?
I GO IN A DIFFERENT WAY.
...WHY?
BECAUSE I DON'T WANT TO ENCOUNTER THE OTHER PEOPLE IN THIS HOUSE.
NOW, GO IN THROUGH HERE.
WHAT?!

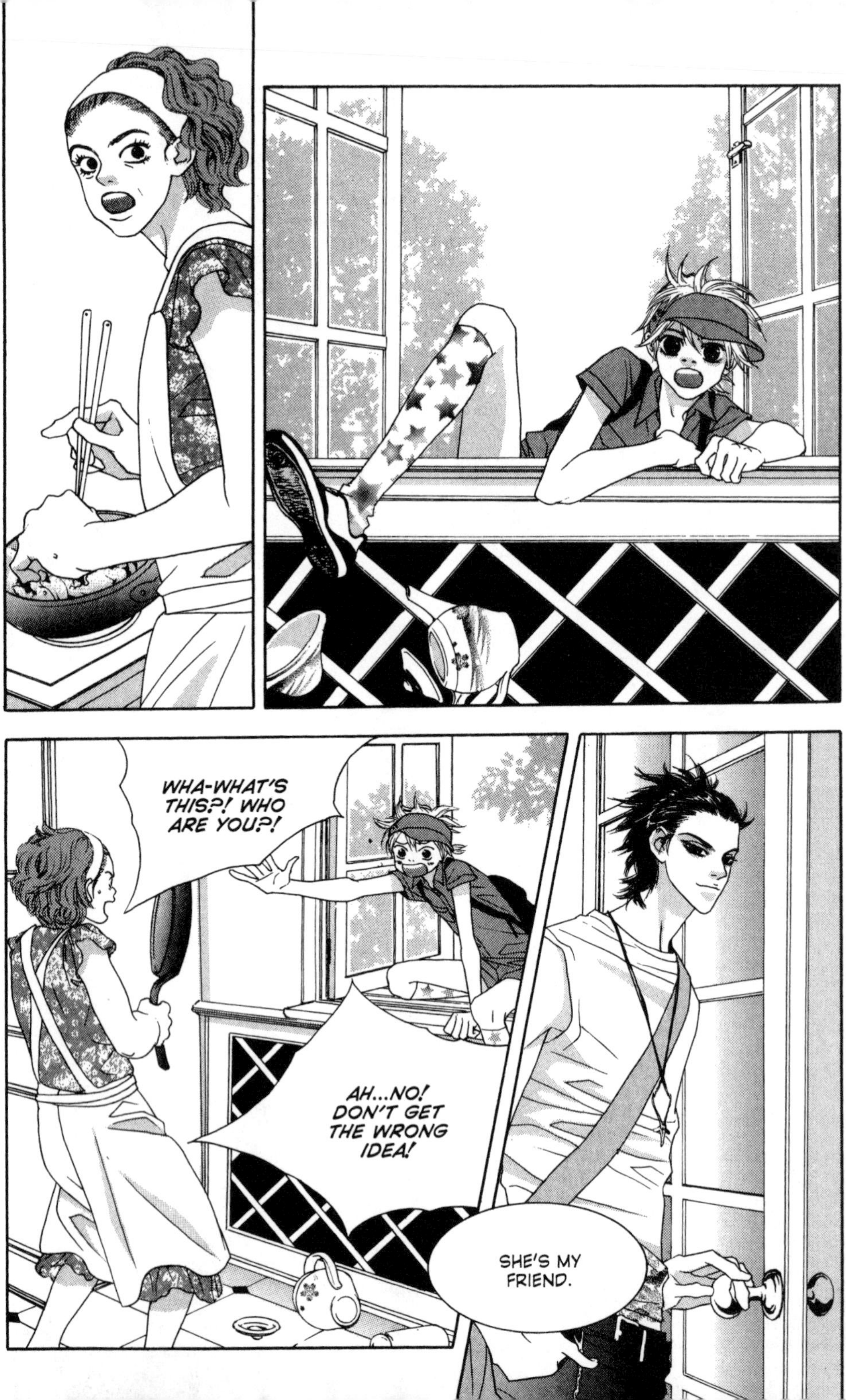
WHA-WHAT'S THIS?! WHO ARE YOU?!
AH...NO! DON'T GET THE WRONG IDEA!
SHE'S MY FRIEND.

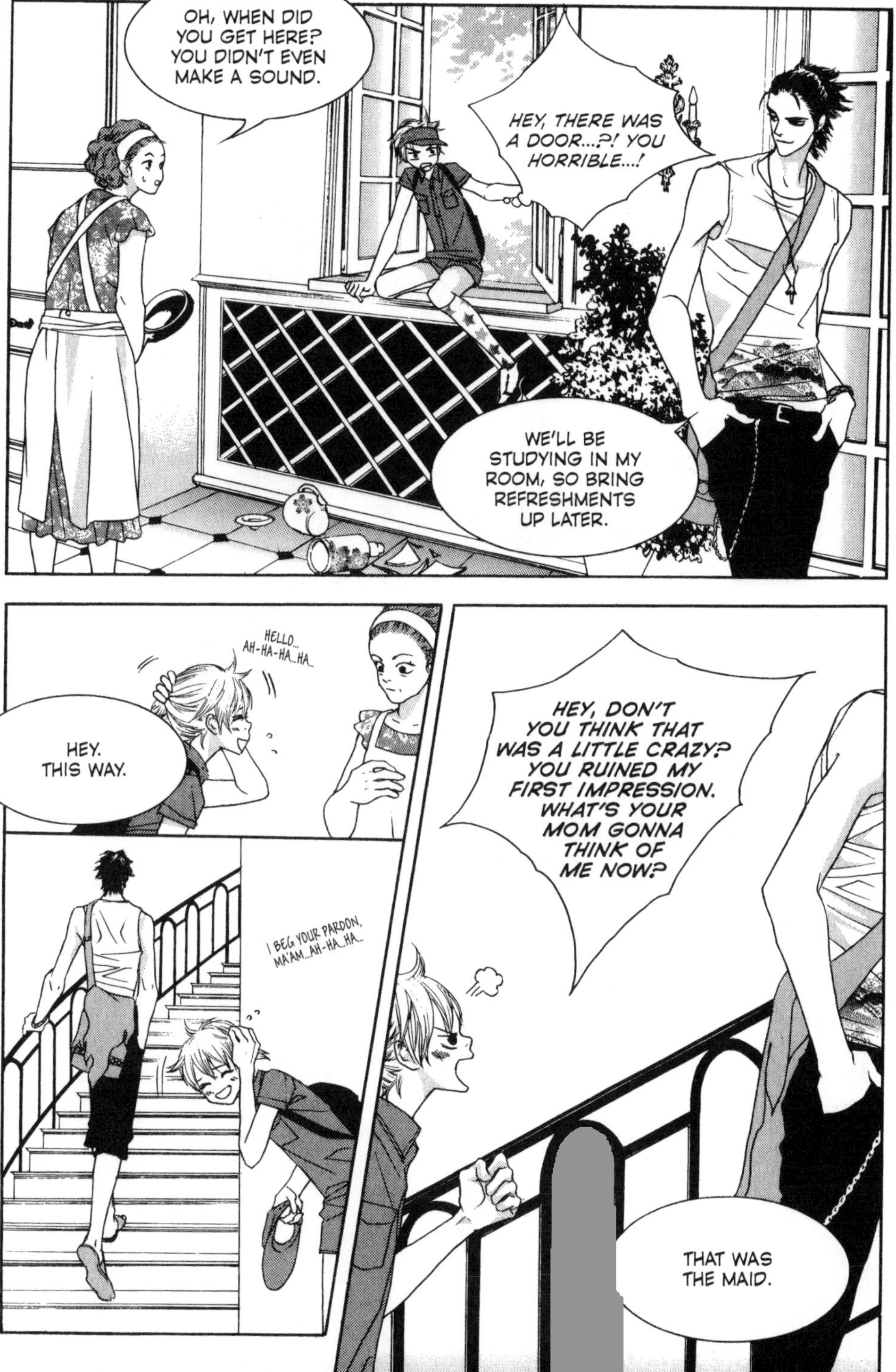
OH, WHEN DID YOU GET HERE? YOU DIDN'T EVEN MAKE A SOUND.
HEY, THERE WAS A DOOR...?! YOU HORRIBLE...!
WE'LL BE STUDYING IN MY ROOM, SO BRING REFRESHMENTS UP LATER.
HELLO... AH-HA-HA..HA..
HEY. THIS WAY.
I BEG YOUR PARDON, MA'AM...AH-HA...HA...
HEY, DON'T YOU THINK THAT WAS A LITTLE CRAZY? YOU RUINED MY FIRST IMPRESSION. WHAT'S YOUR MOM GONNA THINK OF ME NOW?
THAT WAS THE MAID.

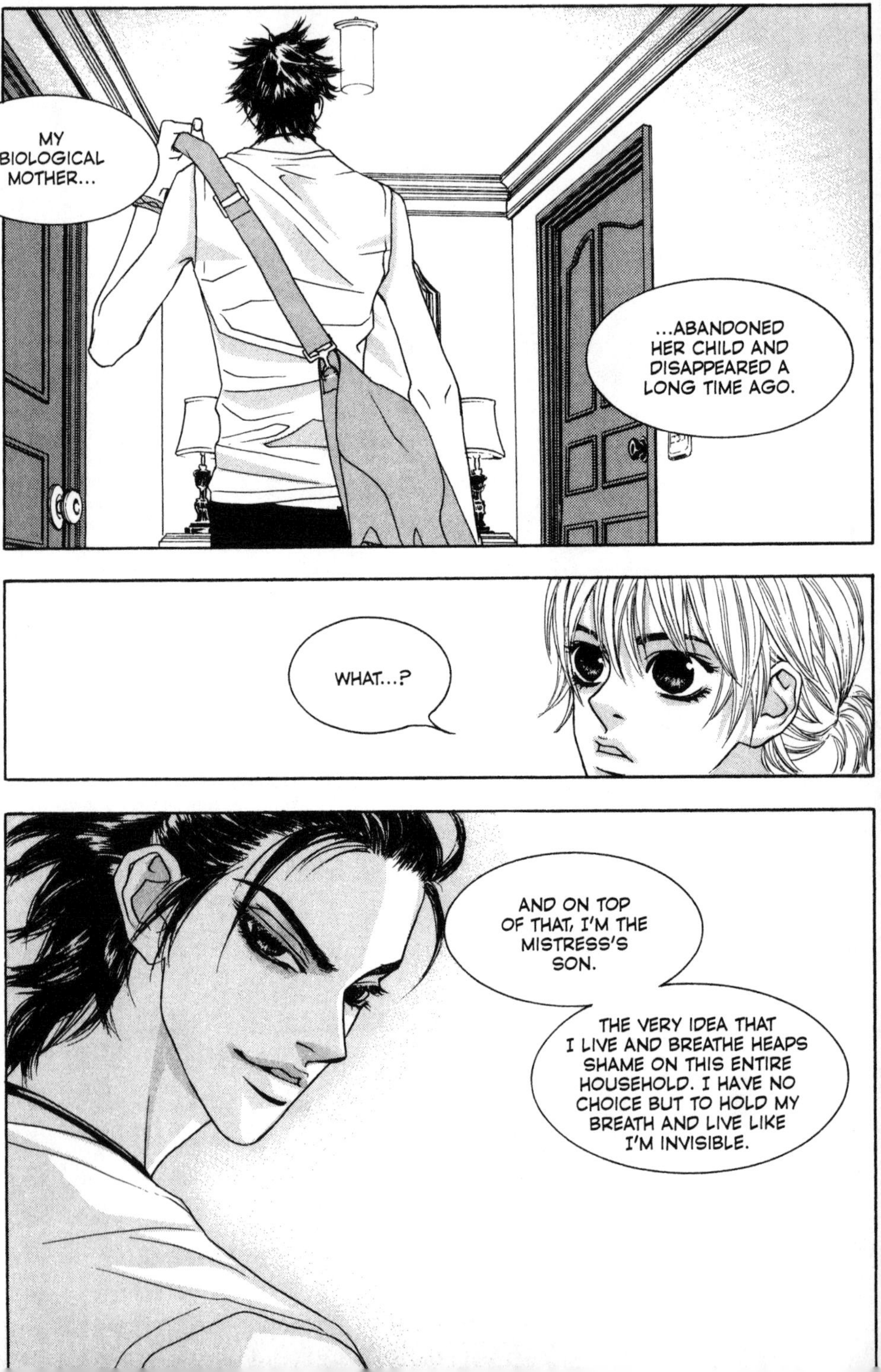
MY BIOLOGICAL MOTHER...
...ABANDONED HER CHILD AND DISAPPEARED A LONG TIME AGO.
WHAT...?
AND ON TOP OF THAT, I'M THE MISTRESS'S SON.
THE VERY IDEA THAT I LIVE AND BREATHE HEAPS SHAME ON THIS ENTIRE HOUSEHOLD. I HAVE NO CHOICE BUT TO HOLD MY BREATH AND LIVE LIKE I'M INVISIBLE.

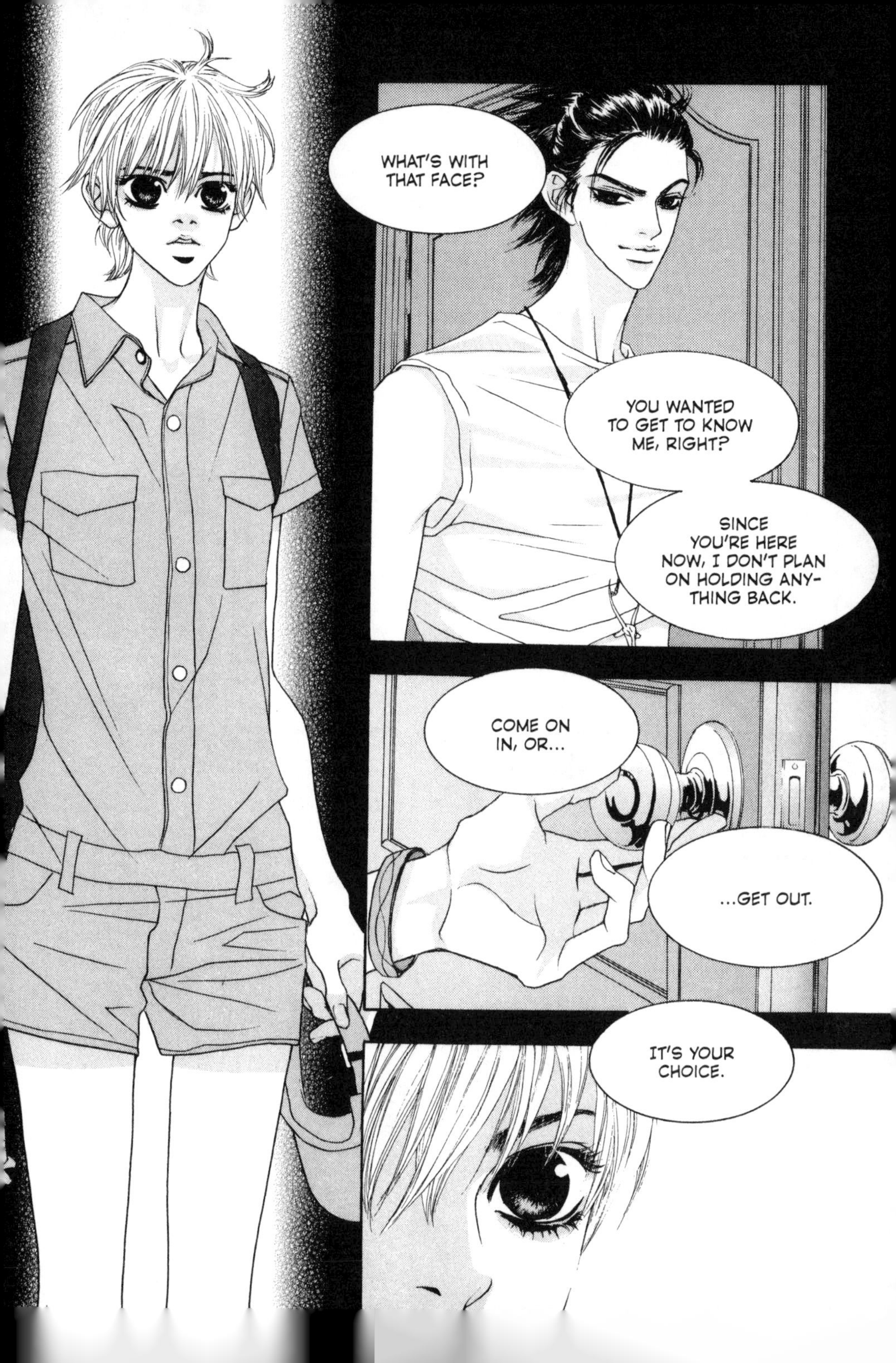
WHAT'S WITH THAT FACE?
YOU WANTED TO GET TO KNOW ME, RIGHT?
SINCE YOU'RE HERE NOW, I DON'T PLAN ON HOLDING ANY-THING BACK.
COME ON IN, OR...
...GET OUT.
IT'S YOUR CHOICE.

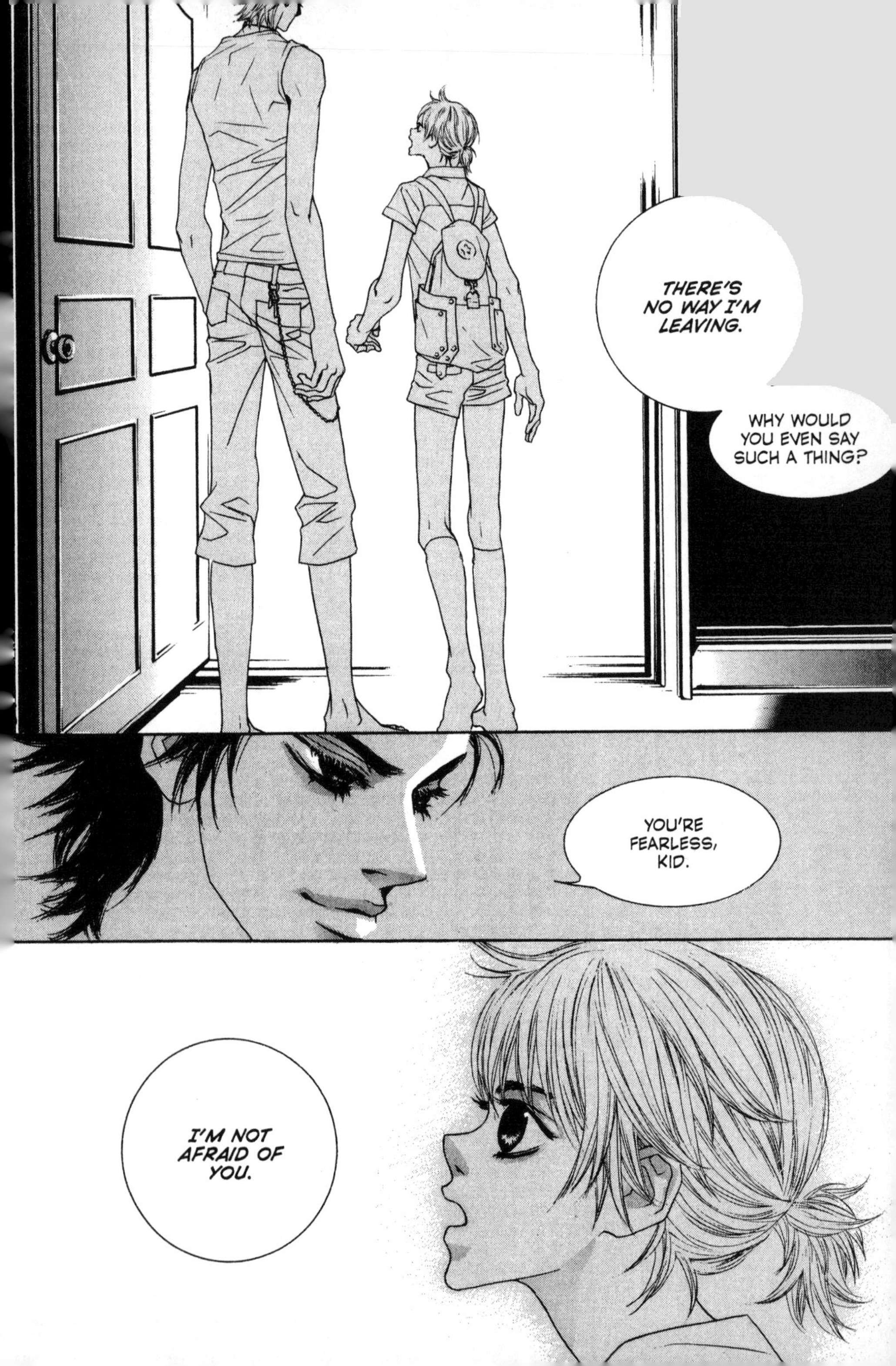

THERE'S NO WAY I'M LEAVING.
WHY WOULD YOU EVEN SAY SUCH A THING?
YOU'RE FEARLESS, KID.
I'M NOT AFRAID OF YOU.

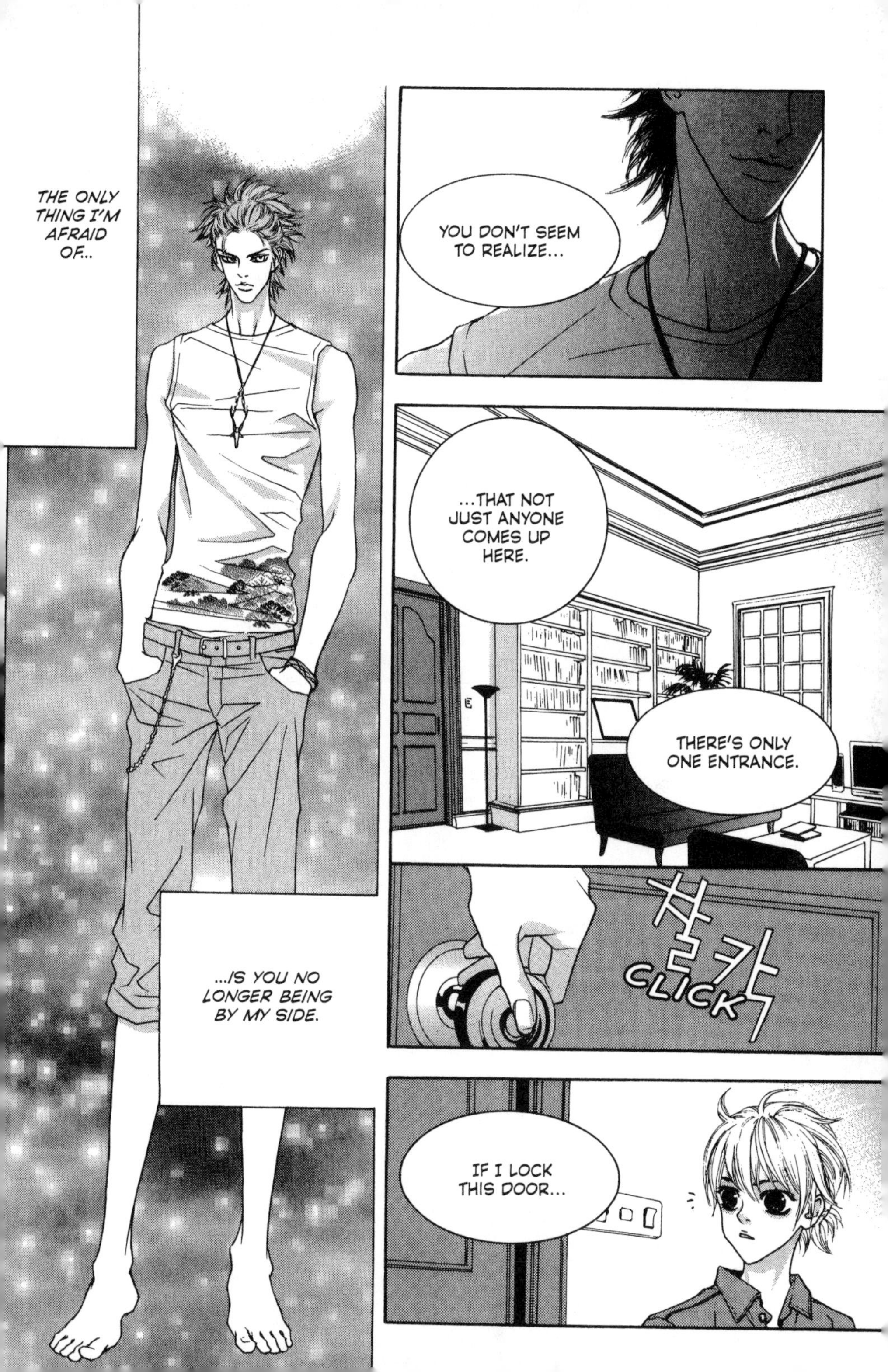
THE ONLY THING I'M AFRAID OF...
...IS YOU NO LONGER BEING BY MY SIDE.
YOU DON'T SEEM TO REALIZE...
...THAT NOT JUST ANYONE COMES UP HERE.
THERE'S ONLY ONE ENTRANCE.
CLICK
IF I LOCK THIS DOOR...

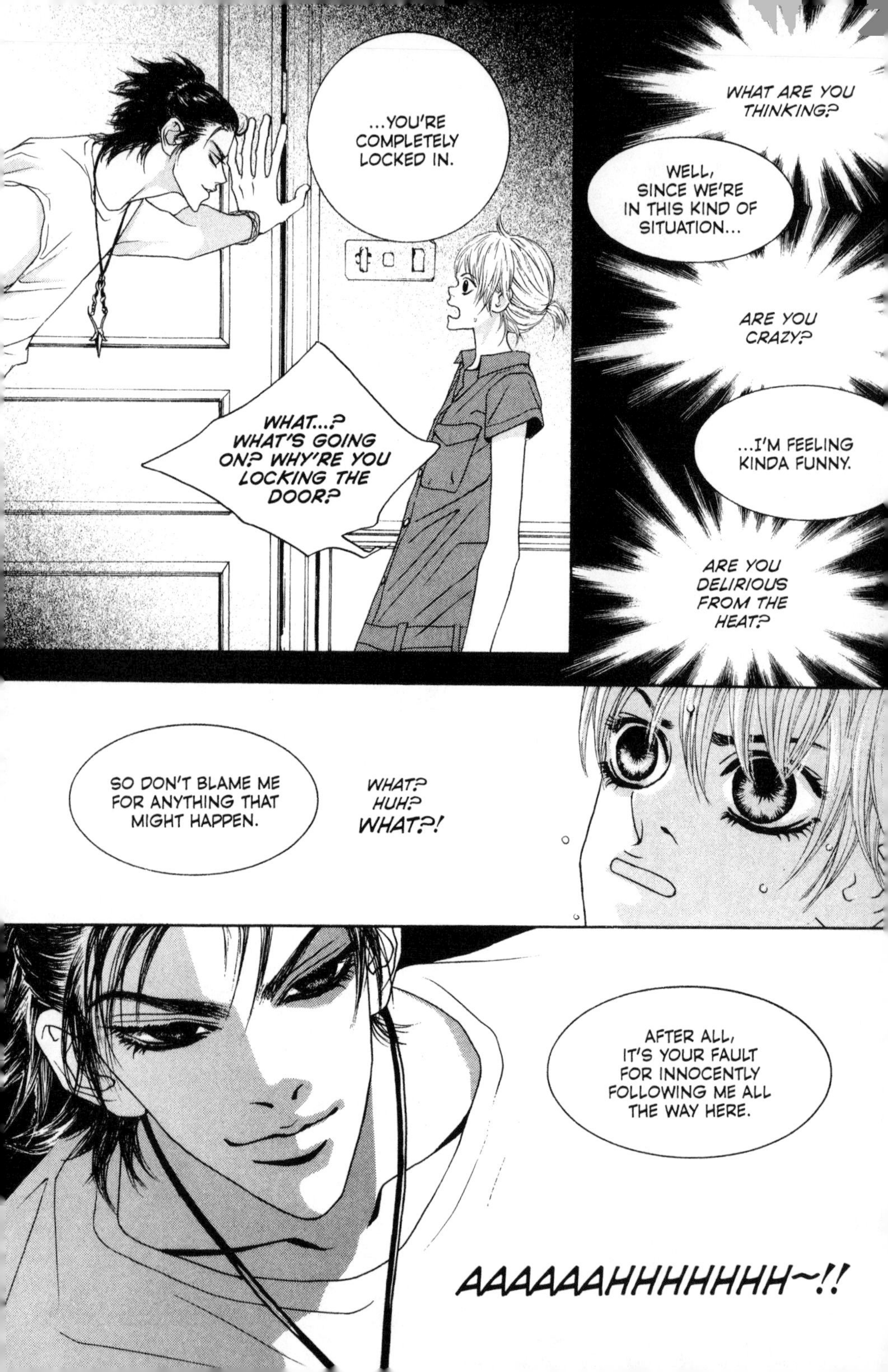
...YOU'RE COMPLETELY LOCKED IN.
WHAT...? WHAT'S GOING ON? WHY'RE YOU LOCKING THE DOOR?
WHAT ARE YOU THINKING?
WELL, SINCE WE'RE IN THIS KIND OF SITUATION...
ARE YOU CRAZY?
...I'M FEELING KINDA FUNNY.
ARE YOU DELIRIOUS FROM THE HEAT?
SO DON'T BLAME ME FOR ANYTHING THAT MIGHT HAPPEN.
WHAT? HUH? WHAT?!
AFTER ALL, IT'S YOUR FAULT FOR INNOCENTLY FOLLOWING ME ALL THE WAY HERE.
AAAAAAHHHHHHH~!!

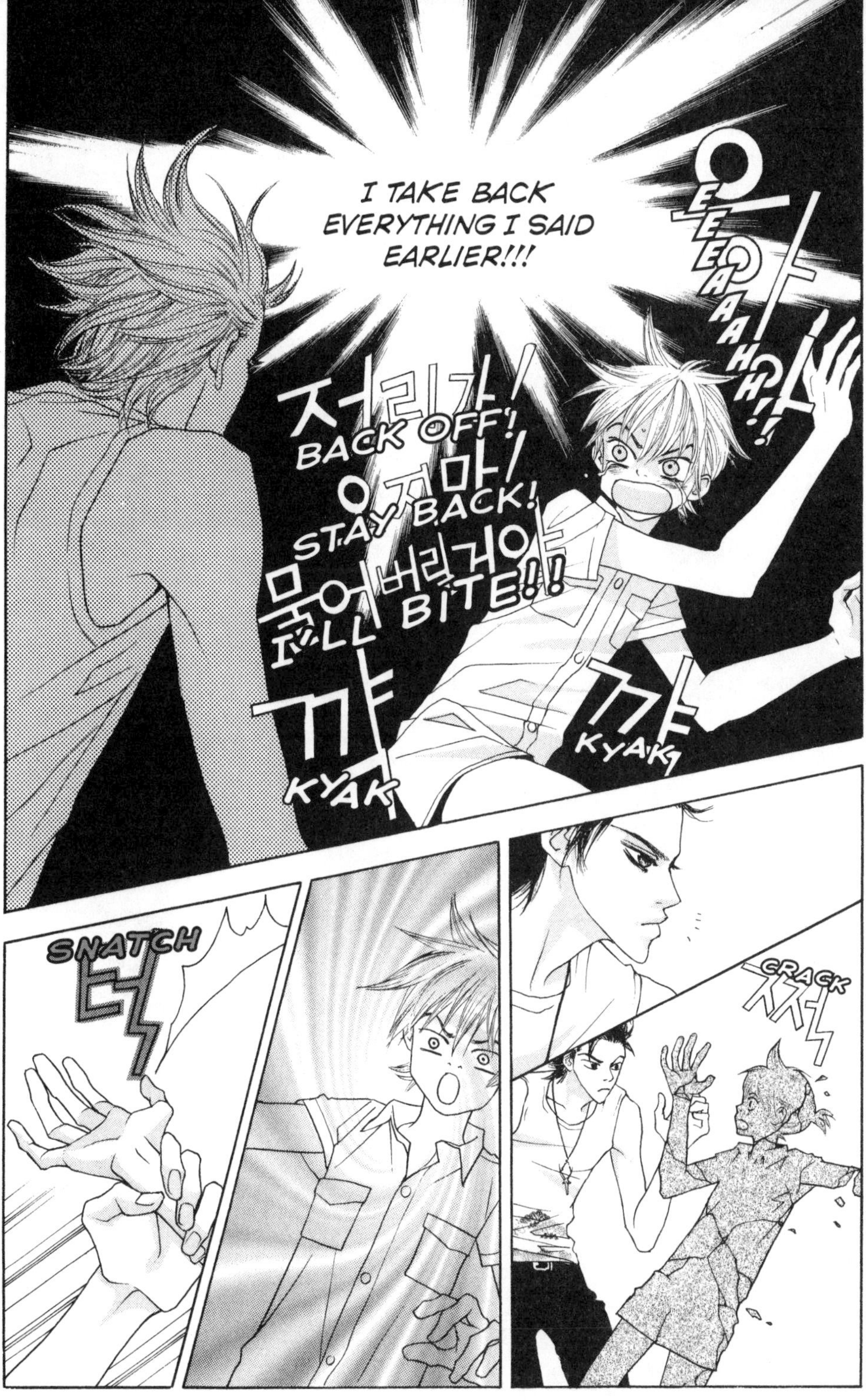

I TAKE BACK EVERYTHING I SAID EARLIER!!!
으악
EEEAAAHHH!!!
저리가!
BACK OFF!
오지마!
STAY BACK!
물어버릴거야!
I'LL BITE!!
꺄
KYAK
꺄
KYAK
SNATCH
CRACK

I CAN'T BELIEVE YOU! YOU PERVERT! WOLF! BEAST!

I HAVEN'T EVEN DONE ANYTHING YET. I WAS JUST JOKING. YOU'RE OVERREACTING.

JUST DON'T COME NEAR ME FOR NOW! STAY AT LEAST TWO METERS AWAY AT ALL TIMES!

OH, STOP FREAKING OUT. I'M NOT INCLINED TO JUMP ON A BRAT WITH THE BODY OF AN ELEMENTARY SCHOOLBOY.

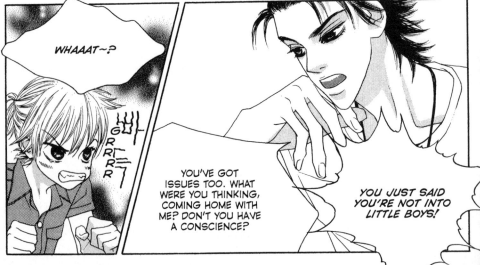

WHAAAT~?

YOU'VE GOT ISSUES TOO. WHAT WERE YOU THINKING, COMING HOME WITH ME? DON'T YOU HAVE A CONSCIENCE?

YOU JUST SAID YOU'RE NOT INTO LITTLE BOYS!

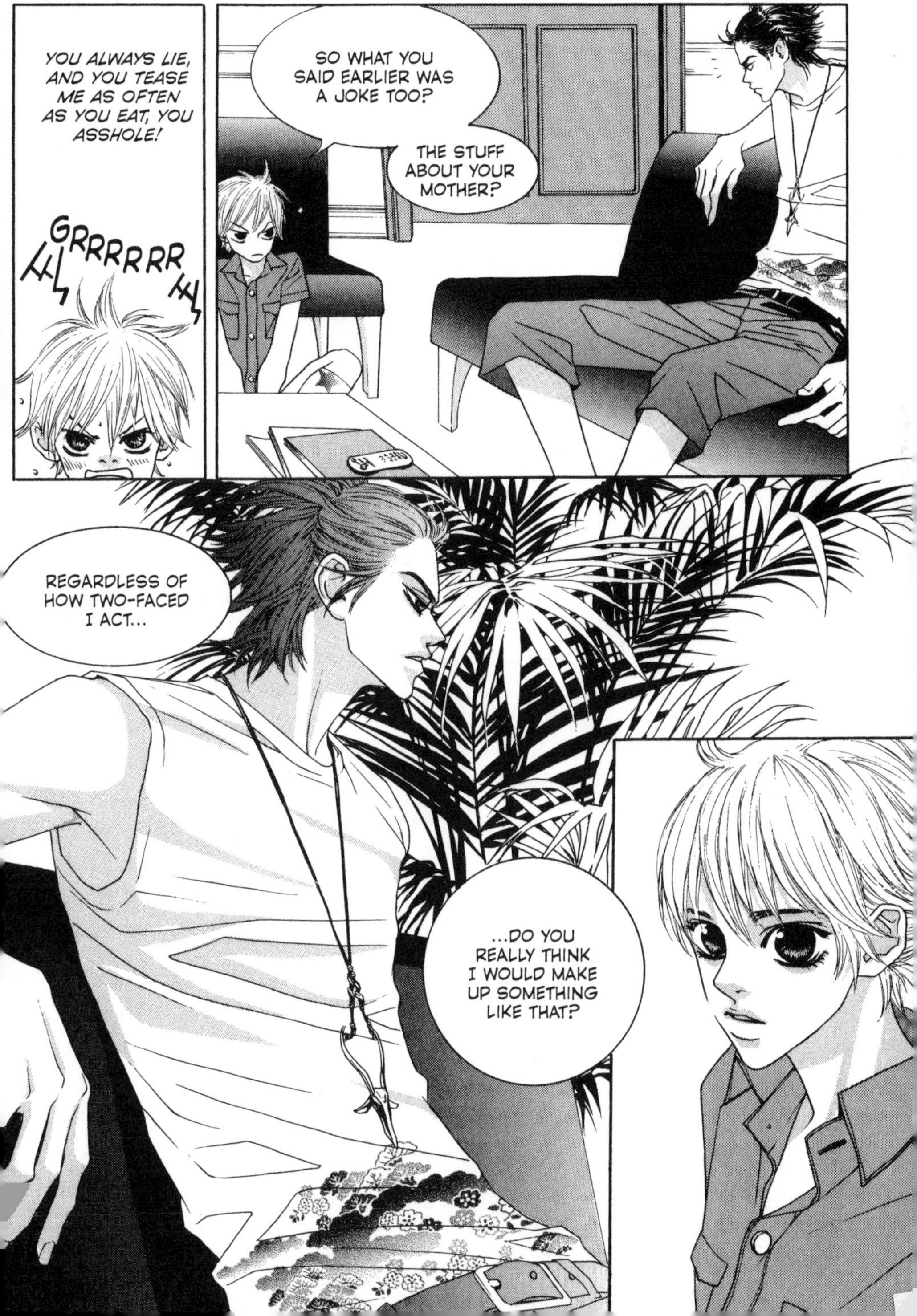
YOU ALWAYS LIE, AND YOU TEASE ME AS OFTEN AS YOU EAT, YOU ASSHOLE!
GRRRRRRR
SO WHAT YOU SAID EARLIER WAS A JOKE TOO?
THE STUFF ABOUT YOUR MOTHER?
REGARDLESS OF HOW TWO-FACED I ACT...
...DO YOU REALLY THINK I WOULD MAKE UP SOMETHING LIKE THAT?

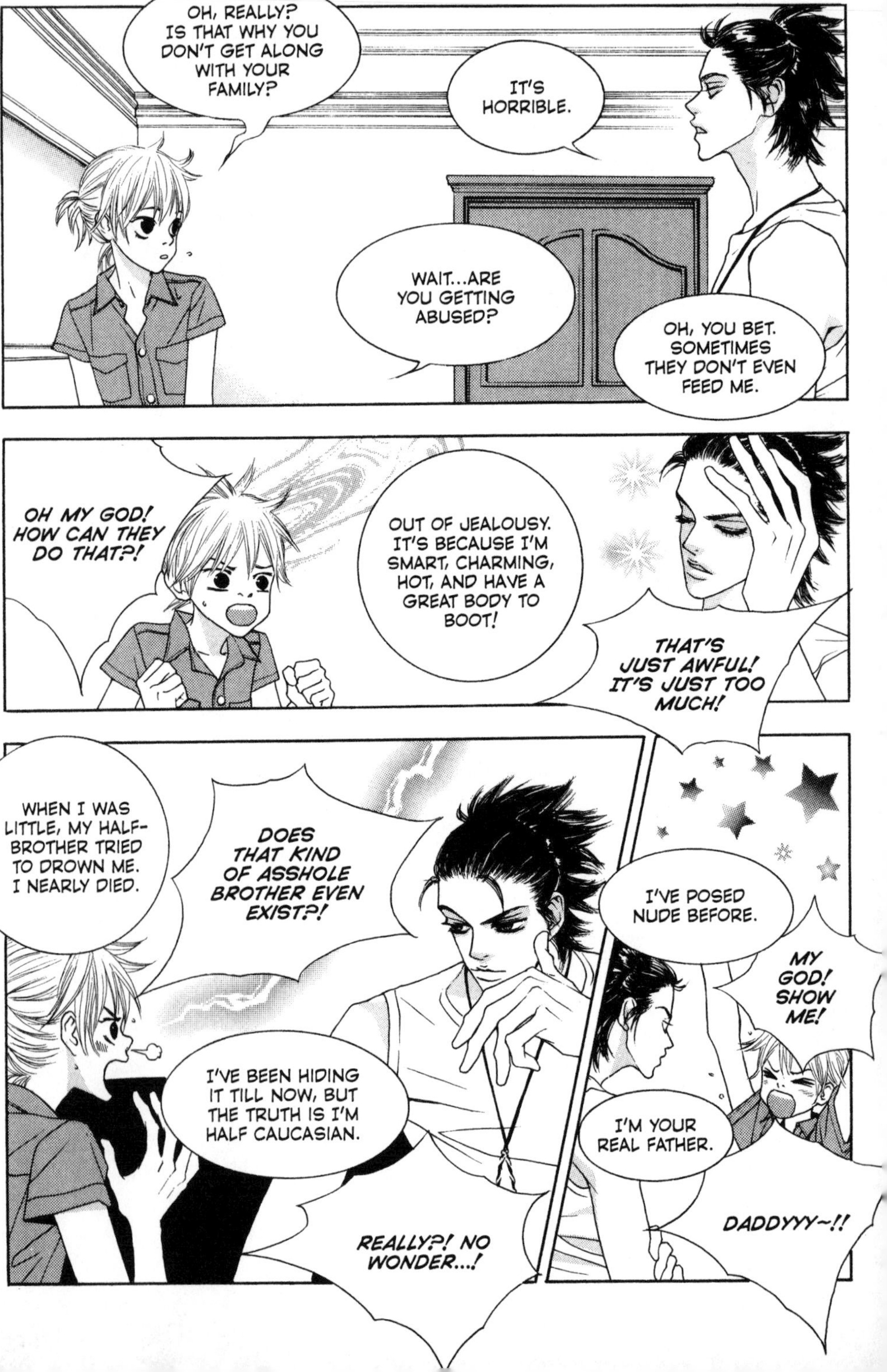
OH, REALLY? IS THAT WHY YOU DON'T GET ALONG WITH YOUR FAMILY?
IT'S HORRIBLE.
WAIT...ARE YOU GETTING ABUSED?
OH, YOU BET. SOMETIMES THEY DON'T EVEN FEED ME.
OH MY GOD! HOW CAN THEY DO THAT?!
OUT OF JEALOUSY. IT'S BECAUSE I'M SMART, CHARMING, HOT, AND HAVE A GREAT BODY TO BOOT!
THAT'S JUST AWFUL! IT'S JUST TOO MUCH!
WHEN I WAS LITTLE, MY HALF-BROTHER TRIED TO DROWN ME. I NEARLY DIED.
DOES THAT KIND OF ASSHOLE BROTHER EVEN EXIST?!
I'VE BEEN HIDING IT TILL NOW, BUT THE TRUTH IS I'M HALF CAUCASIAN.
REALLY?! NO WONDER...!
I'VE POSED NUDE BEFORE.
MY GOD! SHOW ME!
I'M YOUR REAL FATHER.
DADDYYY~!!

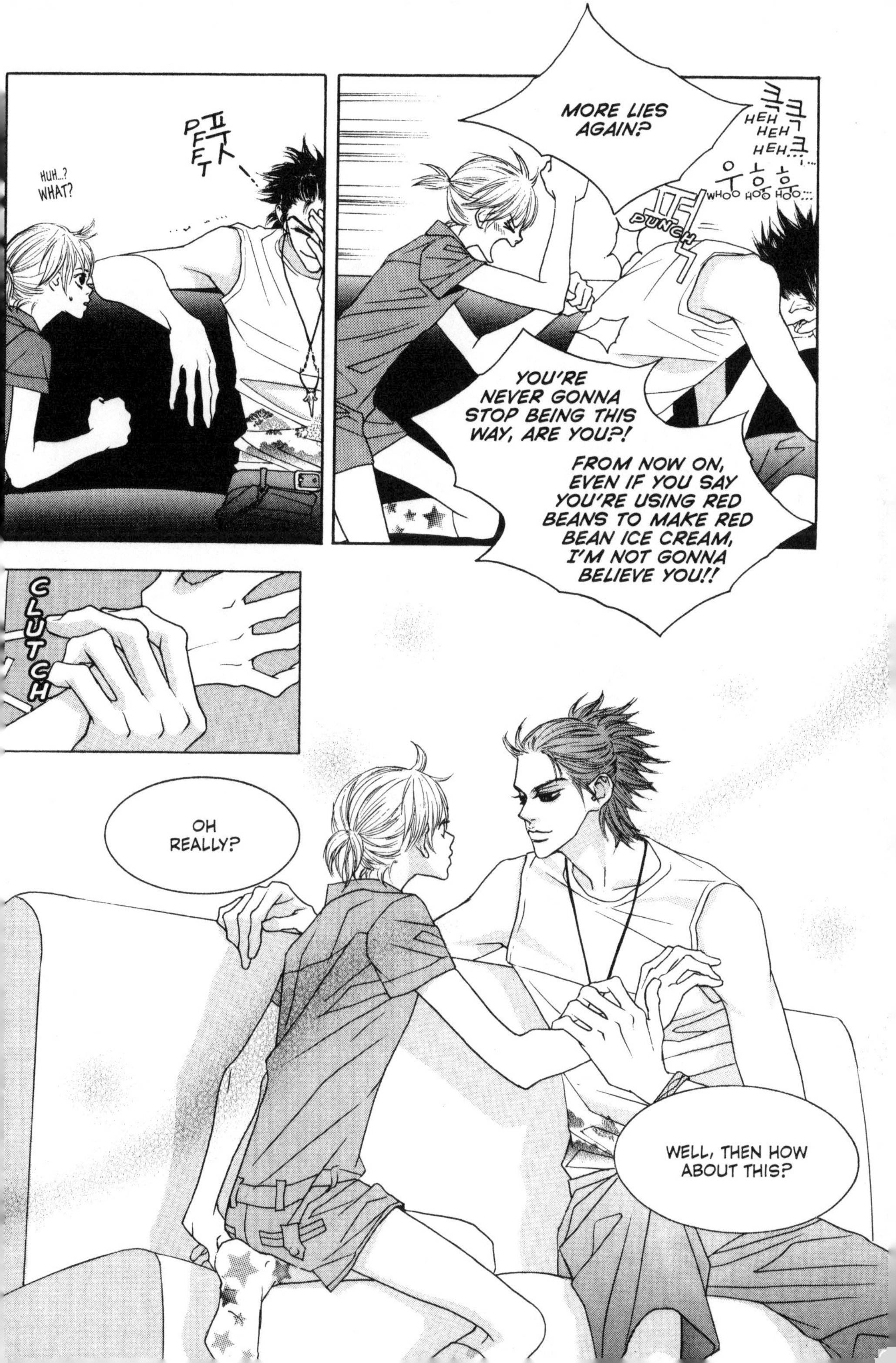
HUH...? WHAT?
PFFT
MORE LIES AGAIN?
HEH HEH HEH
WHOO HOO HOO
PUNCH
YOU'RE NEVER GONNA STOP BEING THIS WAY, ARE YOU?!
FROM NOW ON, EVEN IF YOU SAY YOU'RE USING RED BEANS TO MAKE RED BEAN ICE CREAM, I'M NOT GONNA BELIEVE YOU!!
CLUTCH
OH REALLY?
WELL, THEN HOW ABOUT THIS?

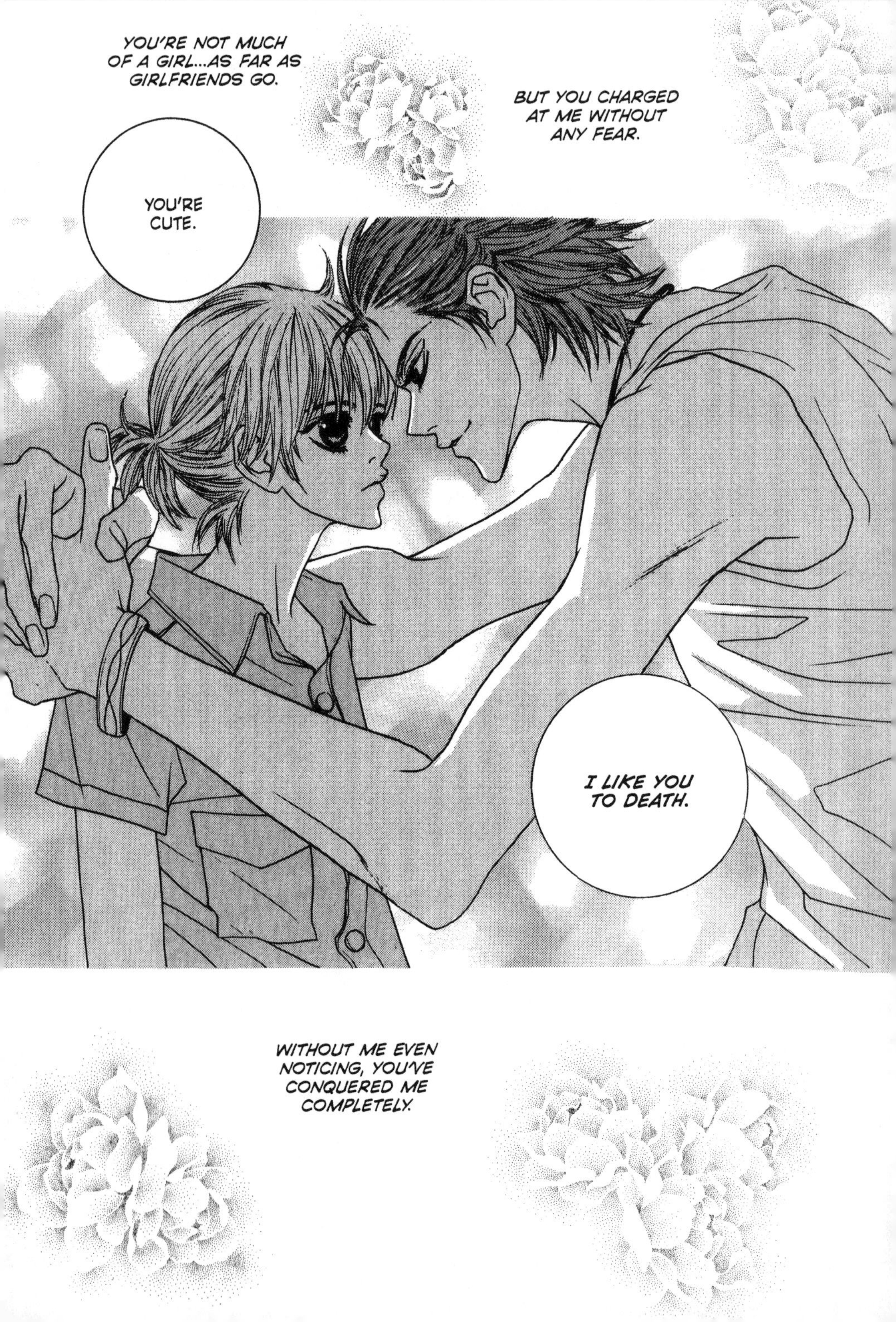
YOU'RE NOT MUCH OF A GIRL...AS FAR AS GIRLFRIENDS GO.
BUT YOU CHARGED AT ME WITHOUT ANY FEAR.
YOU'RE CUTE.
I LIKE YOU TO DEATH.
WITHOUT ME EVEN NOTICING, YOU'VE CONQUERED ME COMPLETELY.

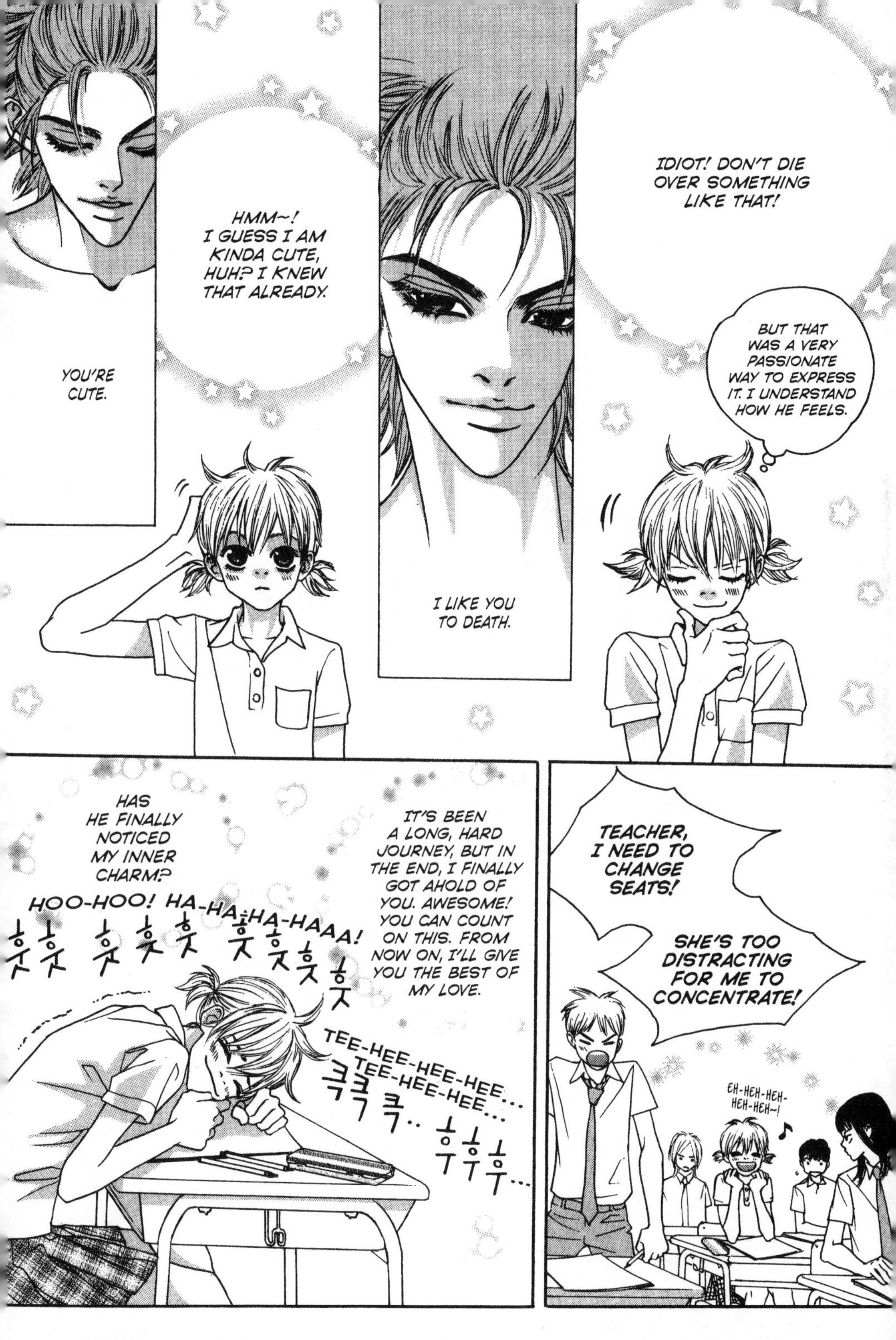

YOU'RE CUTE.
HMM~! I GUESS I AM KINDA CUTE, HUH? I KNEW THAT ALREADY.
I LIKE YOU TO DEATH.
IDIOT! DON'T DIE OVER SOMETHING LIKE THAT!
BUT THAT WAS A VERY PASSIONATE WAY TO EXPRESS IT. I UNDERSTAND HOW HE FEELS.
HAS HE FINALLY NOTICED MY INNER CHARM?
HOO-HOO! HA-HA-HA-HAAA!
IT'S BEEN A LONG, HARD JOURNEY, BUT IN THE END, I FINALLY GOT AHOLD OF YOU. AWESOME! YOU CAN COUNT ON THIS. FROM NOW ON, I'LL GIVE YOU THE BEST OF MY LOVE.
TEE-HEE-HEE-HEE... TEE-HEE-HEE...
큭큭 큭.. 후후후...
TEACHER, I NEED TO CHANGE SEATS!
SHE'S TOO DISTRACTING FOR ME TO CONCENTRATE!
EH-HEH-HEH-HEH-HEH~!

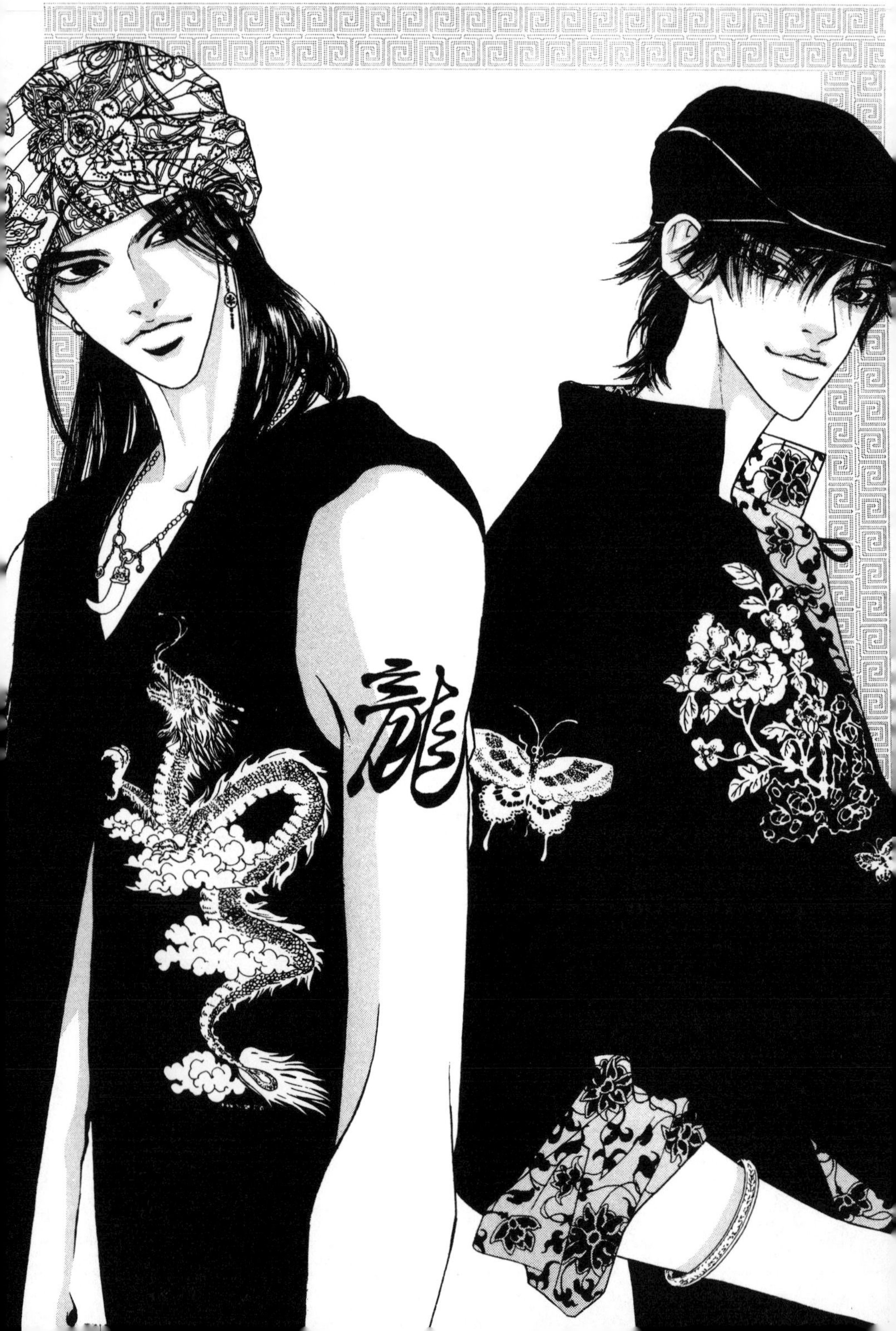
龍

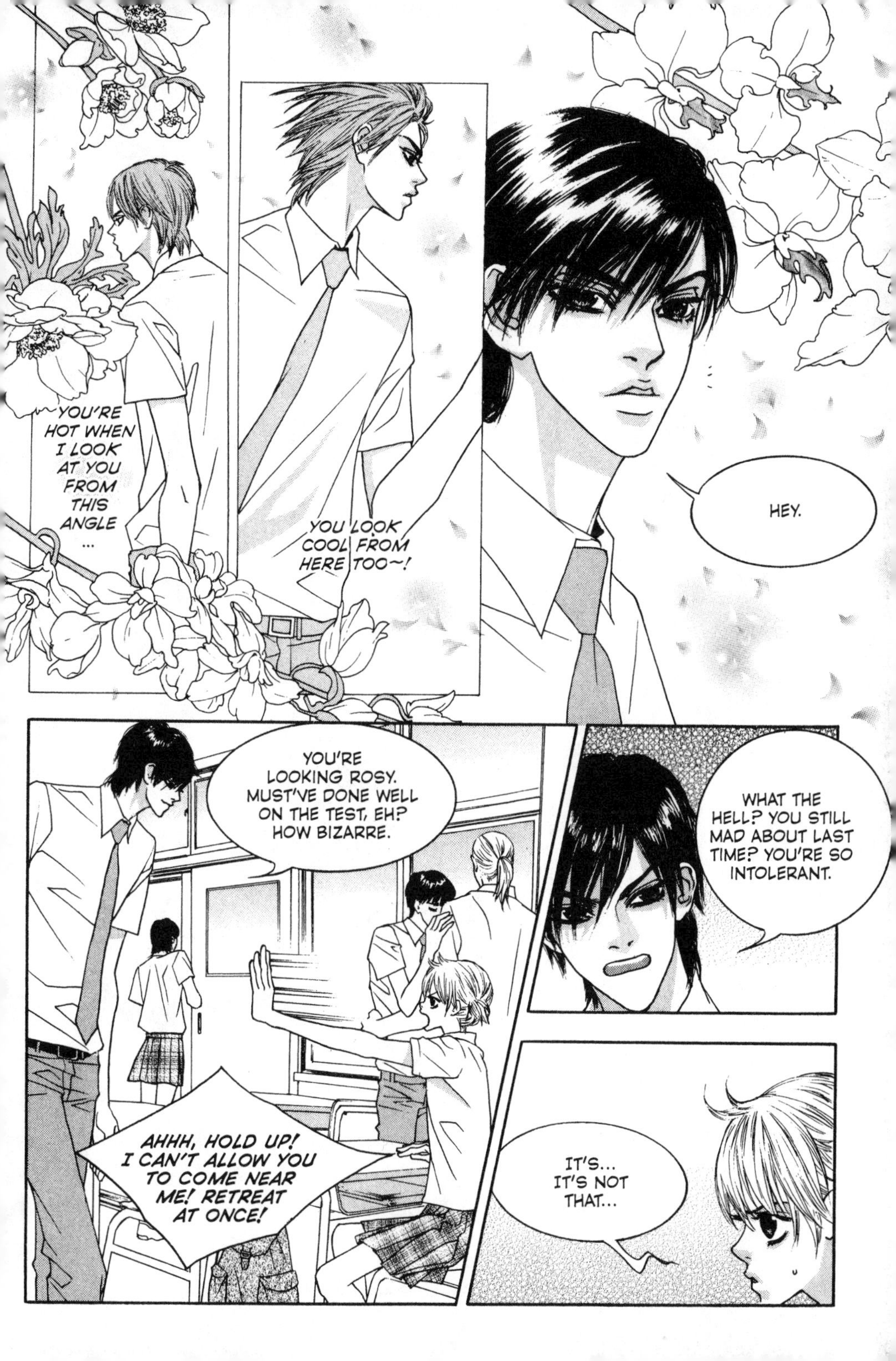
YOU'RE HOT WHEN I LOOK AT YOU FROM THIS ANGLE ...
YOU LOOK COOL FROM HERE TOO~!
HEY.
YOU'RE LOOKING ROSY. MUST'VE DONE WELL ON THE TEST, EH? HOW BIZARRE.
AHHH, HOLD UP! I CAN'T ALLOW YOU TO COME NEAR ME! RETREAT AT ONCE!
WHAT THE HELL? YOU STILL MAD ABOUT LAST TIME? YOU'RE SO INTOLERANT.
IT'S... IT'S NOT THAT...

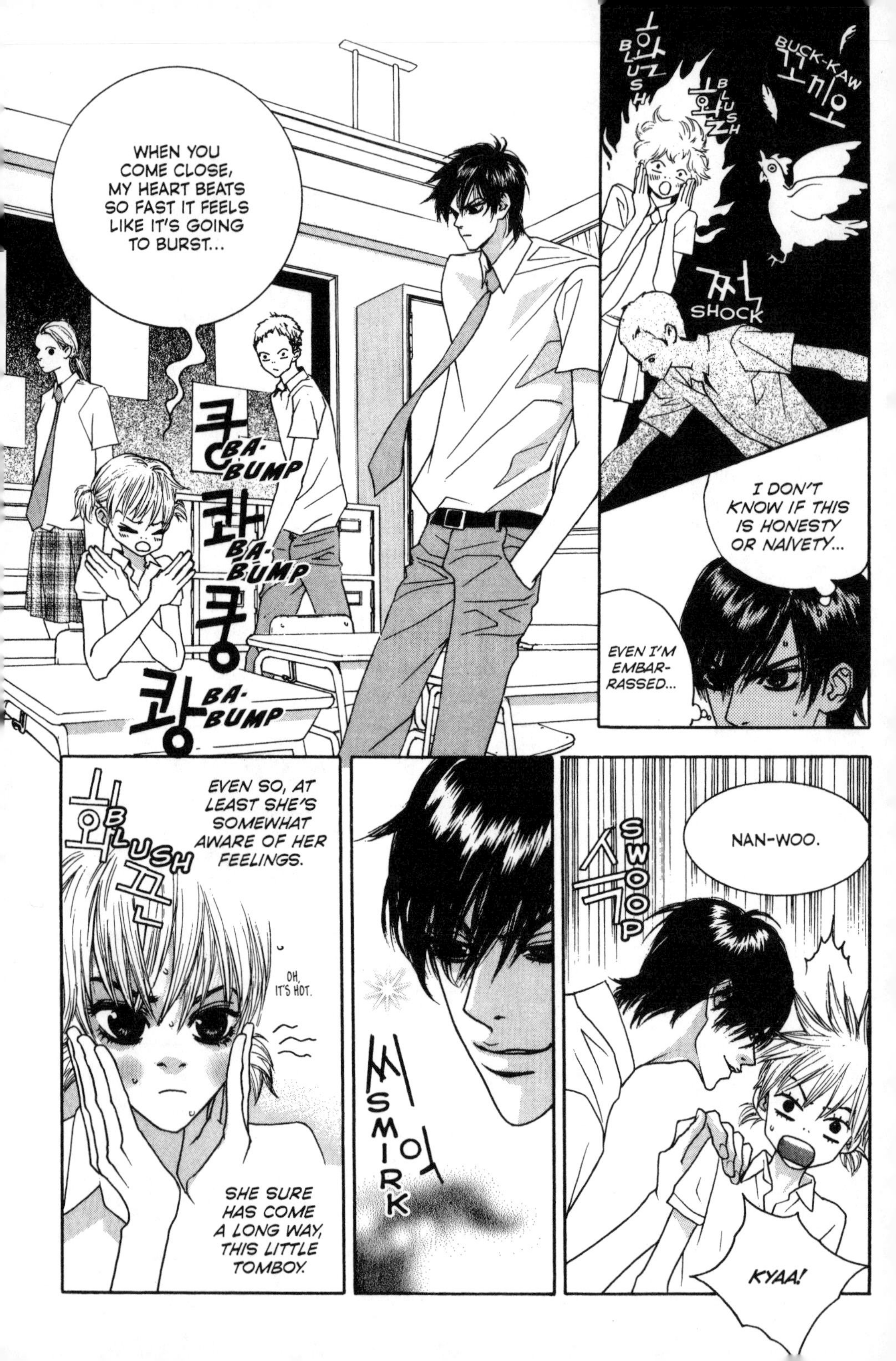

WHEN YOU COME CLOSE, MY HEART BEATS SO FAST IT FEELS LIKE IT'S GOING TO BURST...
쿵 BA-BUMP
쾅 BA-BUMP
쿵
쾅 BA-BUMP
BLUSH
BLUSH
꼬끼오 BUCK-KAW
SHOCK
I DON'T KNOW IF THIS IS HONESTY OR NAIVETY...
EVEN I'M EMBAR-RASSED...
BLUSH
EVEN SO, AT LEAST SHE'S SOMEWHAT AWARE OF HER FEELINGS.
OH, IT'S HOT.
SHE SURE HAS COME A LONG WAY, THIS LITTLE TOMBOY.
SMIRK
SWOOP
NAN-WOO.
KYAA!

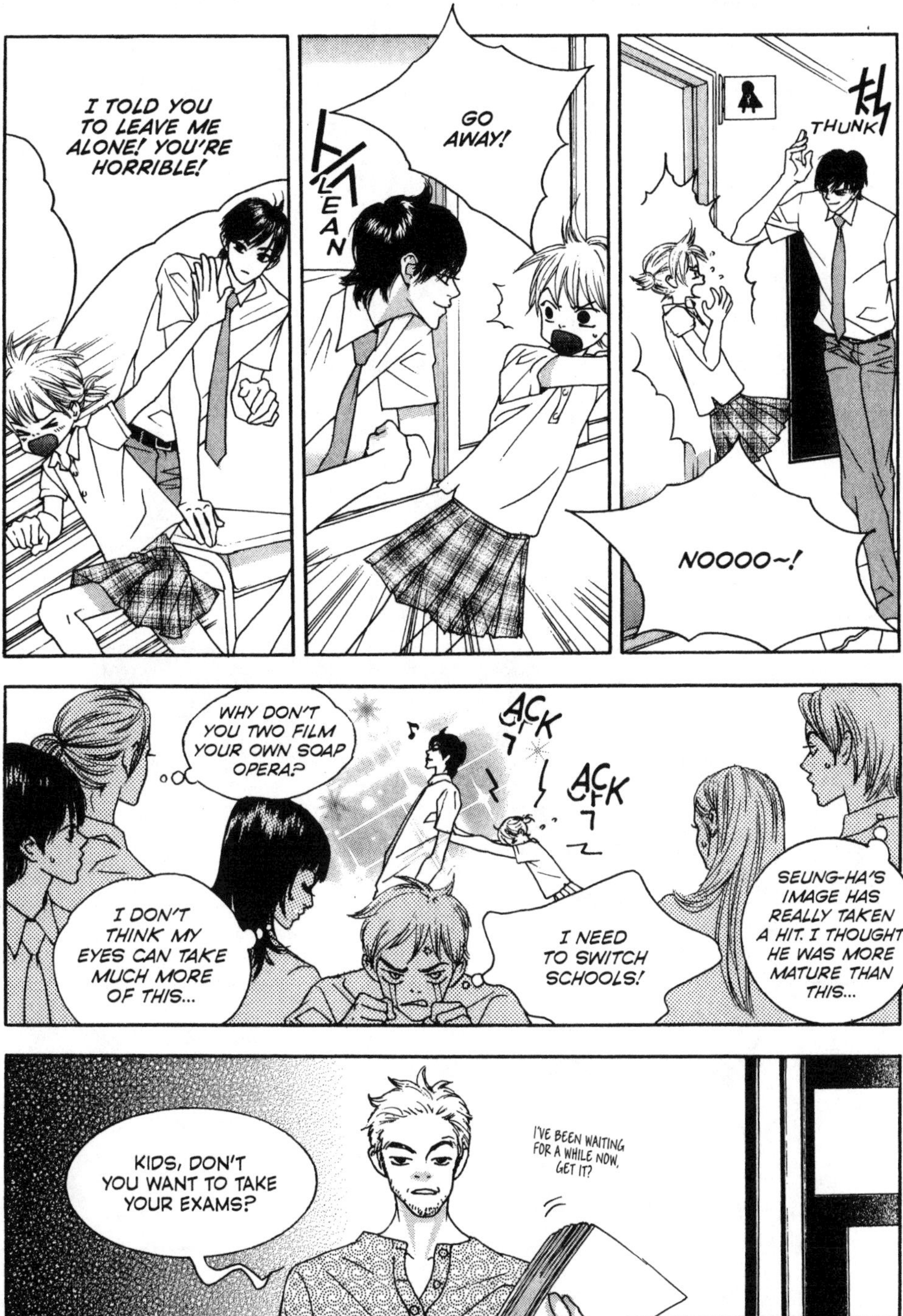

I TOLD YOU TO LEAVE ME ALONE! YOU'RE HORRIBLE!
LEAN
GO AWAY!
THUNK
NOOOO~!
WHY DON'T YOU TWO FILM YOUR OWN SOAP OPERA?
ACK
ACK
I DON'T THINK MY EYES CAN TAKE MUCH MORE OF THIS...
I NEED TO SWITCH SCHOOLS!
SEUNG-HA'S IMAGE HAS REALLY TAKEN A HIT. I THOUGHT HE WAS MORE MATURE THAN THIS...
KIDS, DON'T YOU WANT TO TAKE YOUR EXAMS?
I'VE BEEN WAITING FOR A WHILE NOW, GET IT?
THEY'RE HAVING THEIR FINAL EXAMS.

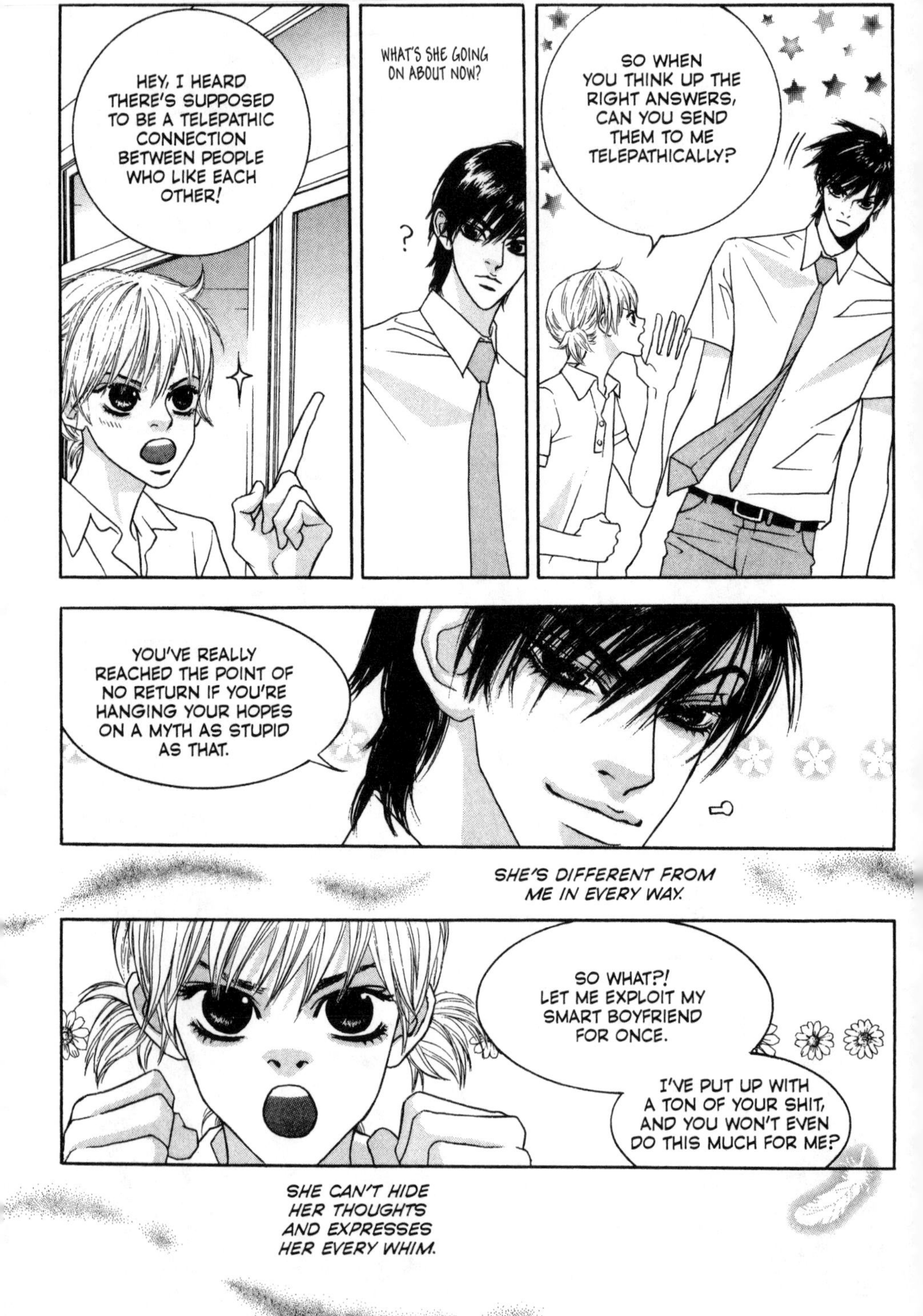

HEY, I HEARD THERE'S SUPPOSED TO BE A TELEPATHIC CONNECTION BETWEEN PEOPLE WHO LIKE EACH OTHER!
WHAT'S SHE GOING ON ABOUT NOW?
?
SO WHEN YOU THINK UP THE RIGHT ANSWERS, CAN YOU SEND THEM TO ME TELEPATHICALLY?
YOU'VE REALLY REACHED THE POINT OF NO RETURN IF YOU'RE HANGING YOUR HOPES ON A MYTH AS STUPID AS THAT.
SHE'S DIFFERENT FROM ME IN EVERY WAY.
SO WHAT?! LET ME EXPLOIT MY SMART BOYFRIEND FOR ONCE.
I'VE PUT UP WITH A TON OF YOUR SHIT, AND YOU WON'T EVEN DO THIS MUCH FOR ME?
SHE CAN'T HIDE HER THOUGHTS AND EXPRESSES HER EVERY WHIM.

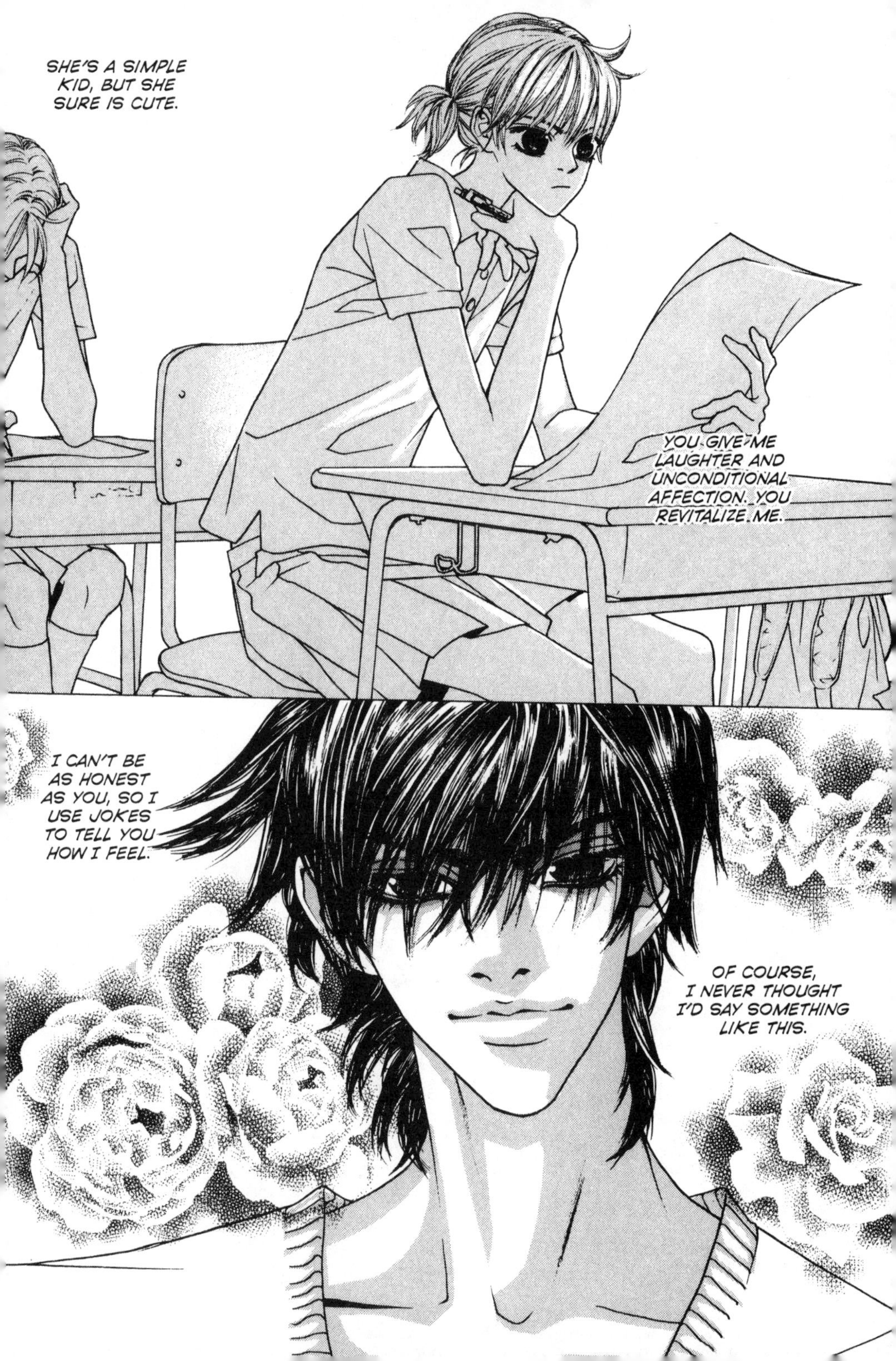
SHE'S A SIMPLE KID, BUT SHE SURE IS CUTE.
YOU GIVE ME LAUGHTER AND UNCONDITIONAL AFFECTION. YOU REVITALIZE ME.
I CAN'T BE AS HONEST AS YOU, SO I USE JOKES TO TELL YOU HOW I FEEL.
OF COURSE, I NEVER THOUGHT I'D SAY SOMETHING LIKE THIS.

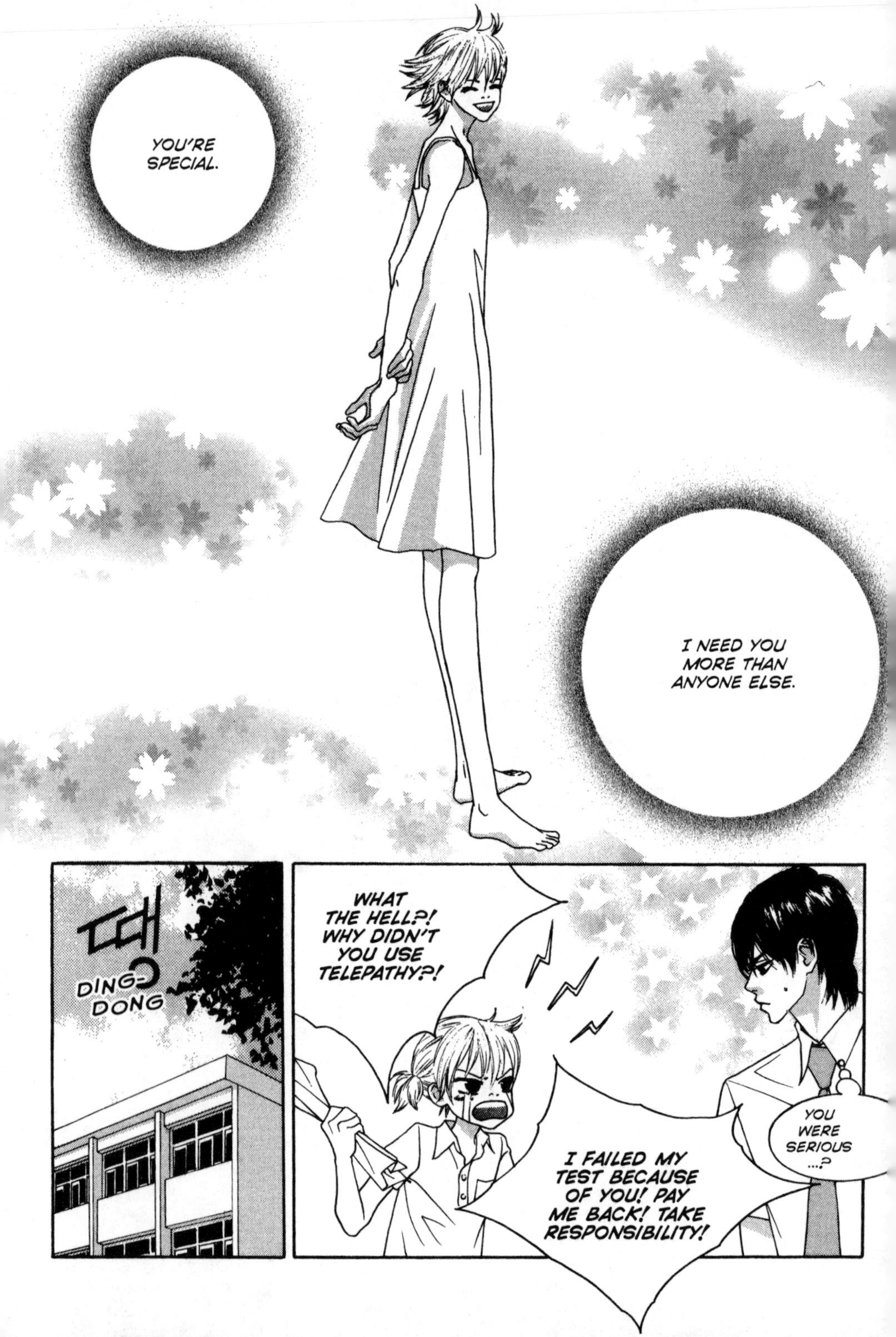
YOU'RE SPECIAL.
I NEED YOU MORE THAN ANYONE ELSE.
DING-DONG
WHAT THE HELL?! WHY DIDN'T YOU USE TELEPATHY?!
YOU WERE SERIOUS ...?
I FAILED MY TEST BECAUSE OF YOU! PAY ME BACK! TAKE RESPONSIBILITY!

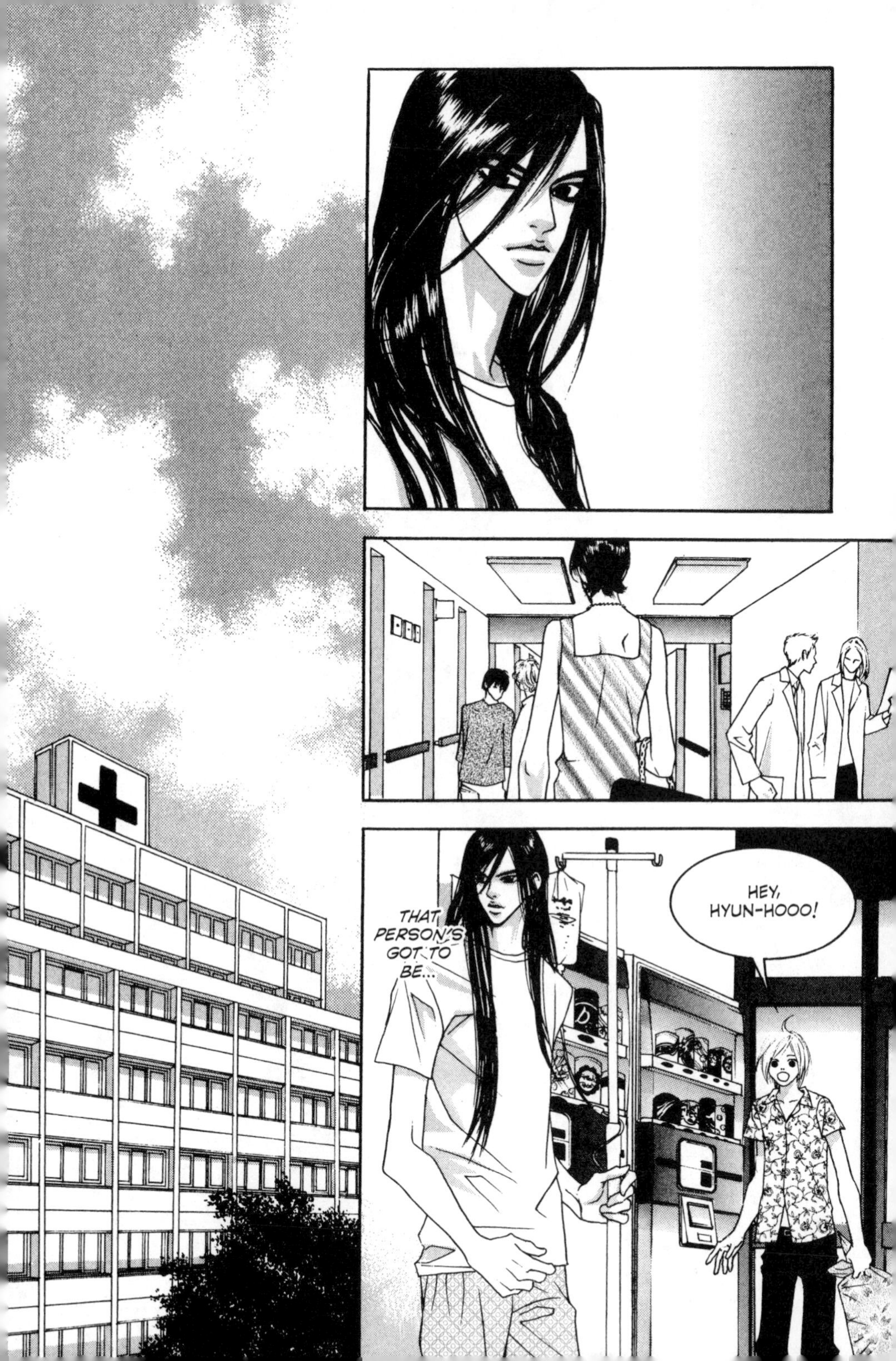
THAT PERSON'S GOT TO BE...
HEY, HYUN-HOOO!

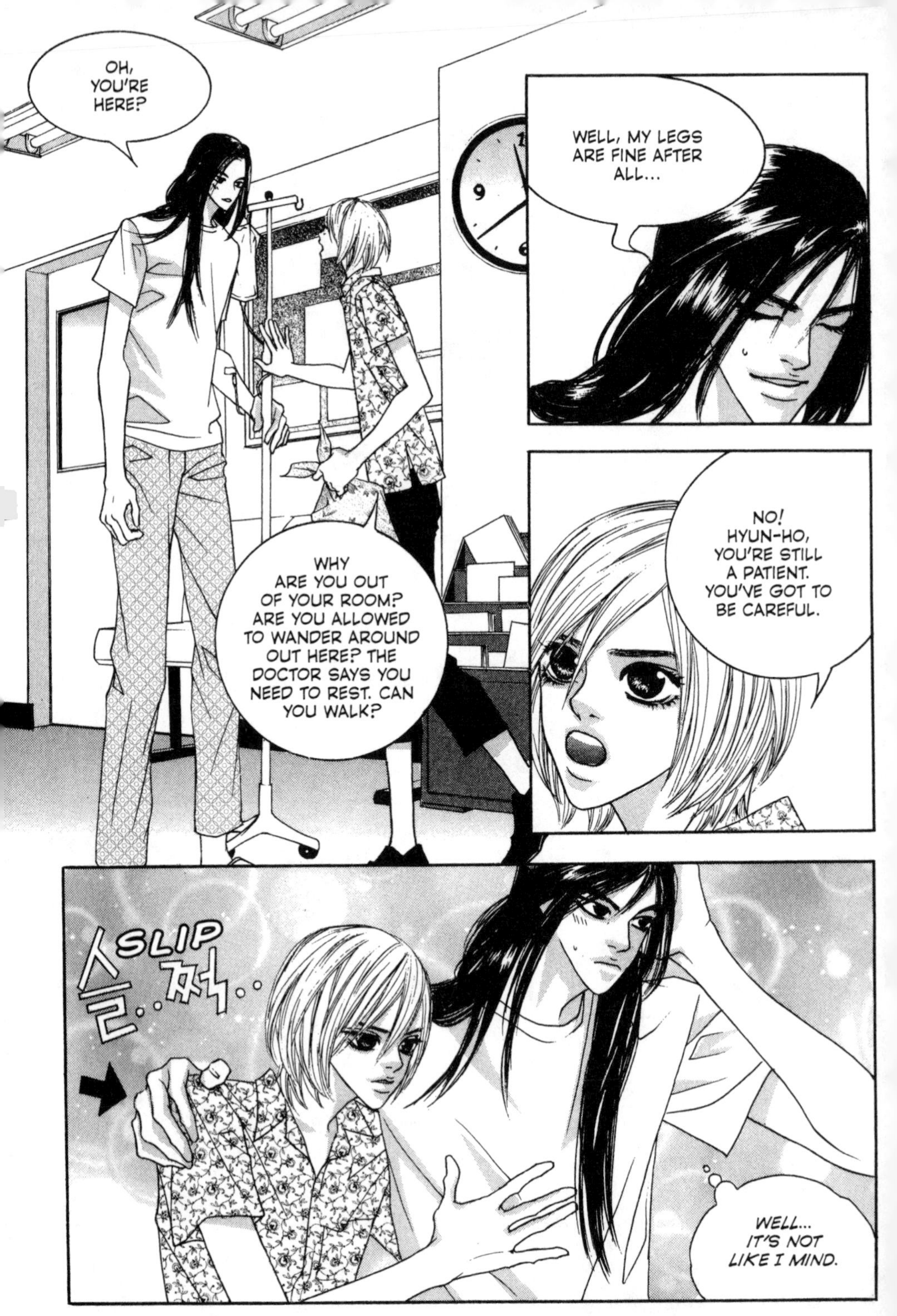
OH, YOU'RE HERE?
WHY ARE YOU OUT OF YOUR ROOM? ARE YOU ALLOWED TO WANDER AROUND OUT HERE? THE DOCTOR SAYS YOU NEED TO REST. CAN YOU WALK?
WELL, MY LEGS ARE FINE AFTER ALL...
NO! HYUN-HO, YOU'RE STILL A PATIENT. YOU'VE GOT TO BE CAREFUL.
SLIP
슬..쩍..
WELL... IT'S NOT LIKE I MIND.

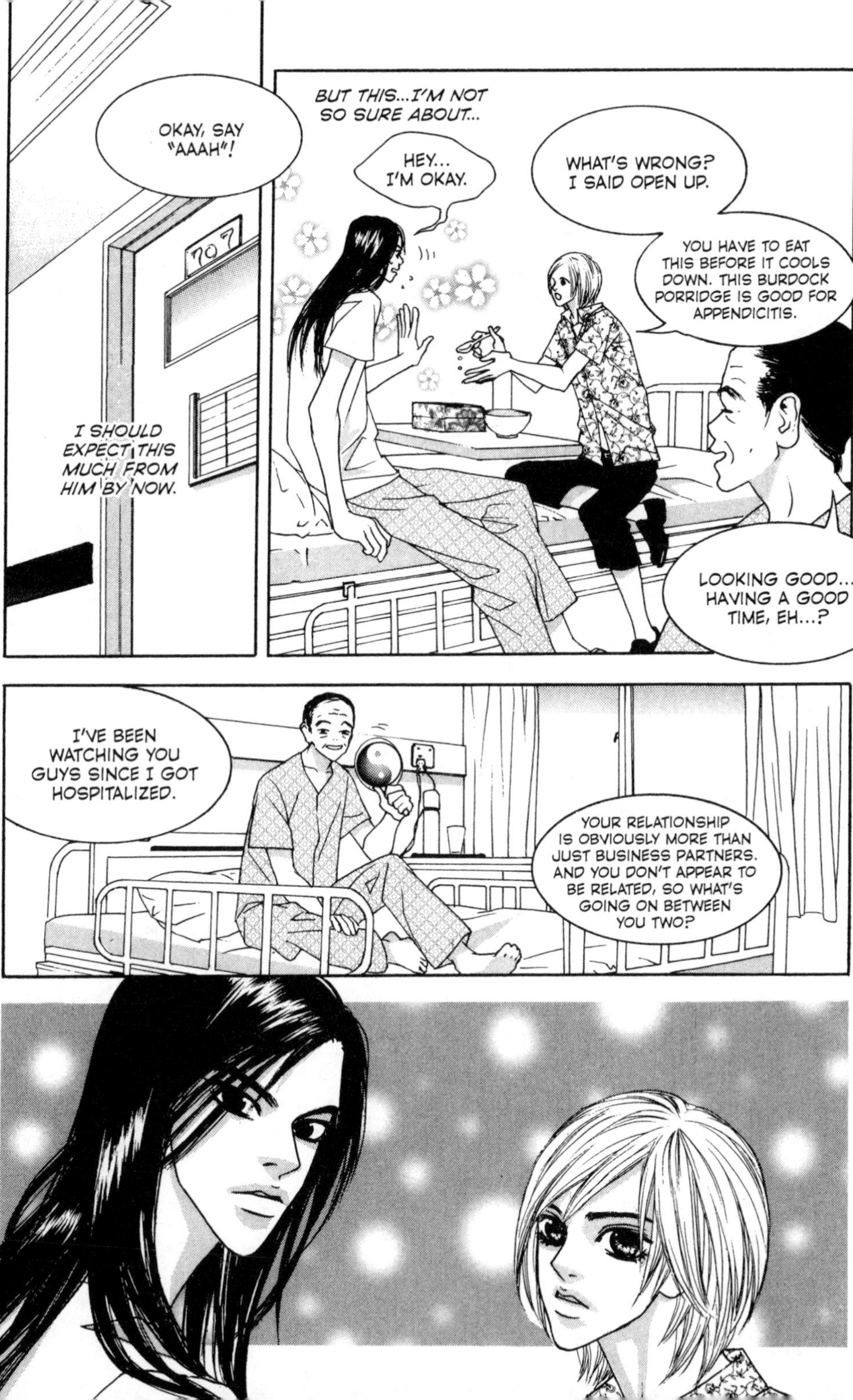
OKAY, SAY "AAAH"!
I SHOULD EXPECT THIS MUCH FROM HIM BY NOW.
BUT THIS...I'M NOT SO SURE ABOUT...
HEY... I'M OKAY.
WHAT'S WRONG? I SAID OPEN UP.
YOU HAVE TO EAT THIS BEFORE IT COOLS DOWN. THIS BURDOCK PORRIDGE IS GOOD FOR APPENDICITIS.
LOOKING GOOD... HAVING A GOOD TIME, EH...?
I'VE BEEN WATCHING YOU GUYS SINCE I GOT HOSPITALIZED.
YOUR RELATIONSHIP IS OBVIOUSLY MORE THAN JUST BUSINESS PARTNERS. AND YOU DON'T APPEAR TO BE RELATED, SO WHAT'S GOING ON BETWEEN YOU TWO?

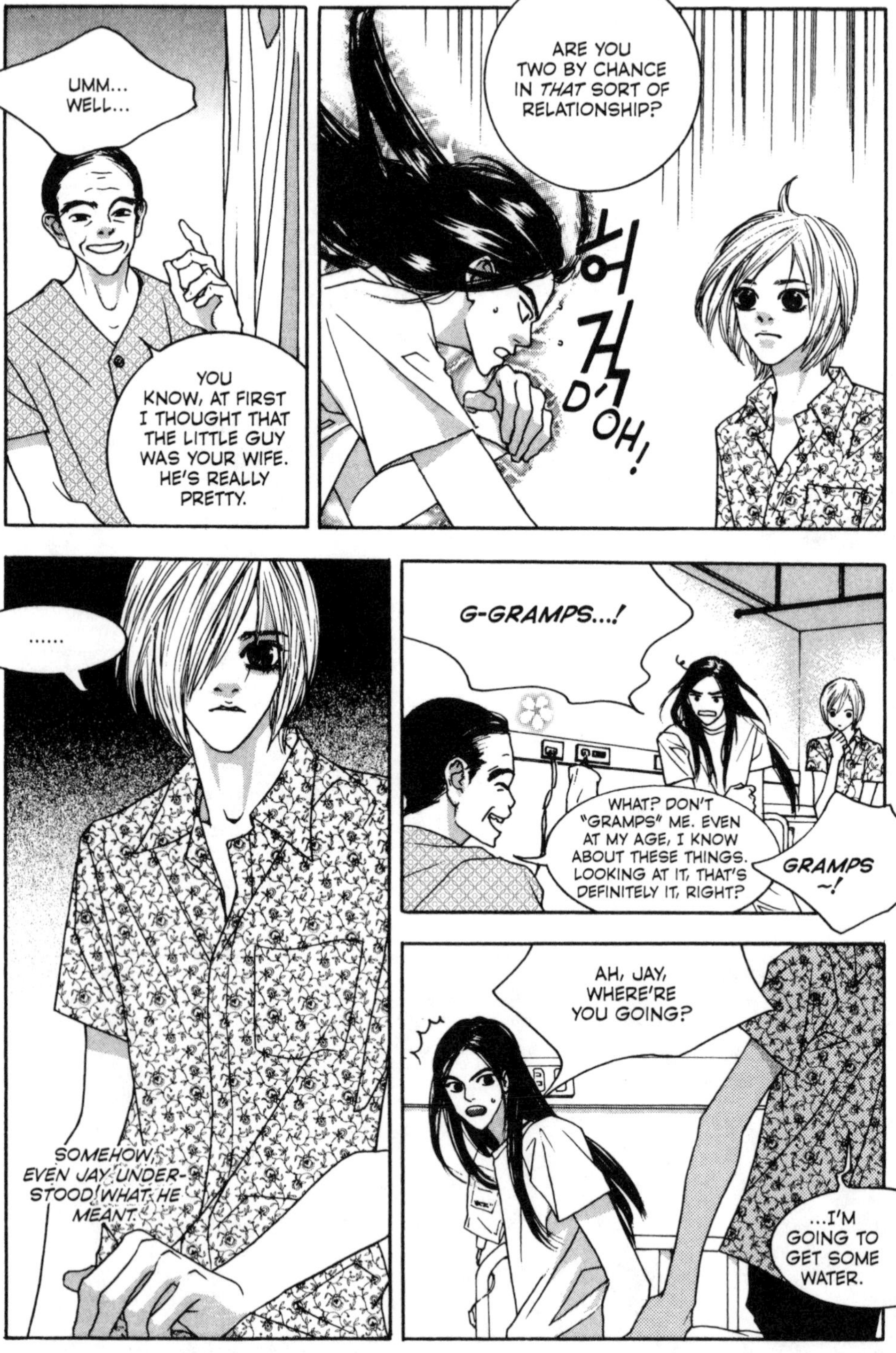
UMM... WELL...
YOU KNOW, AT FIRST I THOUGHT THAT THE LITTLE GUY WAS YOUR WIFE. HE'S REALLY PRETTY.
ARE YOU TWO BY CHANCE IN *THAT* SORT OF RELATIONSHIP?
D'OH!
......
SOMEHOW, EVEN JAY UNDERSTOOD WHAT HE MEANT.
G-GRAMPS...!
WHAT? DON'T "GRAMPS" ME. EVEN AT MY AGE, I KNOW ABOUT THESE THINGS. LOOKING AT IT, THAT'S DEFINITELY IT, RIGHT?
GRAMPS ~!
AH, JAY, WHERE'RE YOU GOING?
...I'M GOING TO GET SOME WATER.

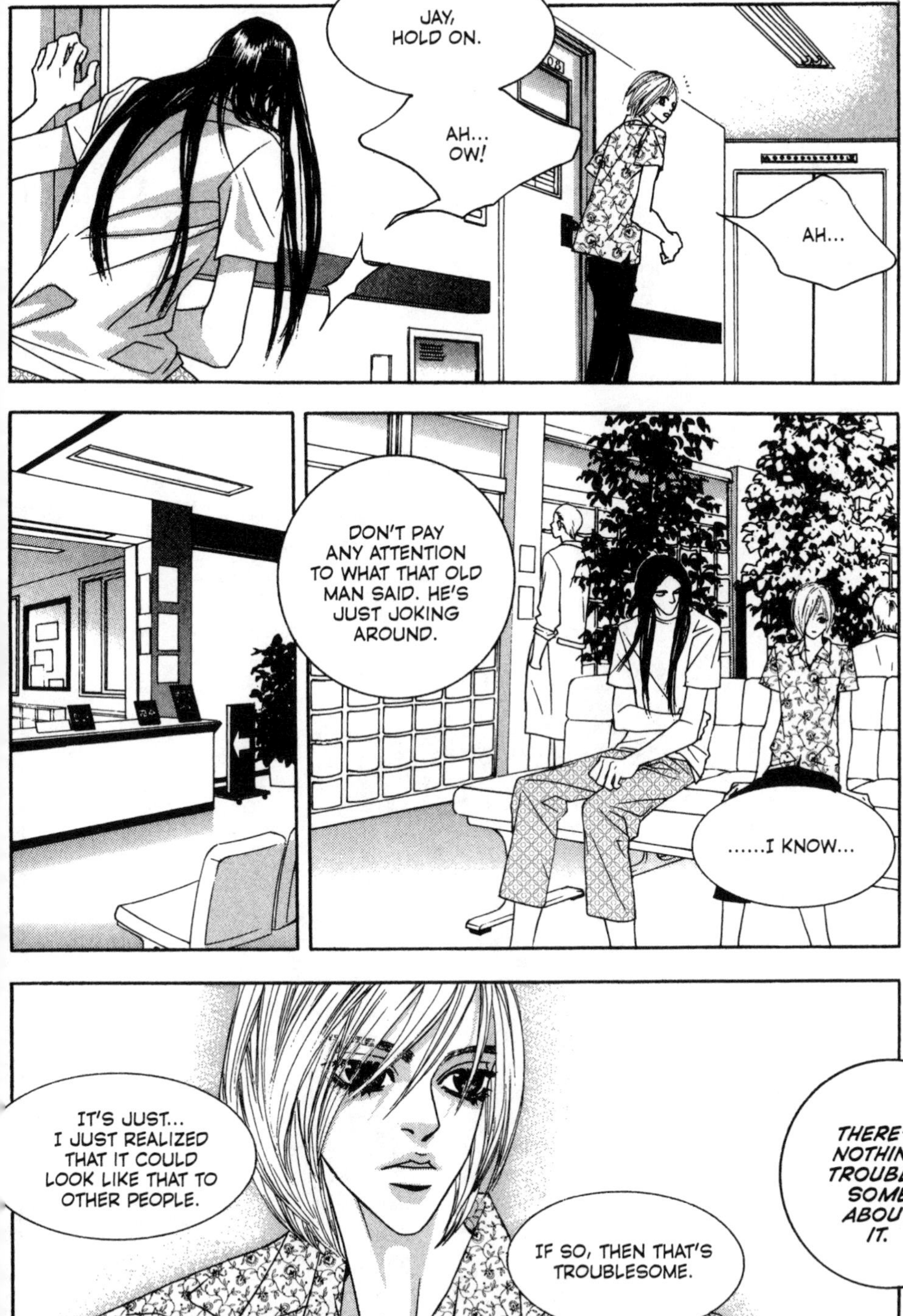
JAY, HOLD ON.
AH... OW!
AH...
DON'T PAY ANY ATTENTION TO WHAT THAT OLD MAN SAID. HE'S JUST JOKING AROUND.
......I KNOW...
IT'S JUST... I JUST REALIZED THAT IT COULD LOOK LIKE THAT TO OTHER PEOPLE.
IF SO, THEN THAT'S TROUBLESOME.
THERE'S NOTHING TROUBLE-SOME ABOUT IT.

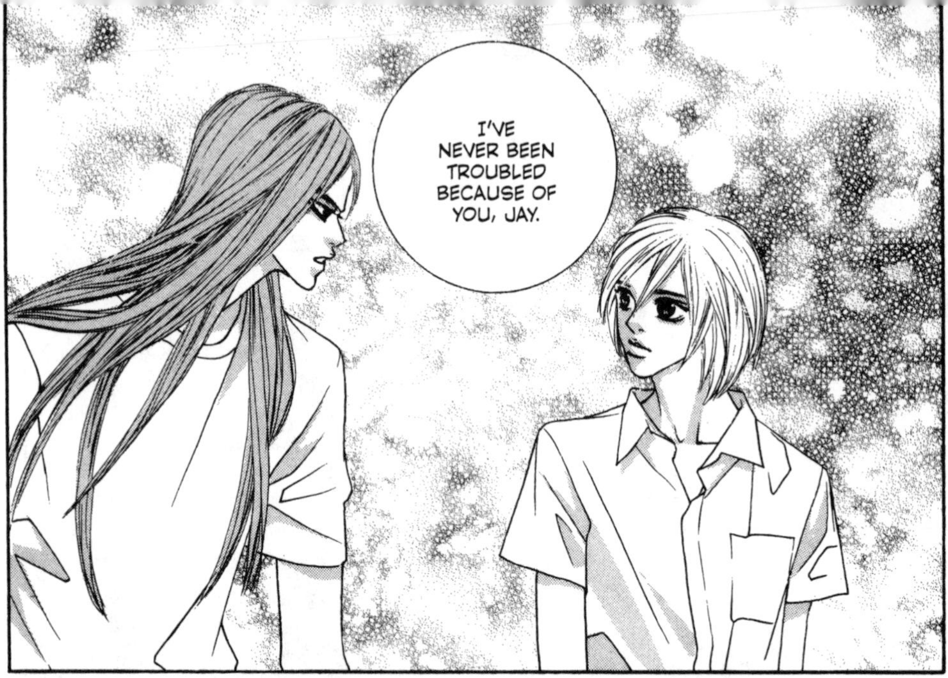
I'VE NEVER BEEN TROUBLED BECAUSE OF YOU, JAY.

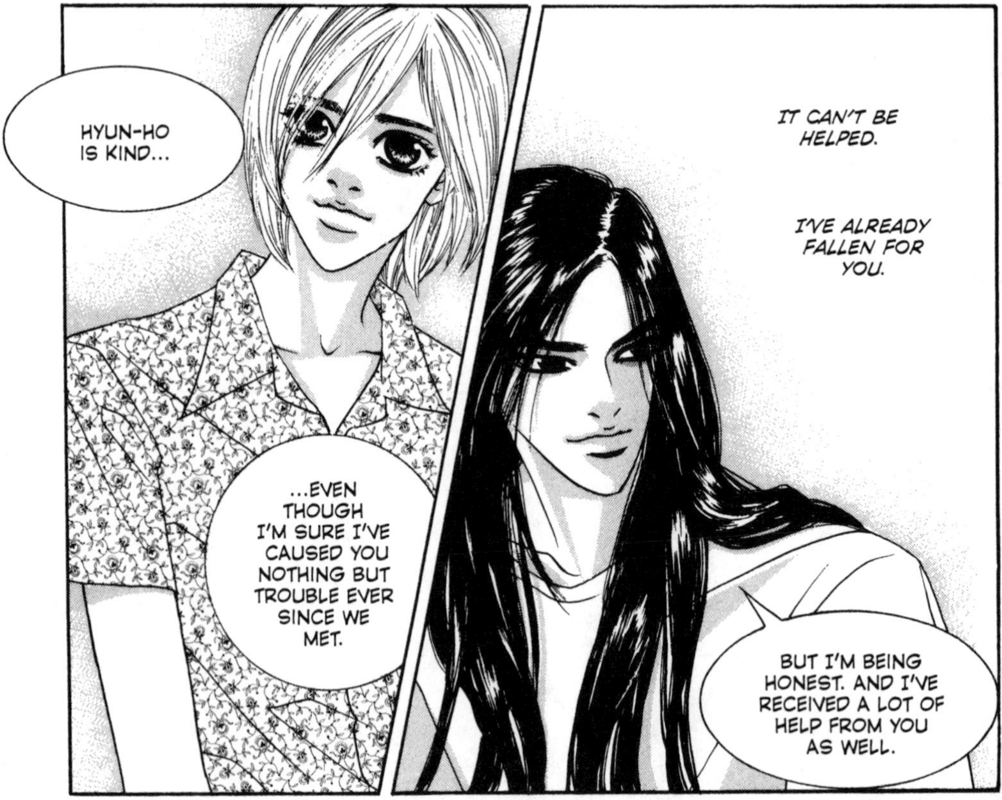
HYUN-HO IS KIND...
...EVEN THOUGH I'M SURE I'VE CAUSED YOU NOTHING BUT TROUBLE EVER SINCE WE MET.
IT CAN'T BE HELPED.
I'VE ALREADY FALLEN FOR YOU.
BUT I'M BEING HONEST. AND I'VE RECEIVED A LOT OF HELP FROM YOU AS WELL.

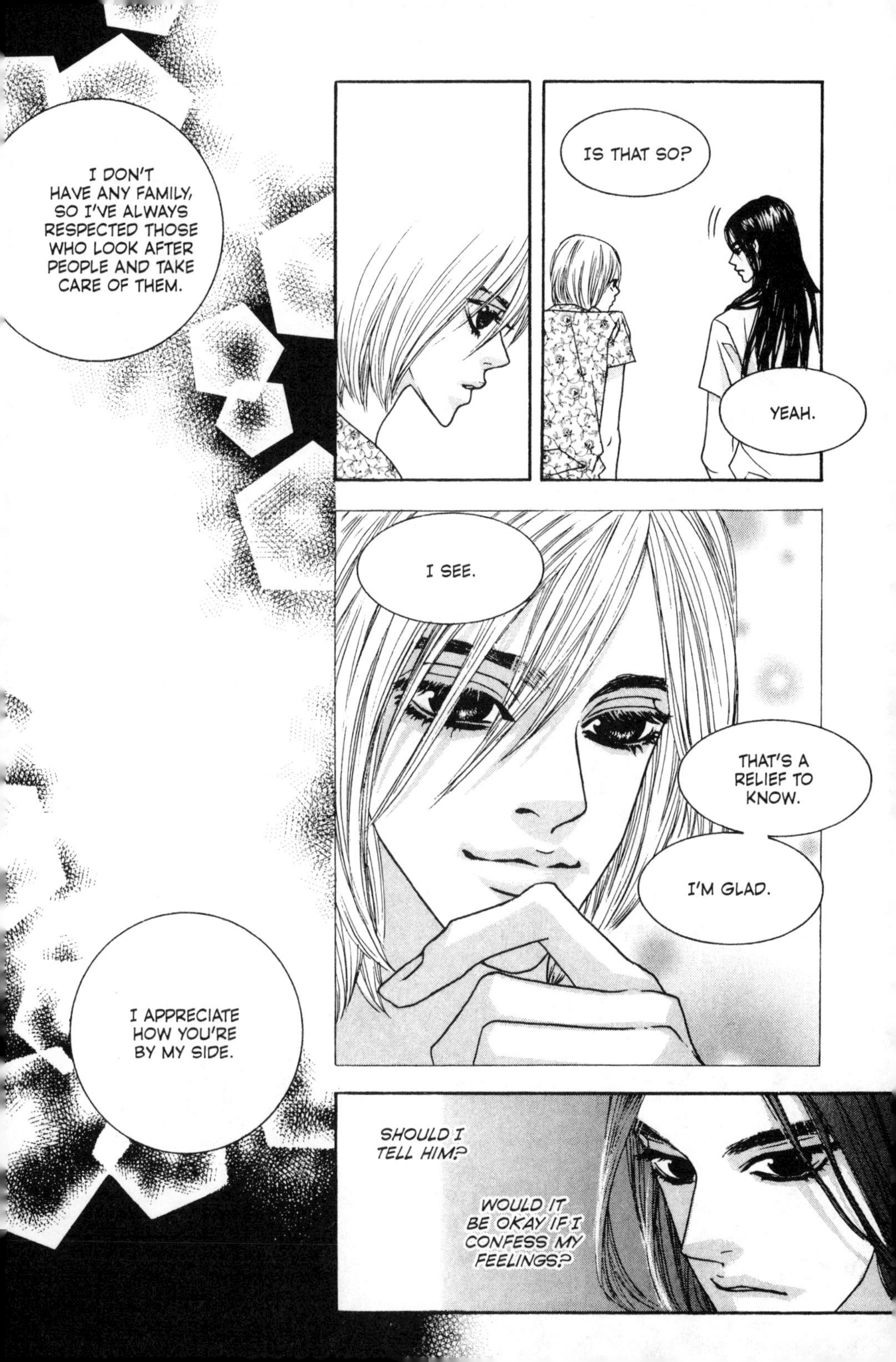
I DON'T HAVE ANY FAMILY, SO I'VE ALWAYS RESPECTED THOSE WHO LOOK AFTER PEOPLE AND TAKE CARE OF THEM.
IS THAT SO?
YEAH.
I SEE.
THAT'S A RELIEF TO KNOW.
I'M GLAD.
I APPRECIATE HOW YOU'RE BY MY SIDE.
SHOULD I TELL HIM?
WOULD IT BE OKAY IF I CONFESS MY FEELINGS?

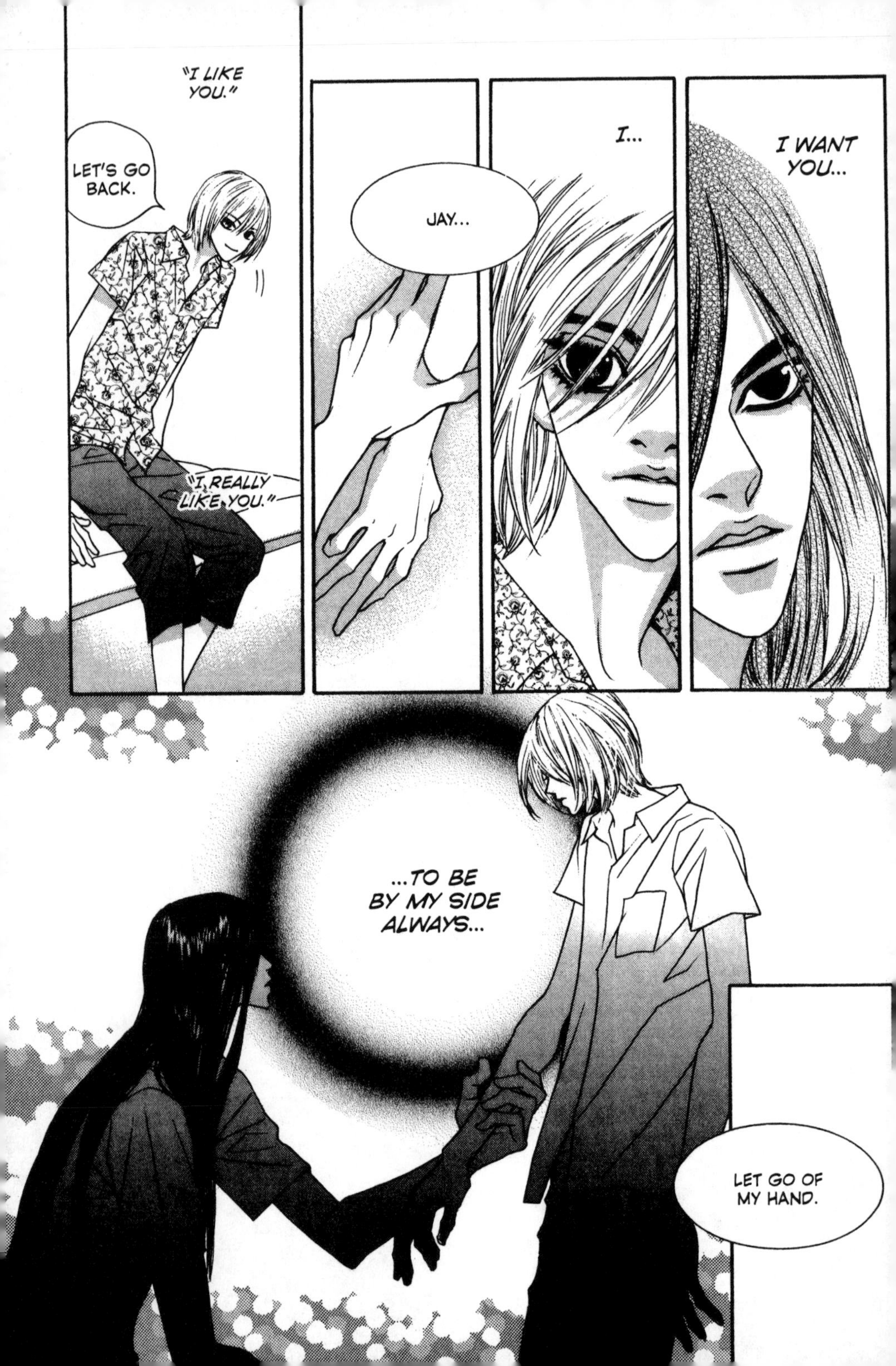
"I LIKE YOU."
LET'S GO BACK.
"I REALLY LIKE YOU."
JAY...
I...
I WANT YOU...
...TO BE BY MY SIDE ALWAYS...
LET GO OF MY HAND.

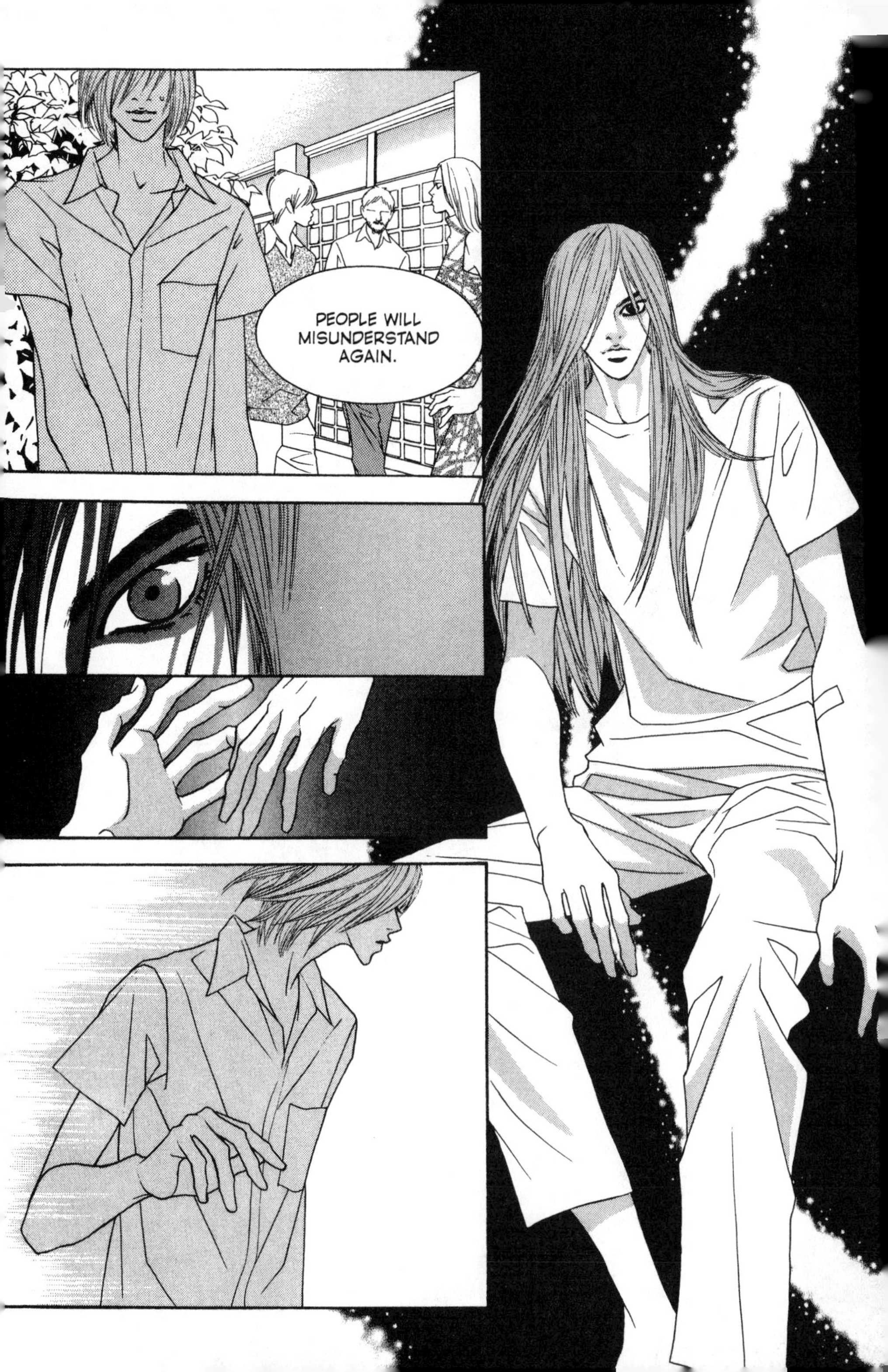
PEOPLE WILL MISUNDERSTAND AGAIN.

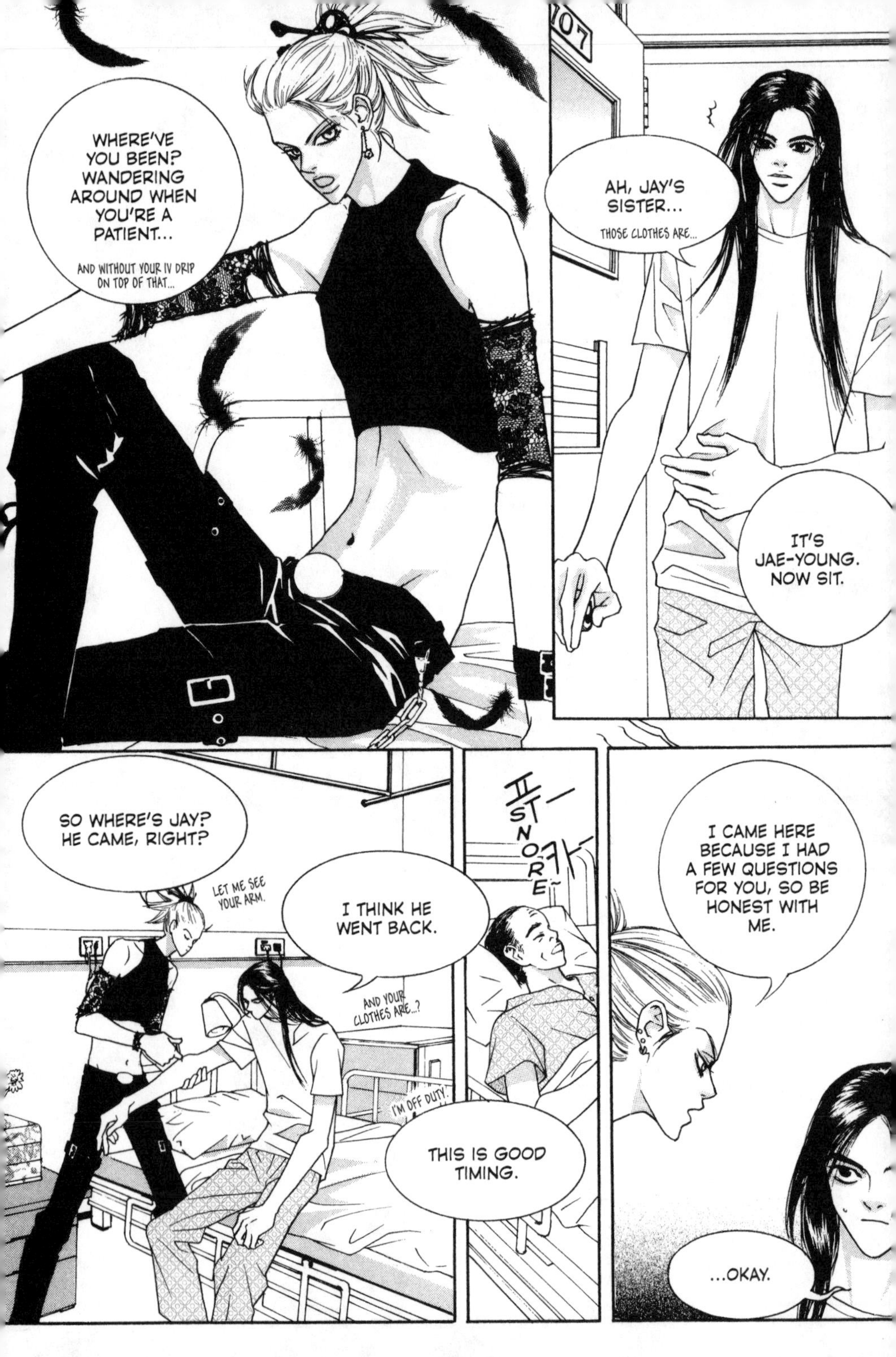
WHERE'VE YOU BEEN? WANDERING AROUND WHEN YOU'RE A PATIENT...
AND WITHOUT YOUR IV DRIP ON TOP OF THAT...
AH, JAY'S SISTER...
THOSE CLOTHES ARE...
IT'S JAE-YOUNG. NOW SIT.
SO WHERE'S JAY? HE CAME, RIGHT?
LET ME SEE YOUR ARM.
I THINK HE WENT BACK.
AND YOUR CLOTHES ARE...?
I'M OFF DUTY.
THIS IS GOOD TIMING.
SNORE~
I CAME HERE BECAUSE I HAD A FEW QUESTIONS FOR YOU, SO BE HONEST WITH ME.
...OKAY.

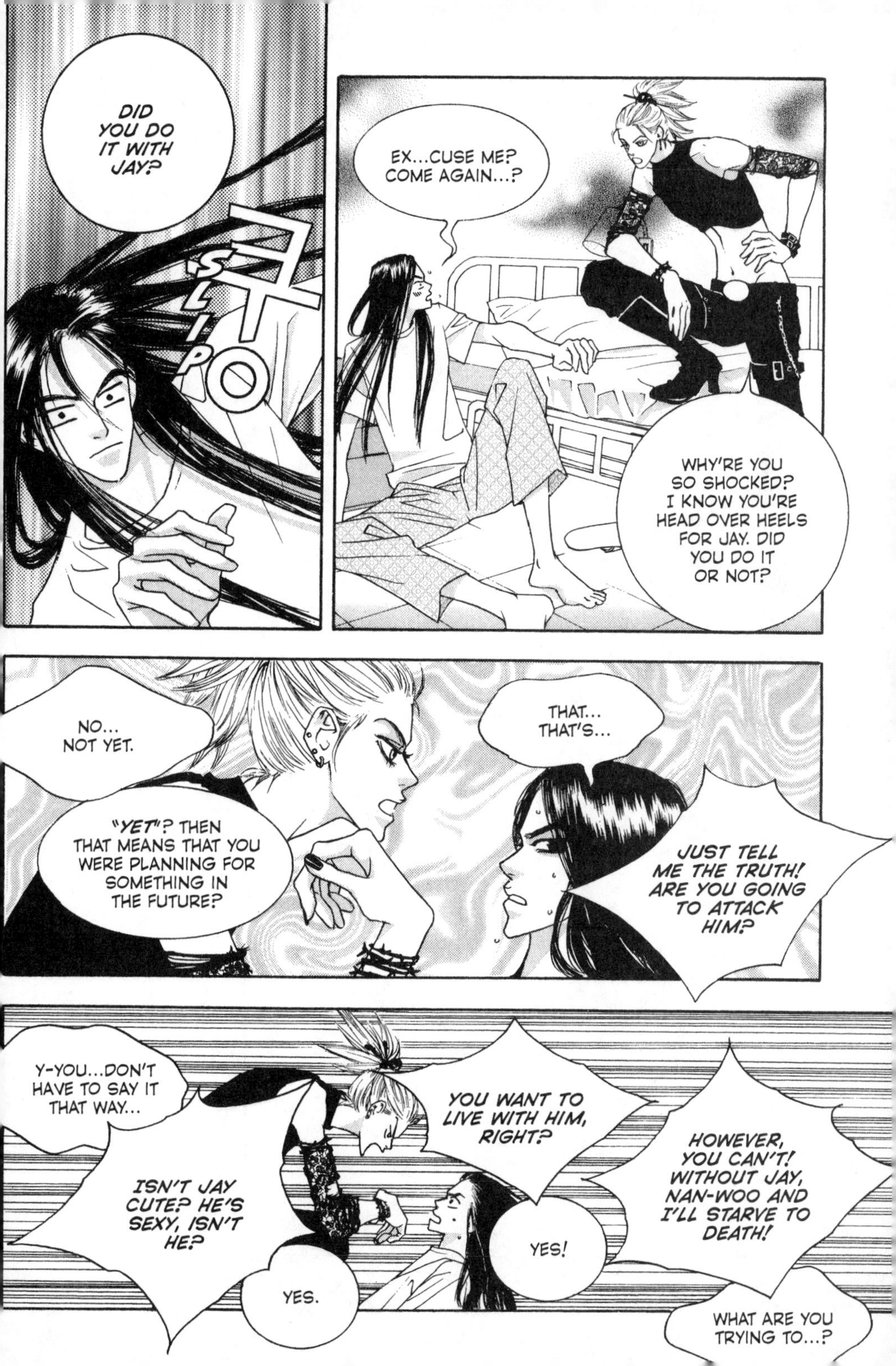
DID YOU DO IT WITH JAY?
SLIP
EX...CUSE ME? COME AGAIN...?
WHY'RE YOU SO SHOCKED? I KNOW YOU'RE HEAD OVER HEELS FOR JAY. DID YOU DO IT OR NOT?
NO... NOT YET.
THAT... THAT'S...
"YET"? THEN THAT MEANS THAT YOU WERE PLANNING FOR SOMETHING IN THE FUTURE?
JUST TELL ME THE TRUTH! ARE YOU GOING TO ATTACK HIM?
Y-YOU...DON'T HAVE TO SAY IT THAT WAY...
YOU WANT TO LIVE WITH HIM, RIGHT?
ISN'T JAY CUTE? HE'S SEXY, ISN'T HE?
YES!
YES.
HOWEVER, YOU CAN'T! WITHOUT JAY, NAN-WOO AND I'LL STARVE TO DEATH!
WHAT ARE YOU TRYING TO...?

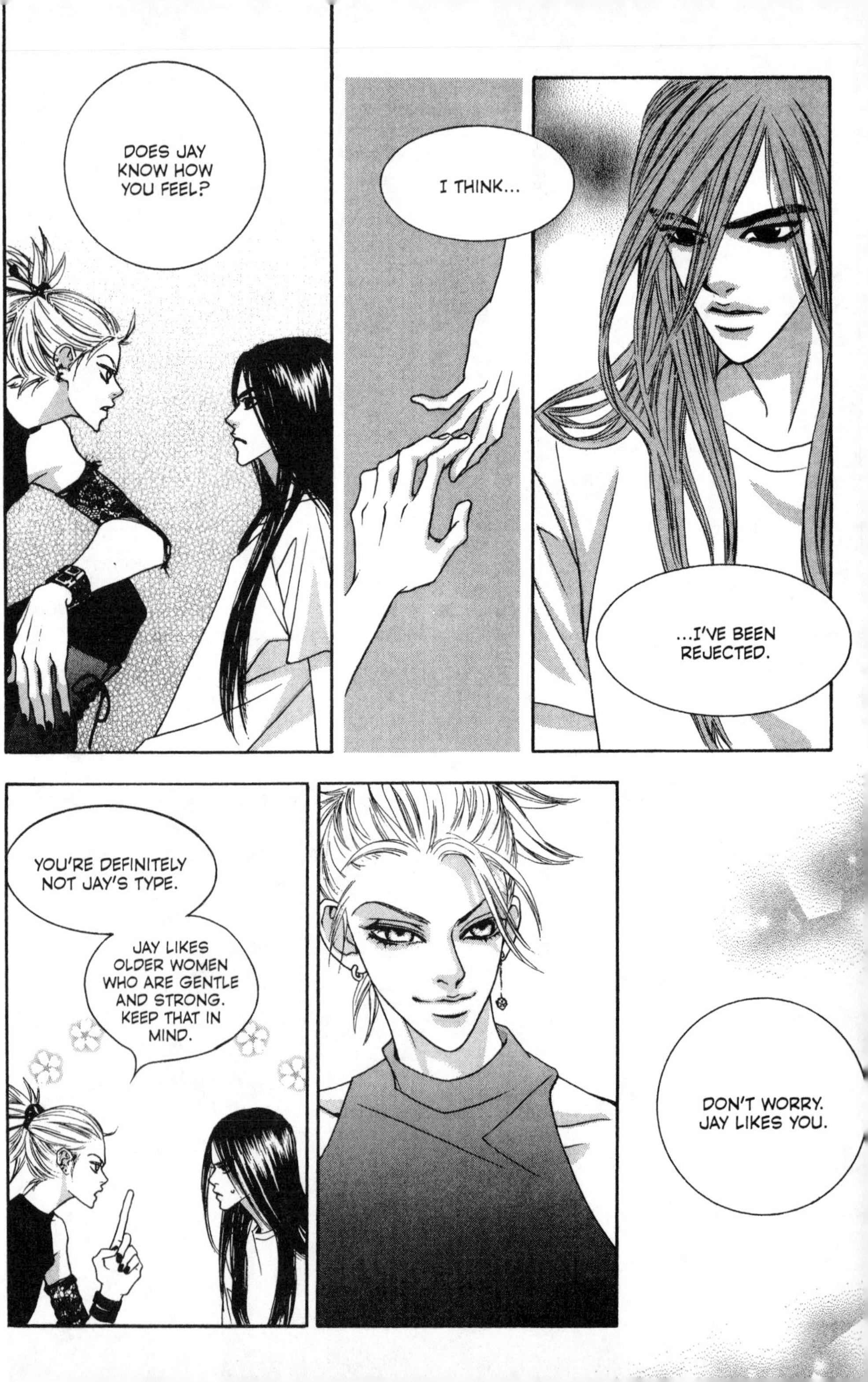
DOES JAY KNOW HOW YOU FEEL?
I THINK...
...I'VE BEEN REJECTED.
YOU'RE DEFINITELY NOT JAY'S TYPE.
JAY LIKES OLDER WOMEN WHO ARE GENTLE AND STRONG. KEEP THAT IN MIND.
DON'T WORRY. JAY LIKES YOU.

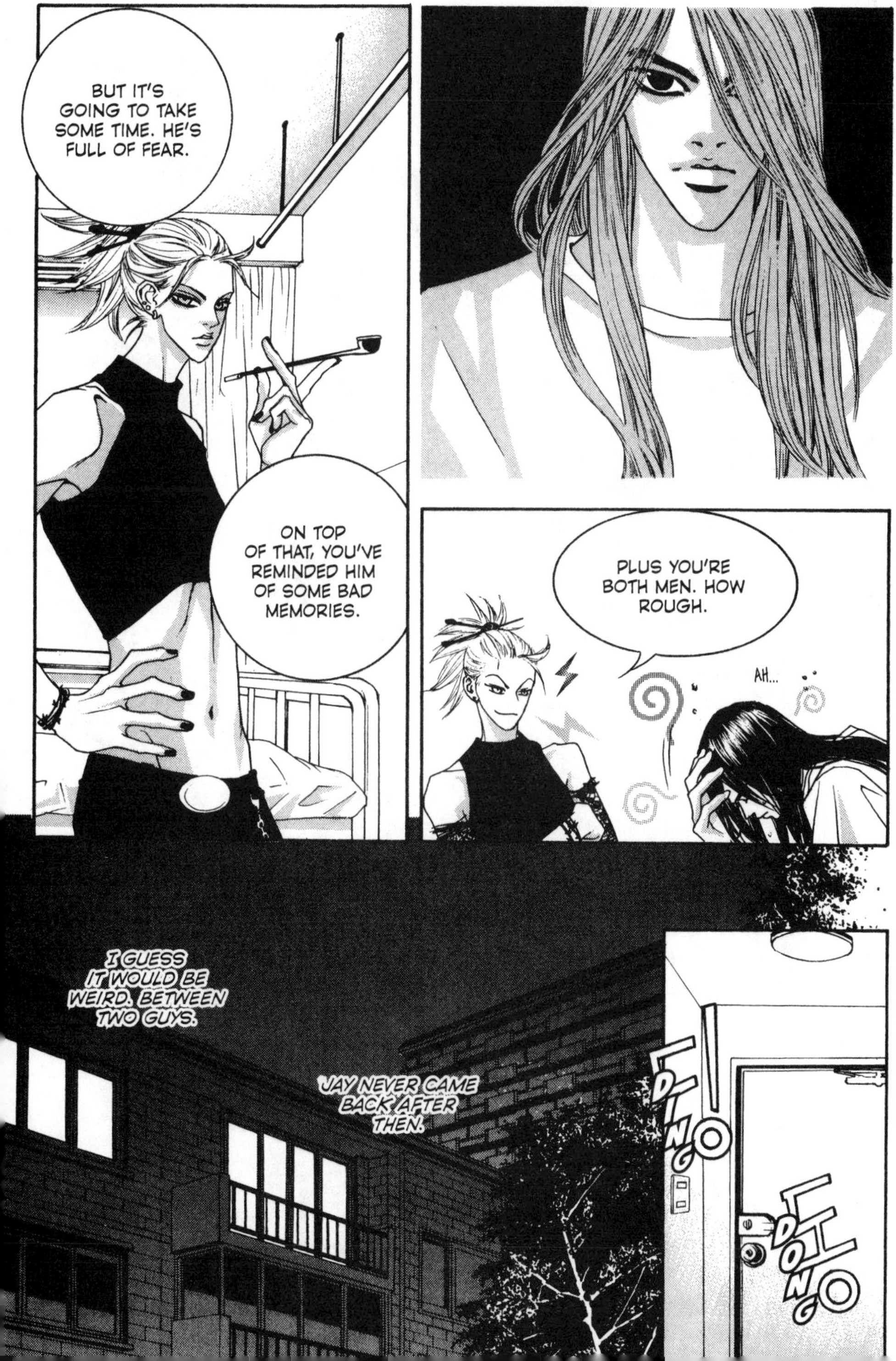
BUT IT'S GOING TO TAKE SOME TIME. HE'S FULL OF FEAR.
ON TOP OF THAT, YOU'VE REMINDED HIM OF SOME BAD MEMORIES.
PLUS YOU'RE BOTH MEN. HOW ROUGH.
AH...
I GUESS IT WOULD BE WEIRD, BETWEEN TWO GUYS.
JAY NEVER CAME BACK AFTER THEN.
DING
DONG

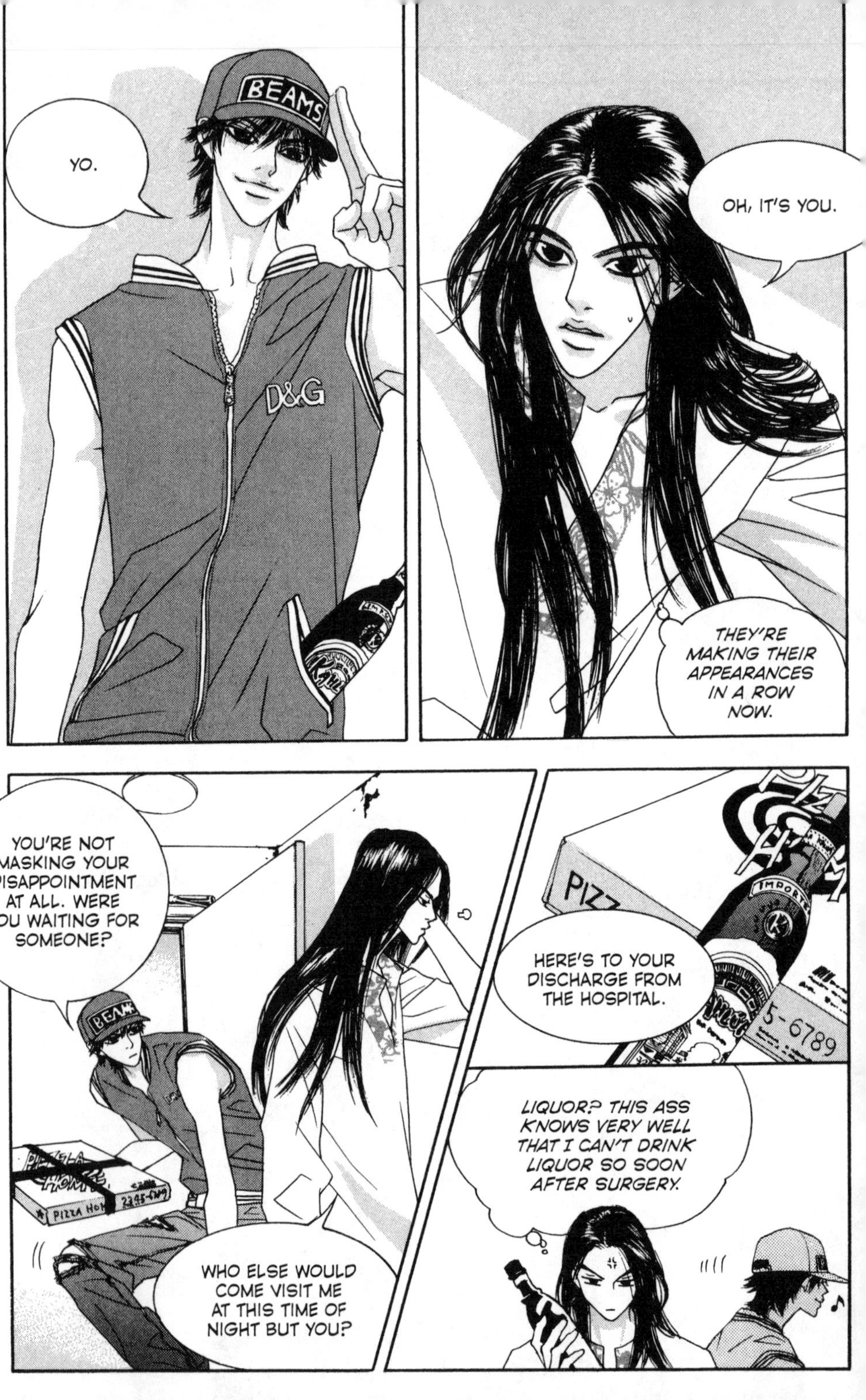
YO.
OH, IT'S YOU.
THEY'RE MAKING THEIR APPEARANCES IN A ROW NOW.
YOU'RE NOT MASKING YOUR DISAPPOINTMENT AT ALL. WERE YOU WAITING FOR SOMEONE?
WHO ELSE WOULD COME VISIT ME AT THIS TIME OF NIGHT BUT YOU?
HERE'S TO YOUR DISCHARGE FROM THE HOSPITAL.
LIQUOR? THIS ASS KNOWS VERY WELL THAT I CAN'T DRINK LIQUOR SO SOON AFTER SURGERY.

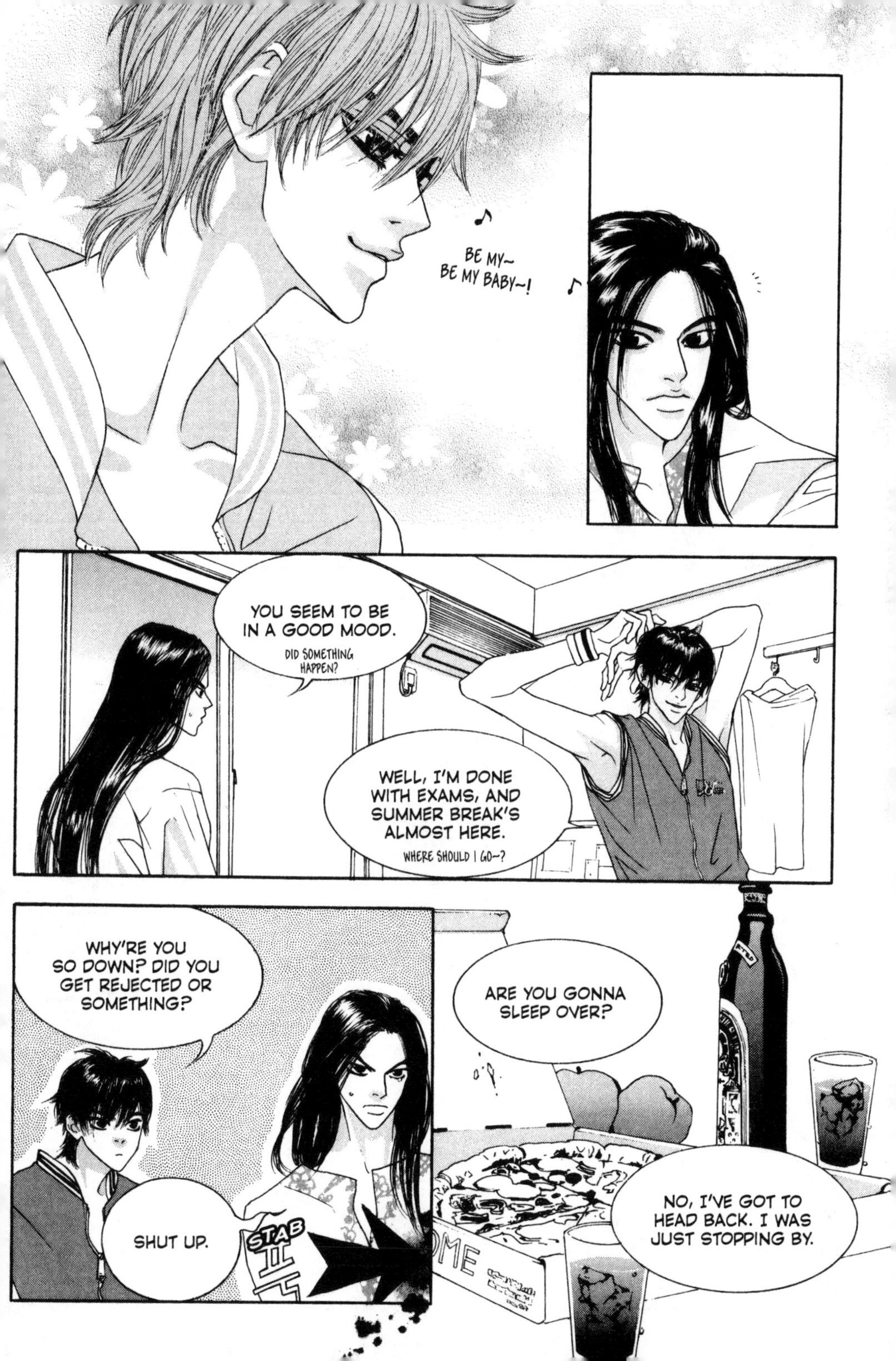
BE MY~
BE MY BABY~!
YOU SEEM TO BE IN A GOOD MOOD.
DID SOMETHING HAPPEN?
WELL, I'M DONE WITH EXAMS, AND SUMMER BREAK'S ALMOST HERE.
WHERE SHOULD I GO~?
WHY'RE YOU SO DOWN? DID YOU GET REJECTED OR SOMETHING?
SHUT UP.
STAB
ARE YOU GONNA SLEEP OVER?
NO, I'VE GOT TO HEAD BACK. I WAS JUST STOPPING BY.

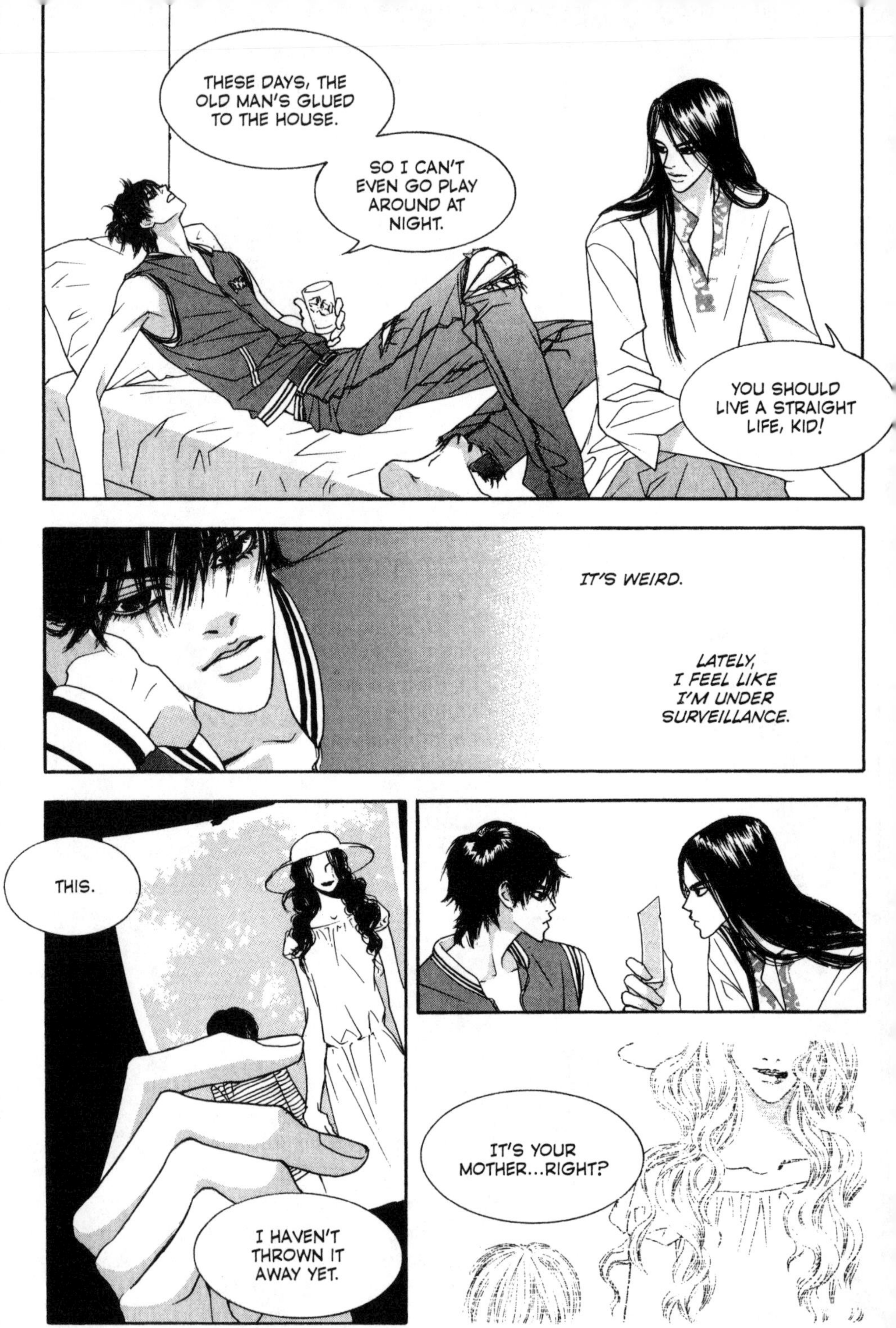
THESE DAYS, THE OLD MAN'S GLUED TO THE HOUSE.
SO I CAN'T EVEN GO PLAY AROUND AT NIGHT.
YOU SHOULD LIVE A STRAIGHT LIFE, KID!
IT'S WEIRD.
LATELY, I FEEL LIKE I'M UNDER SURVEILLANCE.
THIS.
I HAVEN'T THROWN IT AWAY YET.
IT'S YOUR MOTHER...RIGHT?

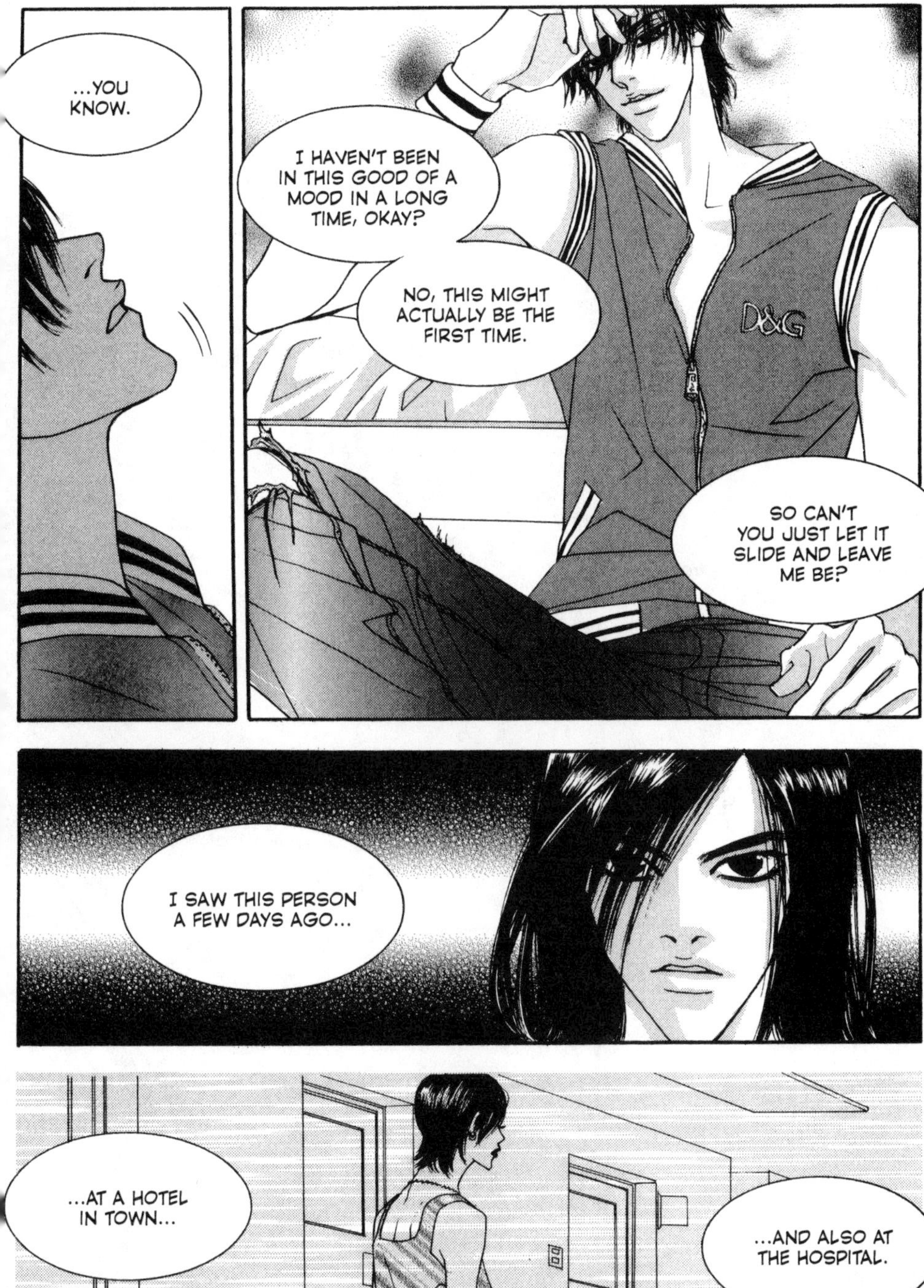
...YOU KNOW.
I HAVEN'T BEEN IN THIS GOOD OF A MOOD IN A LONG TIME, OKAY?
NO, THIS MIGHT ACTUALLY BE THE FIRST TIME.
D&G
SO CAN'T YOU JUST LET IT SLIDE AND LEAVE ME BE?
I SAW THIS PERSON A FEW DAYS AGO...
...AT A HOTEL IN TOWN...
...AND ALSO AT THE HOSPITAL.

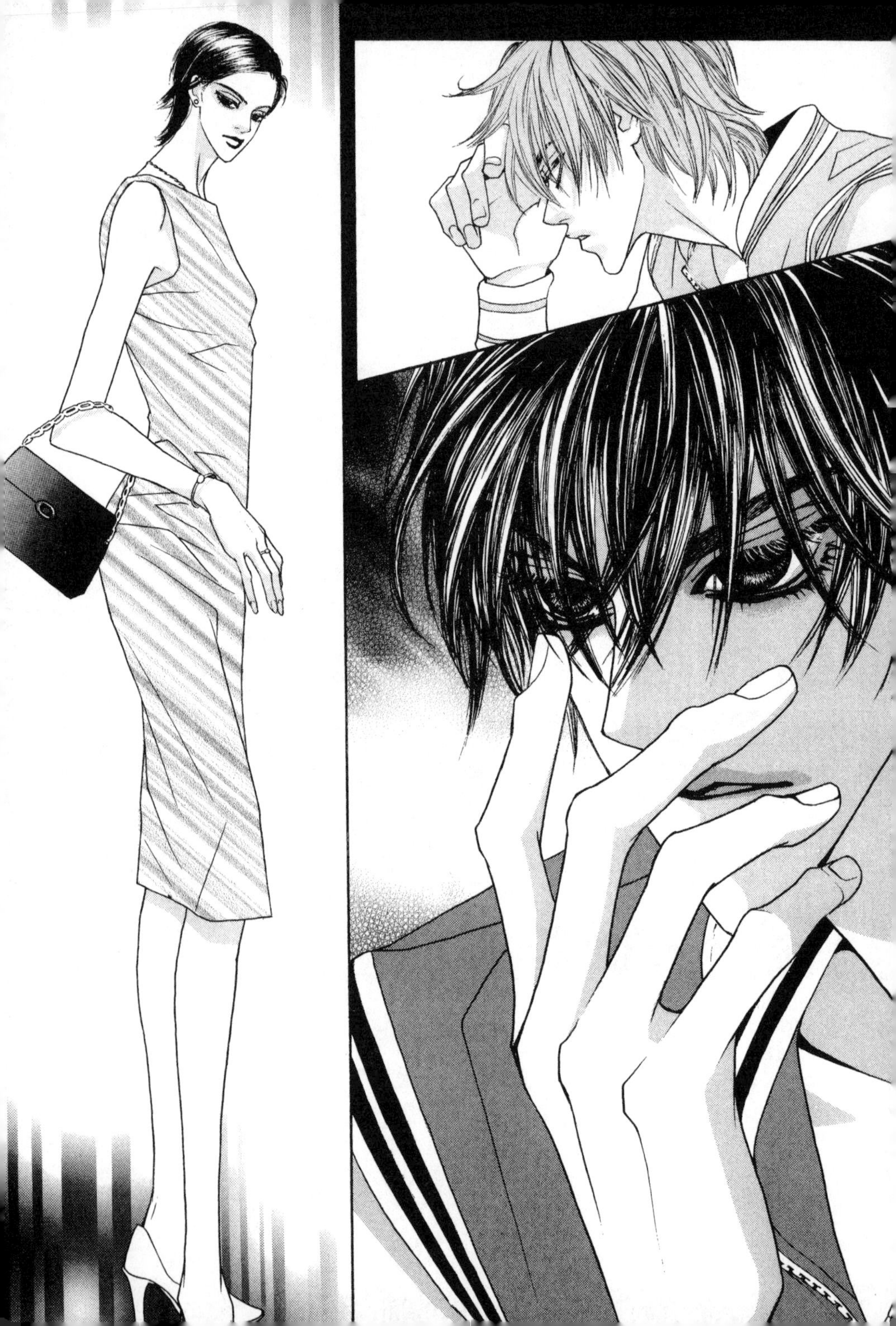

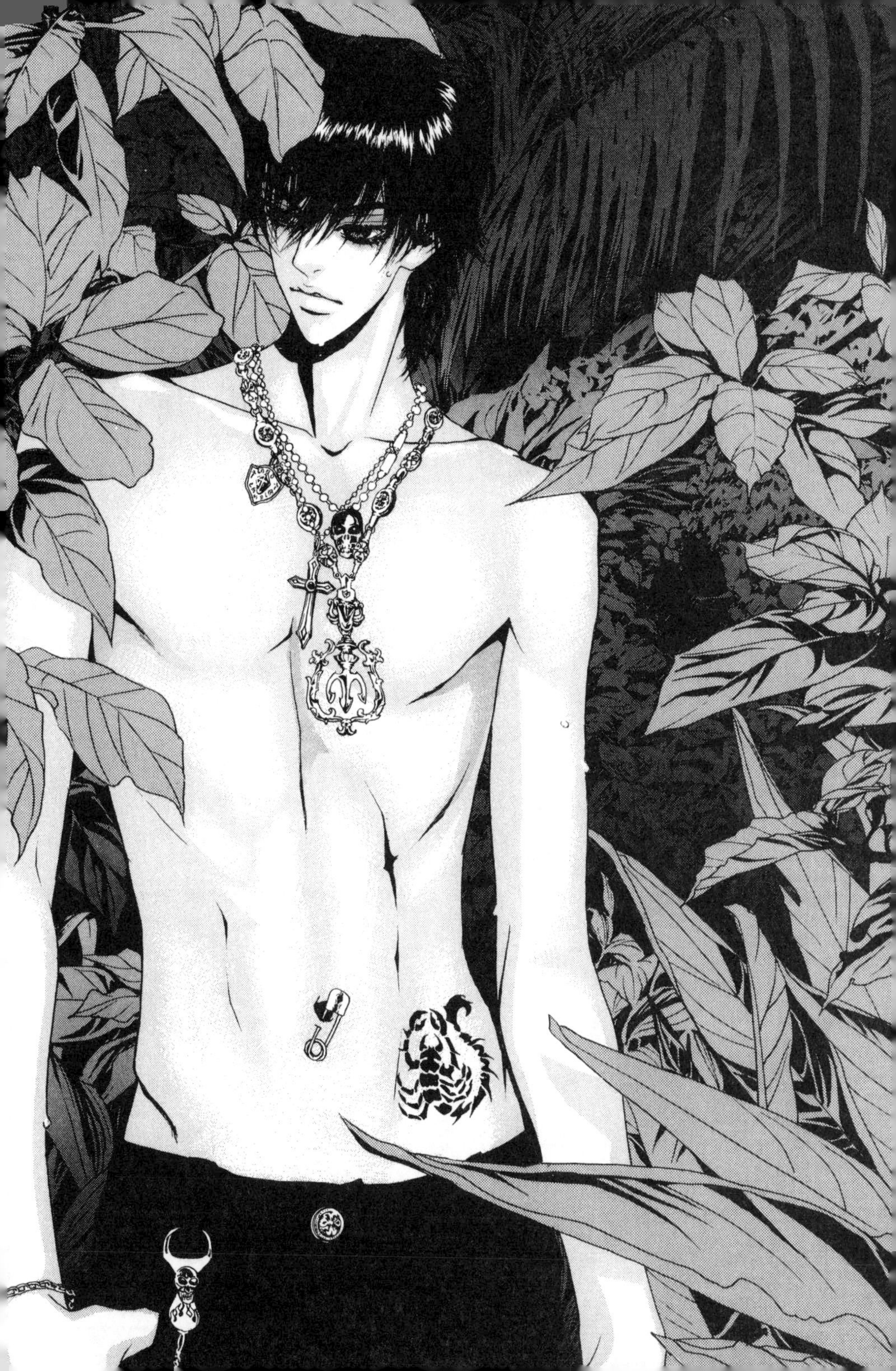

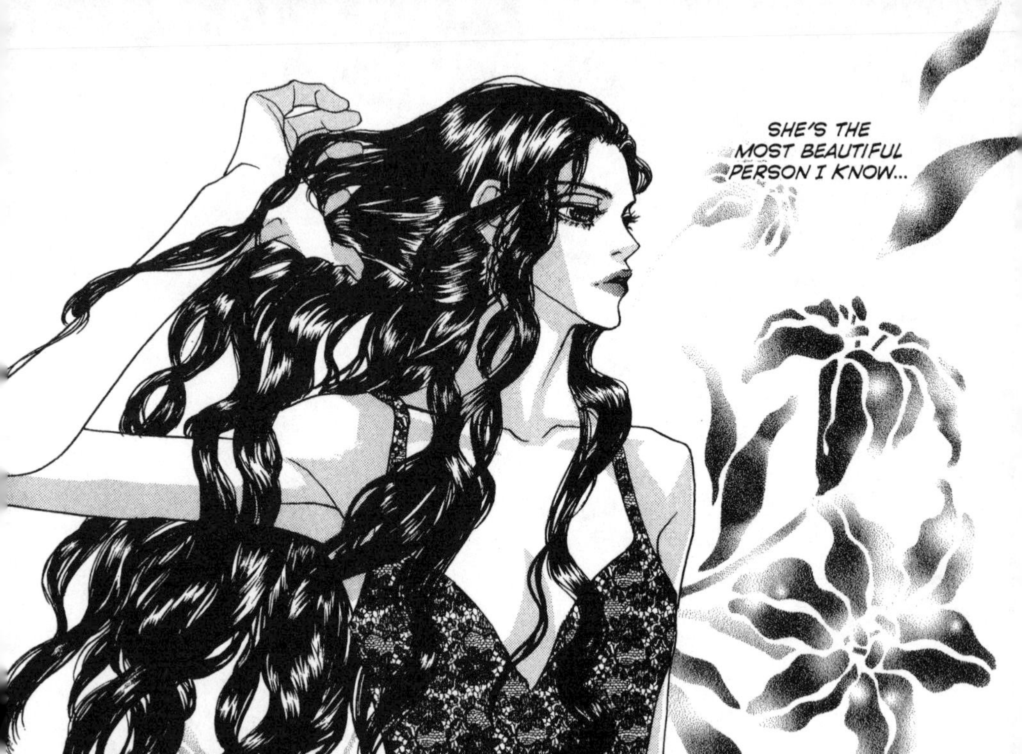
SHE'S THE MOST BEAUTIFUL PERSON I KNOW...
...YET THE MOST VICIOUS.

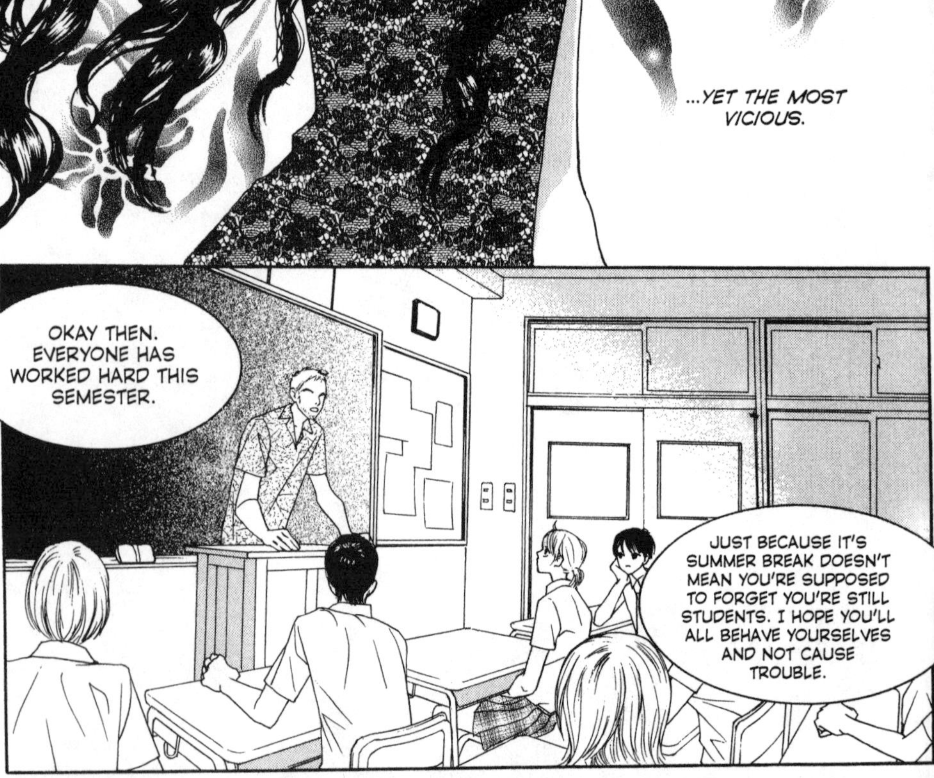
OKAY THEN. EVERYONE HAS WORKED HARD THIS SEMESTER.
JUST BECAUSE IT'S SUMMER BREAK DOESN'T MEAN YOU'RE SUPPOSED TO FORGET YOU'RE STILL STUDENTS. I HOPE YOU'LL ALL BEHAVE YOURSELVES AND NOT CAUSE TROUBLE.

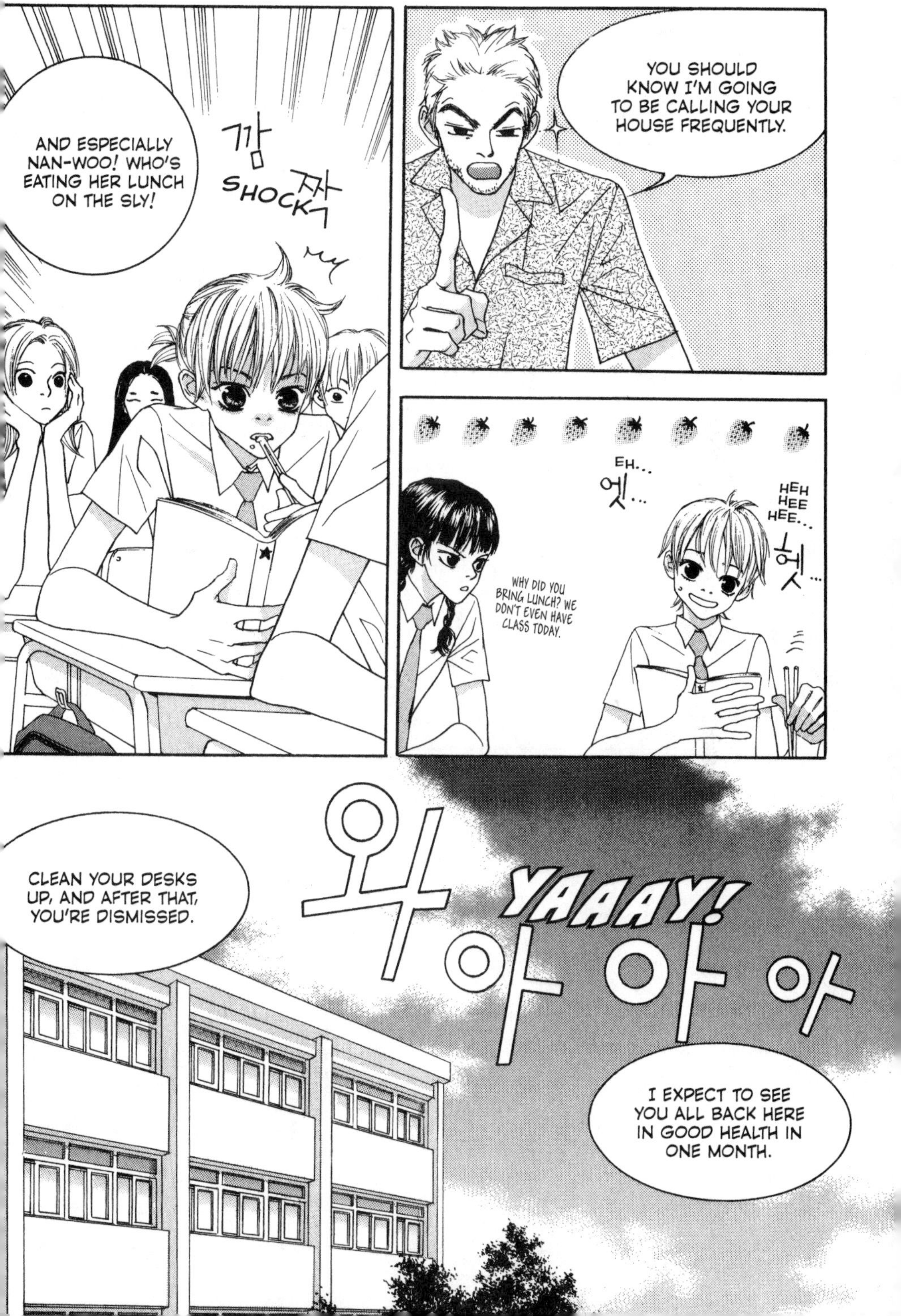
AND ESPECIALLY NAN-WOO! WHO'S EATING HER LUNCH ON THE SLY!
깜 SHOCK 짝
YOU SHOULD KNOW I'M GOING TO BE CALLING YOUR HOUSE FREQUENTLY.
EH... 엣...
WHY DID YOU BRING LUNCH? WE DON'T EVEN HAVE CLASS TODAY.
HEH HEE HEE... 헤...
CLEAN YOUR DESKS UP, AND AFTER THAT, YOU'RE DISMISSED.
와 YAAAY! 아 아 아
I EXPECT TO SEE YOU ALL BACK HERE IN GOOD HEALTH IN ONE MONTH.

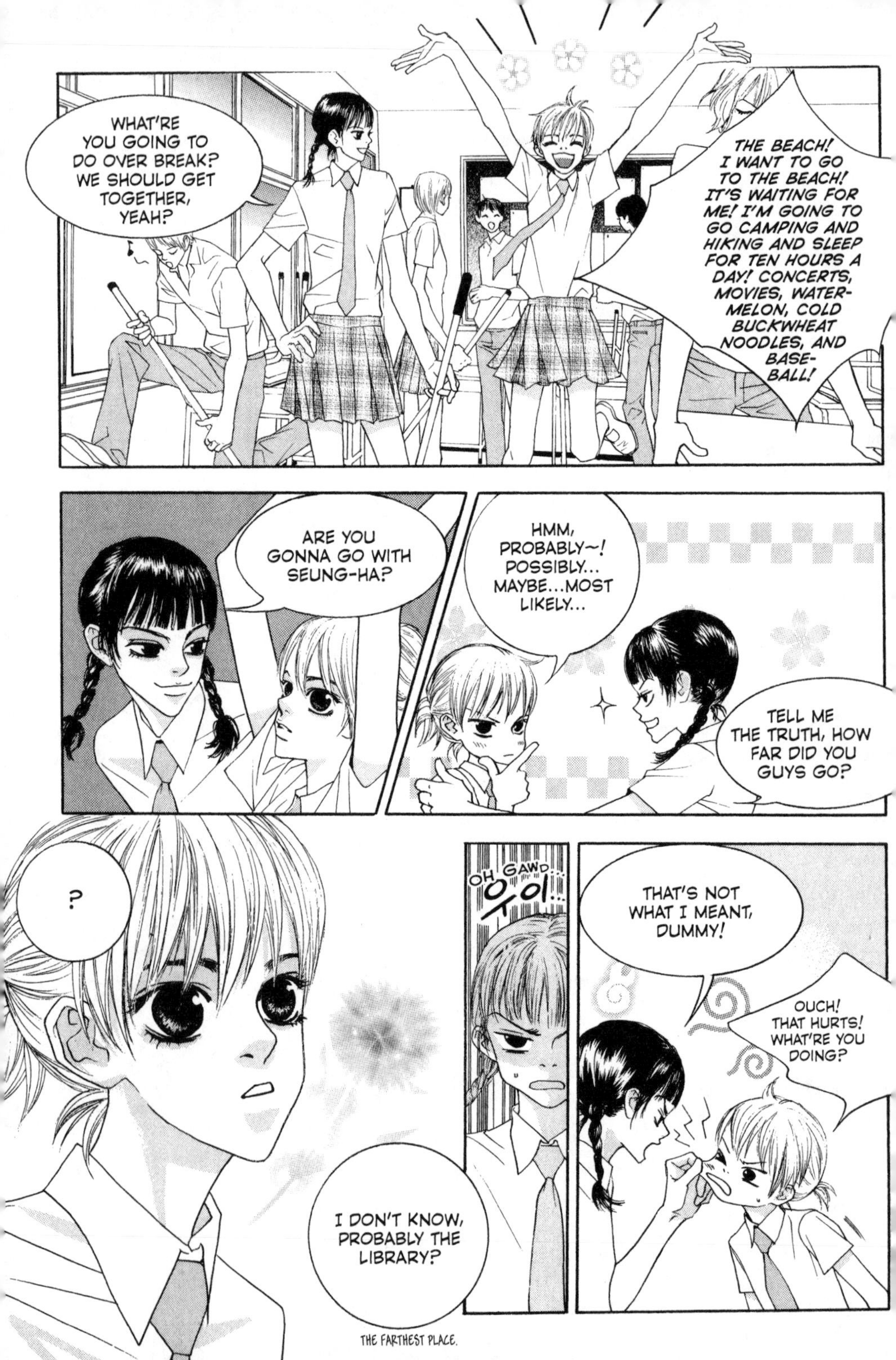
WHAT'RE YOU GOING TO DO OVER BREAK? WE SHOULD GET TOGETHER, YEAH?
THE BEACH! I WANT TO GO TO THE BEACH! IT'S WAITING FOR ME! I'M GOING TO GO CAMPING AND HIKING AND SLEEP FOR TEN HOURS A DAY! CONCERTS, MOVIES, WATER-MELON, COLD BUCKWHEAT NOODLES, AND BASE-BALL!
ARE YOU GONNA GO WITH SEUNG-HA?
HMM, PROBABLY~! POSSIBLY... MAYBE...MOST LIKELY...
TELL ME THE TRUTH, HOW FAR DID YOU GUYS GO?
?
I DON'T KNOW, PROBABLY THE LIBRARY?
THE FARTHEST PLACE.
OH GAWD...
우이!...
THAT'S NOT WHAT I MEANT, DUMMY!
OUCH! THAT HURTS! WHAT'RE YOU DOING?

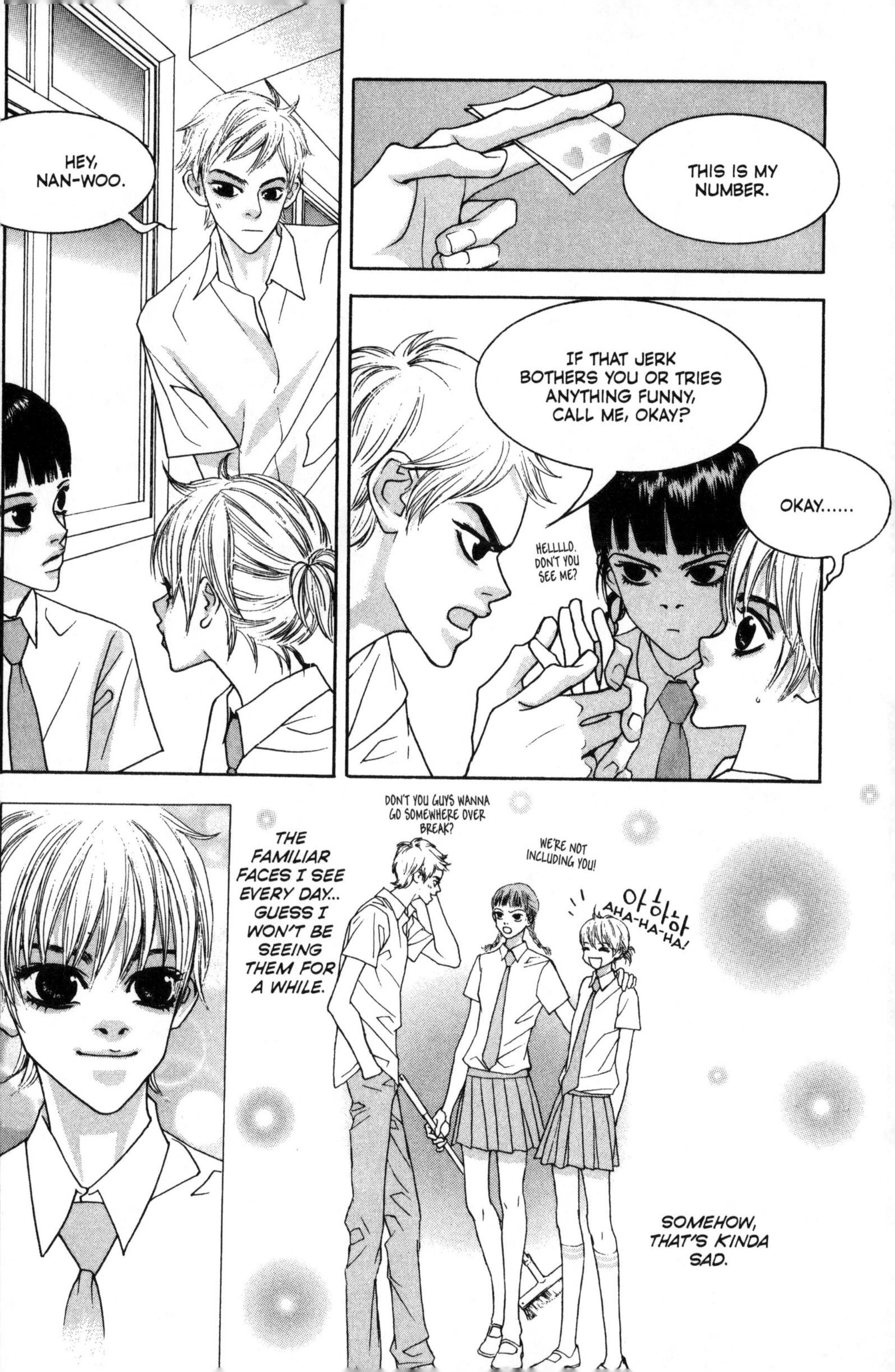
HEY, NAN-WOO.
THIS IS MY NUMBER.
IF THAT JERK BOTHERS YOU OR TRIES ANYTHING FUNNY, CALL ME, OKAY?
HELLLLO. DON'T YOU SEE ME?
OKAY......
THE FAMILIAR FACES I SEE EVERY DAY... GUESS I WON'T BE SEEING THEM FOR A WHILE.
DON'T YOU GUYS WANNA GO SOMEWHERE OVER BREAK?
WE'RE NOT INCLUDING YOU!
아하하
AHA-HA-HA!
SOMEHOW, THAT'S KINDA SAD.

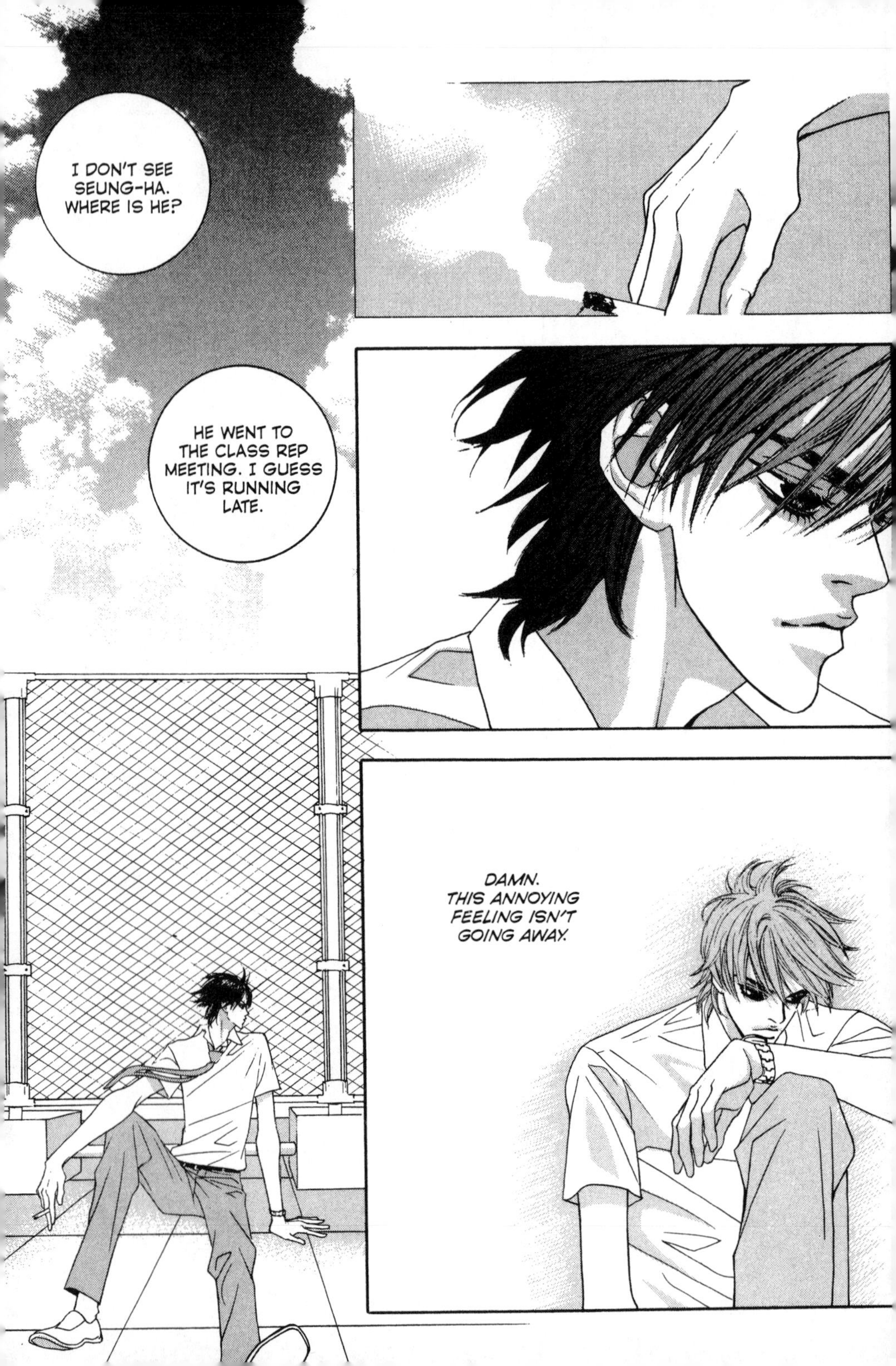
I DON'T SEE SEUNG-HA. WHERE IS HE?
HE WENT TO THE CLASS REP MEETING. I GUESS IT'S RUNNING LATE.
DAMN. THIS ANNOYING FEELING ISN'T GOING AWAY.

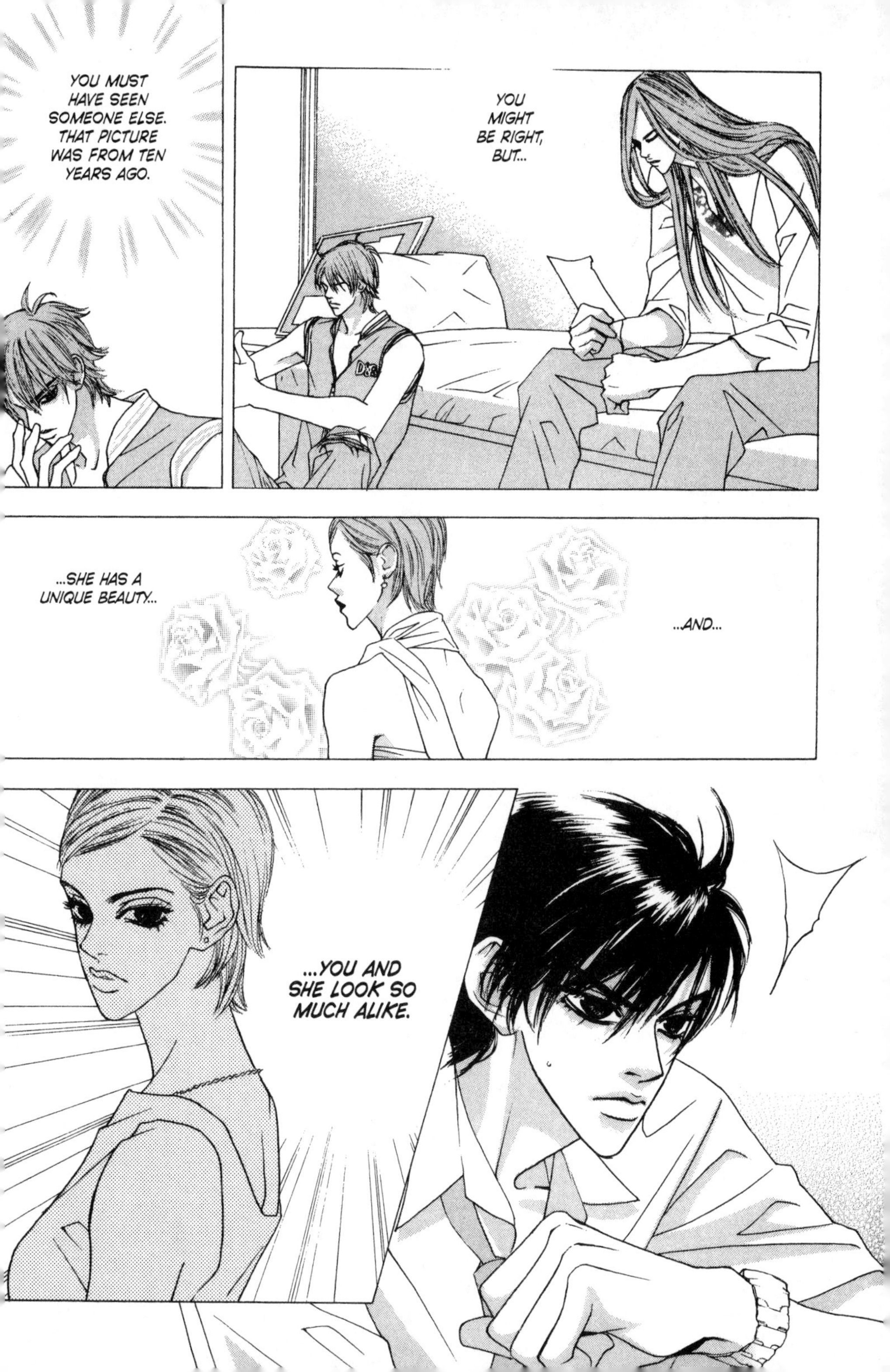
YOU MUST HAVE SEEN SOMEONE ELSE. THAT PICTURE WAS FROM TEN YEARS AGO.
YOU MIGHT BE RIGHT, BUT...
...SHE HAS A UNIQUE BEAUTY...
...AND...
...YOU AND SHE LOOK SO MUCH ALIKE.

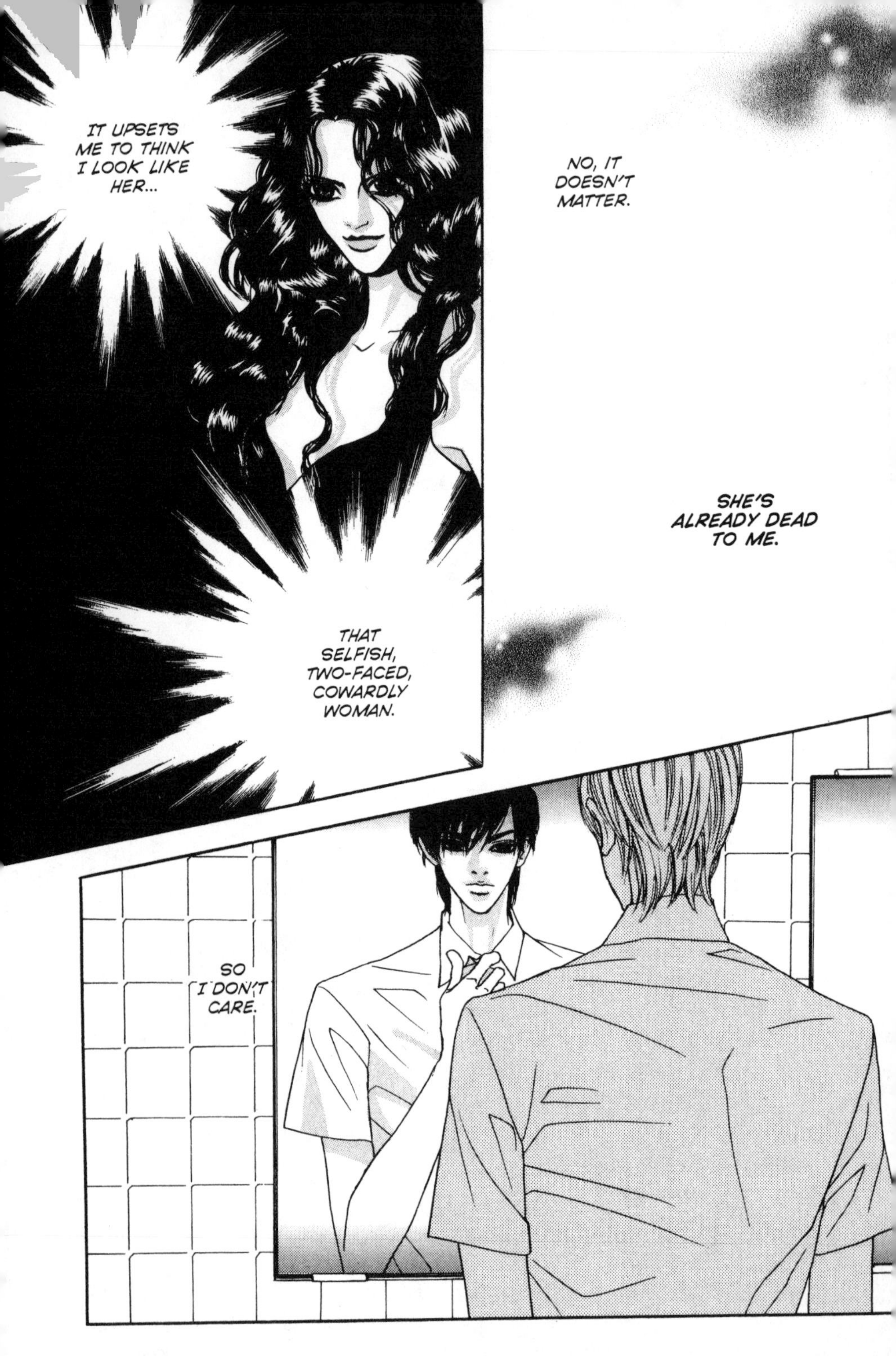
IT UPSETS ME TO THINK I LOOK LIKE HER...
THAT SELFISH, TWO-FACED, COWARDLY WOMAN.
NO, IT DOESN'T MATTER.
SHE'S ALREADY DEAD TO ME.
SO I DON'T CARE.

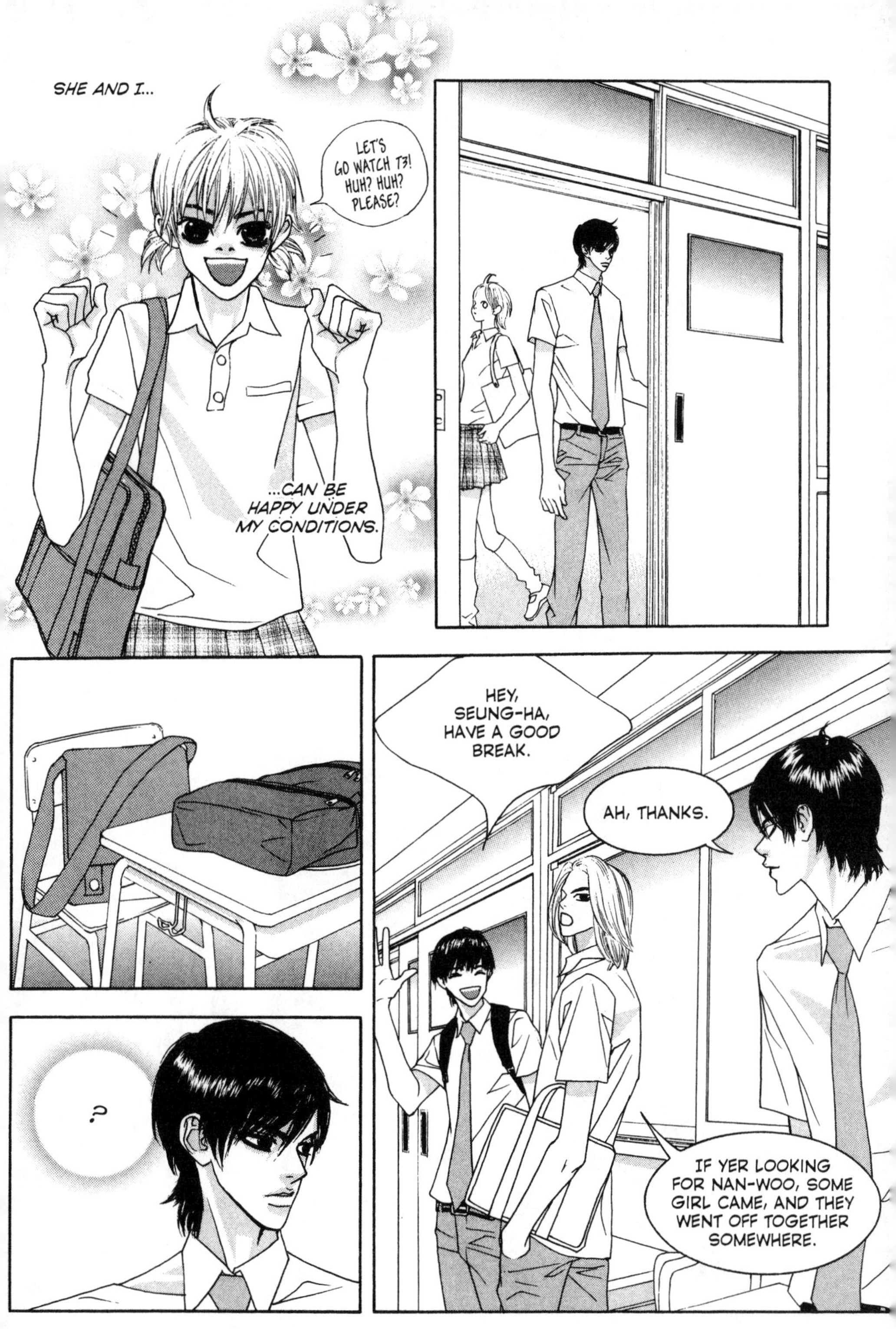
SHE AND I...
LET'S GO WATCH T3! HUH? HUH? PLEASE?
...CAN BE HAPPY UNDER MY CONDITIONS.
?
HEY, SEUNG-HA, HAVE A GOOD BREAK.
AH, THANKS.
IF YER LOOKING FOR NAN-WOO, SOME GIRL CAME, AND THEY WENT OFF TOGETHER SOMEWHERE.

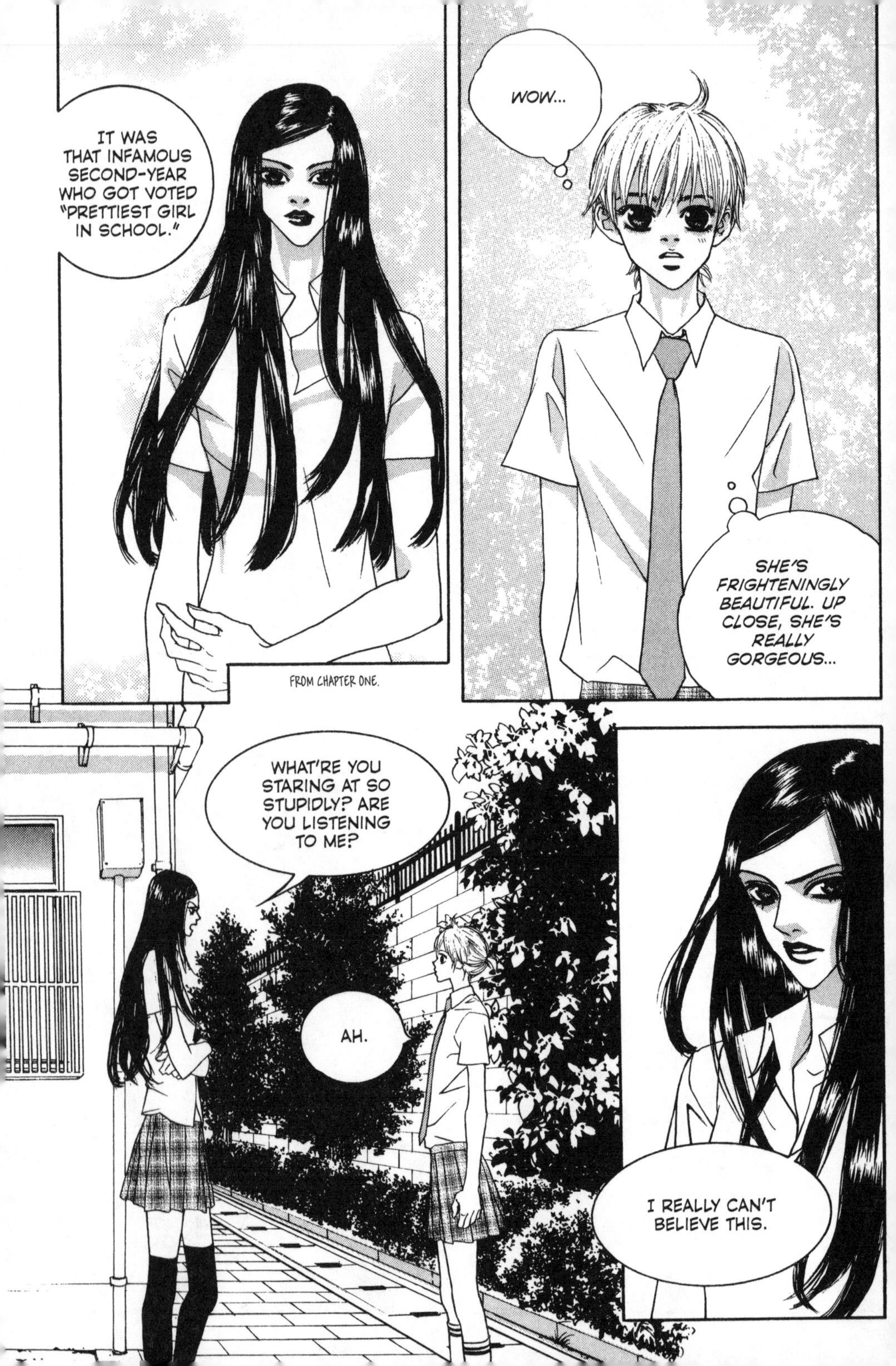
IT WAS THAT INFAMOUS SECOND-YEAR WHO GOT VOTED "PRETTIEST GIRL IN SCHOOL."
FROM CHAPTER ONE.
WOW...
SHE'S FRIGHTENINGLY BEAUTIFUL. UP CLOSE, SHE'S REALLY GORGEOUS...
WHAT'RE YOU STARING AT SO STUPIDLY? ARE YOU LISTENING TO ME?
AH.
I REALLY CAN'T BELIEVE THIS.

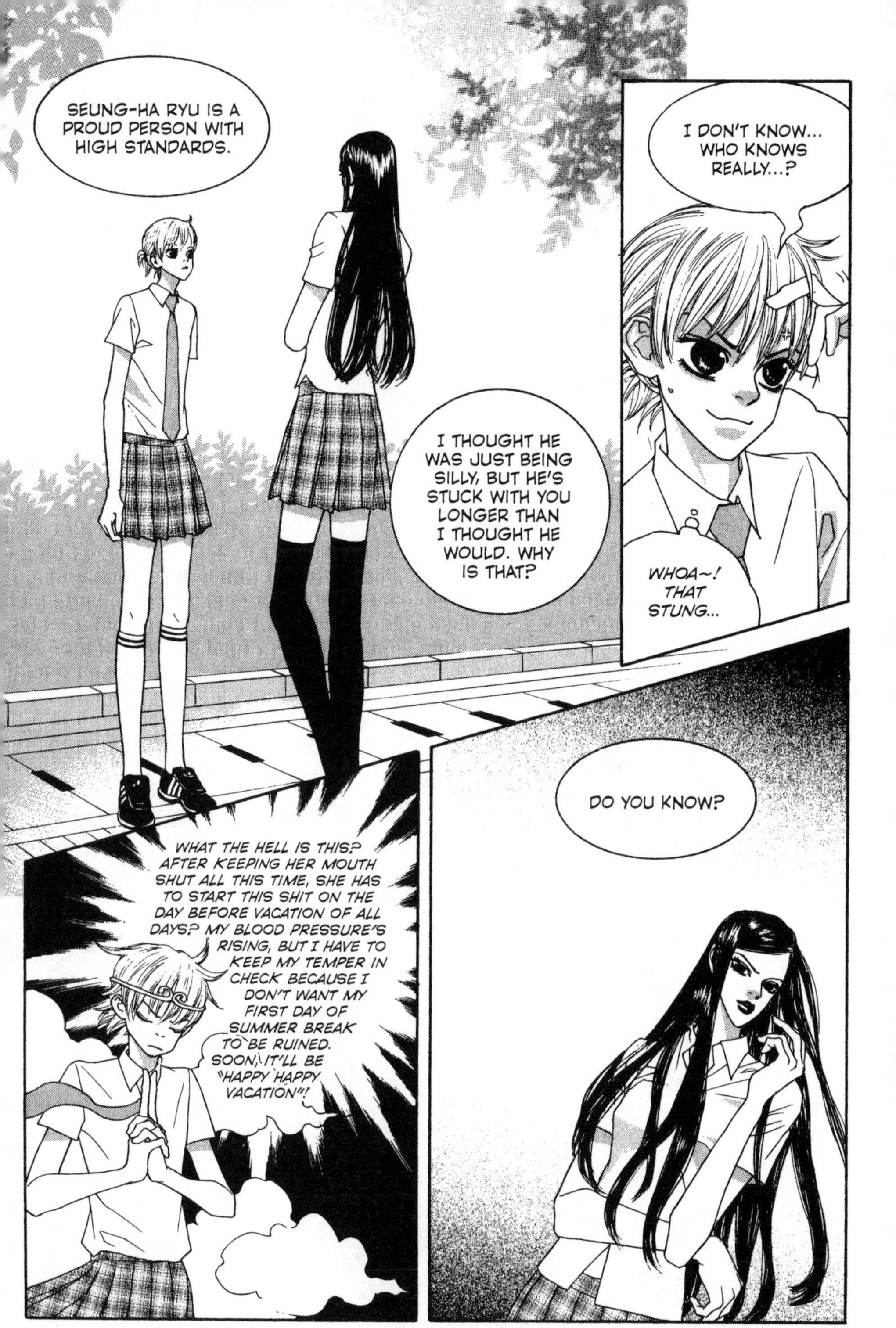
SEUNG-HA RYU IS A PROUD PERSON WITH HIGH STANDARDS.
I THOUGHT HE WAS JUST BEING SILLY, BUT HE'S STUCK WITH YOU LONGER THAN I THOUGHT HE WOULD. WHY IS THAT?
I DON'T KNOW... WHO KNOWS REALLY...?
WHOA~! THAT STUNG...
WHAT THE HELL IS THIS? AFTER KEEPING HER MOUTH SHUT ALL THIS TIME, SHE HAS TO START THIS SHIT ON THE DAY BEFORE VACATION OF ALL DAYS? MY BLOOD PRESSURE'S RISING, BUT I HAVE TO KEEP MY TEMPER IN CHECK BECAUSE I DON'T WANT MY FIRST DAY OF SUMMER BREAK TO BE RUINED. SOON, IT'LL BE "HAPPY HAPPY VACATION"!
DO YOU KNOW?

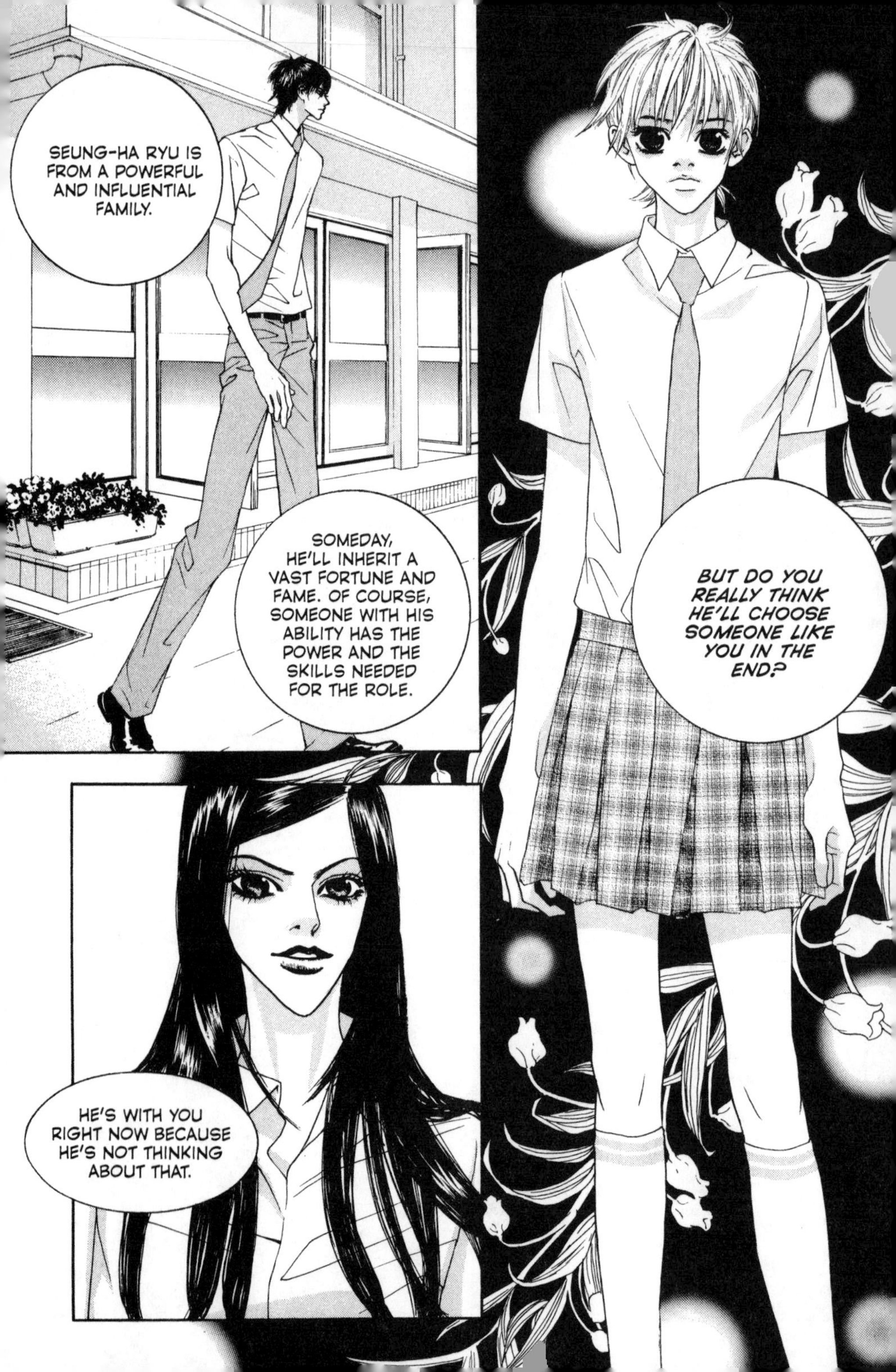
SEUNG-HA RYU IS FROM A POWERFUL AND INFLUENTIAL FAMILY.
SOMEDAY, HE'LL INHERIT A VAST FORTUNE AND FAME. OF COURSE, SOMEONE WITH HIS ABILITY HAS THE POWER AND THE SKILLS NEEDED FOR THE ROLE.
HE'S WITH YOU RIGHT NOW BECAUSE HE'S NOT THINKING ABOUT THAT.
BUT DO YOU REALLY THINK HE'LL CHOOSE SOMEONE LIKE YOU IN THE END?

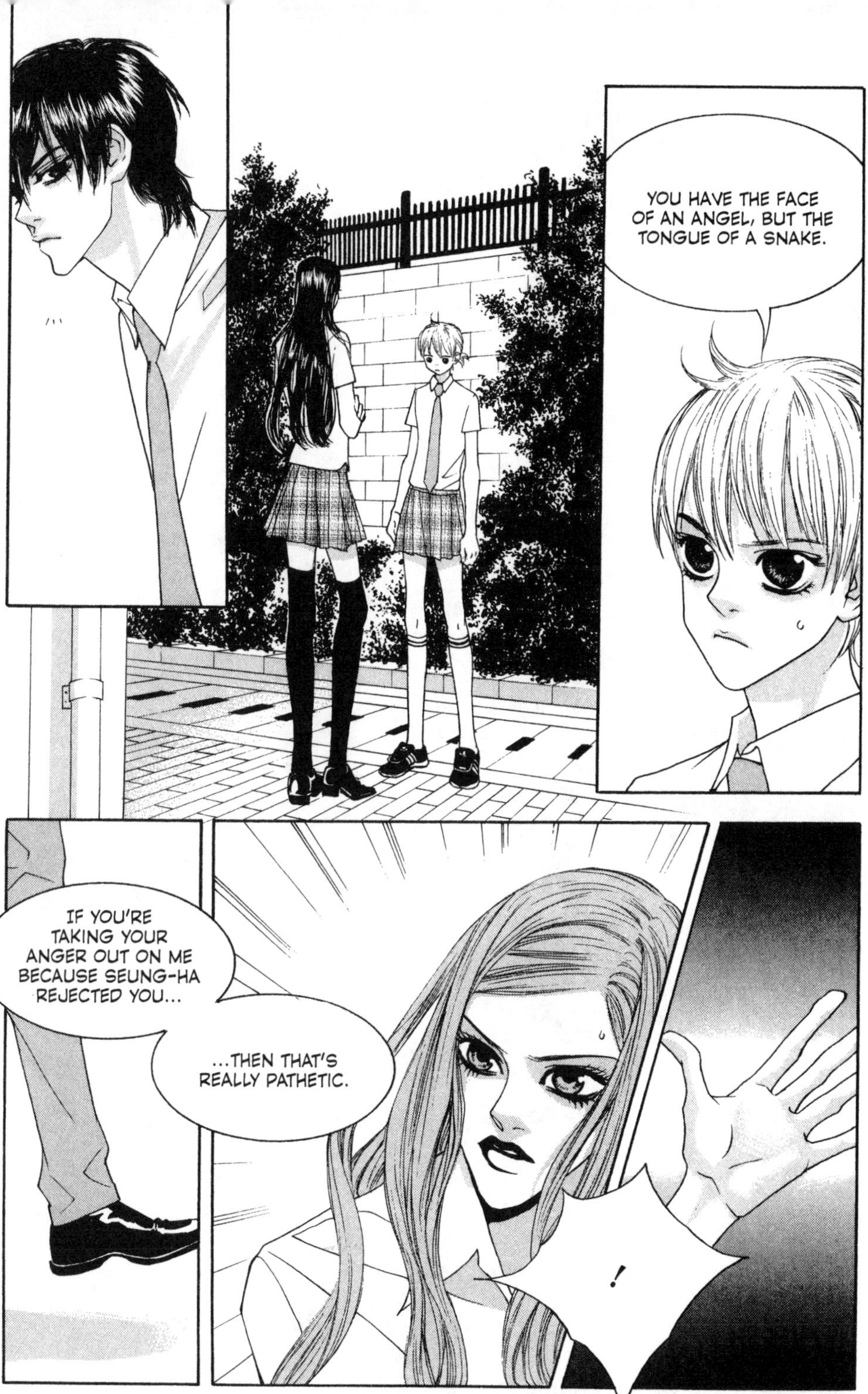
YOU HAVE THE FACE OF AN ANGEL, BUT THE TONGUE OF A SNAKE.
IF YOU'RE TAKING YOUR ANGER OUT ON ME BECAUSE SEUNG-HA REJECTED YOU...
...THEN THAT'S REALLY PATHETIC.
!

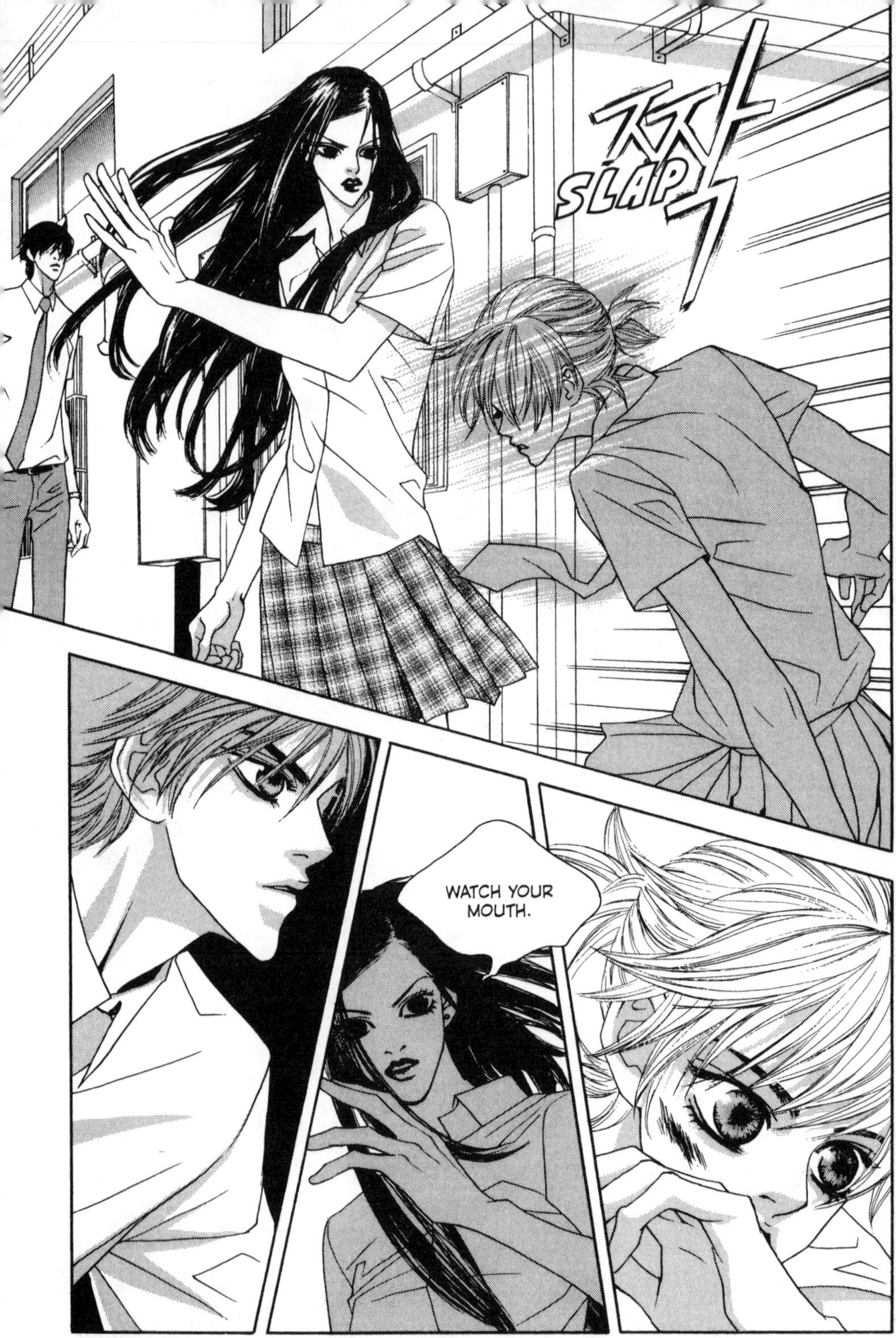
SLAP
WATCH YOUR MOUTH.

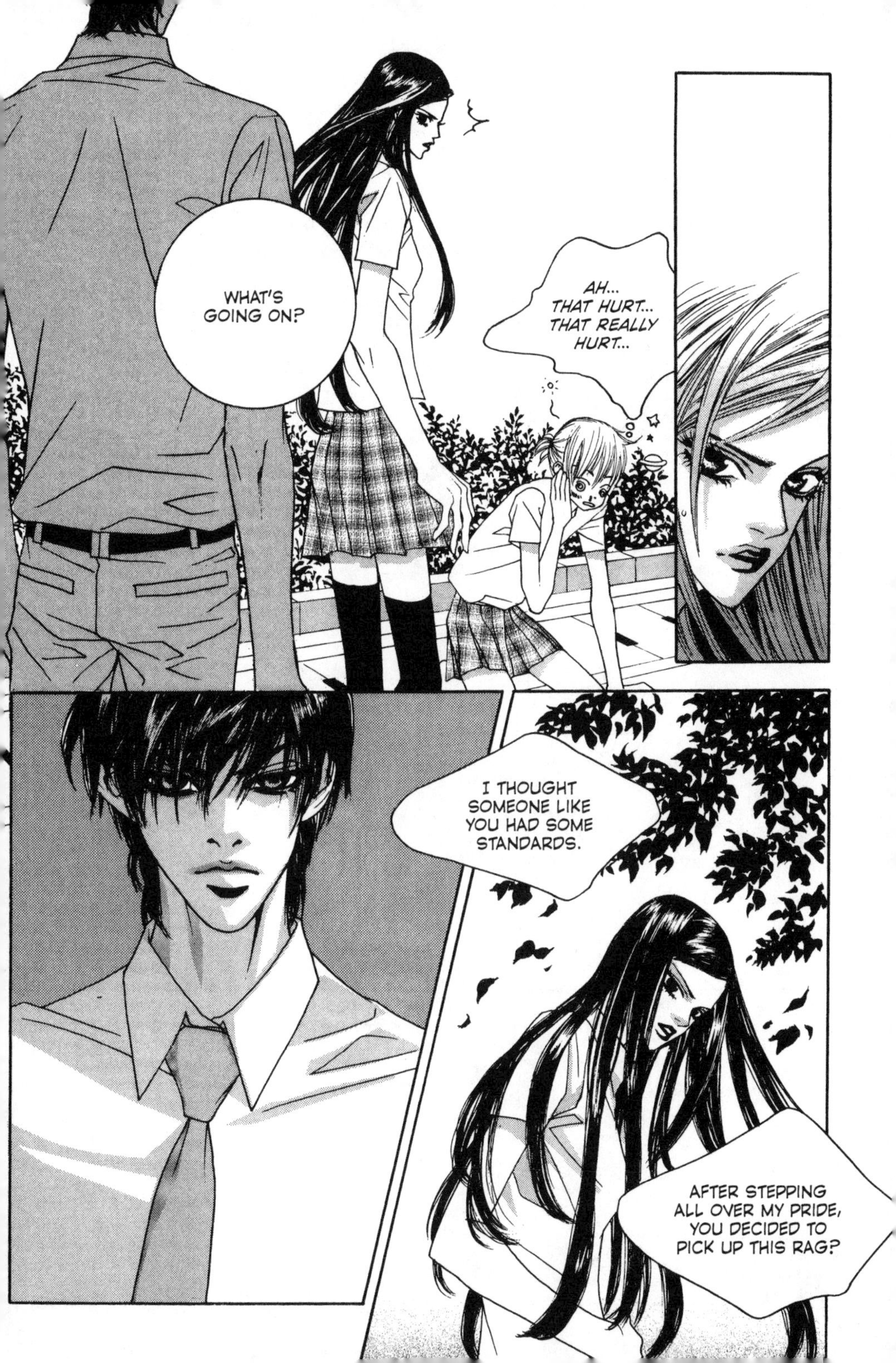
WHAT'S GOING ON?
AH... THAT HURT... THAT REALLY HURT...
I THOUGHT SOMEONE LIKE YOU HAD SOME STANDARDS.
AFTER STEPPING ALL OVER MY PRIDE, YOU DECIDED TO PICK UP THIS RAG?

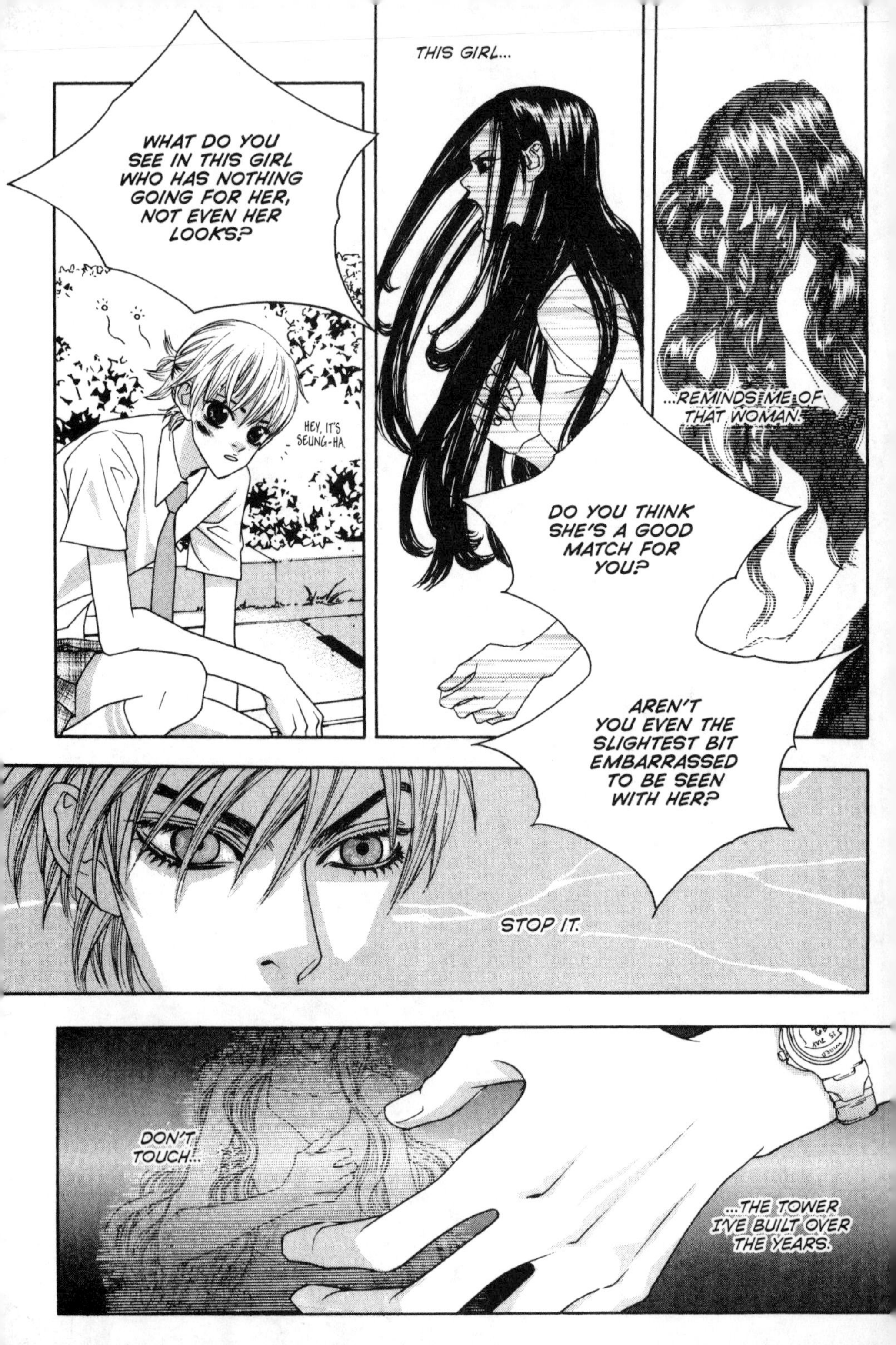
WHAT DO YOU SEE IN THIS GIRL WHO HAS NOTHING GOING FOR HER, NOT EVEN HER LOOKS?
HEY, IT'S SEUNG-HA.
THIS GIRL...
...REMINDS ME OF THAT WOMAN.
DO YOU THINK SHE'S A GOOD MATCH FOR YOU?
AREN'T YOU EVEN THE SLIGHTEST BIT EMBARRASSED TO BE SEEN WITH HER?
STOP IT.
DON'T TOUCH...
...THE TOWER I'VE BUILT OVER THE YEARS.

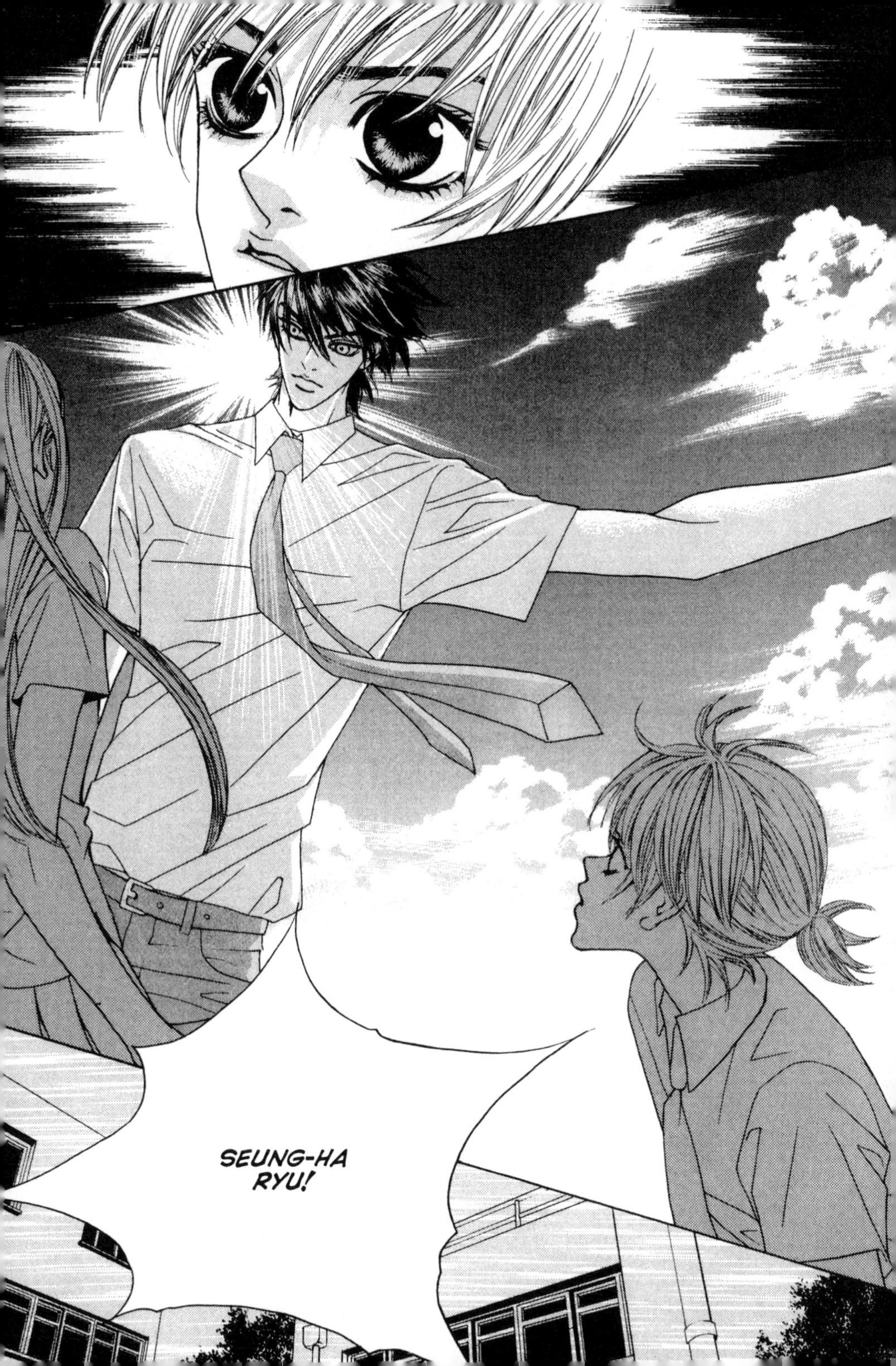
SEUNG-HA
RYU!

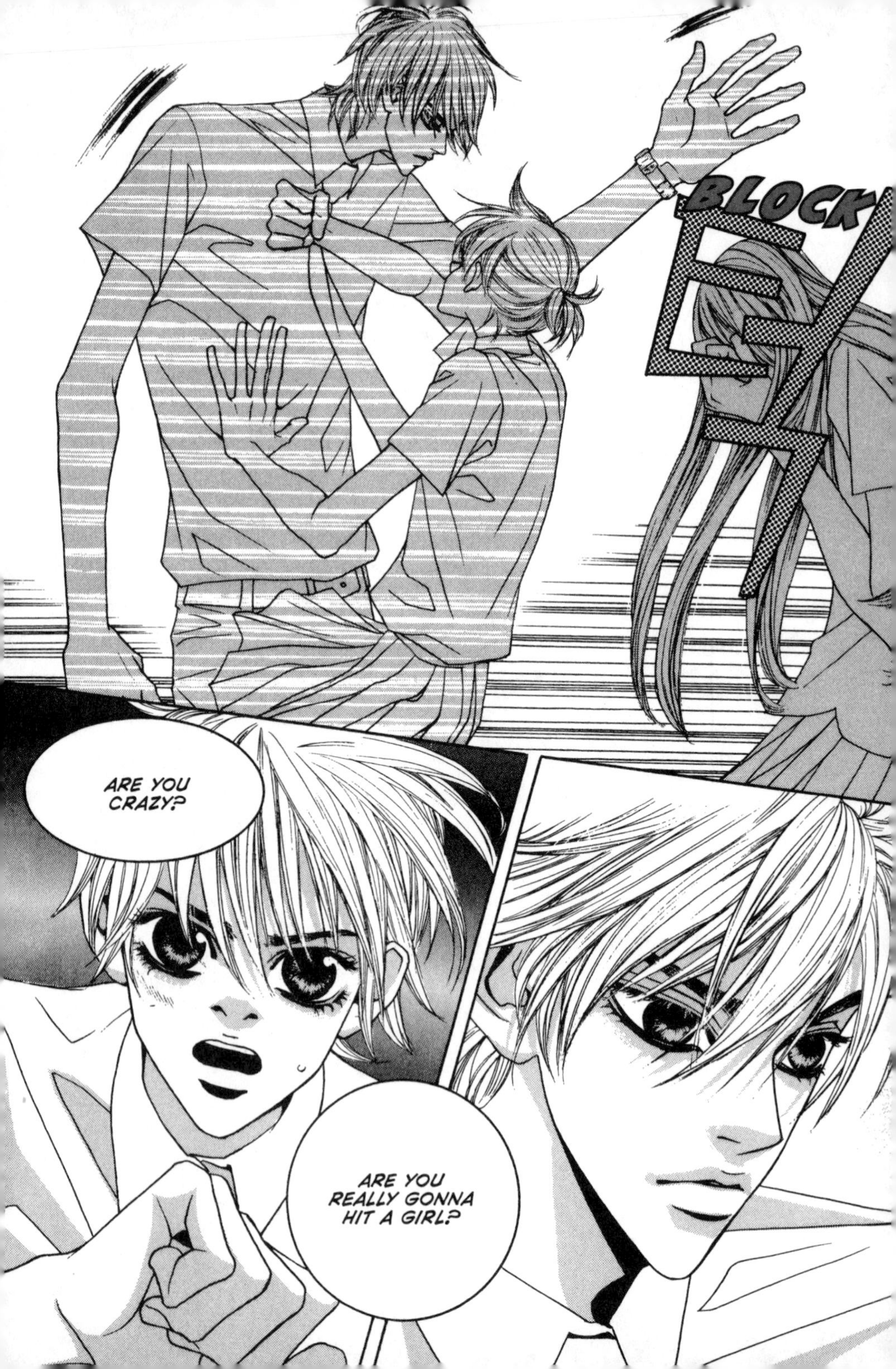
BLOCK
ARE YOU CRAZY?
ARE YOU REALLY GONNA HIT A GIRL?

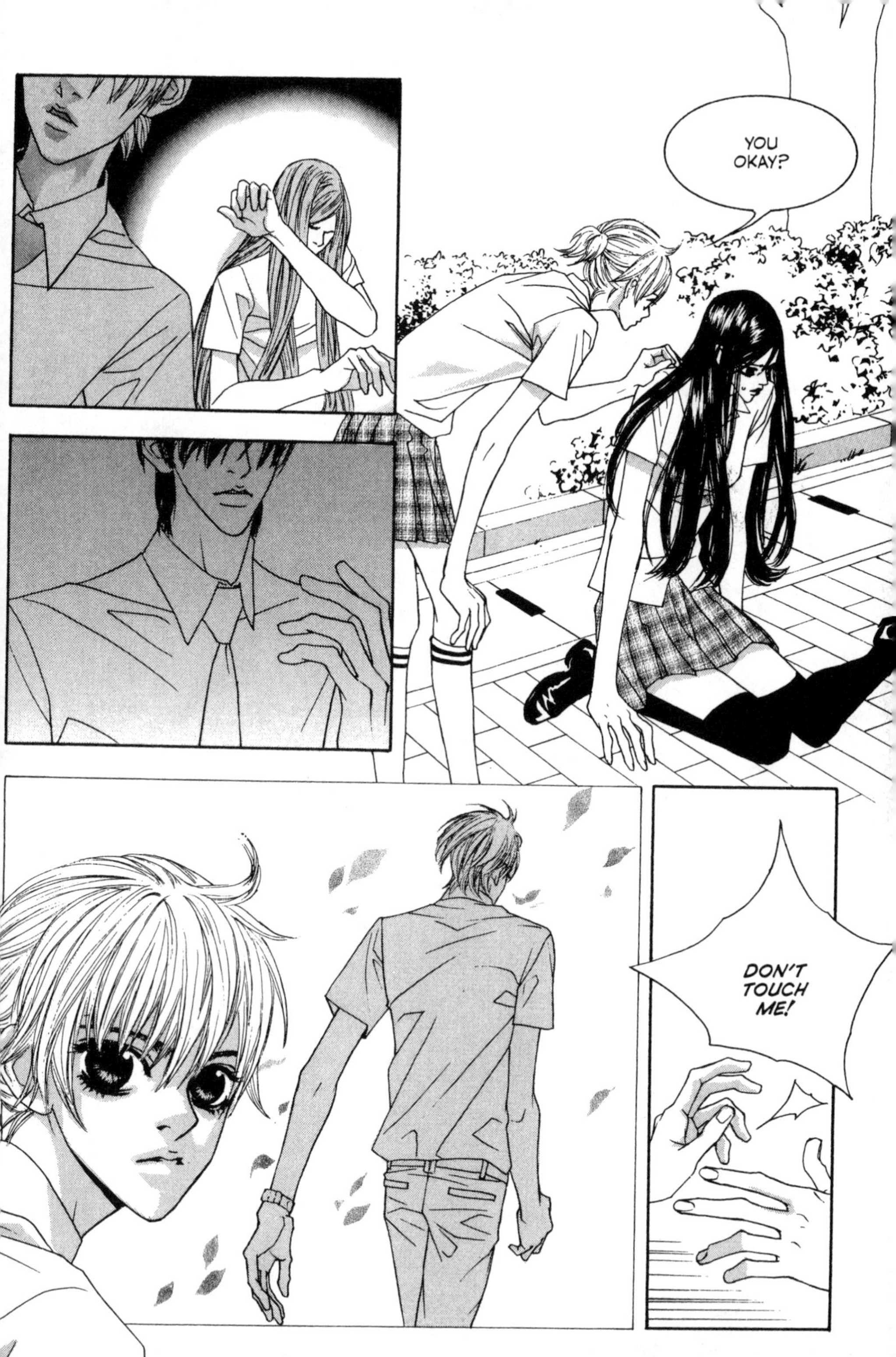
YOU OKAY?
DON'T TOUCH ME!

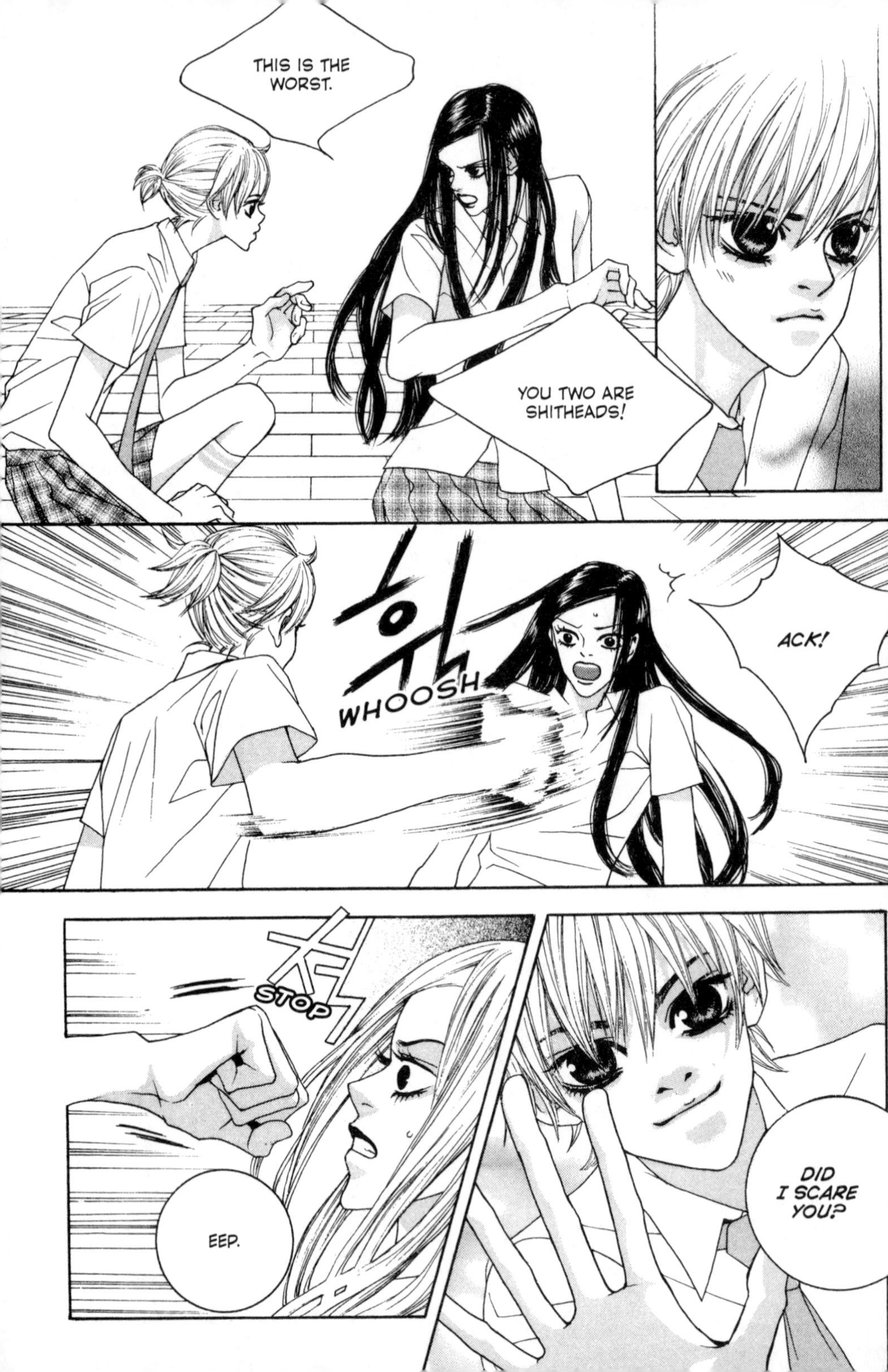
THIS IS THE WORST.
YOU TWO ARE SHITHEADS!
휘
WHOOSH
ACK!
STOP
EEP.
DID I SCARE YOU?

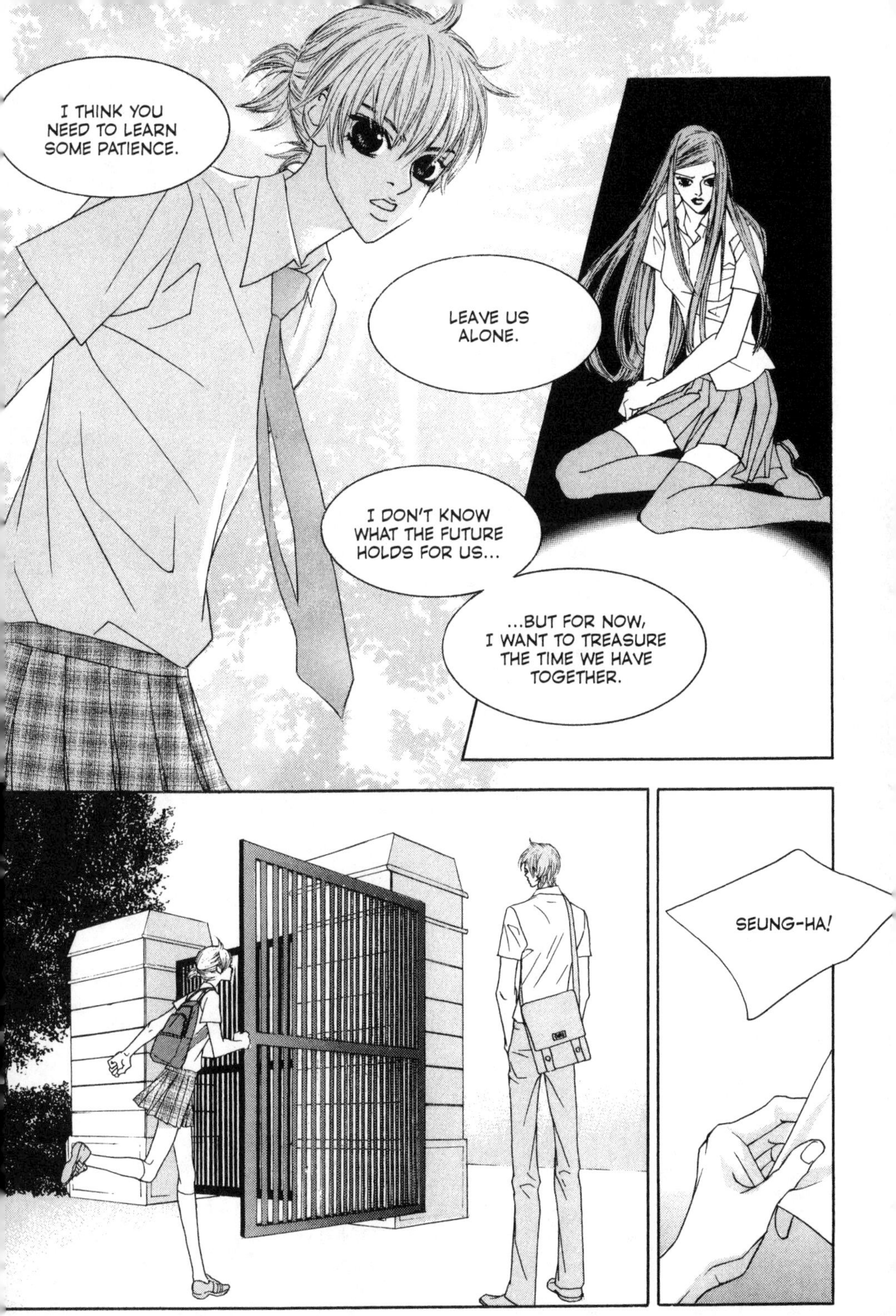
I THINK YOU NEED TO LEARN SOME PATIENCE.
LEAVE US ALONE.
I DON'T KNOW WHAT THE FUTURE HOLDS FOR US...
...BUT FOR NOW, I WANT TO TREASURE THE TIME WE HAVE TOGETHER.
SEUNG-HA!

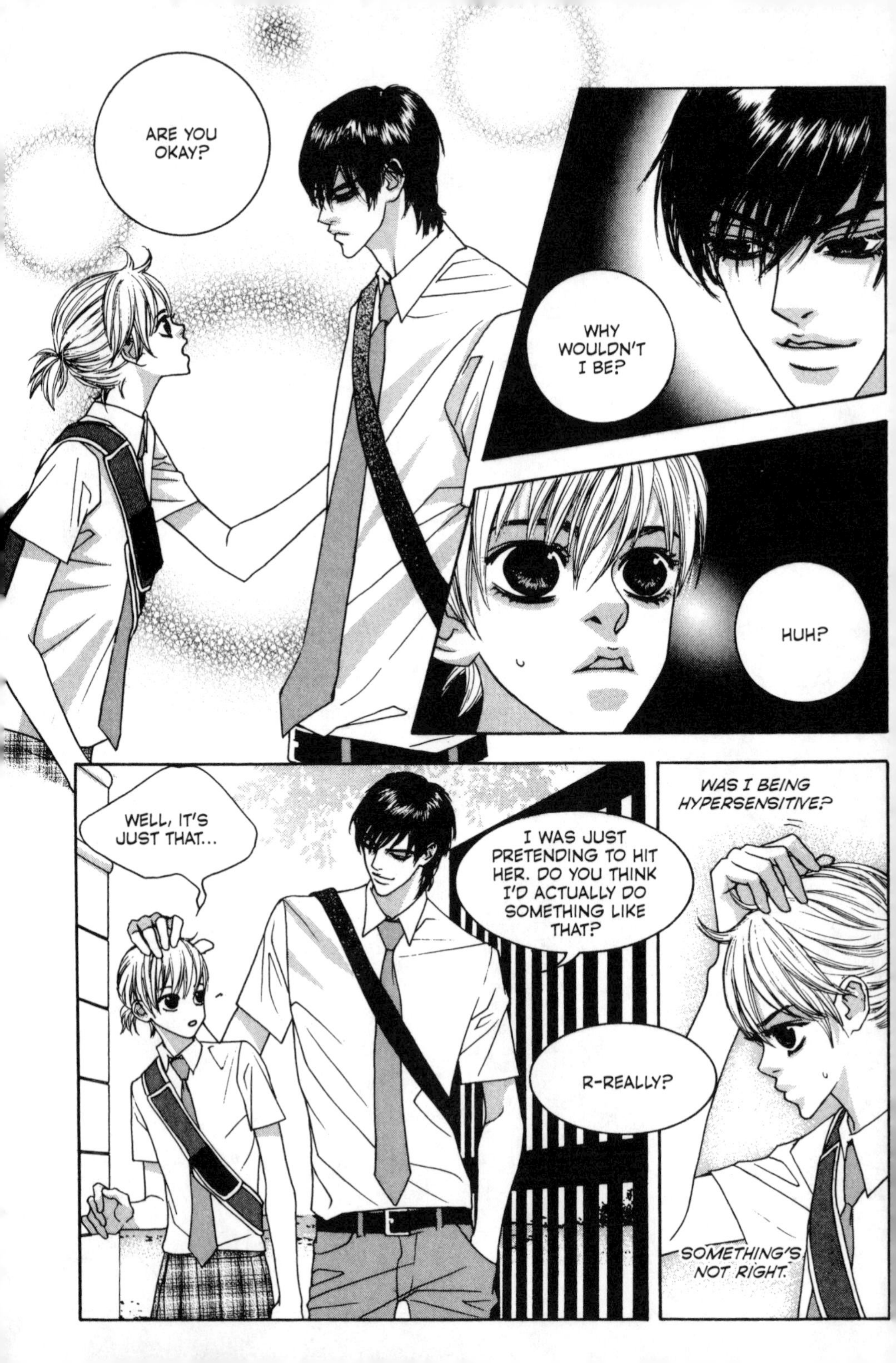
ARE YOU OKAY?
WHY WOULDN'T I BE?
HUH?
WELL, IT'S JUST THAT...
I WAS JUST PRETENDING TO HIT HER. DO YOU THINK I'D ACTUALLY DO SOMETHING LIKE THAT?
R-REALLY?
WAS I BEING HYPERSENSITIVE?
SOMETHING'S NOT RIGHT.

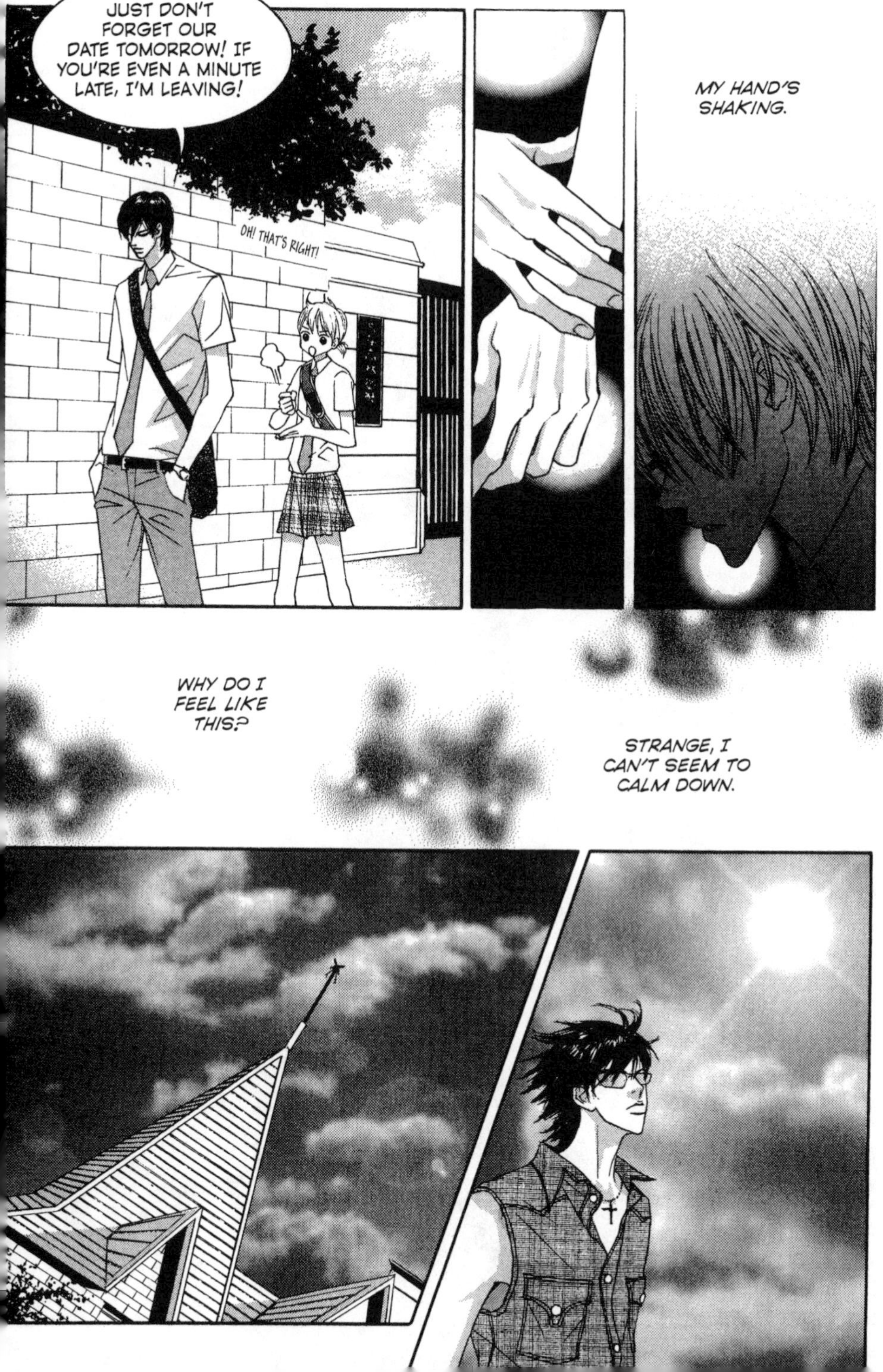
JUST DON'T FORGET OUR DATE TOMORROW! IF YOU'RE EVEN A MINUTE LATE, I'M LEAVING!
OH! THAT'S RIGHT!
MY HAND'S SHAKING.
WHY DO I FEEL LIKE THIS?
STRANGE, I CAN'T SEEM TO CALM DOWN.

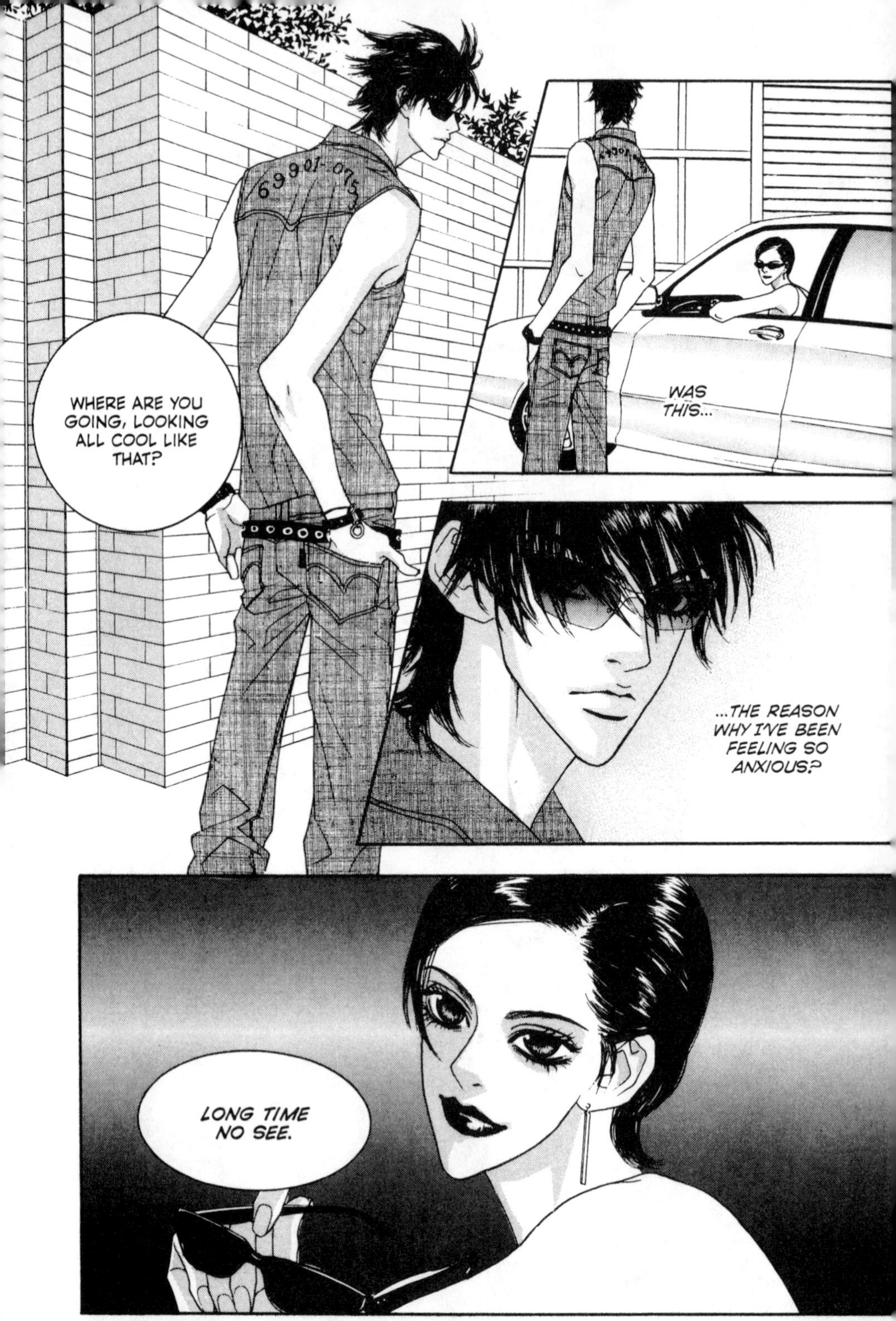
WHERE ARE YOU GOING, LOOKING ALL COOL LIKE THAT?
WAS THIS...
...THE REASON WHY I'VE BEEN FEELING SO ANXIOUS?
LONG TIME NO SEE.

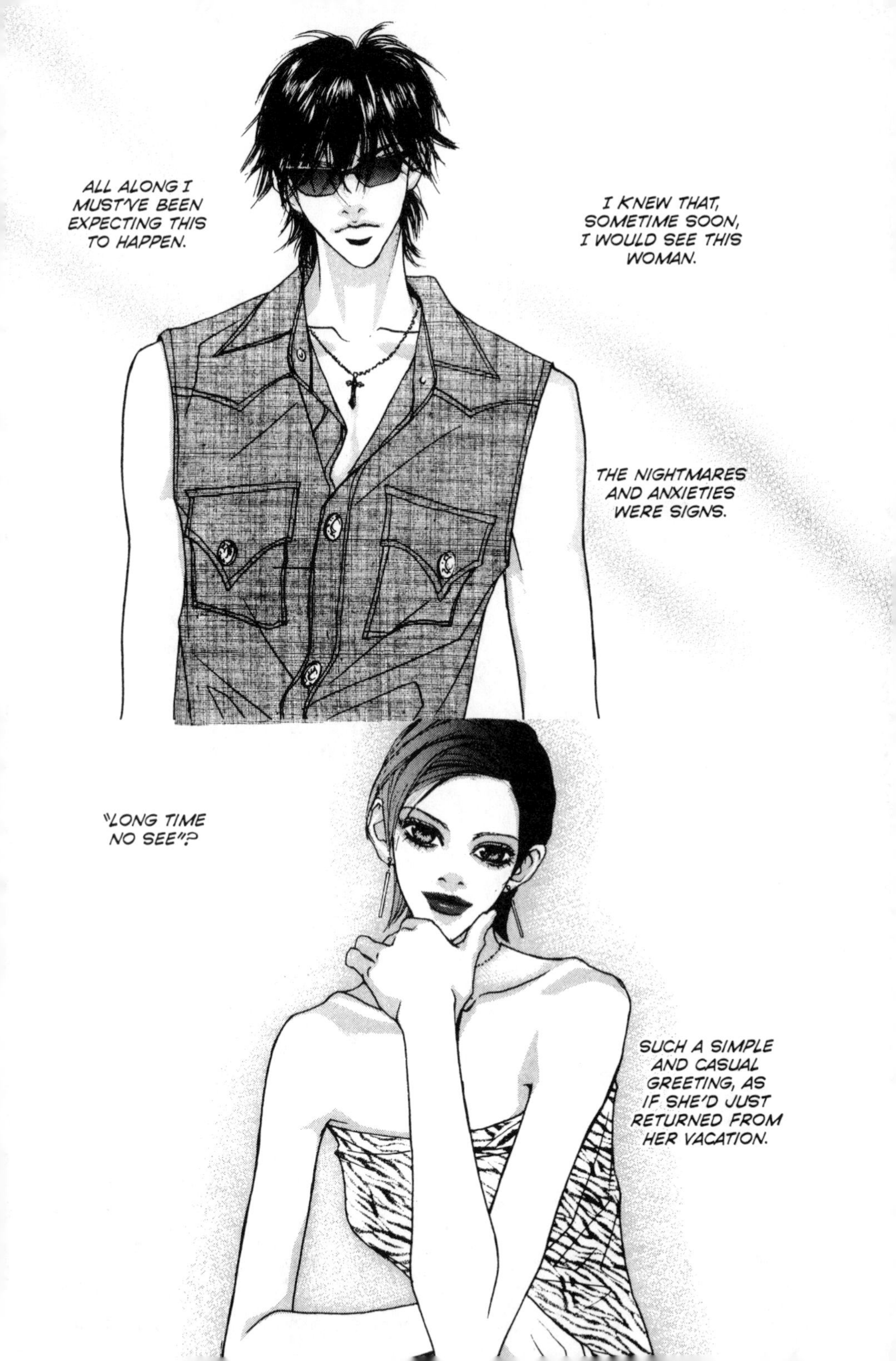
ALL ALONG I MUST'VE BEEN EXPECTING THIS TO HAPPEN.
I KNEW THAT, SOMETIME SOON, I WOULD SEE THIS WOMAN.
THE NIGHTMARES AND ANXIETIES WERE SIGNS.
"LONG TIME NO SEE"?
SUCH A SIMPLE AND CASUAL GREETING, AS IF SHE'D JUST RETURNED FROM HER VACATION.

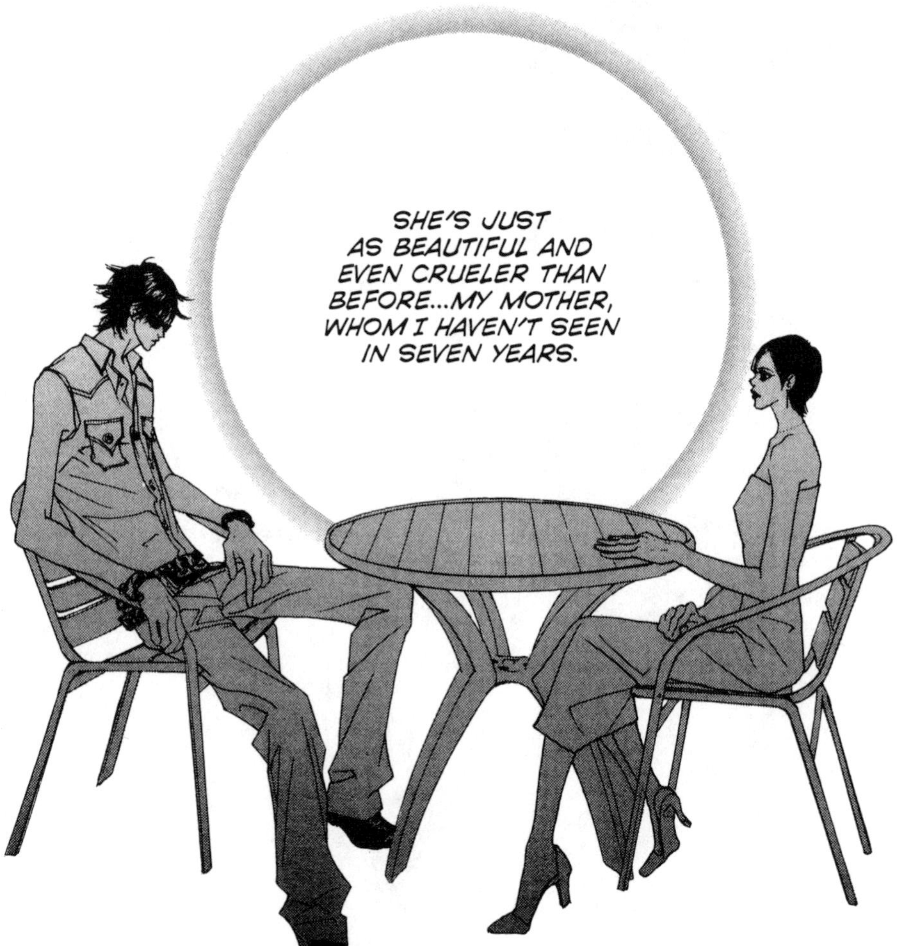
SHE'S JUST AS BEAUTIFUL AND EVEN CRUELER THAN BEFORE...MY MOTHER, WHOM I HAVEN'T SEEN IN SEVEN YEARS.
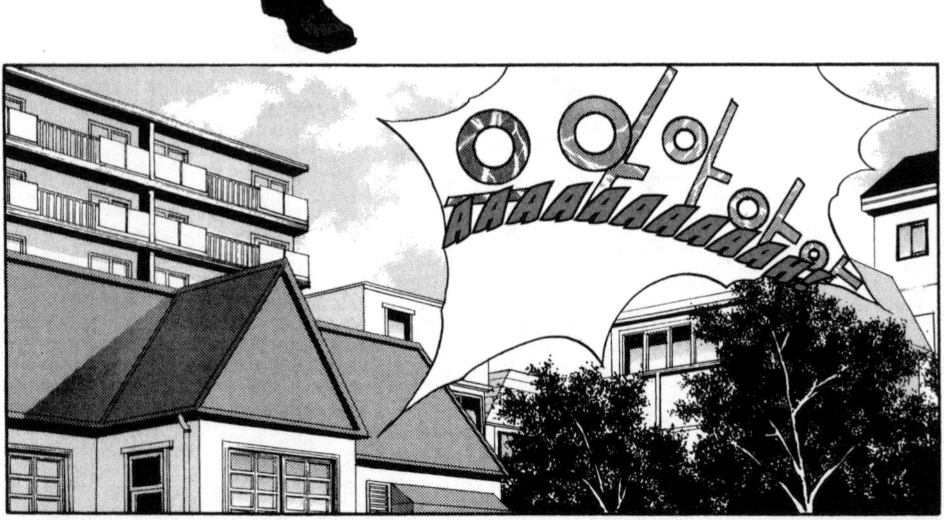
AAAAAAAAAAAH!!

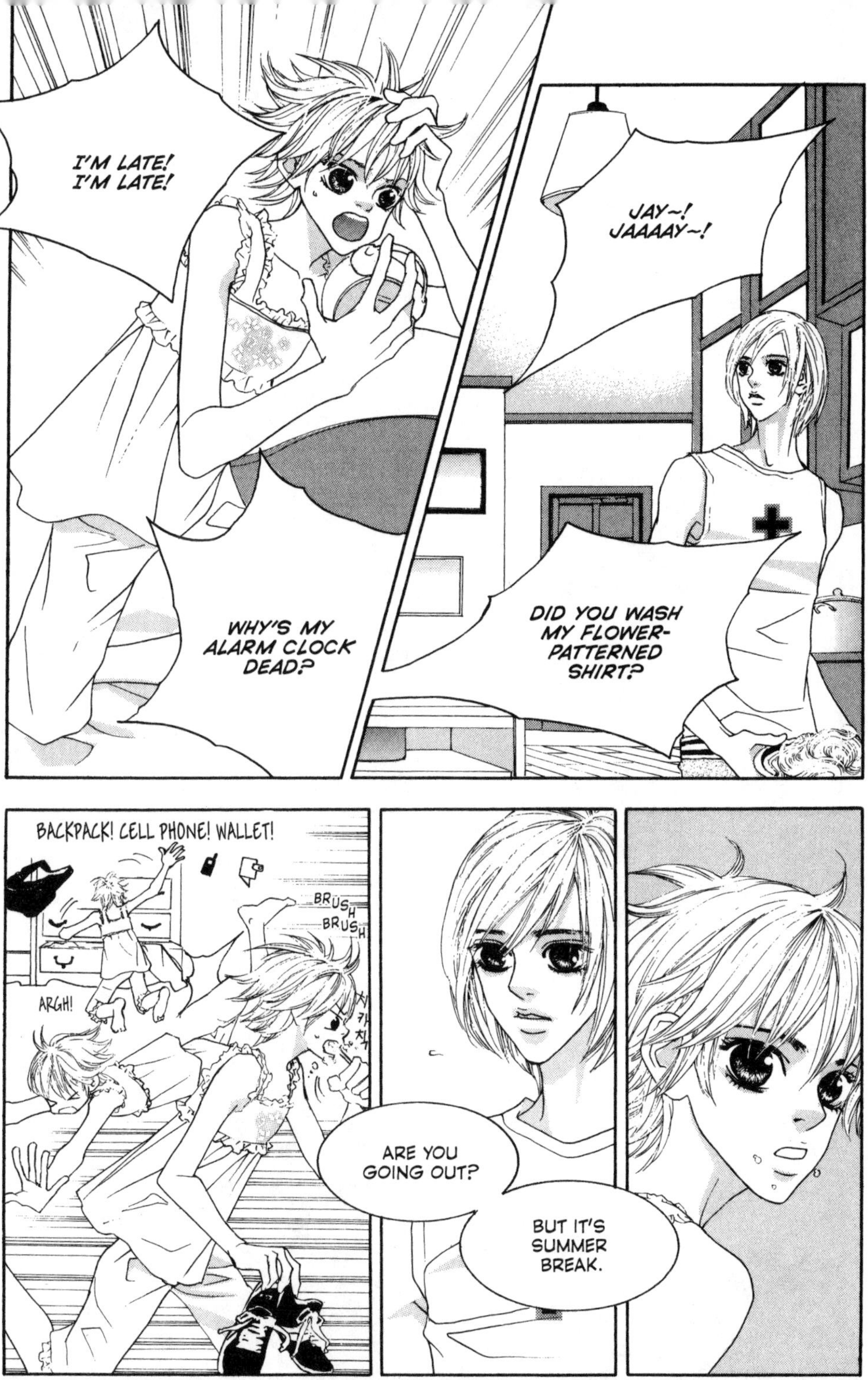
I'M LATE! I'M LATE!
WHY'S MY ALARM CLOCK DEAD?
JAY~! JAAAAY~!
DID YOU WASH MY FLOWER-PATTERNED SHIRT?
BACKPACK! CELL PHONE! WALLET!
BRUSH BRUSH
ARGH!
ARE YOU GOING OUT?
BUT IT'S SUMMER BREAK.

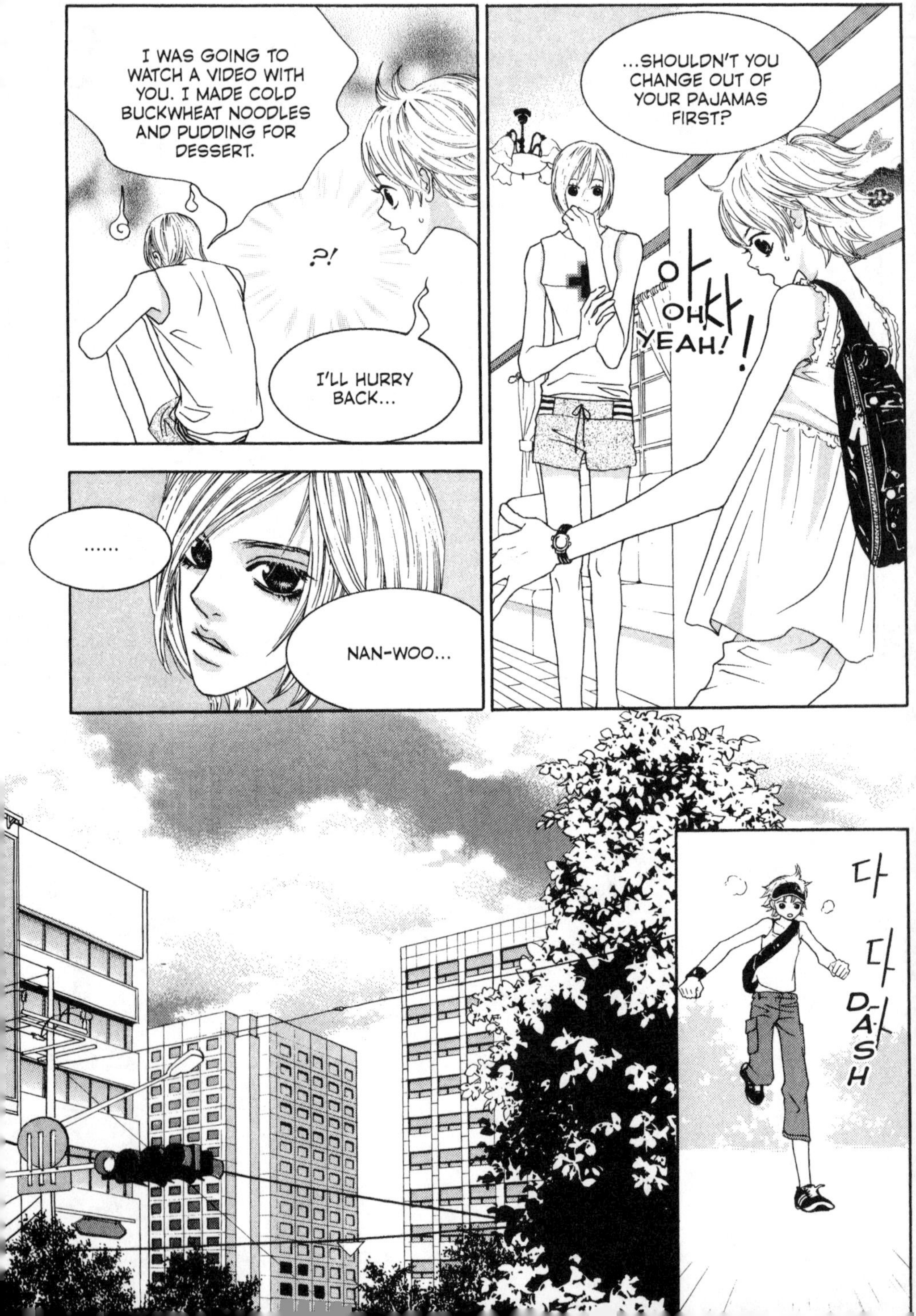
I WAS GOING TO WATCH A VIDEO WITH YOU. I MADE COLD BUCKWHEAT NOODLES AND PUDDING FOR DESSERT.
?!
I'LL HURRY BACK...
...SHOULDN'T YOU CHANGE OUT OF YOUR PAJAMAS FIRST?
아차
OH YEAH!
!
......
NAN-WOO...
다다다
DASH

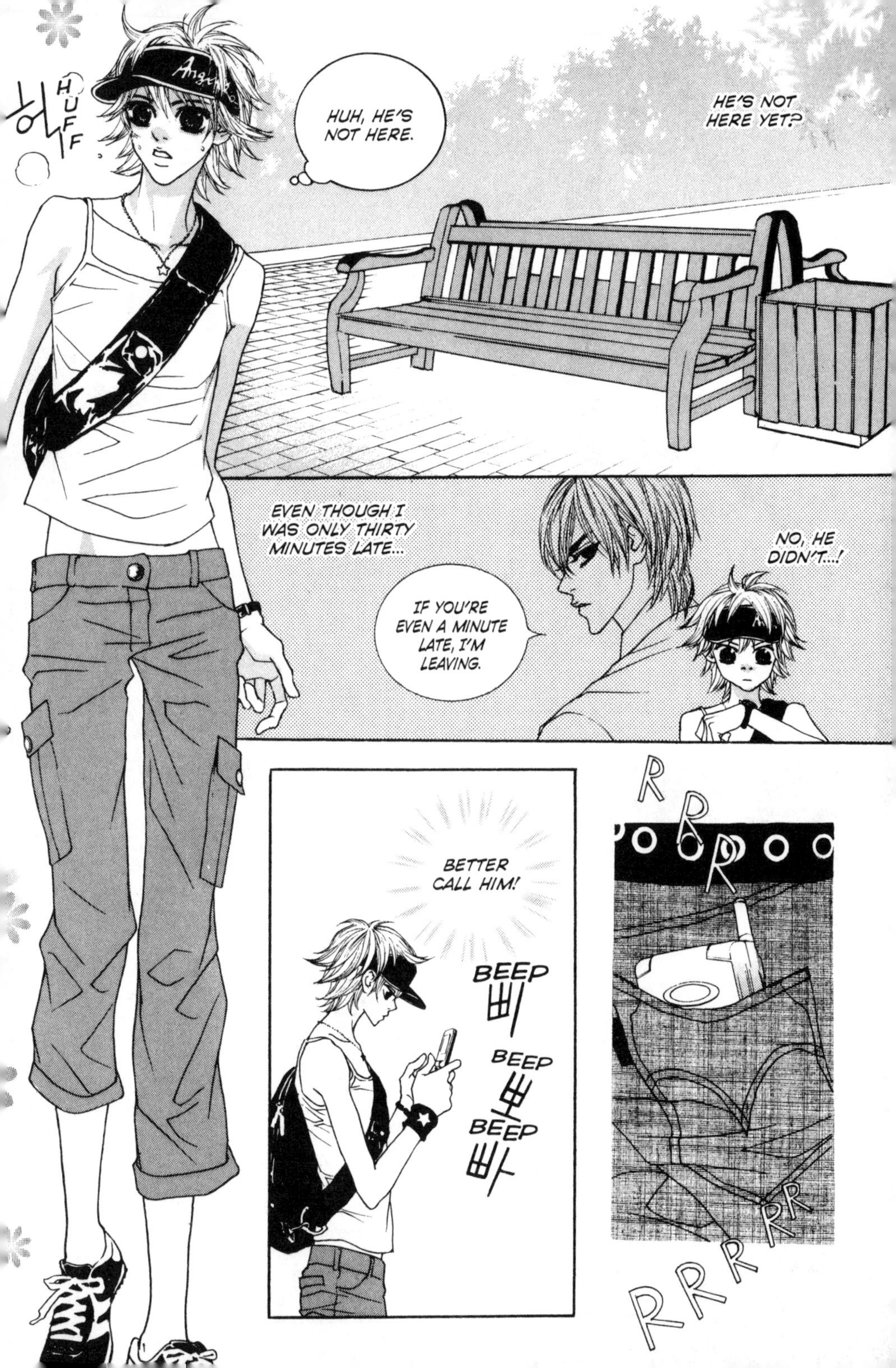
헉
HUFF
HUH, HE'S NOT HERE.
HE'S NOT HERE YET?
EVEN THOUGH I WAS ONLY THIRTY MINUTES LATE...
IF YOU'RE EVEN A MINUTE LATE, I'M LEAVING.
NO, HE DIDN'T...!
BETTER CALL HIM!
BEEP
삐
BEEP
BEEP
빠
RRR
RRRRRRR

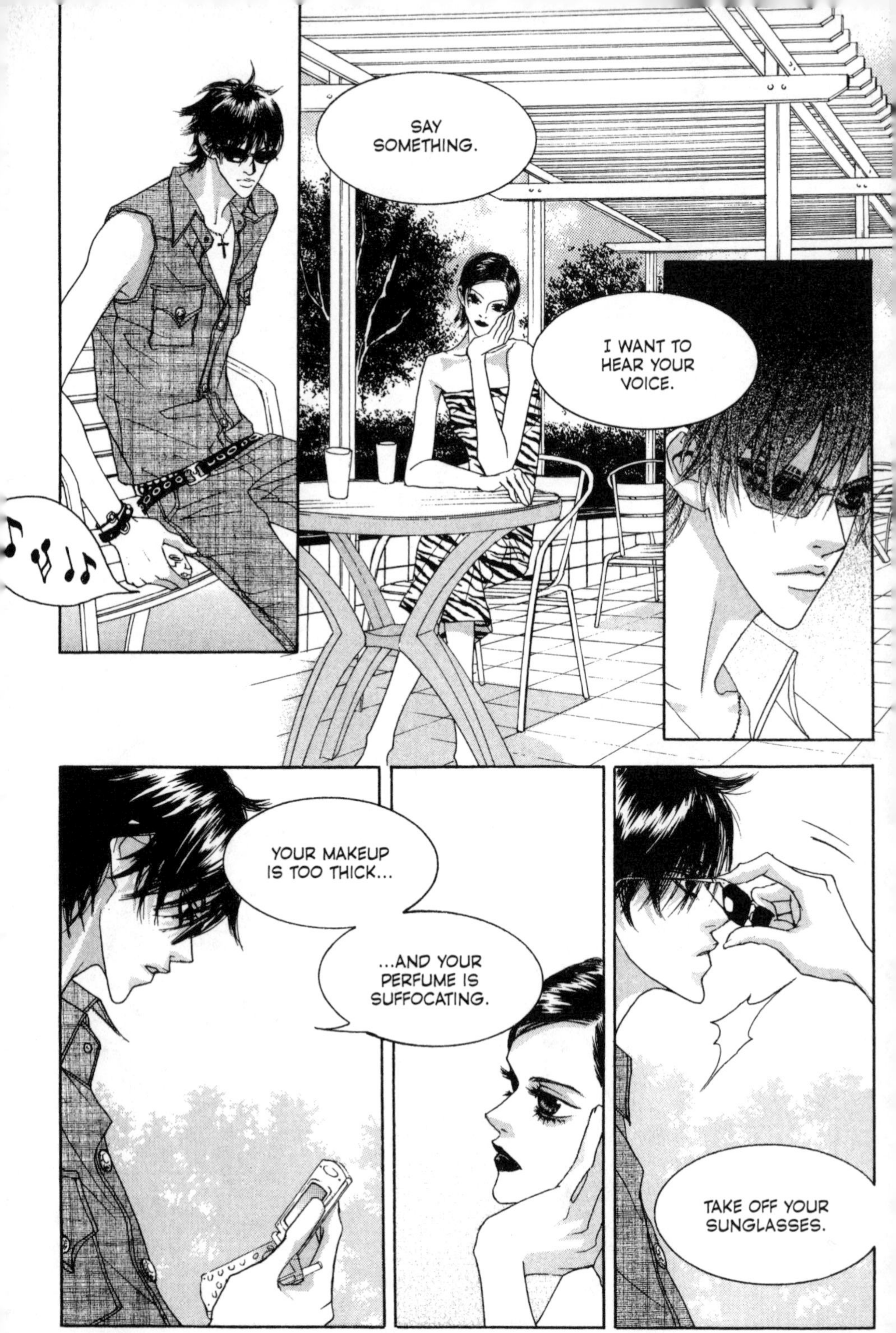
SAY SOMETHING.
I WANT TO HEAR YOUR VOICE.
YOUR MAKEUP IS TOO THICK...
...AND YOUR PERFUME IS SUFFOCATING.
TAKE OFF YOUR SUNGLASSES.

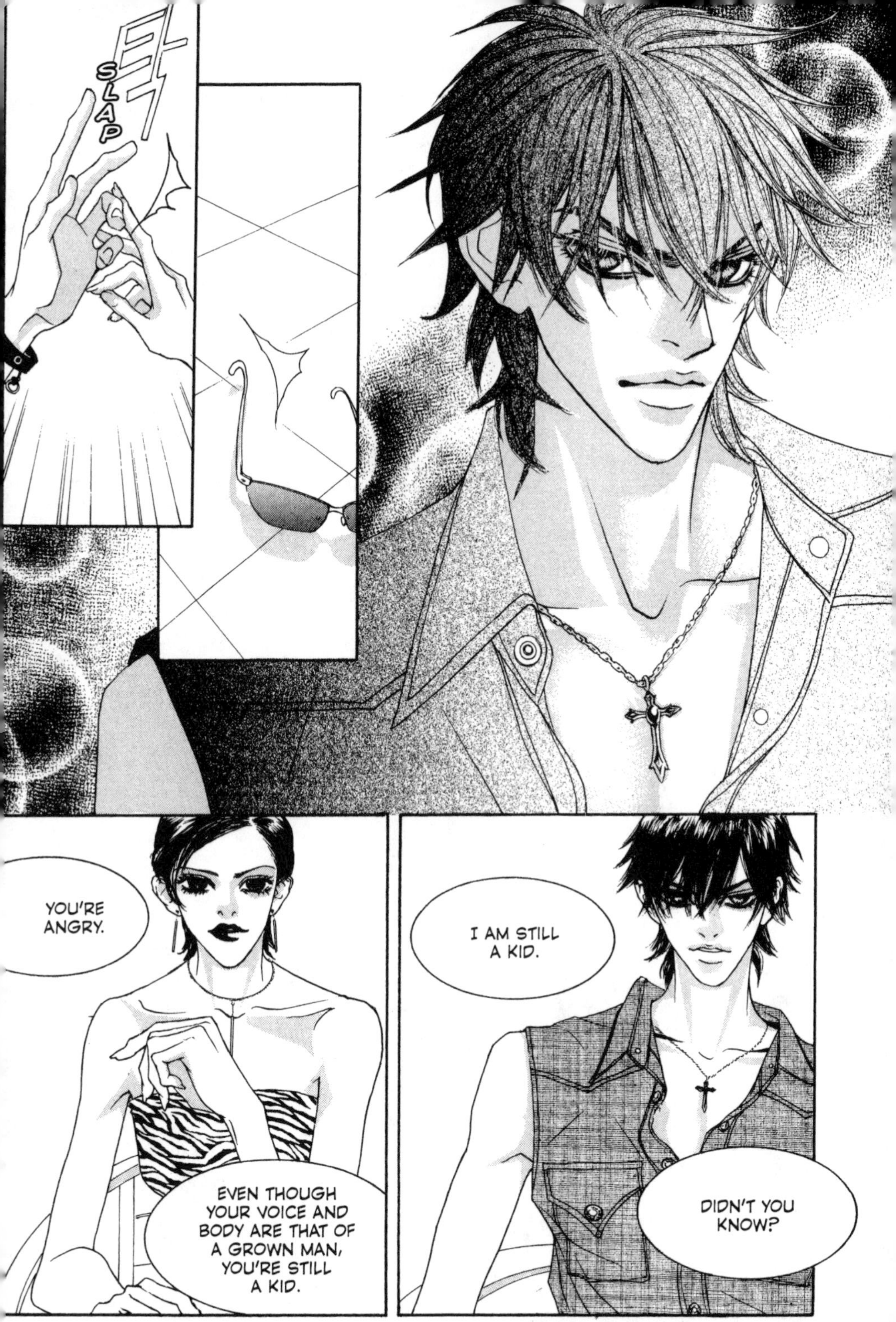
SLAP
YOU'RE ANGRY.
EVEN THOUGH YOUR VOICE AND BODY ARE THAT OF A GROWN MAN, YOU'RE STILL A KID.
I AM STILL A KID.
DIDN'T YOU KNOW?

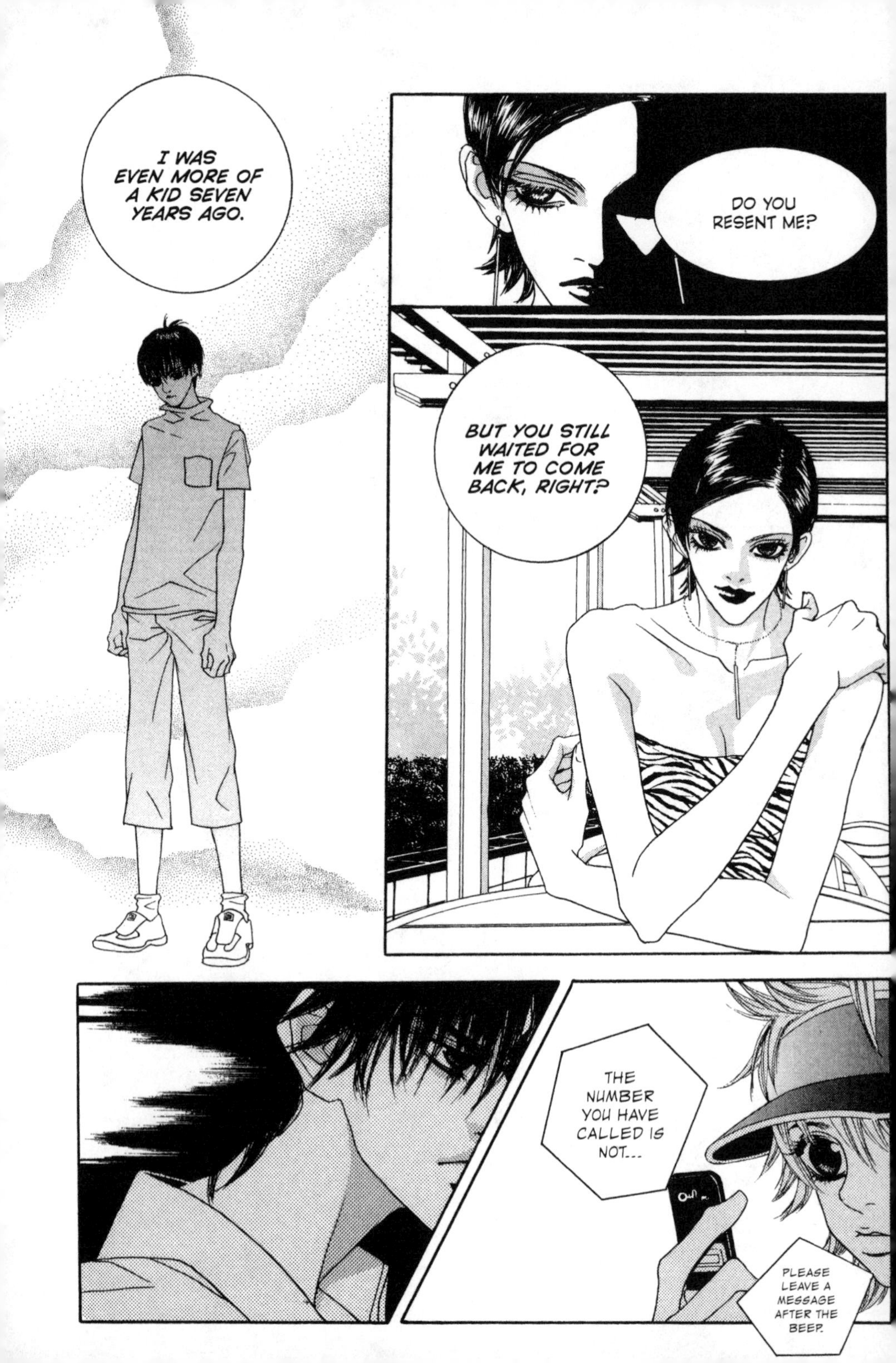
I WAS EVEN MORE OF A KID SEVEN YEARS AGO.
DO YOU RESENT ME?
BUT YOU STILL WAITED FOR ME TO COME BACK, RIGHT?
THE NUMBER YOU HAVE CALLED IS NOT...
PLEASE LEAVE A MESSAGE AFTER THE BEEP.

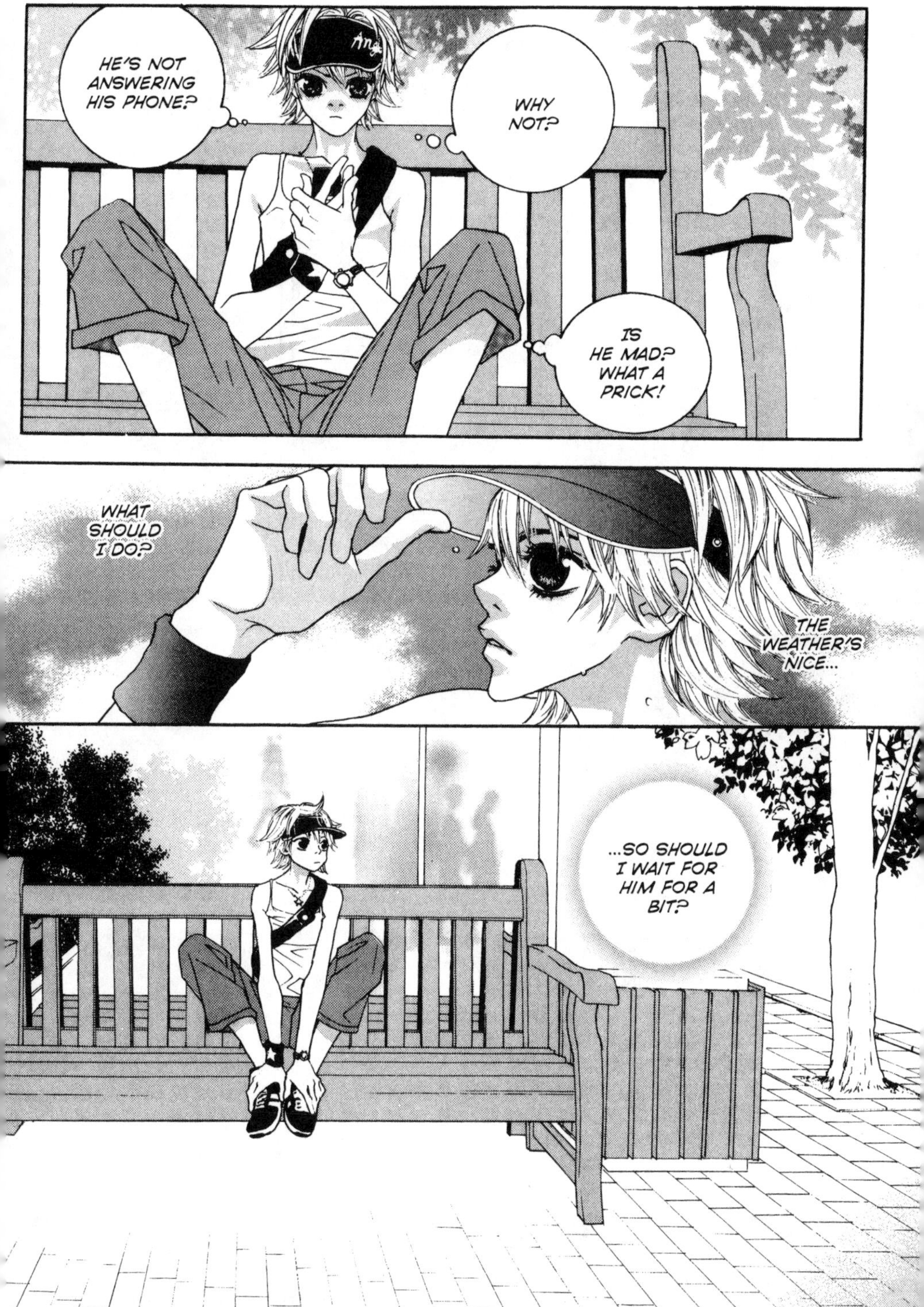

HE'S NOT ANSWERING HIS PHONE?
WHY NOT?
IS HE MAD? WHAT A PRICK!
WHAT SHOULD I DO?
THE WEATHER'S NICE...
...SO SHOULD I WAIT FOR HIM FOR A BIT?

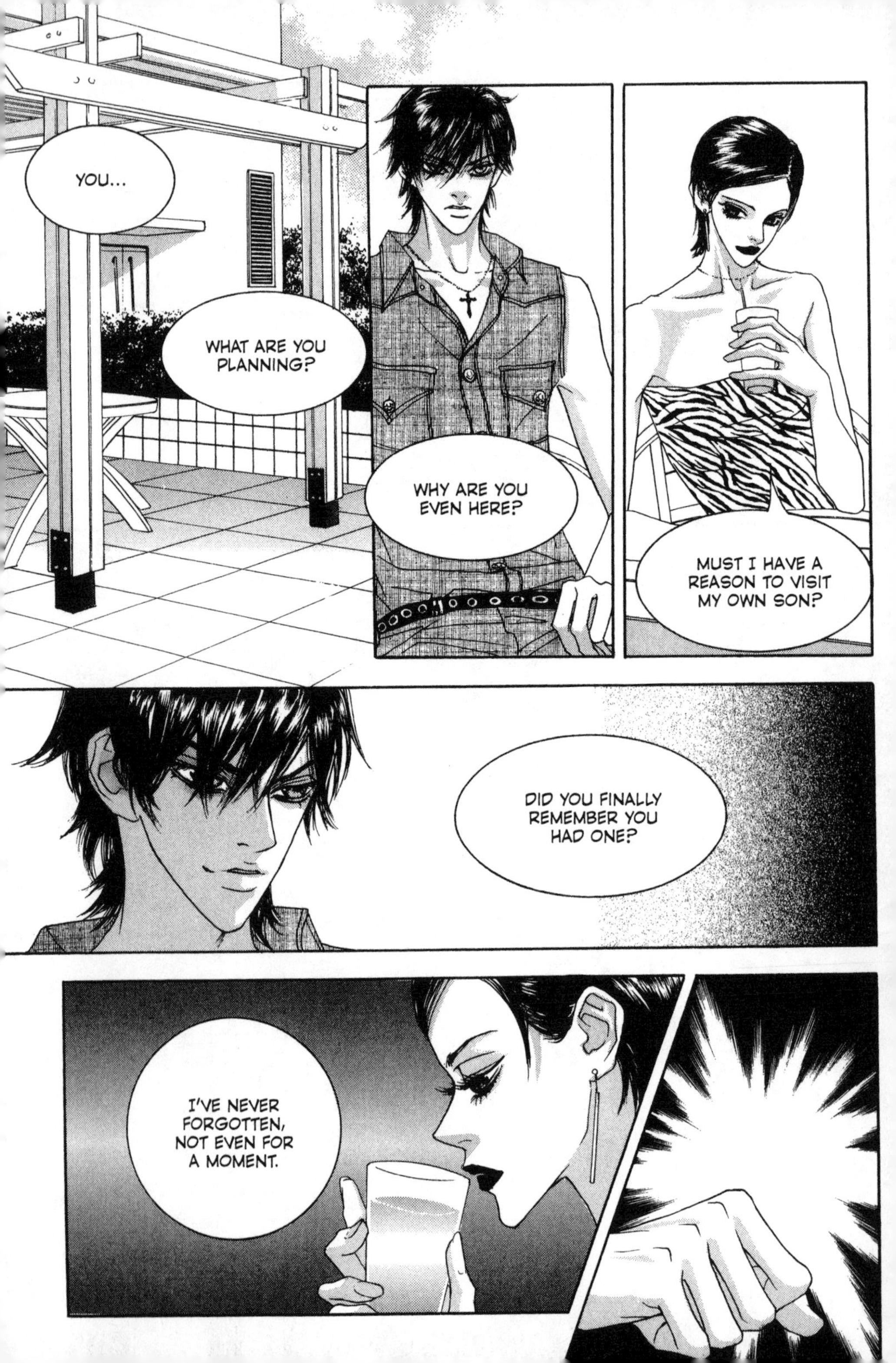
YOU...
WHAT ARE YOU PLANNING?
WHY ARE YOU EVEN HERE?
MUST I HAVE A REASON TO VISIT MY OWN SON?
DID YOU FINALLY REMEMBER YOU HAD ONE?
I'VE NEVER FORGOTTEN, NOT EVEN FOR A MOMENT.

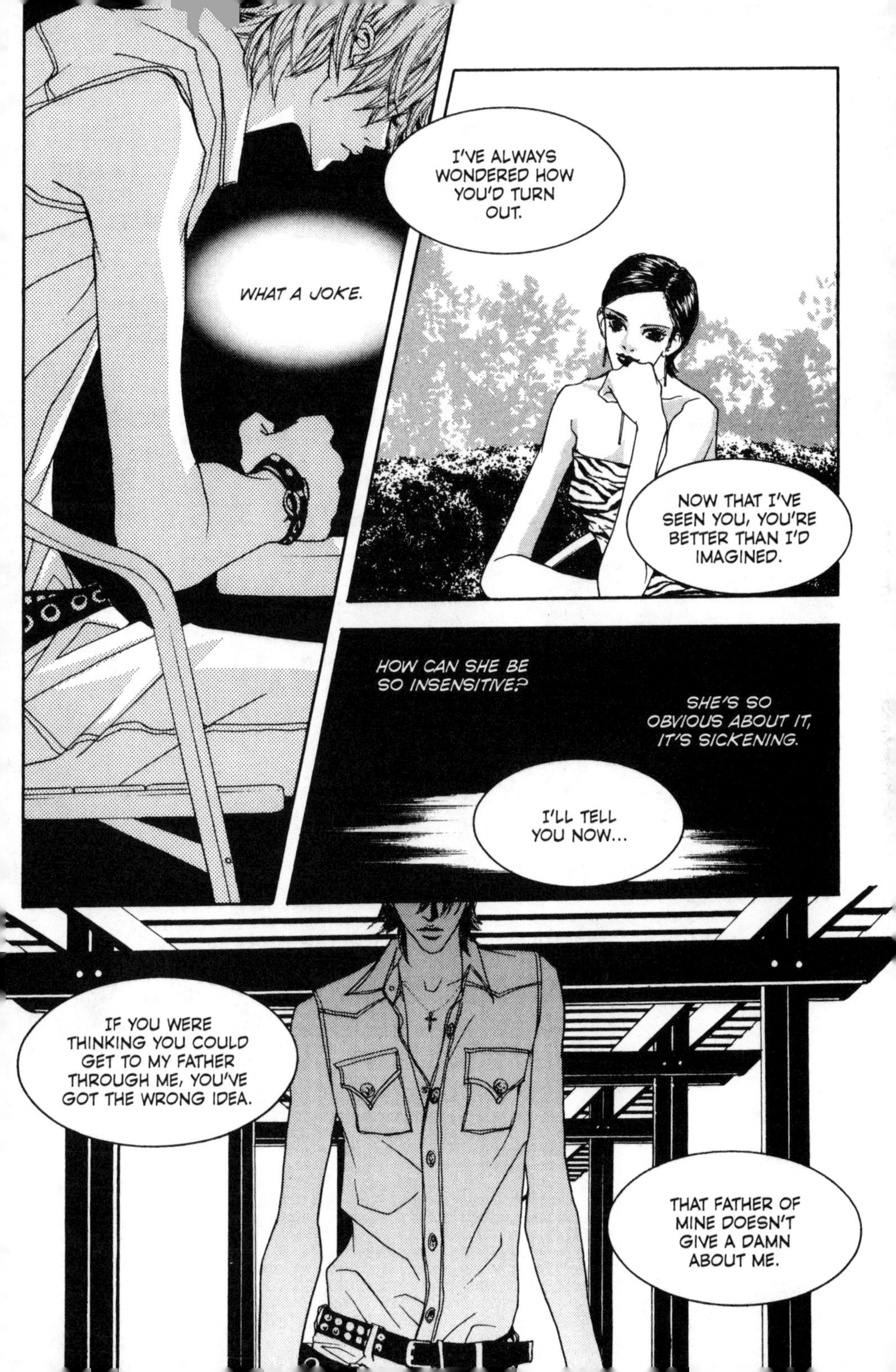
WHAT A JOKE.
I'VE ALWAYS WONDERED HOW YOU'D TURN OUT.
NOW THAT I'VE SEEN YOU, YOU'RE BETTER THAN I'D IMAGINED.
HOW CAN SHE BE SO INSENSITIVE?
SHE'S SO OBVIOUS ABOUT IT, IT'S SICKENING.
I'LL TELL YOU NOW...
IF YOU WERE THINKING YOU COULD GET TO MY FATHER THROUGH ME, YOU'VE GOT THE WRONG IDEA.
THAT FATHER OF MINE DOESN'T GIVE A DAMN ABOUT ME.

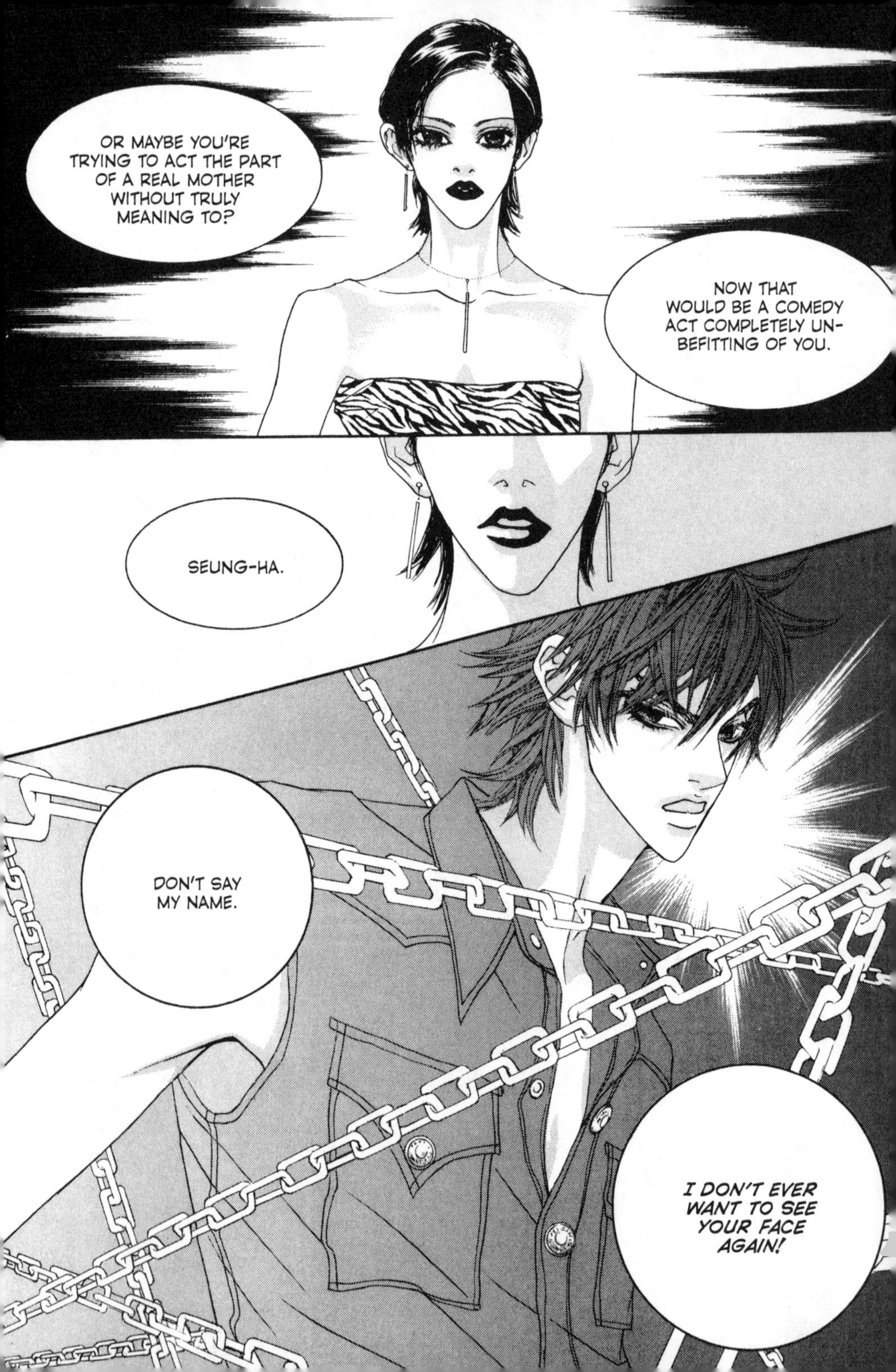
OR MAYBE YOU'RE TRYING TO ACT THE PART OF A REAL MOTHER WITHOUT TRULY MEANING TO?
NOW THAT WOULD BE A COMEDY ACT COMPLETELY UN-BEFITTING OF YOU.
SEUNG-HA.
DON'T SAY MY NAME.
I DON'T EVER WANT TO SEE YOUR FACE AGAIN!

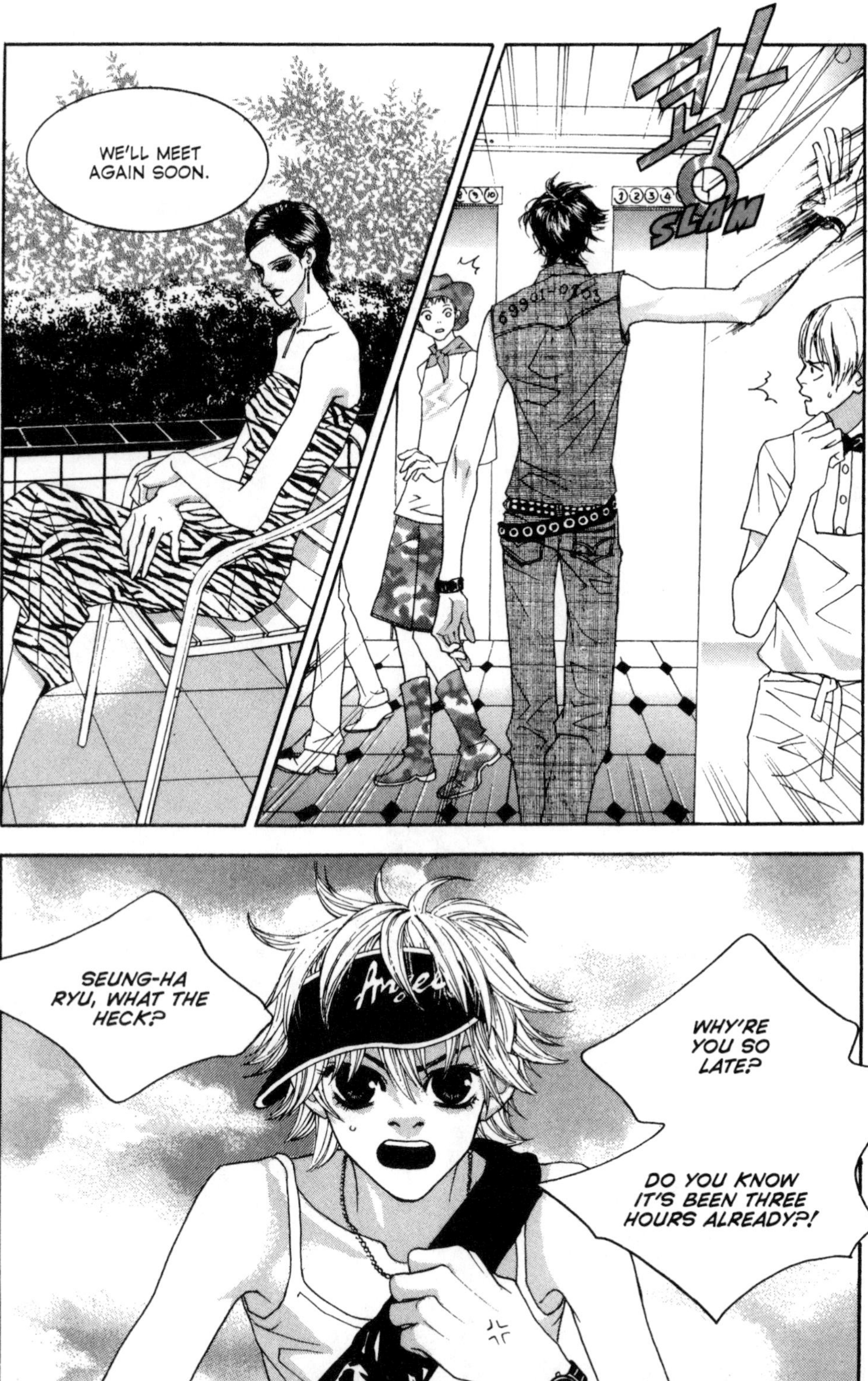

WE'LL MEET AGAIN SOON.
꽝
SLAM
SEUNG-HA RYU, WHAT THE HECK?
WHY'RE YOU SO LATE?
DO YOU KNOW IT'S BEEN THREE HOURS ALREADY?!

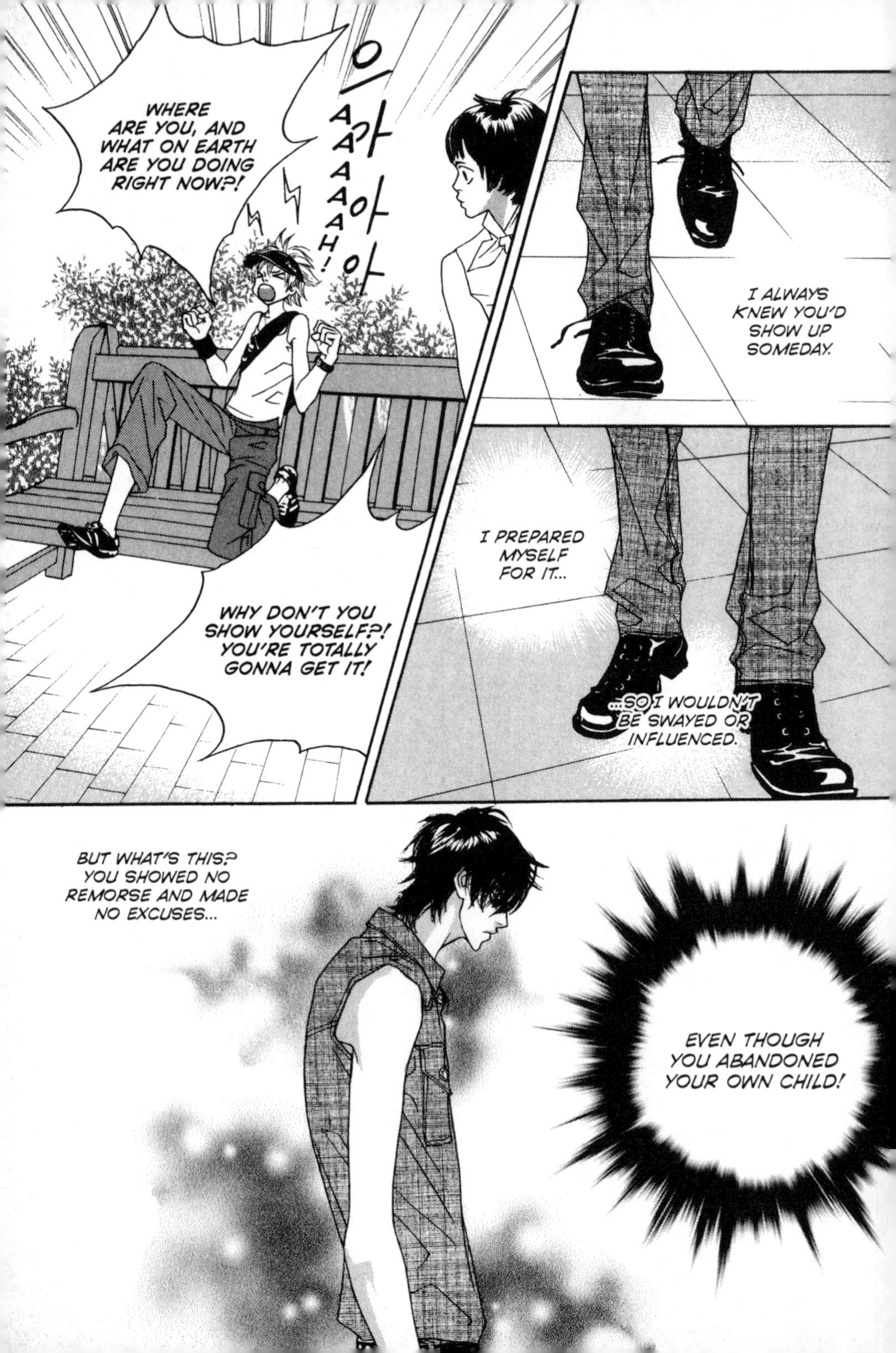
WHERE ARE YOU, AND WHAT ON EARTH ARE YOU DOING RIGHT NOW?!
으아아아
AAAAAAH!
WHY DON'T YOU SHOW YOURSELF?! YOU'RE TOTALLY GONNA GET IT!
I ALWAYS KNEW YOU'D SHOW UP SOMEDAY.
I PREPARED MYSELF FOR IT...
...SO I WOULDN'T BE SWAYED OR INFLUENCED.
BUT WHAT'S THIS? YOU SHOWED NO REMORSE AND MADE NO EXCUSES...
EVEN THOUGH YOU ABANDONED YOUR OWN CHILD!

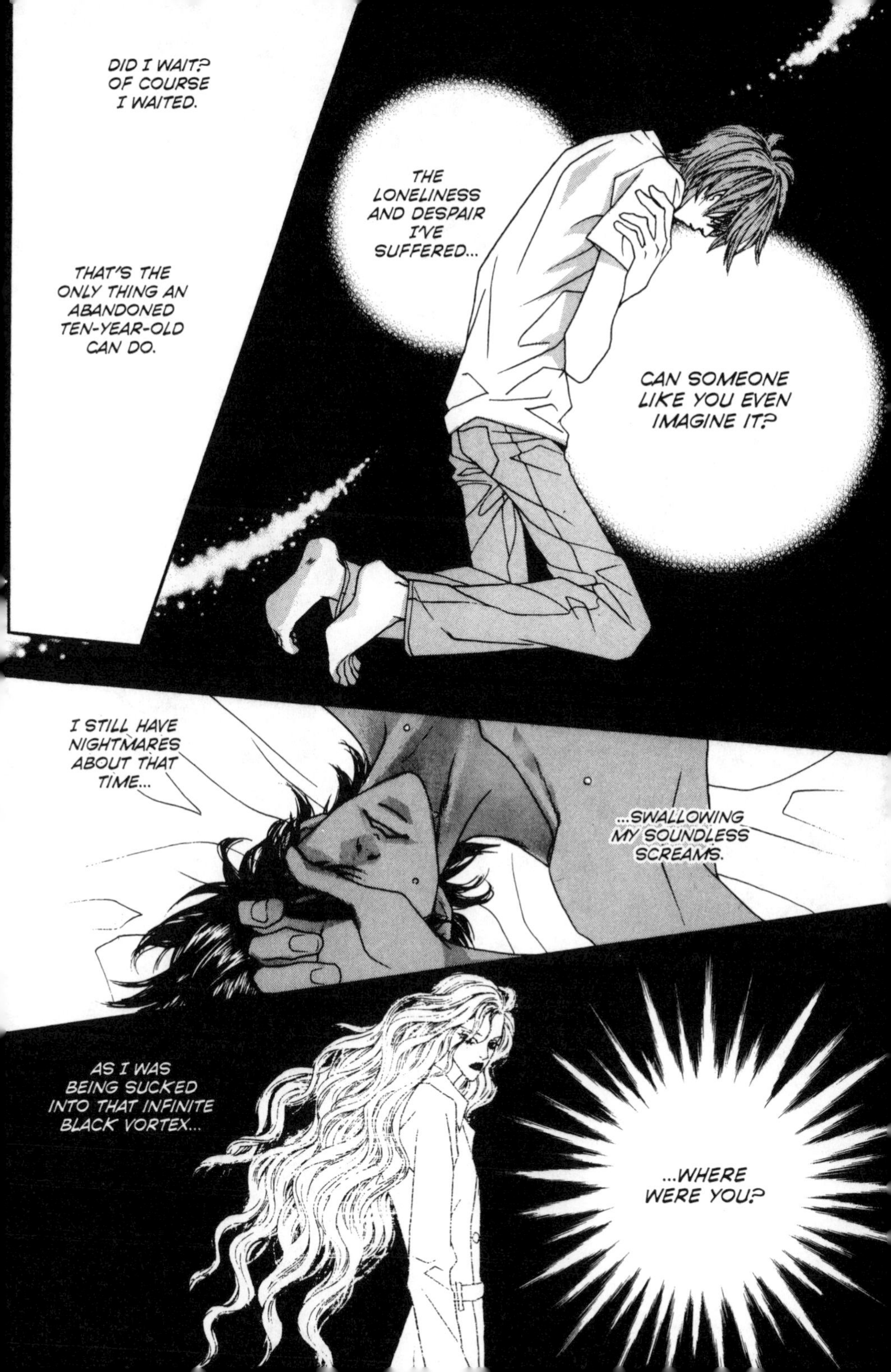

DID I WAIT? OF COURSE I WAITED.
THE LONELINESS AND DESPAIR I'VE SUFFERED...
THAT'S THE ONLY THING AN ABANDONED TEN-YEAR-OLD CAN DO.
CAN SOMEONE LIKE YOU EVEN IMAGINE IT?
I STILL HAVE NIGHTMARES ABOUT THAT TIME...
...SWALLOWING MY SOUNDLESS SCREAMS.
AS I WAS BEING SUCKED INTO THAT INFINITE BLACK VORTEX...
...WHERE WERE YOU?

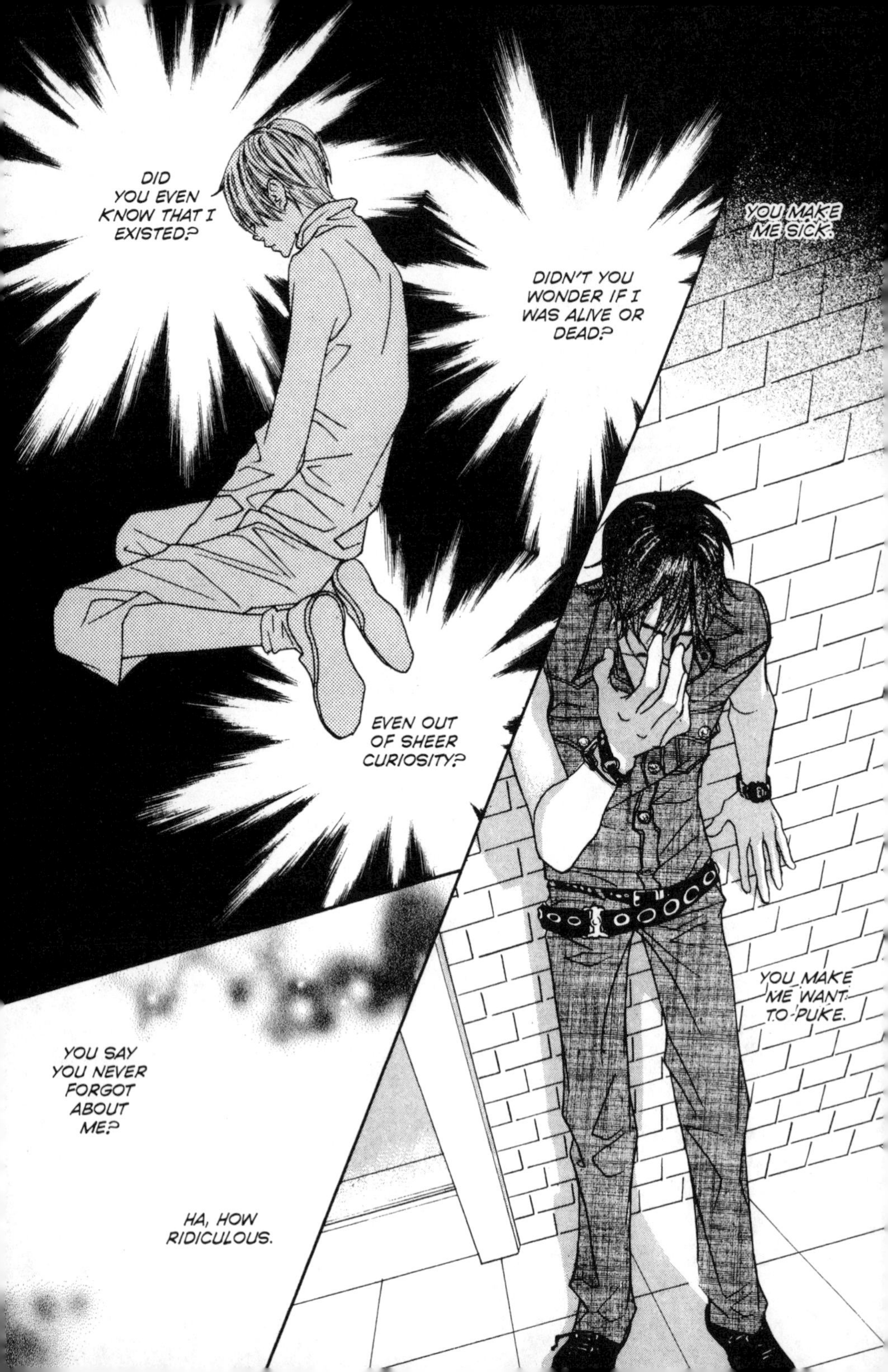
DID YOU EVEN KNOW THAT I EXISTED?
DIDN'T YOU WONDER IF I WAS ALIVE OR DEAD?
EVEN OUT OF SHEER CURIOSITY?
YOU SAY YOU NEVER FORGOT ABOUT ME?
HA, HOW RIDICULOUS.
YOU MAKE ME SICK.
YOU MAKE ME WANT TO PUKE.

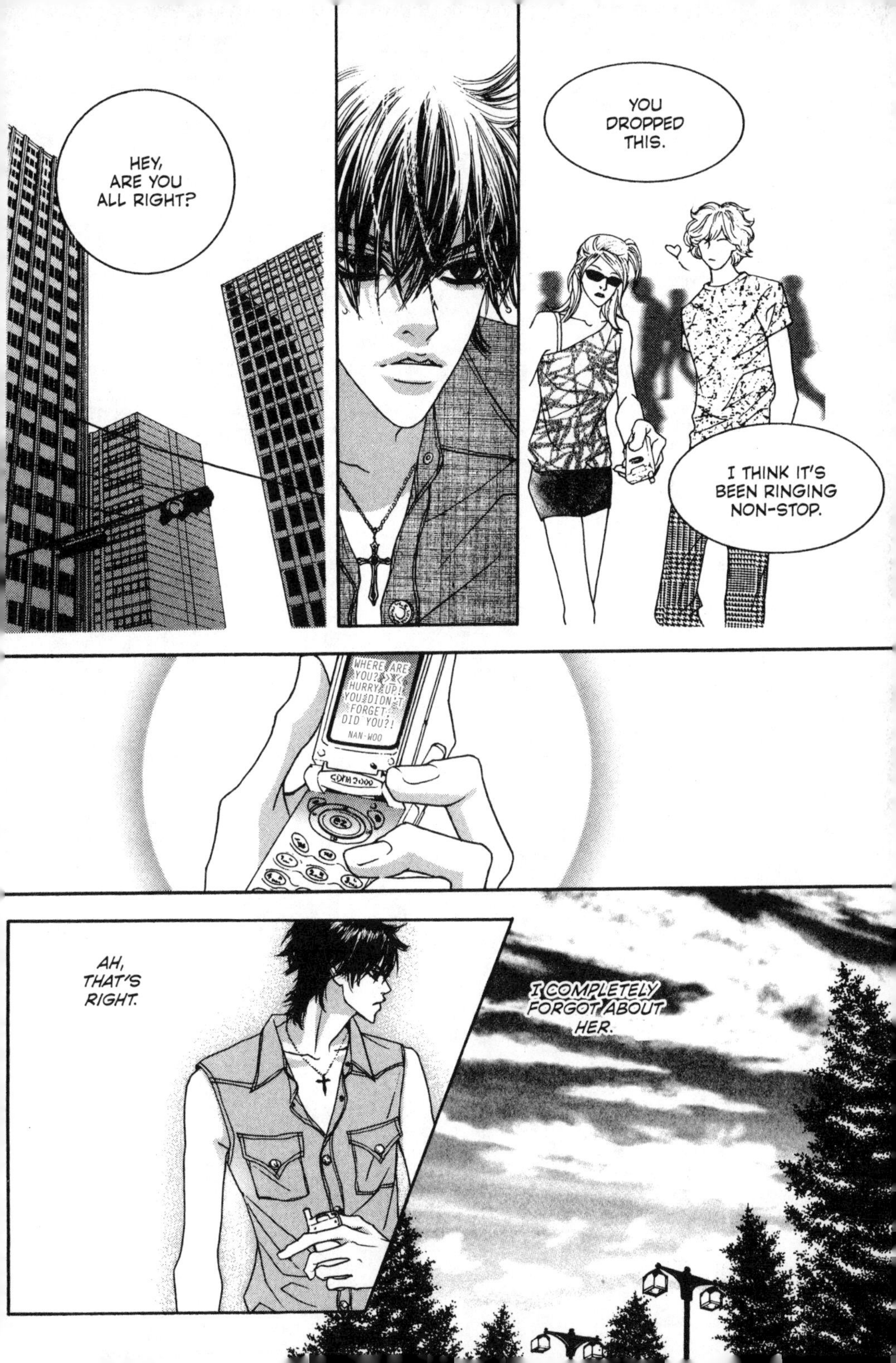
HEY, ARE YOU ALL RIGHT?
YOU DROPPED THIS.
I THINK IT'S BEEN RINGING NON-STOP.
WHERE ARE YOU?! HURRY UP! YOU DIDN'T FORGET DID YOU?!
NAN-WOO
AH, THAT'S RIGHT.
I COMPLETELY FORGOT ABOUT HER.

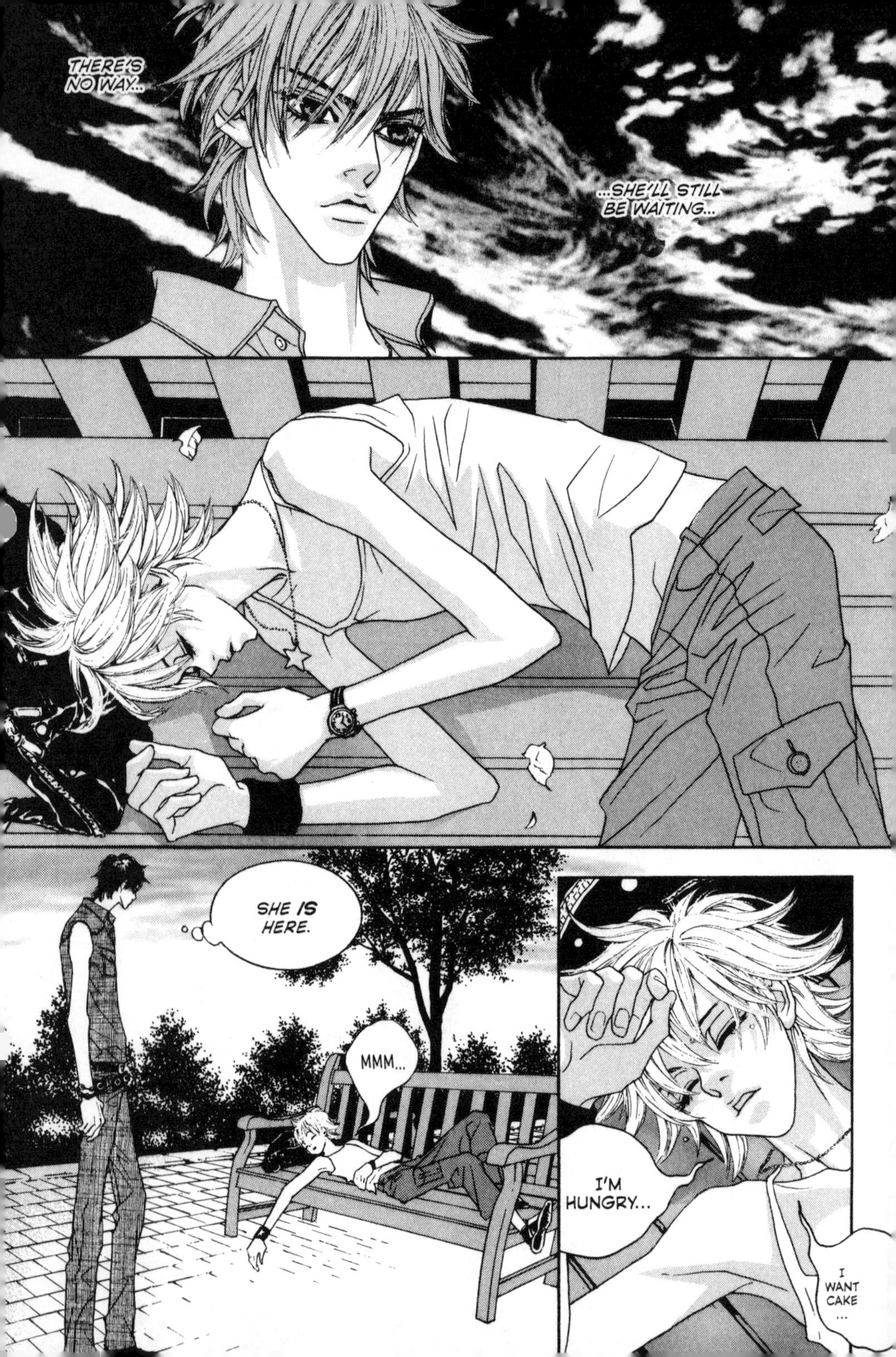
THERE'S NO WAY...
...SHE'LL STILL BE WAITING...
SHE IS HERE.
MMM...
I'M HUNGRY...
I WANT CAKE ...

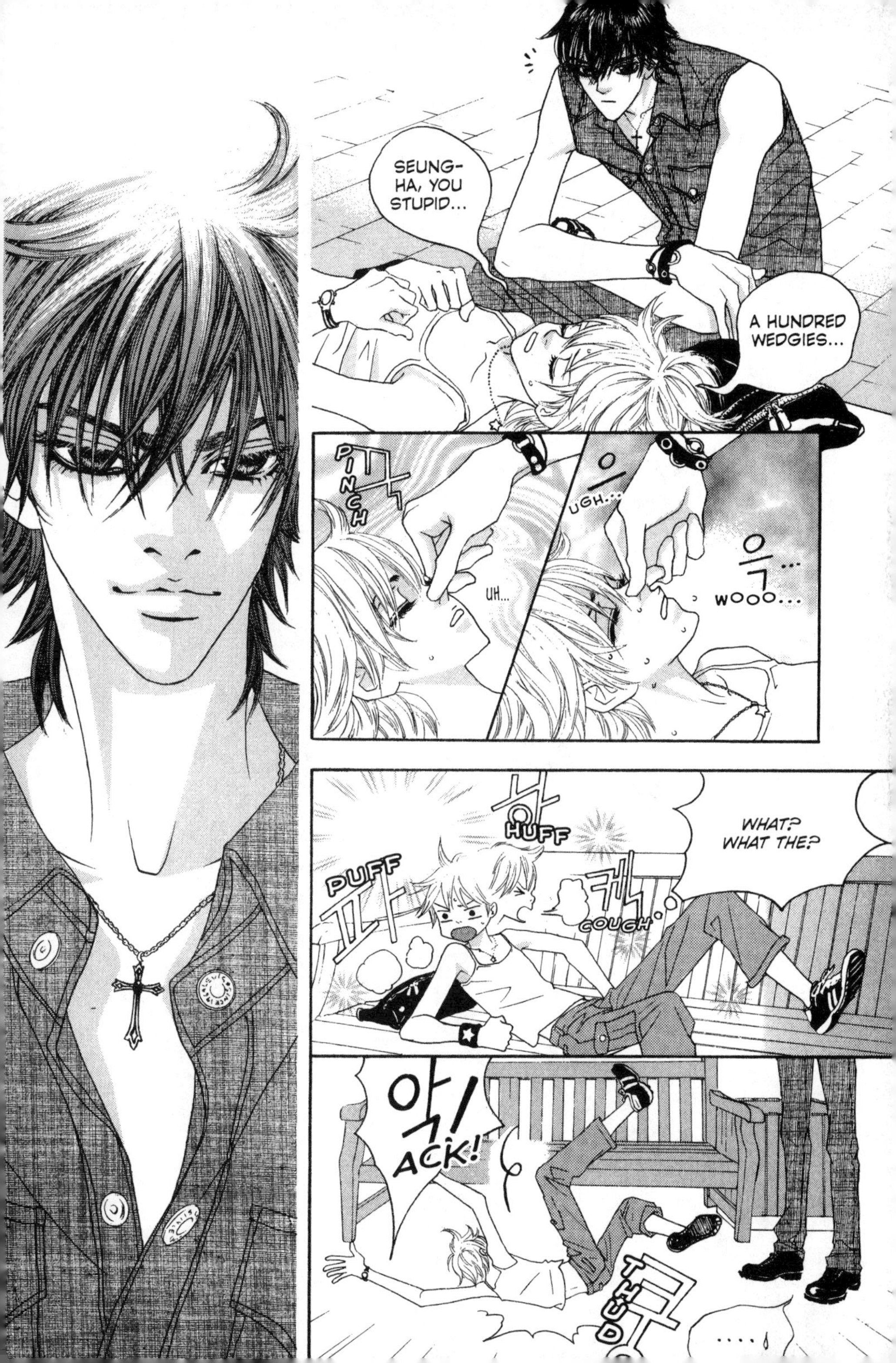
SEUNG-HA, YOU STUPID...
A HUNDRED WEDGIES...
PINCH
UH...
UGH...
WOOO...
HUFF
PUFF
COUGH
WHAT? WHAT THE?
ACK!
THUD
....

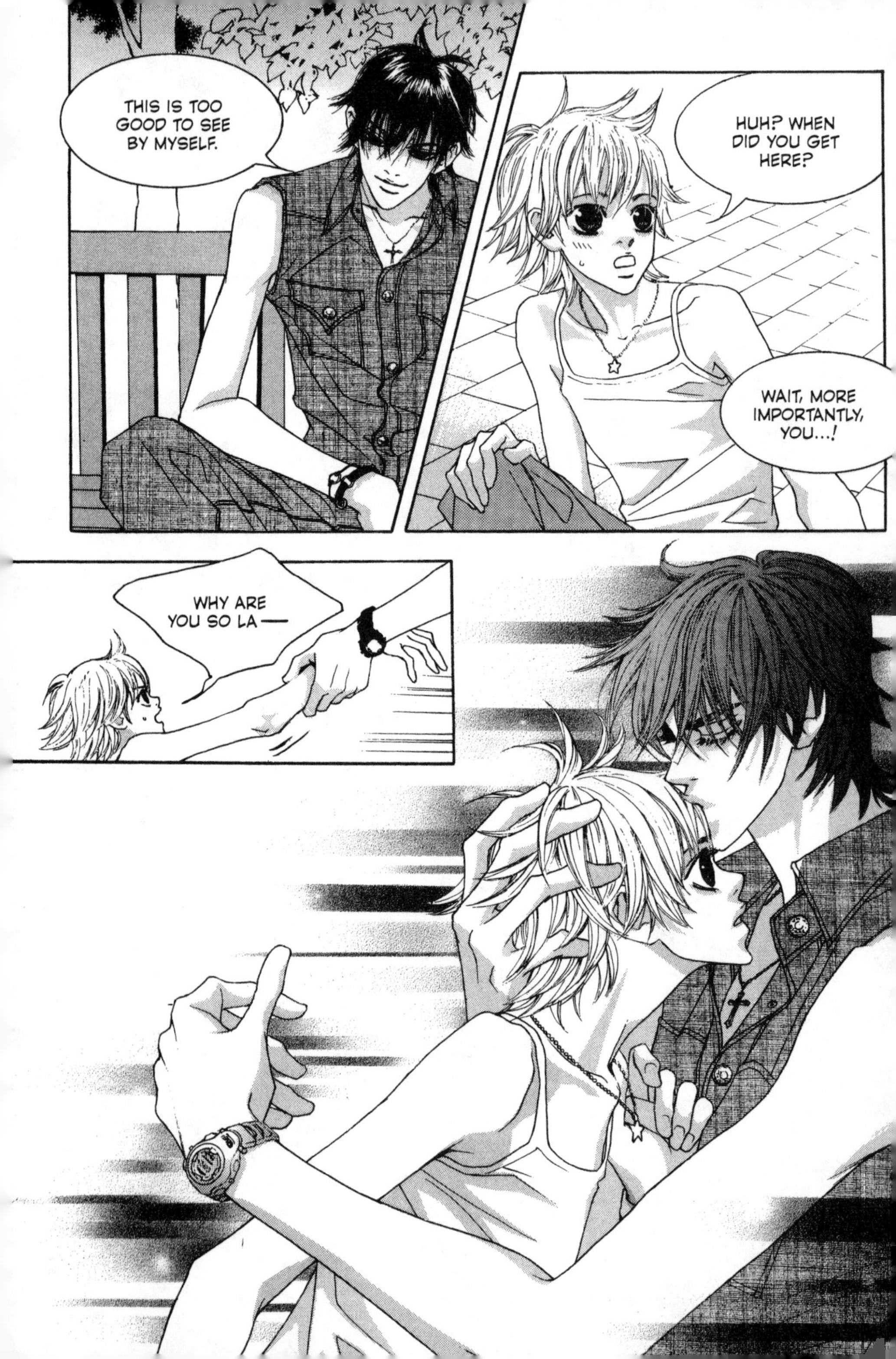
THIS IS TOO GOOD TO SEE BY MYSELF.
HUH? WHEN DID YOU GET HERE?
WAIT, MORE IMPORTANTLY, YOU...!
WHY ARE YOU SO LA—

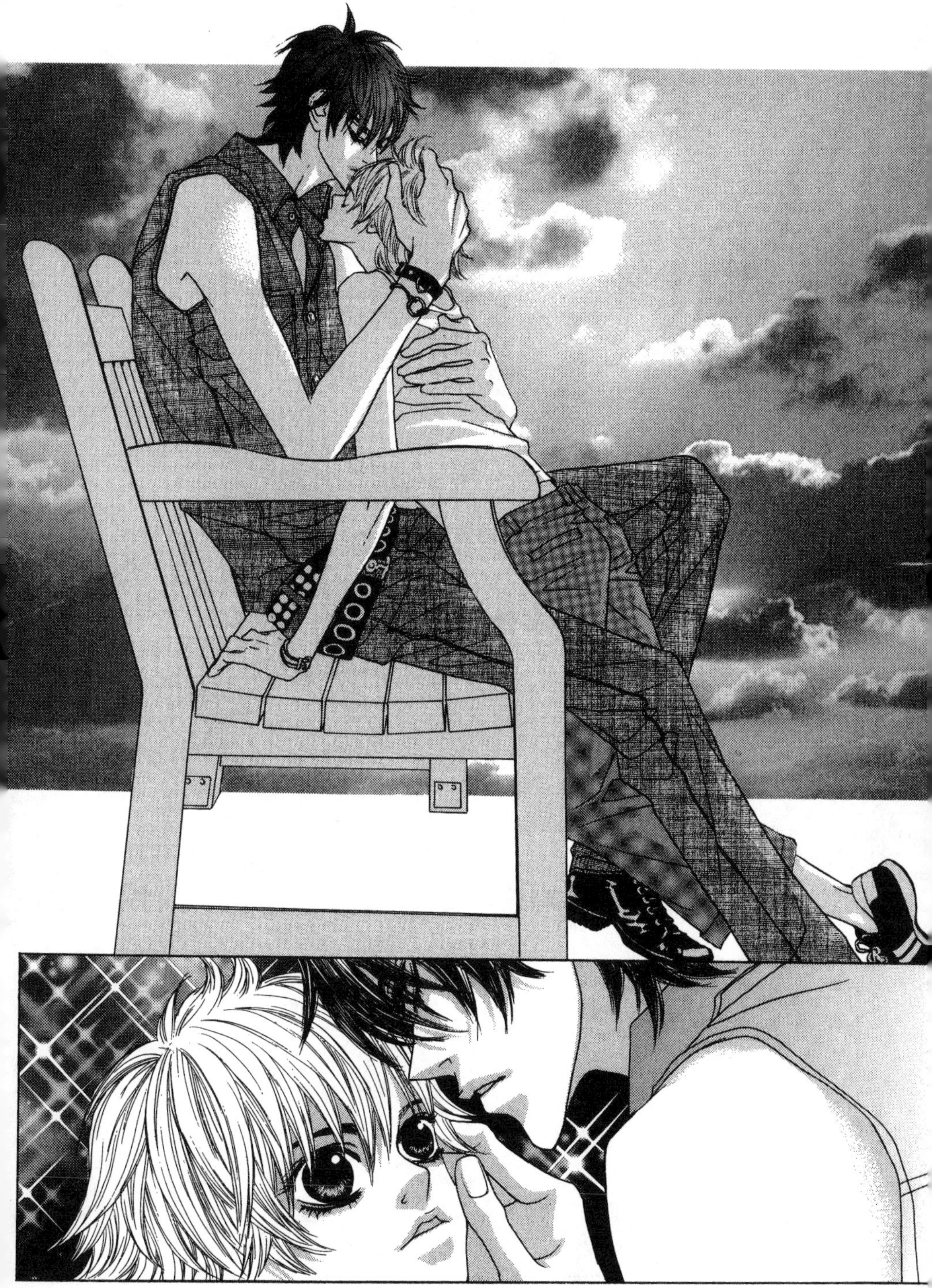

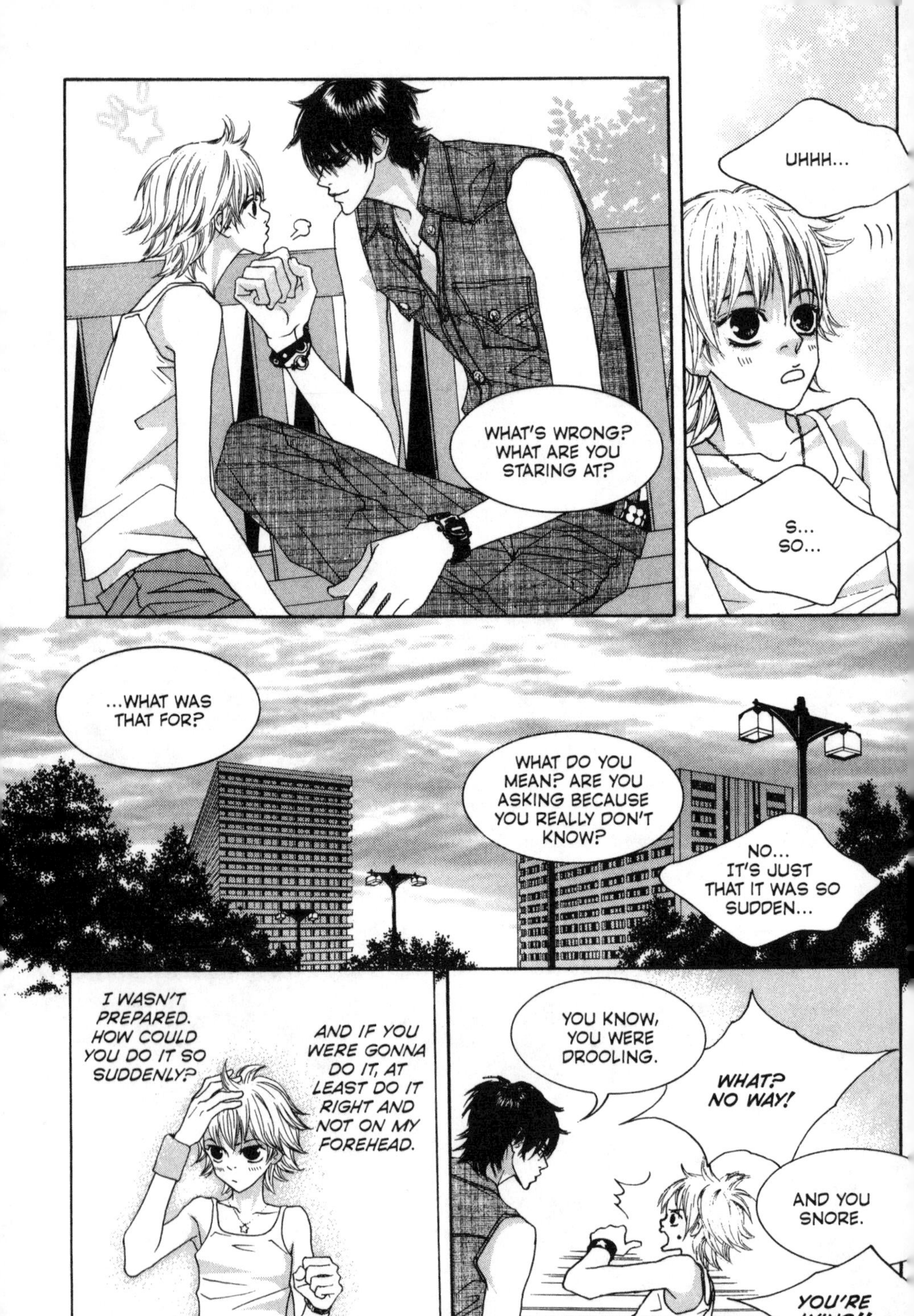
WHAT'S WRONG? WHAT ARE YOU STARING AT?
UHHH...
S... SO...
...WHAT WAS THAT FOR?
WHAT DO YOU MEAN? ARE YOU ASKING BECAUSE YOU REALLY DON'T KNOW?
NO... IT'S JUST THAT IT WAS SO SUDDEN...
I WASN'T PREPARED. HOW COULD YOU DO IT SO SUDDENLY?
AND IF YOU WERE GONNA DO IT, AT LEAST DO IT RIGHT AND NOT ON MY FOREHEAD.
YOU KNOW, YOU WERE DROOLING.
WHAT? NO WAY!
AND YOU SNORE.
YOU'RE LYING!!

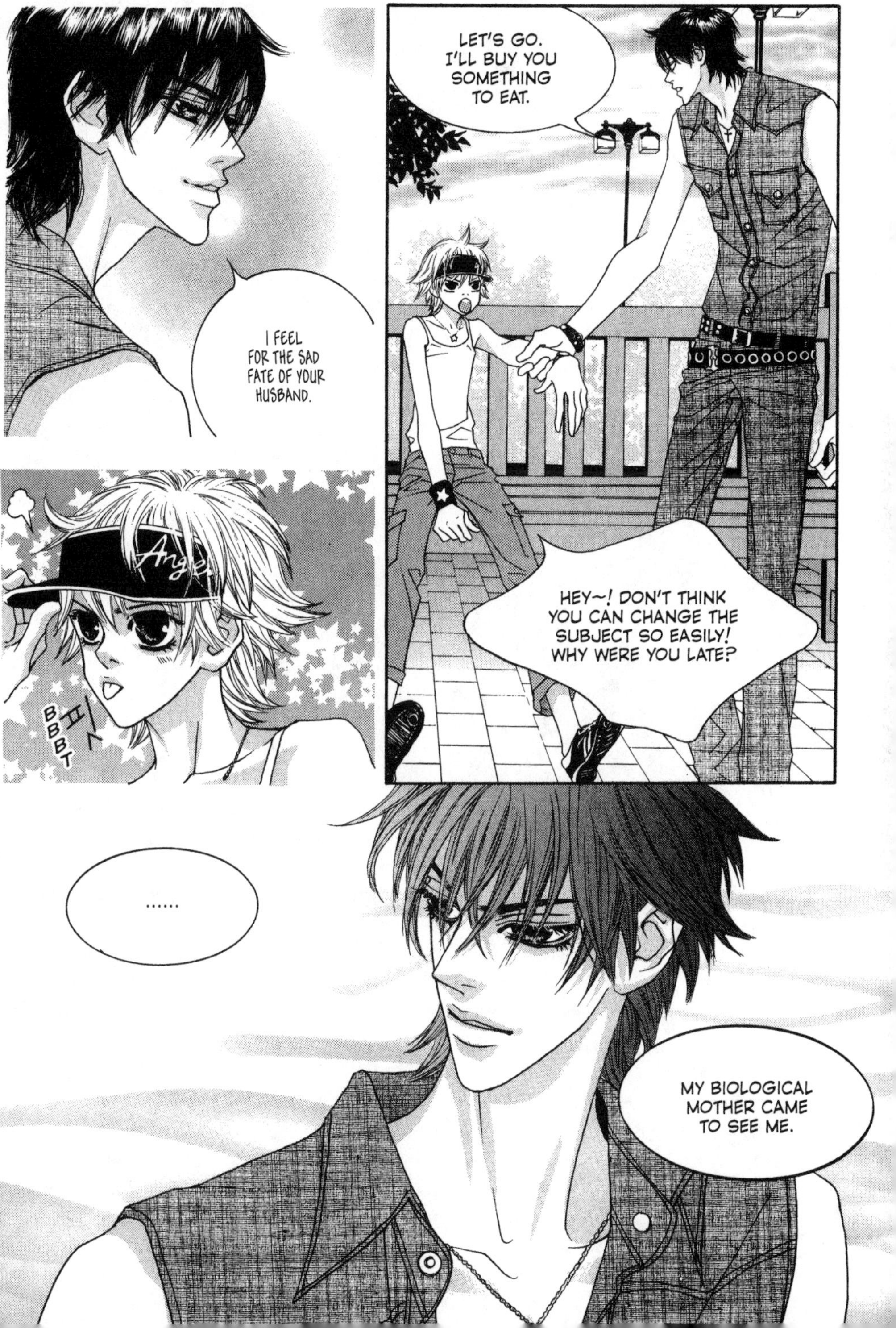
I FEEL FOR THE SAD FATE OF YOUR HUSBAND.
BBBT
LET'S GO. I'LL BUY YOU SOMETHING TO EAT.
HEY~! DON'T THINK YOU CAN CHANGE THE SUBJECT SO EASILY! WHY WERE YOU LATE?
......
MY BIOLOGICAL MOTHER CAME TO SEE ME.

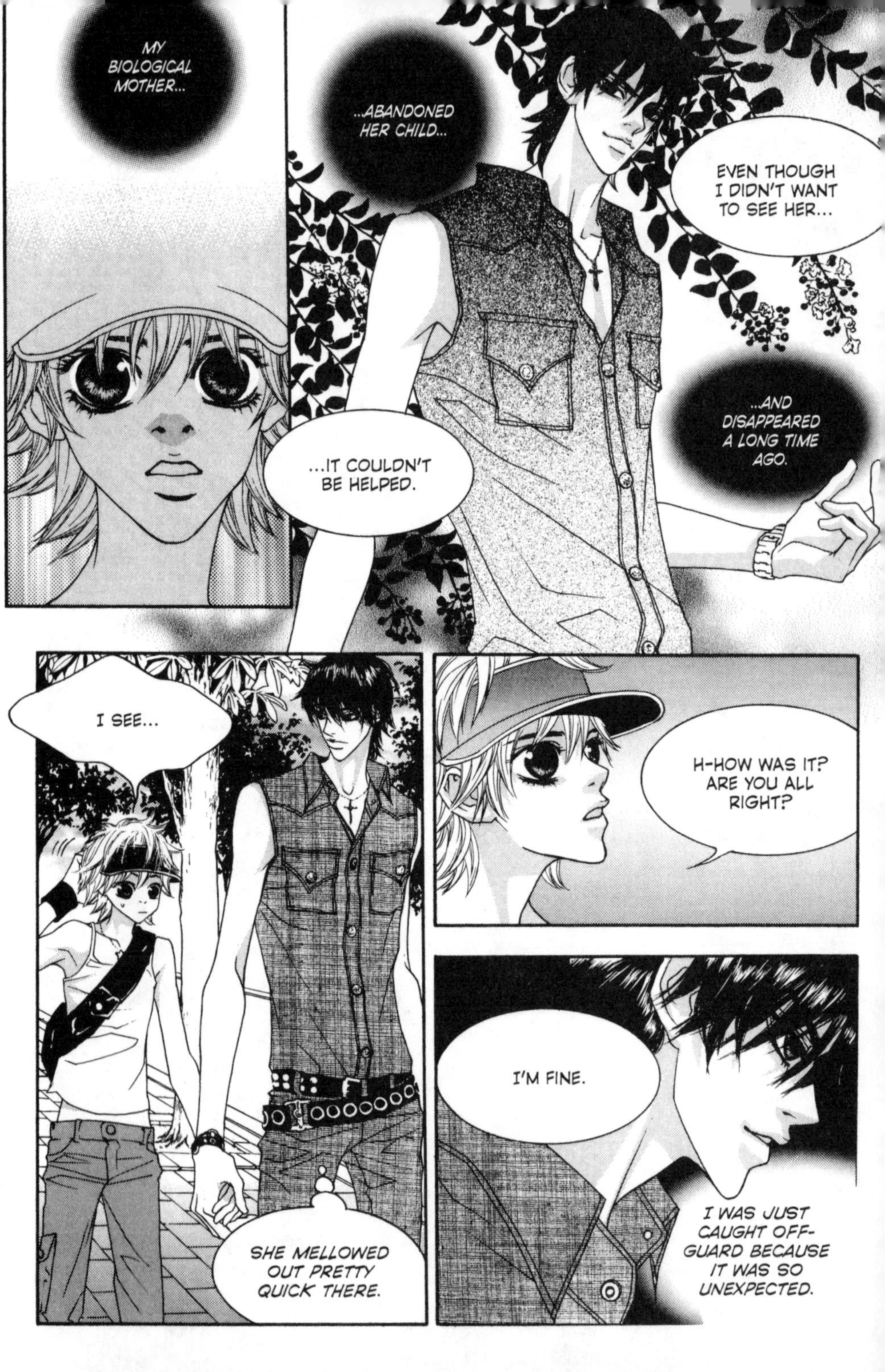
MY BIOLOGICAL MOTHER...
...ABANDONED HER CHILD...
EVEN THOUGH I DIDN'T WANT TO SEE HER...
...AND DISAPPEARED A LONG TIME AGO.
...IT COULDN'T BE HELPED.
I SEE...
H-HOW WAS IT? ARE YOU ALL RIGHT?
SHE MELLOWED OUT PRETTY QUICK THERE.
I'M FINE.
I WAS JUST CAUGHT OFF-GUARD BECAUSE IT WAS SO UNEXPECTED.

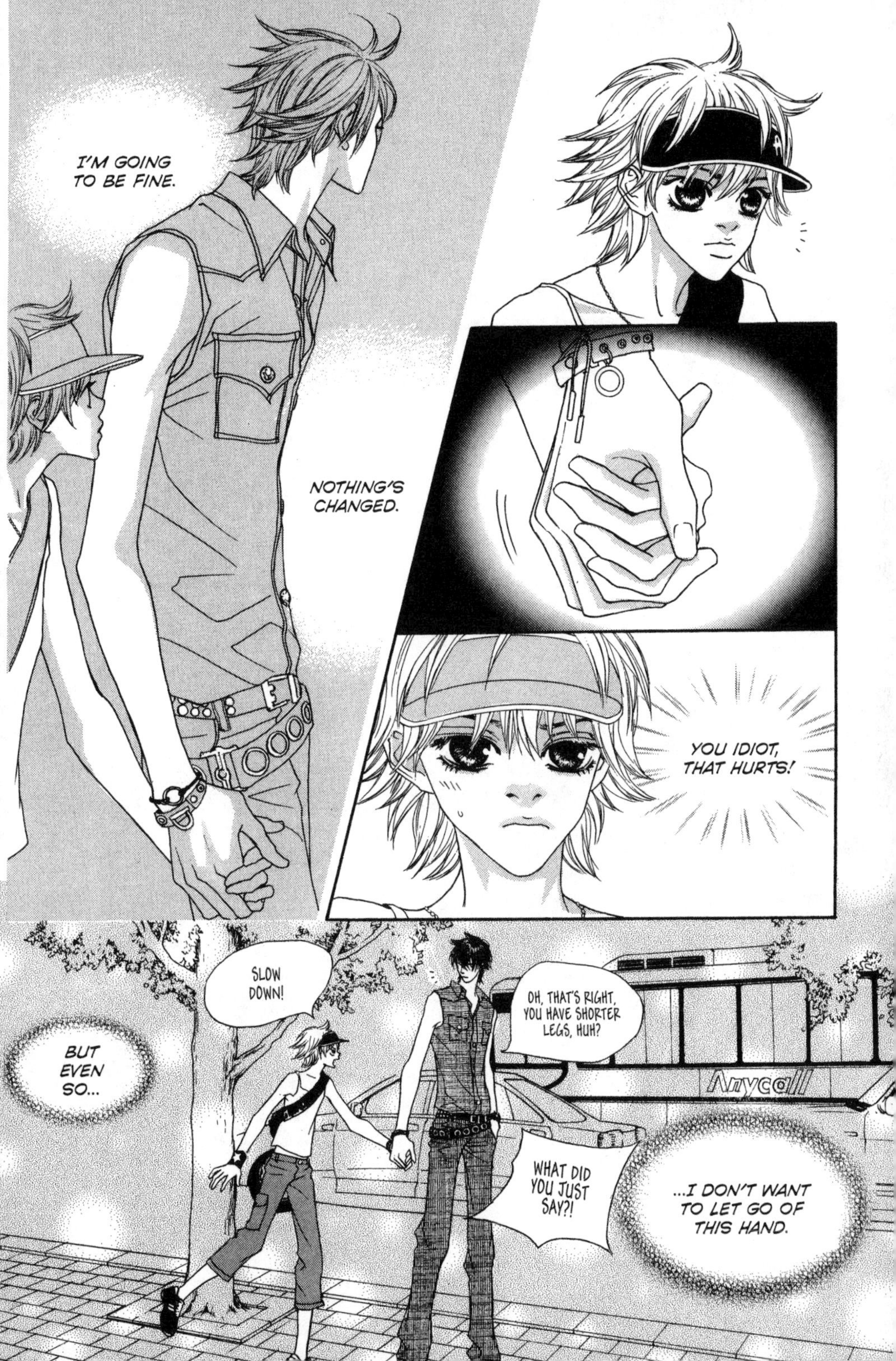
I'M GOING TO BE FINE.
NOTHING'S CHANGED.
YOU IDIOT, THAT HURTS!
BUT EVEN SO...
SLOW DOWN!
OH, THAT'S RIGHT, YOU HAVE SHORTER LEGS, HUH?
WHAT DID YOU JUST SAY?!
...I DON'T WANT TO LET GO OF THIS HAND.
Anycall

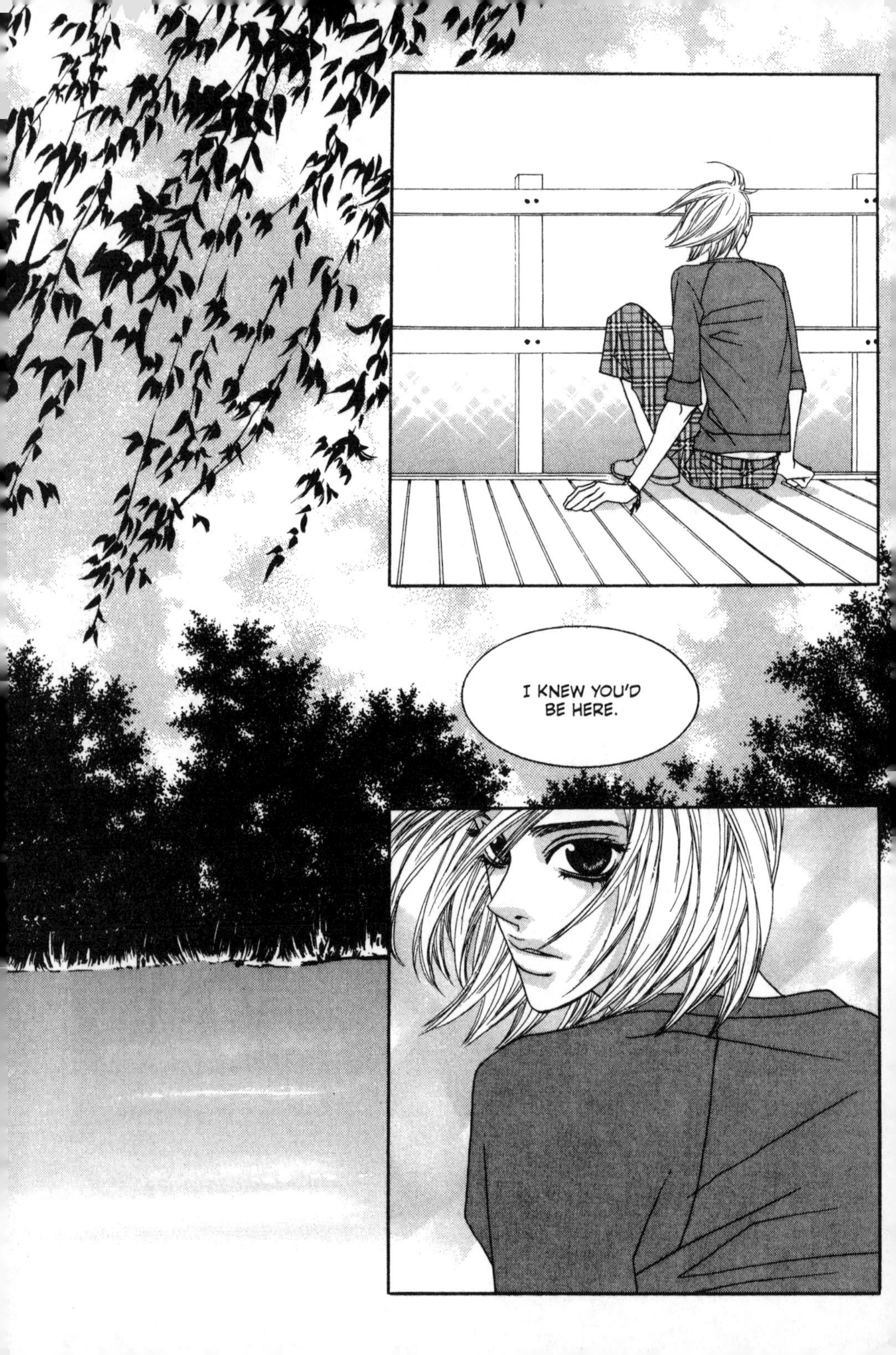
I KNEW YOU'D BE HERE.

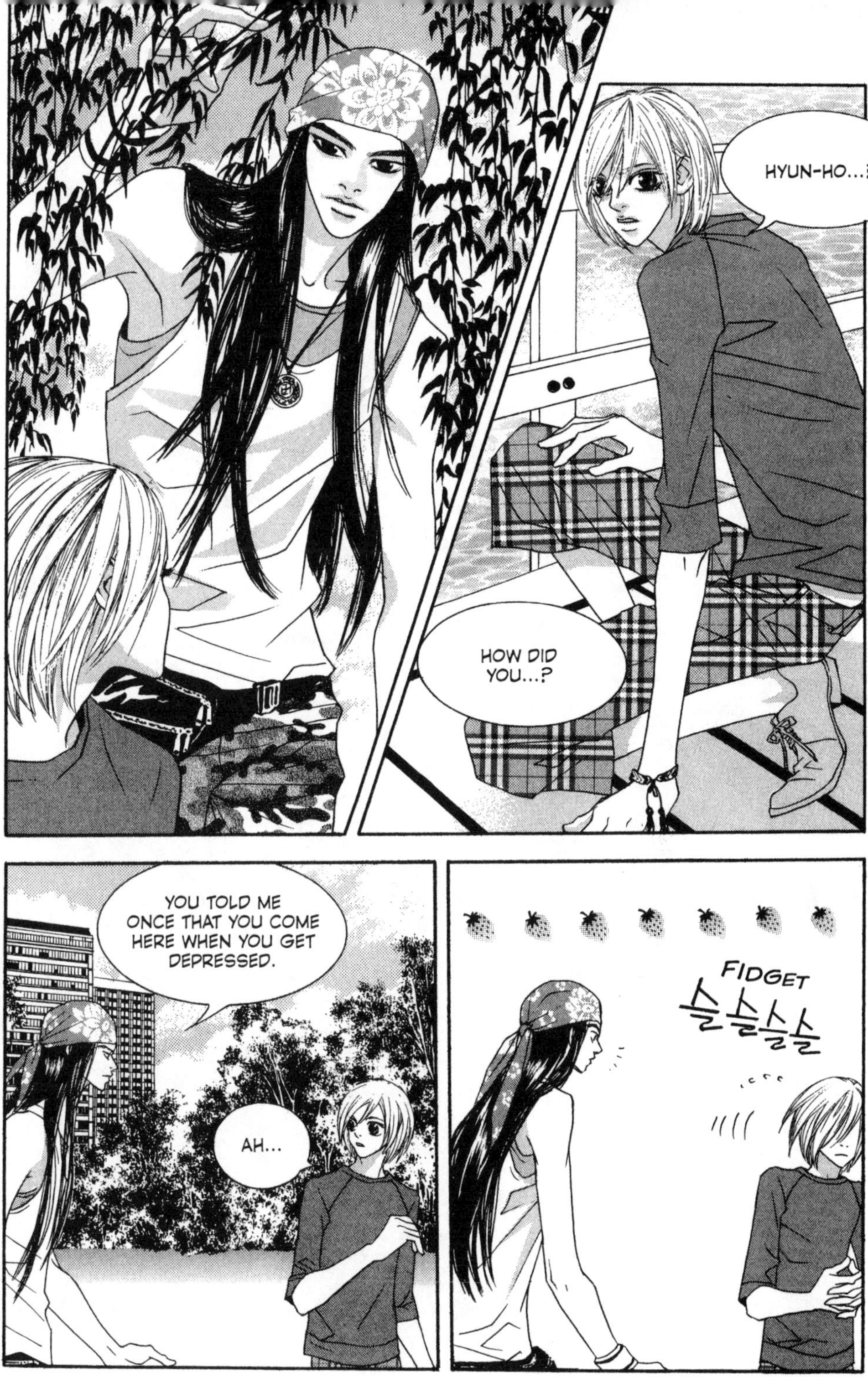
HYUN-HO...?
HOW DID YOU...?
YOU TOLD ME ONCE THAT YOU COME HERE WHEN YOU GET DEPRESSED.
AH...
FIDGET
슬슬슬슬

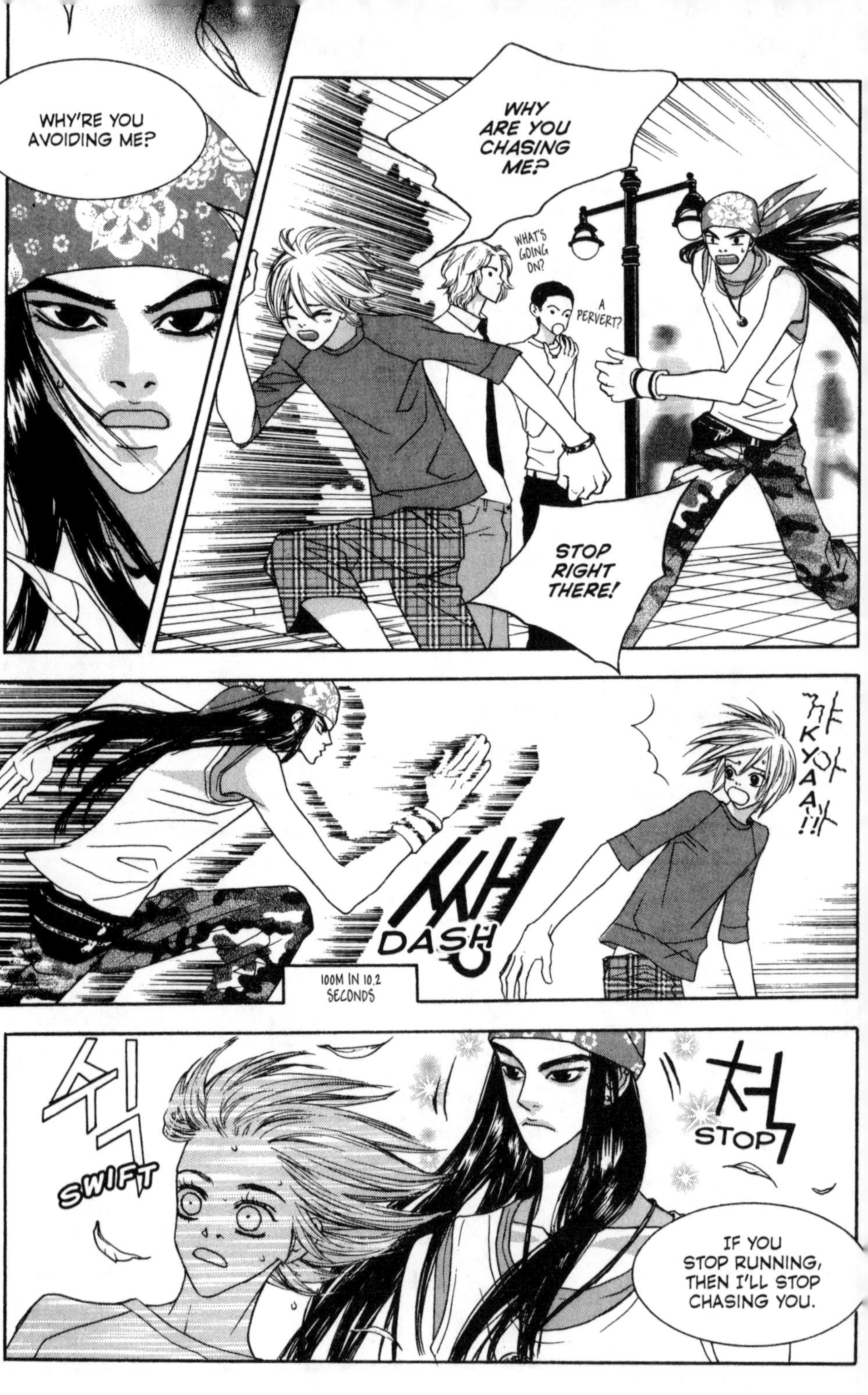
WHY'RE YOU AVOIDING ME?
WHY ARE YOU CHASING ME?
WHAT'S GOING ON?
A PERVERT?
STOP RIGHT THERE!
캬아!!
KYAA!!
쌔
DASH
100M IN 10.2 SECONDS
쉬
SWIFT
척
STOP
IF YOU STOP RUNNING, THEN I'LL STOP CHASING YOU.

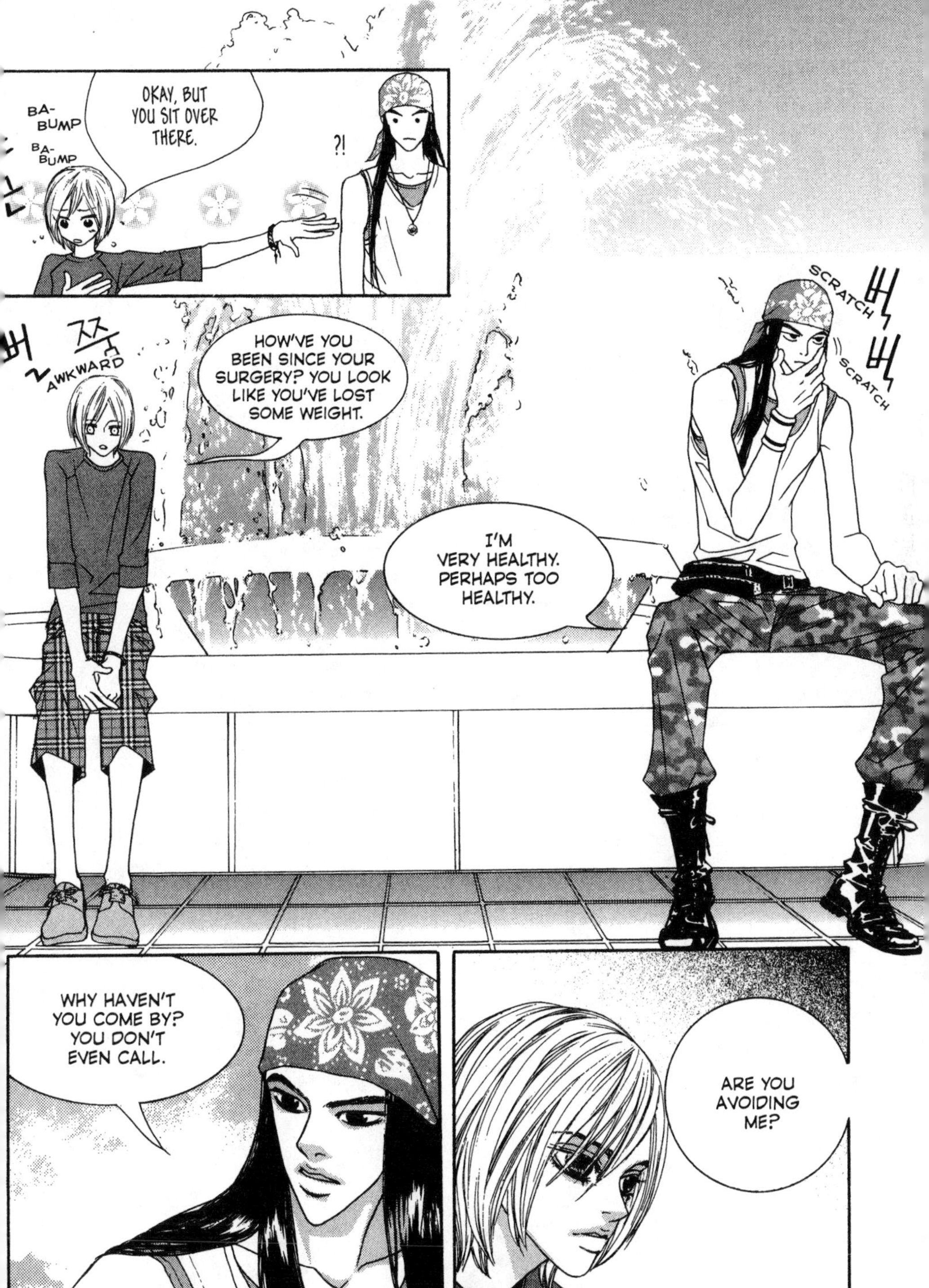
BA-BUMP
BA-BUMP
OKAY, BUT YOU SIT OVER THERE.
?!
AWKWARD
HOW'VE YOU BEEN SINCE YOUR SURGERY? YOU LOOK LIKE YOU'VE LOST SOME WEIGHT.
SCRATCH
SCRATCH
I'M VERY HEALTHY. PERHAPS TOO HEALTHY.
WHY HAVEN'T YOU COME BY? YOU DON'T EVEN CALL.
ARE YOU AVOIDING ME?

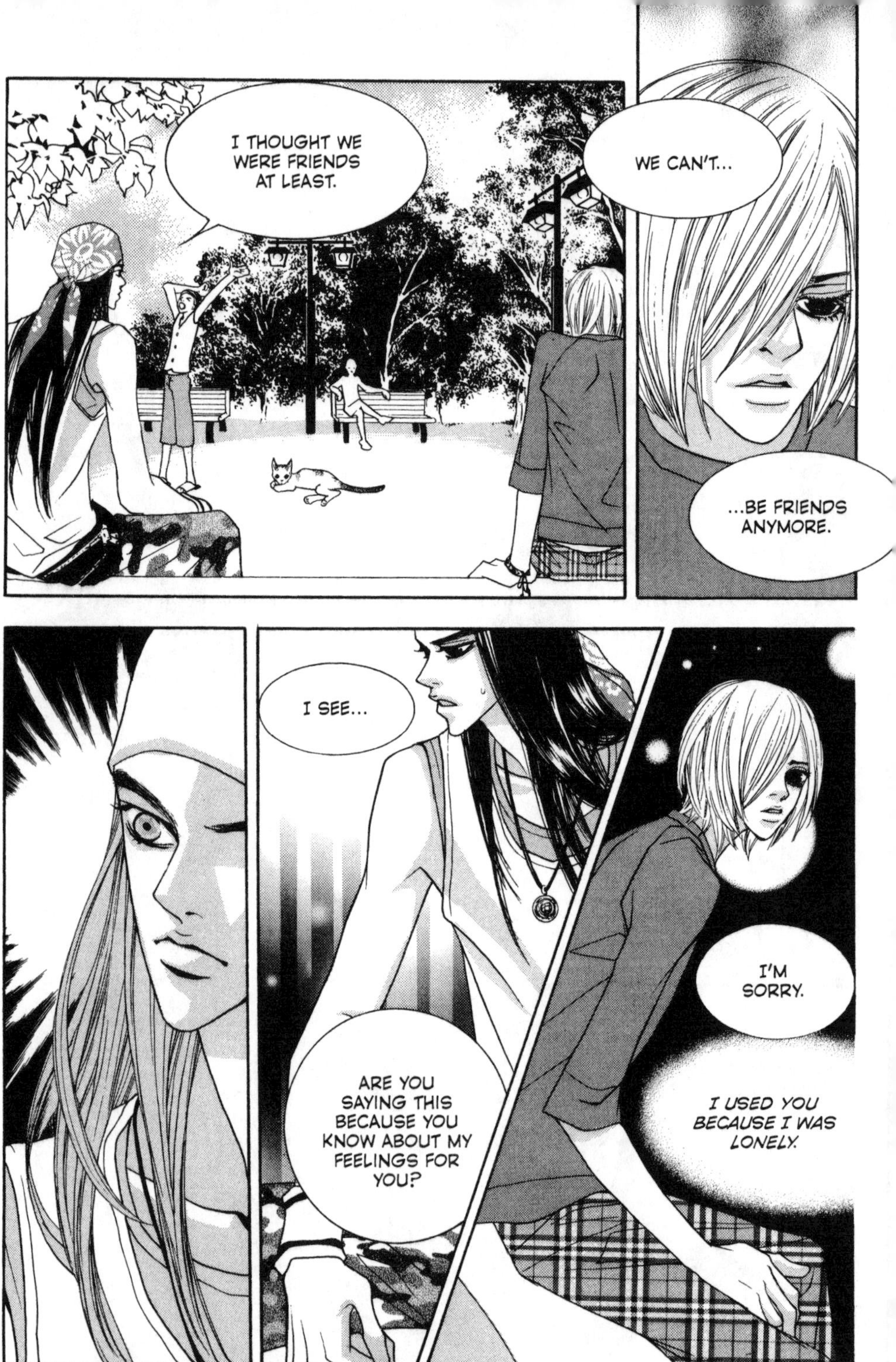
I THOUGHT WE WERE FRIENDS AT LEAST.
WE CAN'T...
...BE FRIENDS ANYMORE.
I SEE...
ARE YOU SAYING THIS BECAUSE YOU KNOW ABOUT MY FEELINGS FOR YOU?
I'M SORRY.
I USED YOU BECAUSE I WAS LONELY.

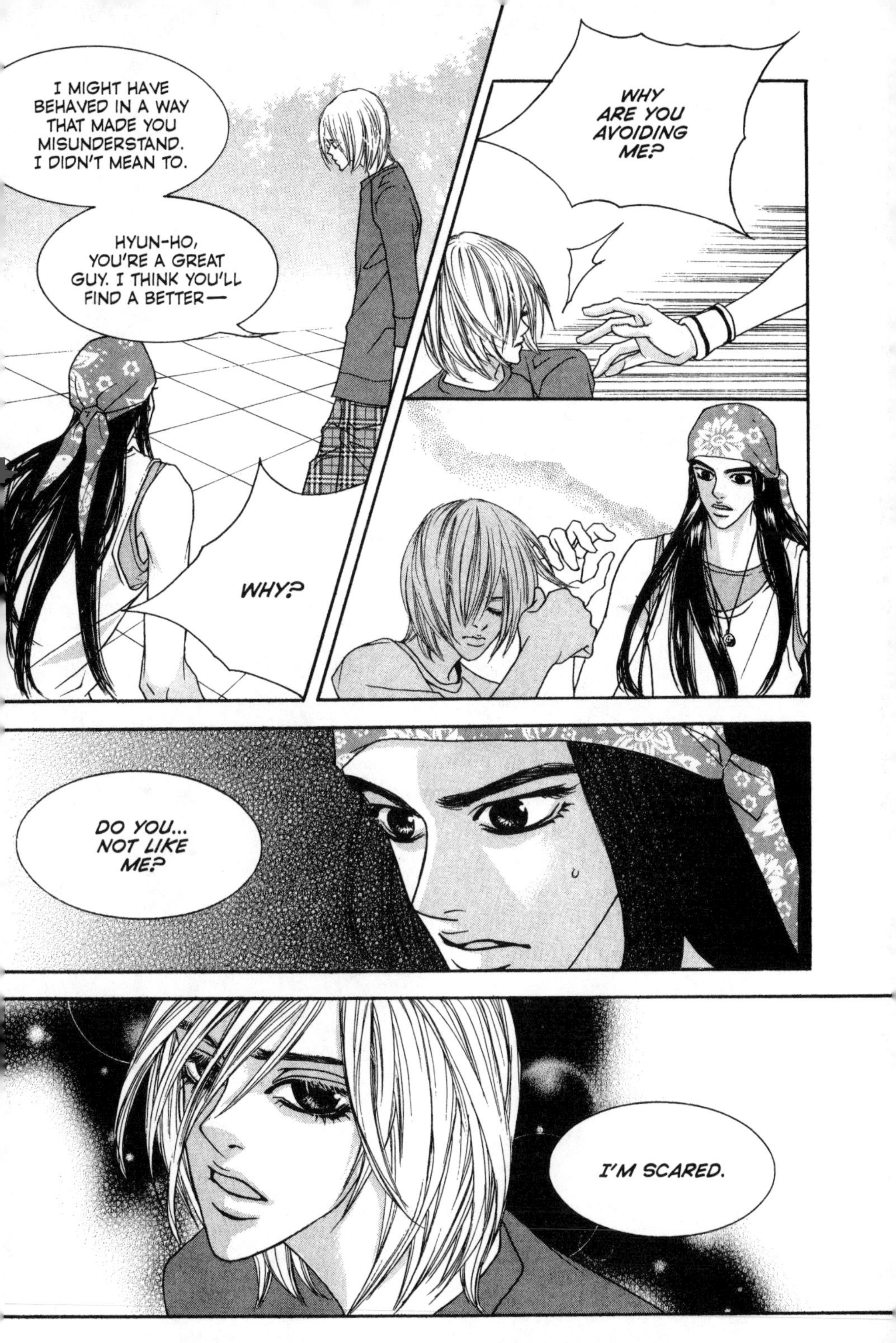
I MIGHT HAVE BEHAVED IN A WAY THAT MADE YOU MISUNDERSTAND. I DIDN'T MEAN TO.
HYUN-HO, YOU'RE A GREAT GUY. I THINK YOU'LL FIND A BETTER—
WHY?
WHY ARE YOU AVOIDING ME?
DO YOU... NOT LIKE ME?
I'M SCARED.

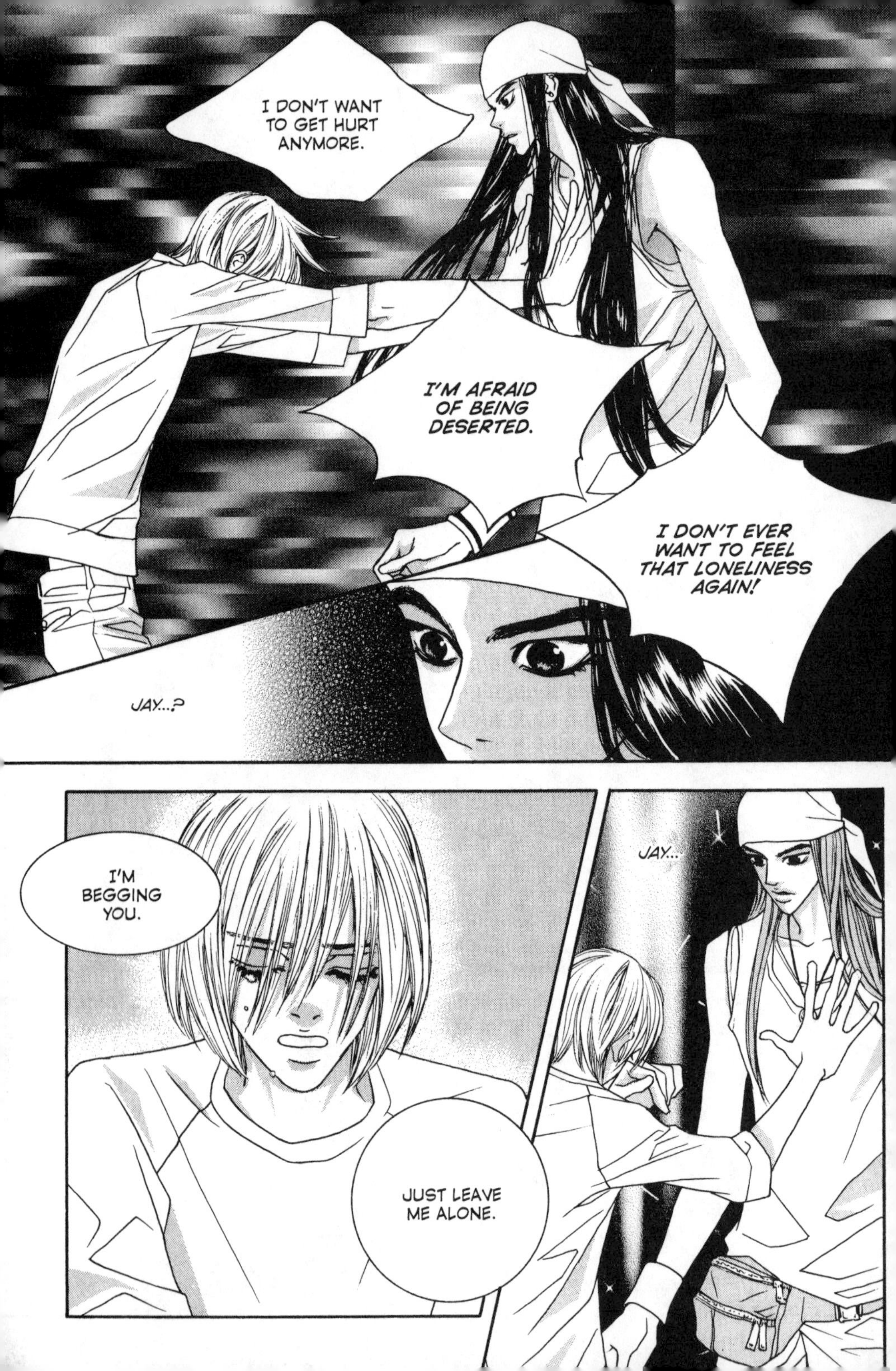
I DON'T WANT TO GET HURT ANYMORE.
I'M AFRAID OF BEING DESERTED.
I DON'T EVER WANT TO FEEL THAT LONELINESS AGAIN!
JAY...?
I'M BEGGING YOU.
JUST LEAVE ME ALONE.
JAY...

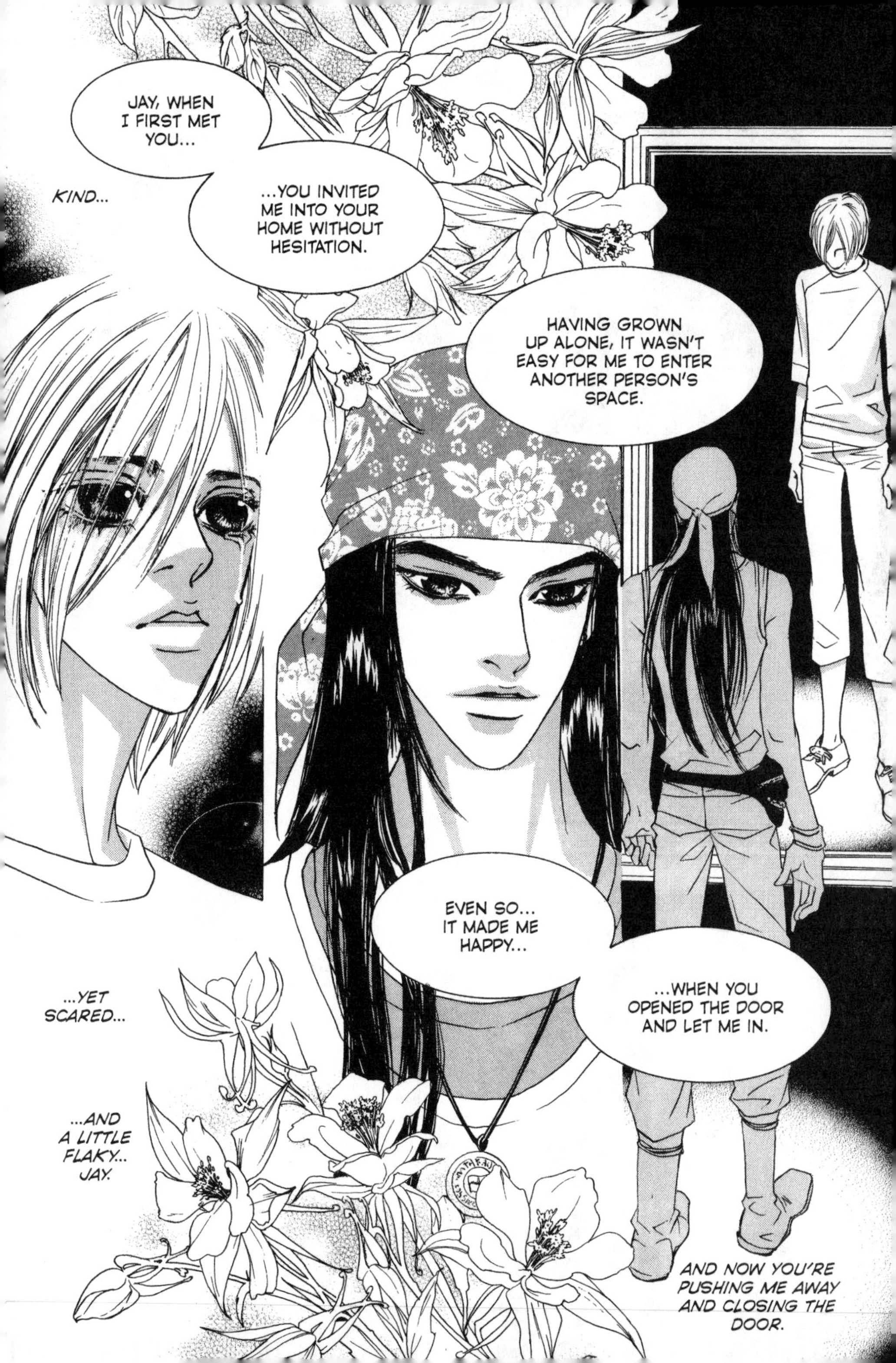
JAY, WHEN I FIRST MET YOU...
...YOU INVITED ME INTO YOUR HOME WITHOUT HESITATION.
KIND...
HAVING GROWN UP ALONE, IT WASN'T EASY FOR ME TO ENTER ANOTHER PERSON'S SPACE.
EVEN SO... IT MADE ME HAPPY...
...WHEN YOU OPENED THE DOOR AND LET ME IN.
...YET SCARED...
...AND A LITTLE FLAKY... JAY.
AND NOW YOU'RE PUSHING ME AWAY AND CLOSING THE DOOR.

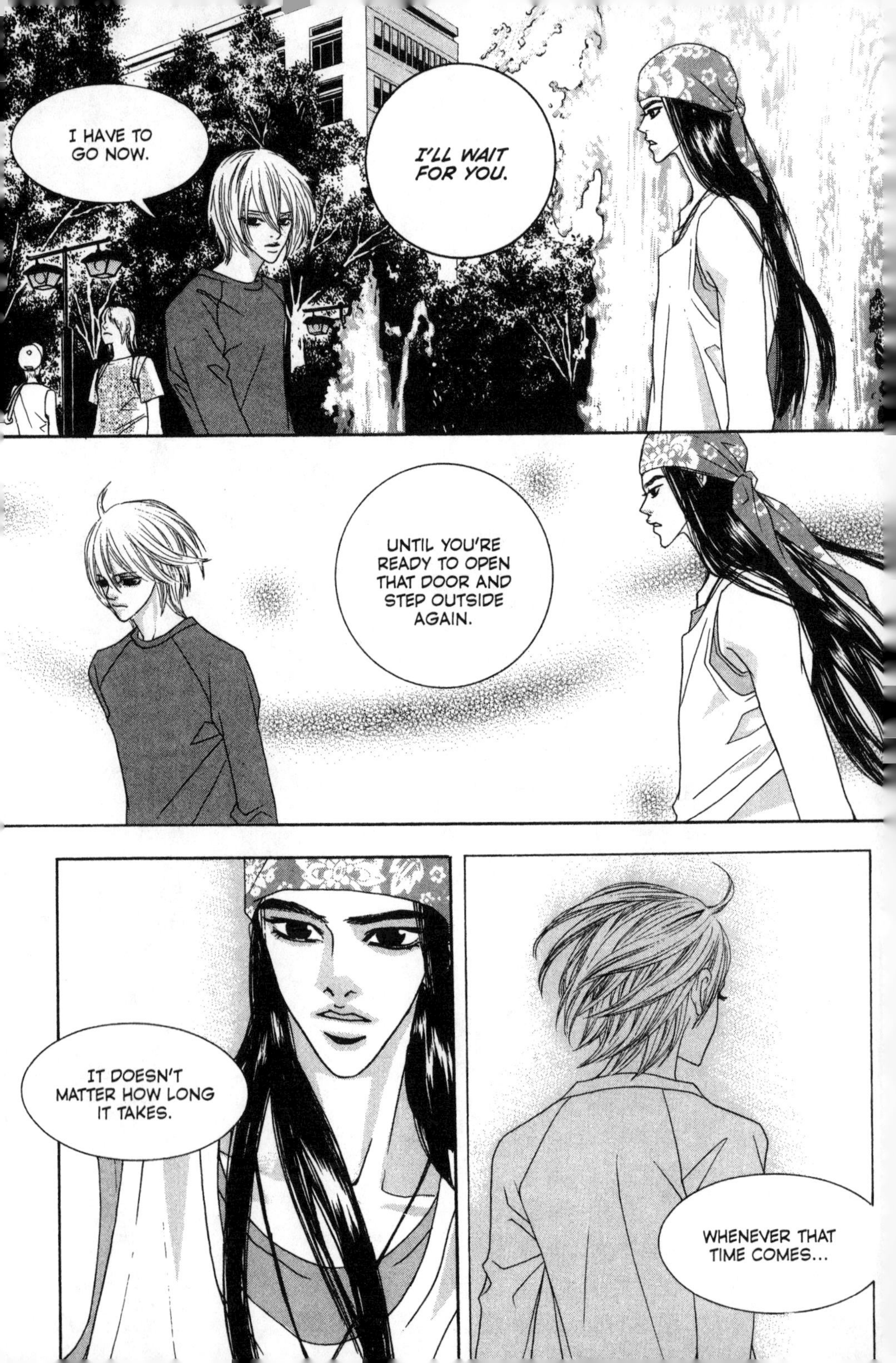
I HAVE TO GO NOW.
I'LL WAIT FOR YOU.
UNTIL YOU'RE READY TO OPEN THAT DOOR AND STEP OUTSIDE AGAIN.
IT DOESN'T MATTER HOW LONG IT TAKES.
WHENEVER THAT TIME COMES...

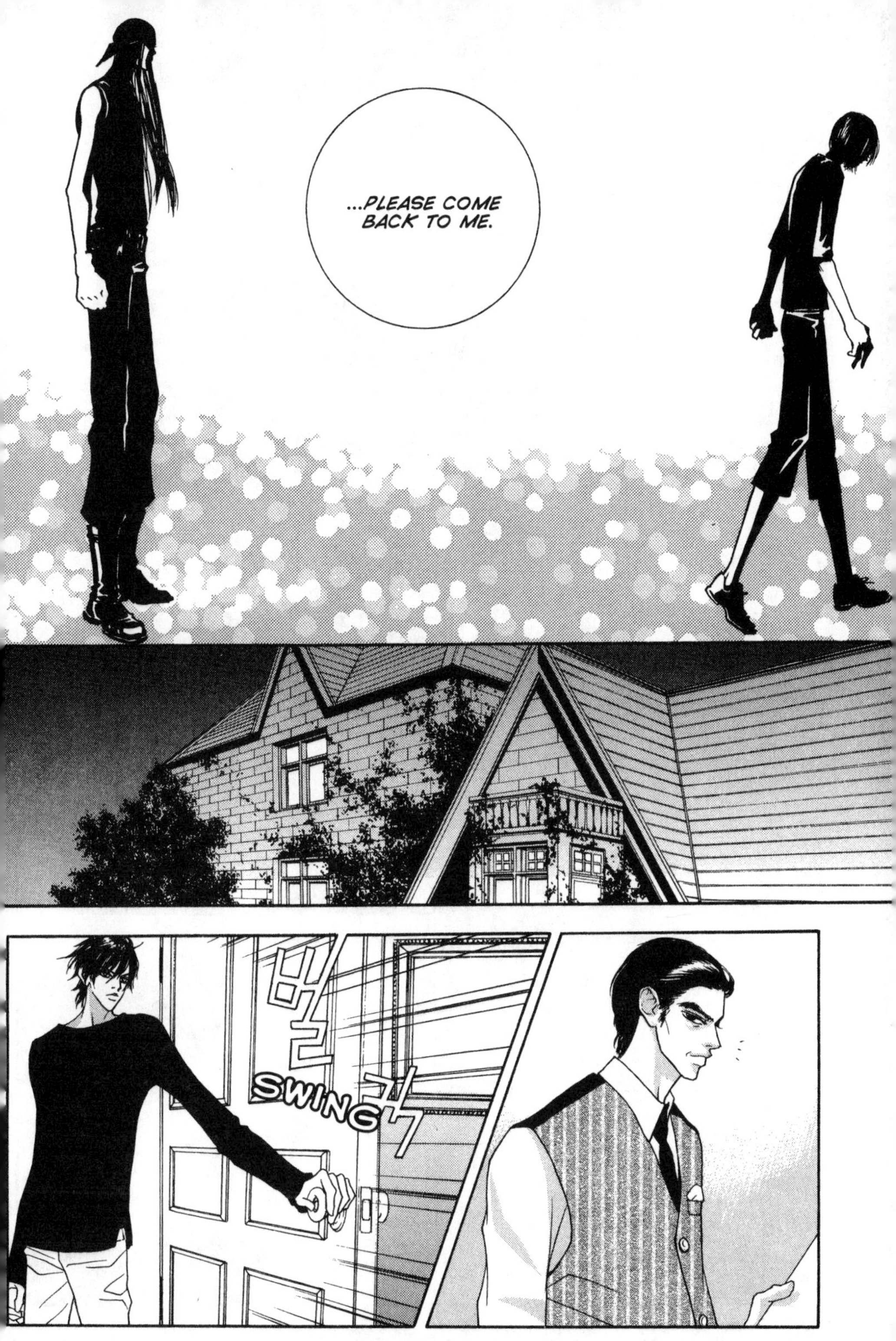
...PLEASE COME BACK TO ME.
벌컥
SWING

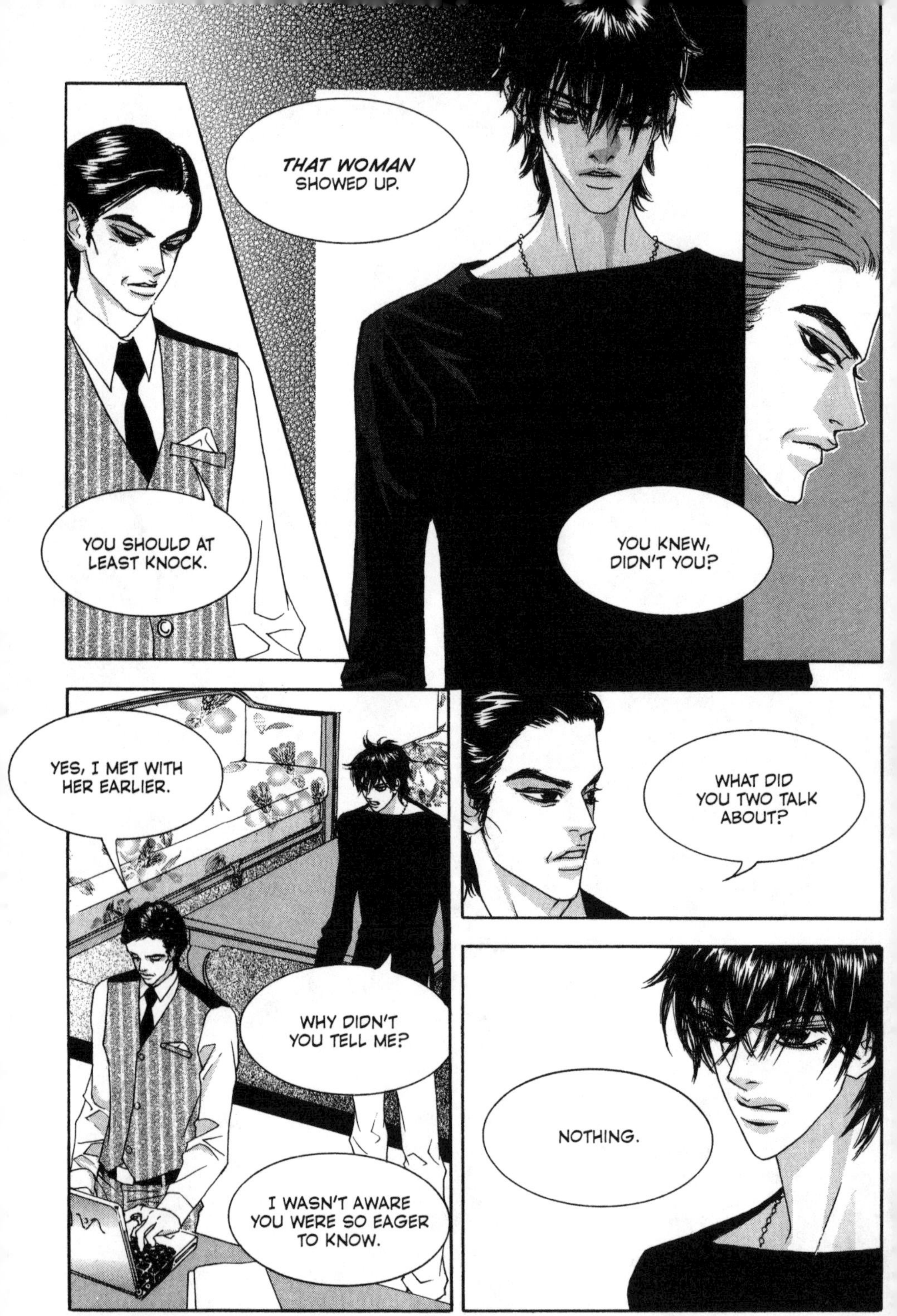
THAT WOMAN SHOWED UP.
YOU SHOULD AT LEAST KNOCK.
YOU KNEW, DIDN'T YOU?
YES, I MET WITH HER EARLIER.
WHY DIDN'T YOU TELL ME?
I WASN'T AWARE YOU WERE SO EAGER TO KNOW.
WHAT DID YOU TWO TALK ABOUT?
NOTHING.

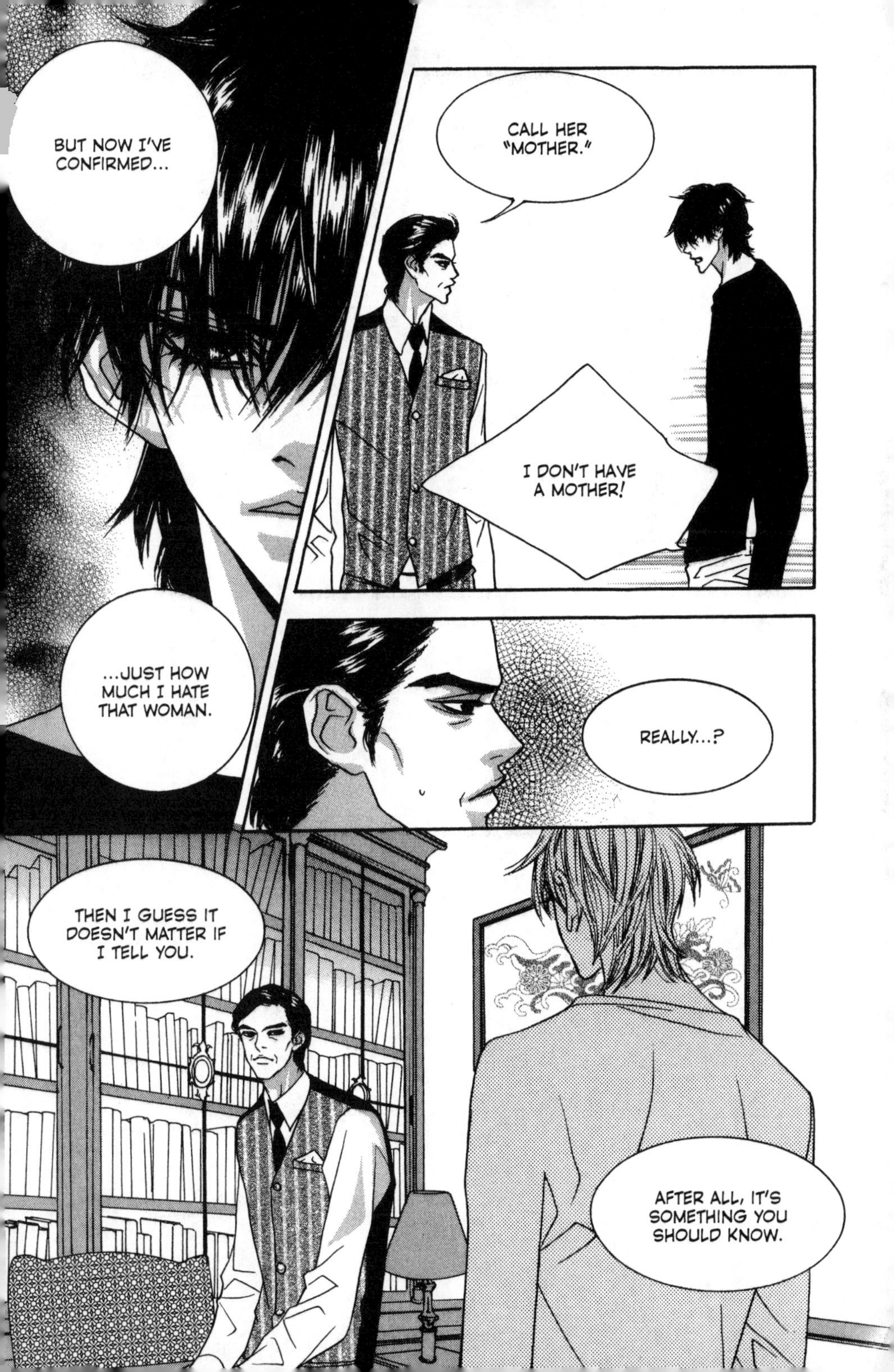
BUT NOW I'VE CONFIRMED...
...JUST HOW MUCH I HATE THAT WOMAN.
CALL HER "MOTHER."
I DON'T HAVE A MOTHER!
REALLY...?
THEN I GUESS IT DOESN'T MATTER IF I TELL YOU.
AFTER ALL, IT'S SOMETHING YOU SHOULD KNOW.

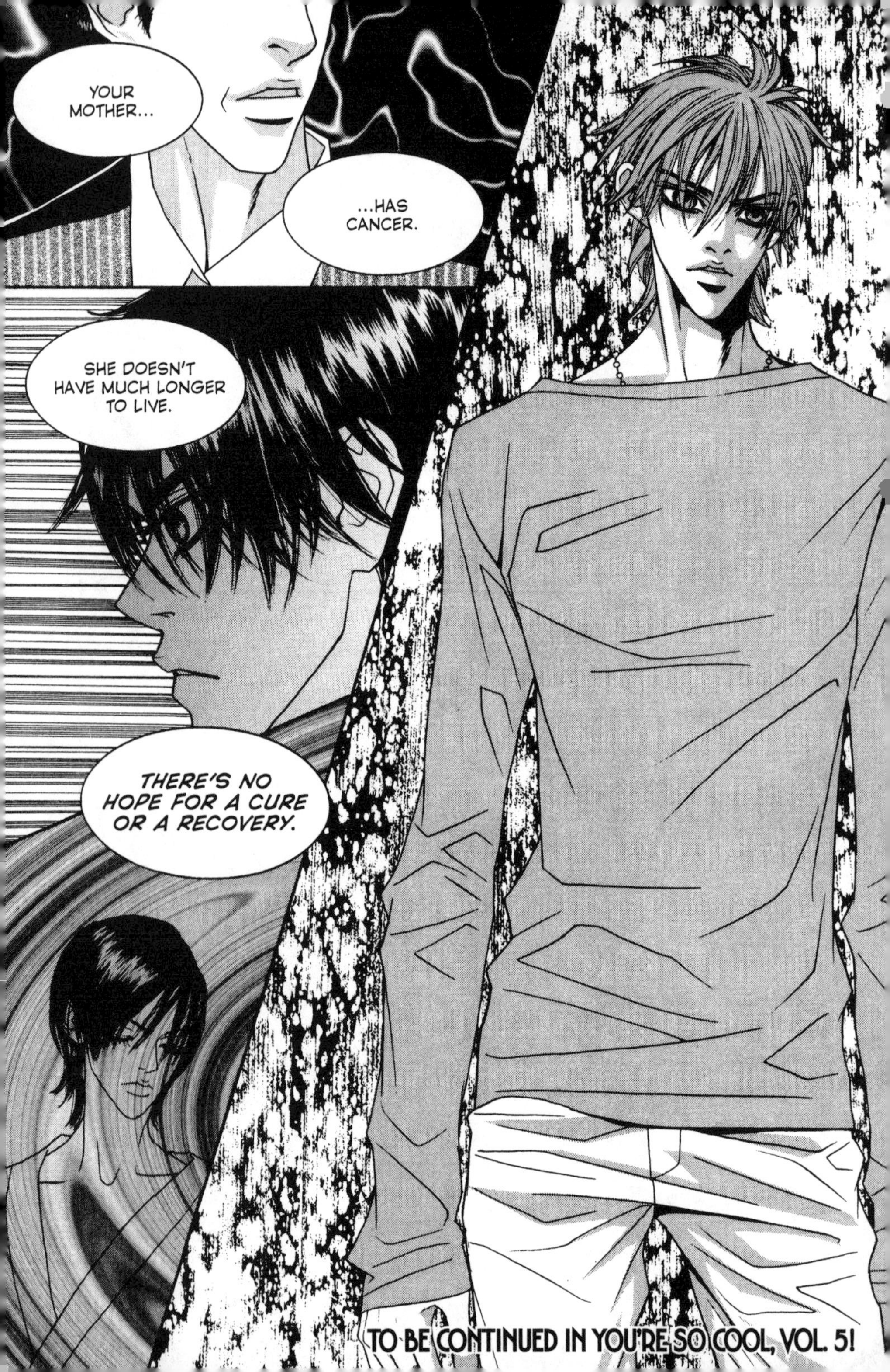
YOUR MOTHER...
...HAS CANCER.
SHE DOESN'T HAVE MUCH LONGER TO LIVE.
THERE'S NO HOPE FOR A CURE OR A RECOVERY.
TO BE CONTINUED IN YOU'RE SO COOL, VOL. 5!

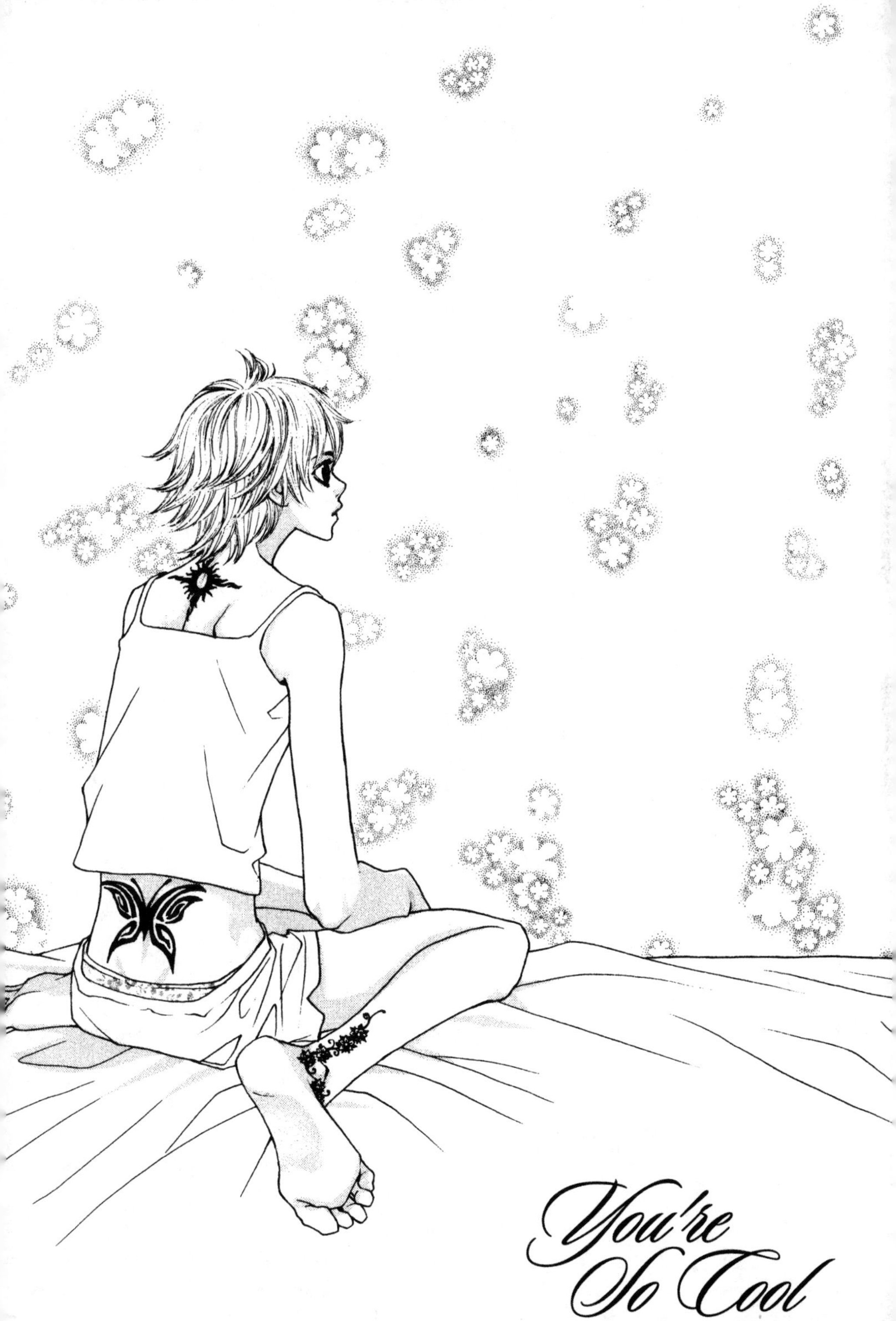
You're
So Cool

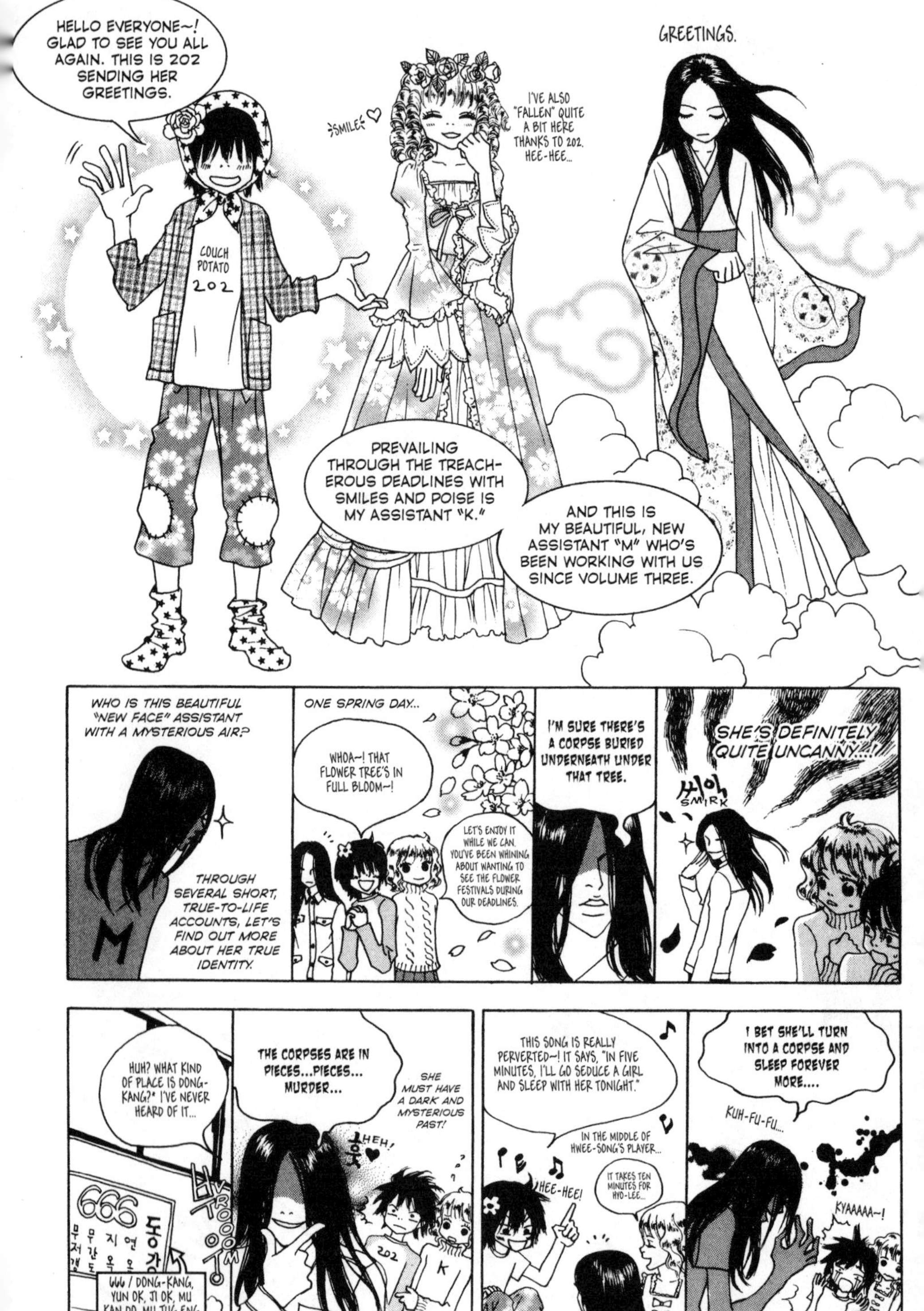
HELLO EVERYONE~! GLAD TO SEE YOU ALL AGAIN. THIS IS 202 SENDING HER GREETINGS.
COUCH POTATO 202
~SMILE~ ♡
I'VE ALSO "FALLEN" QUITE A BIT HERE THANKS TO 202. HEE-HEE...
GREETINGS.
PREVAILING THROUGH THE TREACHEROUS DEADLINES WITH SMILES AND POISE IS MY ASSISTANT "K."
AND THIS IS MY BEAUTIFUL, NEW ASSISTANT "M" WHO'S BEEN WORKING WITH US SINCE VOLUME THREE.
WHO IS THIS BEAUTIFUL "NEW FACE" ASSISTANT WITH A MYSTERIOUS AIR?
M
THROUGH SEVERAL SHORT, TRUE-TO-LIFE ACCOUNTS, LET'S FIND OUT MORE ABOUT HER TRUE IDENTITY.
ONE SPRING DAY...
WHOA~! THAT FLOWER TREE'S IN FULL BLOOM~!
LET'S ENJOY IT WHILE WE CAN. YOU'VE BEEN WHINING ABOUT WANTING TO SEE THE FLOWER FESTIVALS DURING OUR DEADLINES.
I'M SURE THERE'S A CORPSE BURIED UNDERNEATH UNDER THAT TREE.
SHE'S DEFINITELY QUITE UNCANNY...!
씨익 SMIRK
HUH? WHAT KIND OF PLACE IS DONG-KANG?* I'VE NEVER HEARD OF IT...
666
동강
666 / DONG-KANG, YUN OK, JI OK, MU KAN DO, MU JUG ENG
VROOOOM
THE CORPSES ARE IN PIECES...PIECES... MURDER...
훗 HEH! ♥
SHE MUST HAVE A DARK AND MYSTERIOUS PAST!
202
K
THIS SONG IS REALLY PERVERTED~! IT SAYS, "IN FIVE MINUTES, I'LL GO SEDUCE A GIRL AND SLEEP WITH HER TONIGHT."
IN THE MIDDLE OF HWEE-SONG'S PLAYER...
HEE-HEE!
IT TAKES TEN MINUTES FOR HYO-LEE...
I BET SHE'LL TURN INTO A CORPSE AND SLEEP FOREVER MORE....
KUH-FU-FU...
KYAAAAA~!

*DONG-KANG MEANS "PIECES" IN KOREAN.

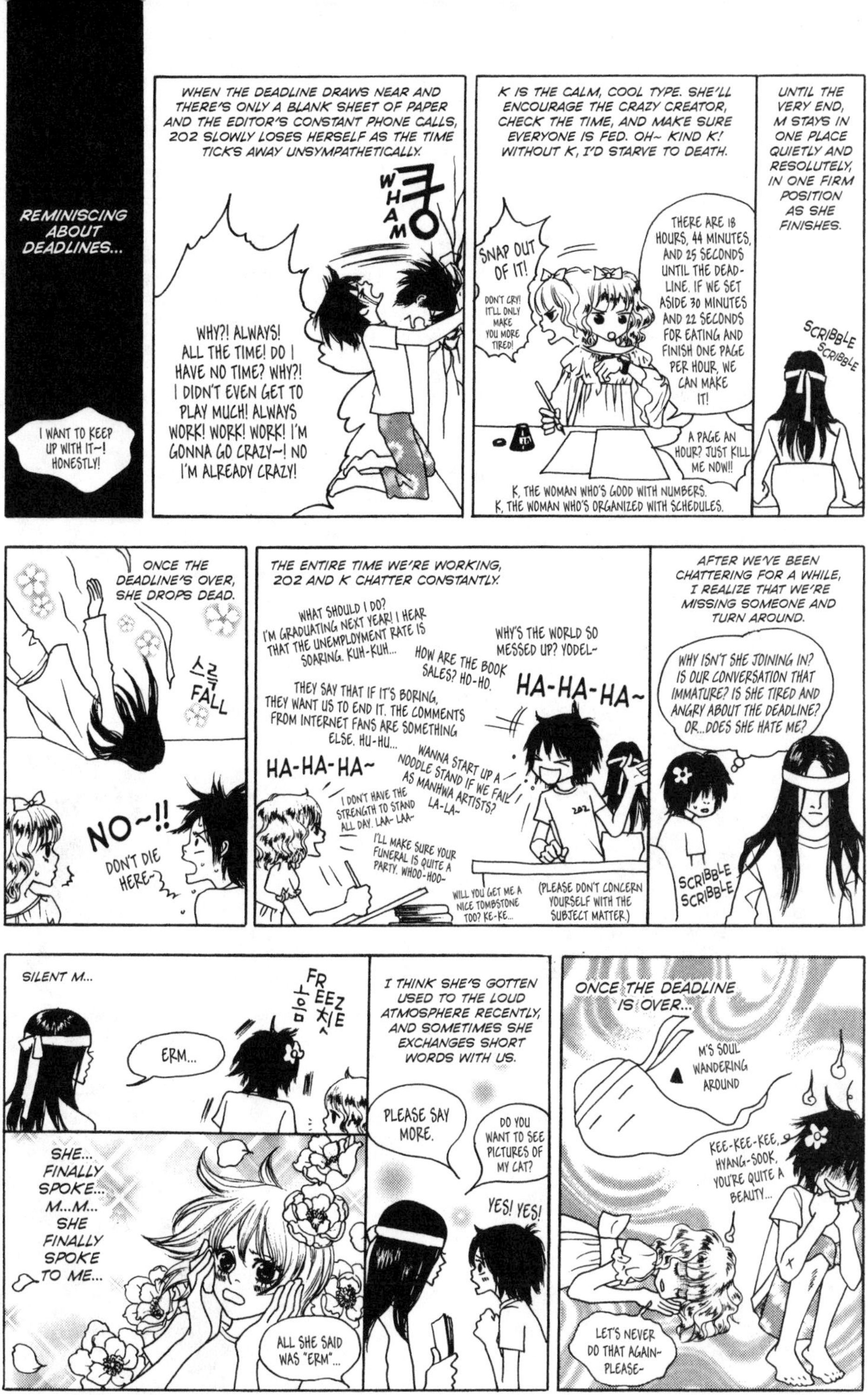
REMINISCING ABOUT DEADLINES...
I WANT TO KEEP UP WITH IT~! HONESTLY!
WHEN THE DEADLINE DRAWS NEAR AND THERE'S ONLY A BLANK SHEET OF PAPER AND THE EDITOR'S CONSTANT PHONE CALLS, 202 SLOWLY LOSES HERSELF AS THE TIME TICKS AWAY UNSYMPATHETICALLY.
WHAM
WHY?! ALWAYS! ALL THE TIME! DO I HAVE NO TIME? WHY?! I DIDN'T EVEN GET TO PLAY MUCH! ALWAYS WORK! WORK! WORK! I'M GONNA GO CRAZY~! NO I'M ALREADY CRAZY!
K IS THE CALM, COOL TYPE. SHE'LL ENCOURAGE THE CRAZY CREATOR, CHECK THE TIME, AND MAKE SURE EVERYONE IS FED. OH~ KIND K! WITHOUT K, I'D STARVE TO DEATH.
SNAP OUT OF IT!
DON'T CRY! IT'LL ONLY MAKE YOU MORE TIRED!
THERE ARE 18 HOURS, 44 MINUTES, AND 25 SECONDS UNTIL THE DEADLINE. IF WE SET ASIDE 30 MINUTES AND 22 SECONDS FOR EATING AND FINISH ONE PAGE PER HOUR, WE CAN MAKE IT!
A PAGE AN HOUR? JUST KILL ME NOW!!
K, THE WOMAN WHO'S GOOD WITH NUMBERS.
K, THE WOMAN WHO'S ORGANIZED WITH SCHEDULES.
UNTIL THE VERY END, M STAYS IN ONE PLACE QUIETLY AND RESOLUTELY, IN ONE FIRM POSITION AS SHE FINISHES.
SCRIBBLE SCRIBBLE
ONCE THE DEADLINE'S OVER, SHE DROPS DEAD.
스륵
FALL
NO~!!
DON'T DIE HERE~
THE ENTIRE TIME WE'RE WORKING, 202 AND K CHATTER CONSTANTLY.
WHAT SHOULD I DO? I'M GRADUATING NEXT YEAR! I HEAR THAT THE UNEMPLOYMENT RATE IS SOARING. KUH-KUH...
WHY'S THE WORLD SO MESSED UP? YODEL~
HOW ARE THE BOOK SALES? HO-HO.
THEY SAY THAT IF IT'S BORING, THEY WANT US TO END IT. THE COMMENTS FROM INTERNET FANS ARE SOMETHING ELSE. HU-HU...
HA-HA-HA~
HA-HA-HA~
WANNA START UP A NOODLE STAND IF WE FAIL AS MANHWA ARTISTS? LA-LA~
I DON'T HAVE THE STRENGTH TO STAND ALL DAY. LAA- LAA~
I'LL MAKE SURE YOUR FUNERAL IS QUITE A PARTY. WHOO-HOO~
WILL YOU GET ME A NICE TOMBSTONE TOO? KE-KE...
(PLEASE DON'T CONCERN YOURSELF WITH THE SUBJECT MATTER.)
202
AFTER WE'VE BEEN CHATTERING FOR A WHILE, I REALIZE THAT WE'RE MISSING SOMEONE AND TURN AROUND.
WHY ISN'T SHE JOINING IN? IS OUR CONVERSATION THAT IMMATURE? IS SHE TIRED AND ANGRY ABOUT THE DEADLINE? OR...DOES SHE HATE ME?
SCRIBBLE SCRIBBLE
SILENT M...
FREEZE
흠칫
ERM...
SHE... FINALLY SPOKE... M...M... SHE FINALLY SPOKE TO ME...
ALL SHE SAID WAS "ERM"...
I THINK SHE'S GOTTEN USED TO THE LOUD ATMOSPHERE RECENTLY, AND SOMETIMES SHE EXCHANGES SHORT WORDS WITH US.
PLEASE SAY MORE.
DO YOU WANT TO SEE PICTURES OF MY CAT?
YES! YES!
ONCE THE DEADLINE IS OVER...
M'S SOUL WANDERING AROUND
KEE-KEE-KEE, HYANG-SOOK, YOU'RE QUITE A BEAUTY...
LET'S NEVER DO THAT AGAIN-PLEASE~

MESSAGE...
From 202

WHEN ONE OF MY BOOKS IS PUBLISHED, I'M VERY HAPPY, YET I ALSO HAVE MANY REGRETS. I WISH I'D WORKED HARDER ON IT AND THAT I HADN'T SKIMMED OVER THINGS THAT I WAS TOO IGNORANT TO NOTICE. EVEN THOUGH I KNOW I DECIDED TO LET CERTAIN THINGS GO WHEN I DIDN'T HAVE ENOUGH TIME OR WAS TOO TIRED, THESE GLARING FLAWS ARE ALL I CAN SEE. UGH... THERE ARE MANY THINGS I LACK, BUT THANK YOU FOR LIKING THIS BOOK ANYWAY.

I WORK OVERNIGHT, BOTHER THE PEOPLE AROUND ME, LIE THROUGH MY TEETH, AND HAVE NO SOCIAL LIFE. I'M ALMOST A HERMIT. AH-HA-HA-HA...

I GIVE MANY THANKS TO K, MY GUARDIAN ANGEL, WHO'S ALWAYS BY MY SIDE WITH PATIENCE AND LOVE. AND MANY THANKS ALSO TO M, THE QUEEN OF SINCERITY AND THOUGHTFULNESS. I TRUST HER COMPLETELY. (THOUGH SHE TURNED INTO A SCARY CHARACTER IN THE MINI COMIC, SHE'S A SWEETIE AND TRULY LOVES ANIME AND MUSIC.) THANK YOU VERY, VERY MUCH, YOU TWO.

YOON-SOOK, CONGRATULATIONS. LET'S WALK TOGETHER DOWN THE ROAD OF DARKNESS. AH-HA-HA-HA...

THOUGH IT WAS ONLY FOR A SHORT TIME, I'VE GROWN FOND OF EDITOR TAE-HYUNG KIM. I'LL FOREVER TREASURE OUR HAPPY MEMORIES.

AFTER HER PREGNANCY, EDITOR JI-EUN YOON HAS BECOME EVEN MORE LADY-LIKE. THANK YOU VERY MUCH, AND I LOOK FORWARD TO CONTINUING TO WORK TOGETHER.

THANK YOU FOR YOUR SUPPORT, EVEN WITH THE DANGER OF BECOMING AN OUTCAST, JI-HAE. THANK YOU~!

MOON-HEE, YOU'VE TOUCHED MY HEART SEVERAL TIMES. SOO-JUNG, ANNA, AND SOO-JIN...AND EVERY ONE FROM THE WHA FAN CLUB, YOU GUYS ARE MY NUMBER ONE FAVORITES. THANK YOU FOR KINDLY WATCHING OVER ME.

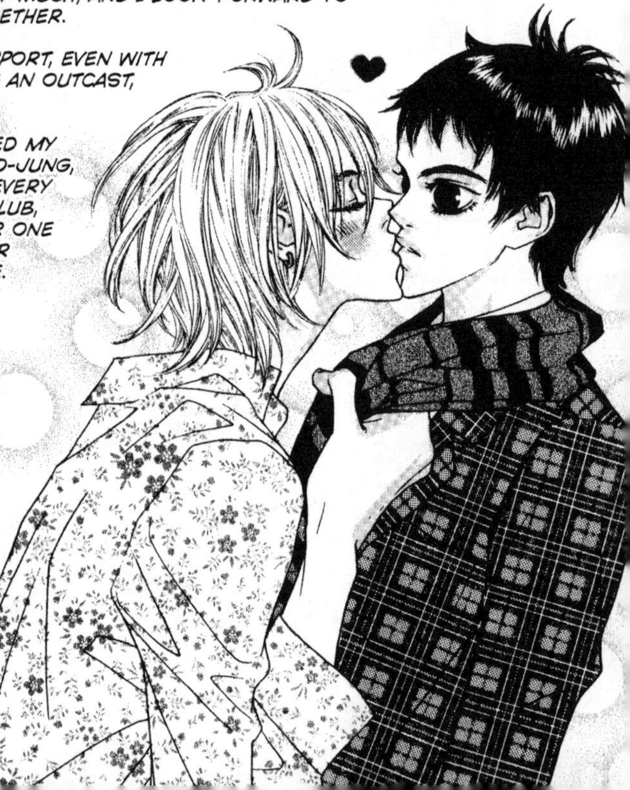

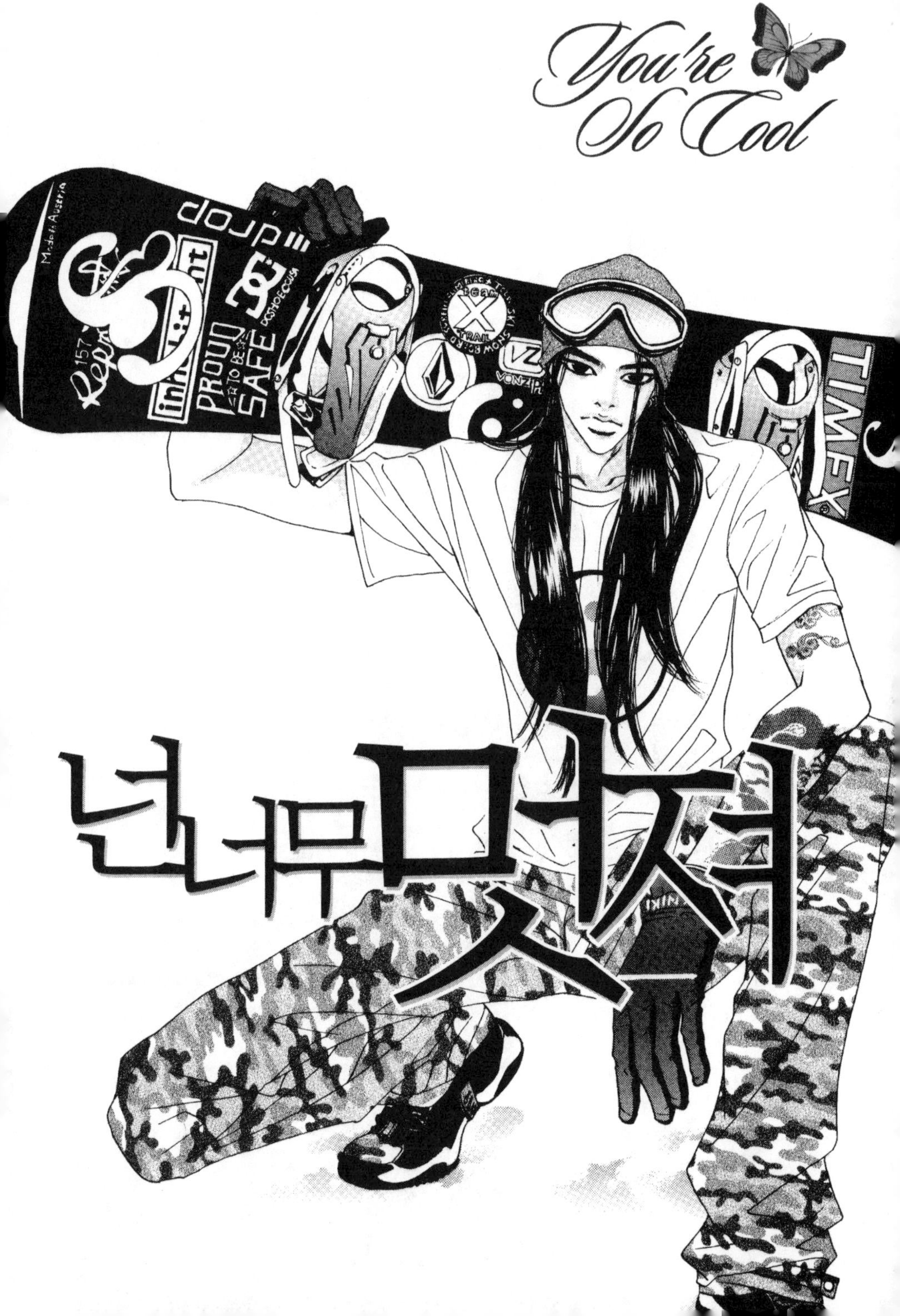
You're So Cool
넌 너무 멋져

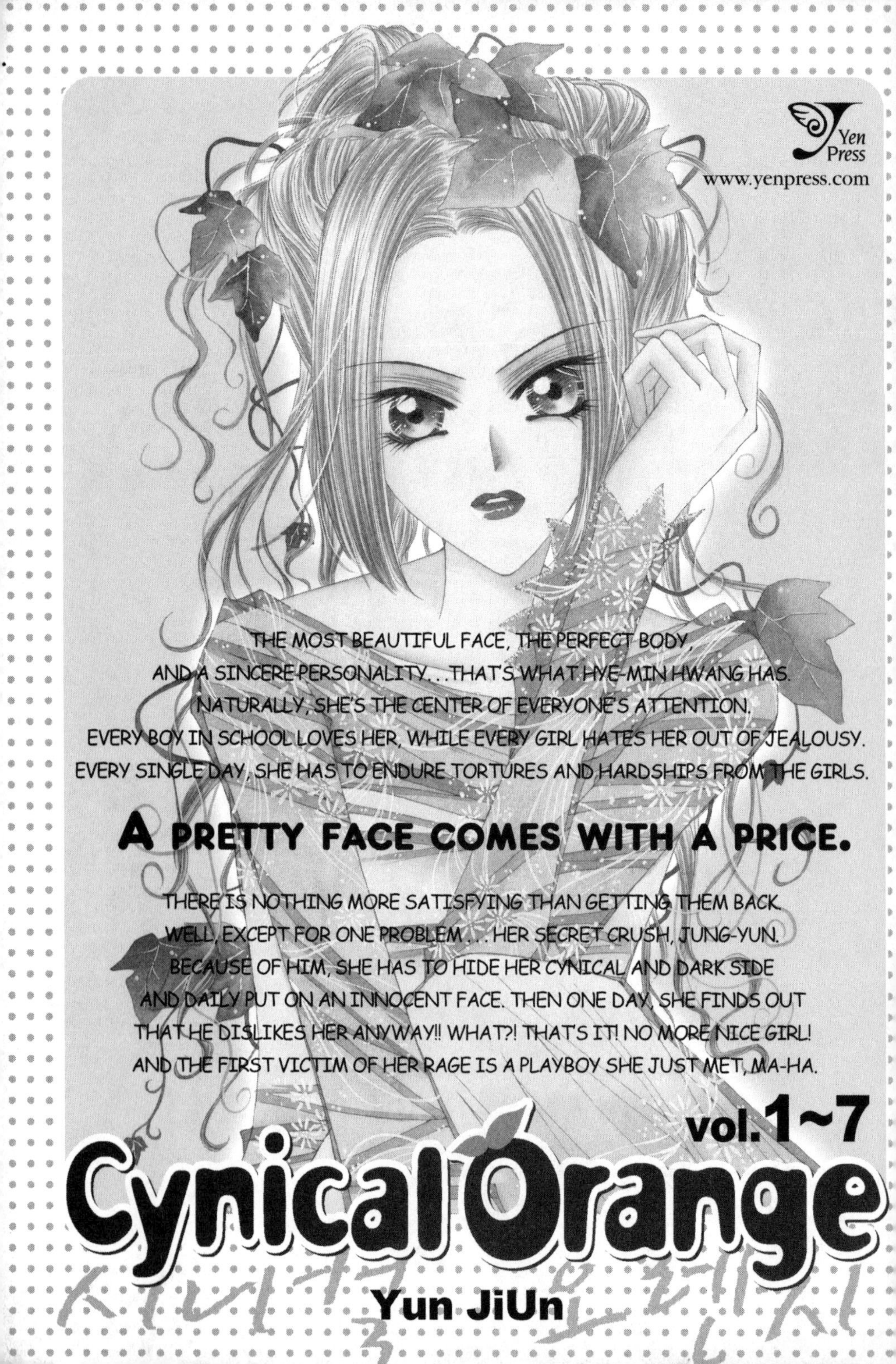
Yen Press
www.yenpress.com
THE MOST BEAUTIFUL FACE, THE PERFECT BODY,
AND A SINCERE PERSONALITY. . .THAT'S WHAT HYE-MIN HWANG HAS.
NATURALLY, SHE'S THE CENTER OF EVERYONE'S ATTENTION.
EVERY BOY IN SCHOOL LOVES HER, WHILE EVERY GIRL HATES HER OUT OF JEALOUSY.
EVERY SINGLE DAY, SHE HAS TO ENDURE TORTURES AND HARDSHIPS FROM THE GIRLS.
A PRETTY FACE COMES WITH A PRICE.
THERE IS NOTHING MORE SATISFYING THAN GETTING THEM BACK.
WELL, EXCEPT FOR ONE PROBLEM . . . HER SECRET CRUSH, JUNG-YUN.
BECAUSE OF HIM, SHE HAS TO HIDE HER CYNICAL AND DARK SIDE
AND DAILY PUT ON AN INNOCENT FACE. THEN ONE DAY, SHE FINDS OUT
THAT HE DISLIKES HER ANYWAY!! WHAT?! THAT'S IT! NO MORE NICE GIRL!
AND THE FIRST VICTIM OF HER RAGE IS A PLAYBOY SHE JUST MET, MA-HA.
vol.1~7
Cynical Orange
Yun JiUn

Totally new Arabian nights, where Shahrazad is a guy!

Everyone knows the story of Shahrazad and her wonderful tales from the Arabian Nights. For one thousand and one nights, the stories that she created entertained the mad Sultan and eventually saved her life. In this version, Shahrazad is a guy who wanted to save his sister from the mad Sultan by disguising himself as a woman. When he puts his life on the line, what kind of strange and unique stories would he tell? This new twist on one of the greatest classical tales might just keep you awake for another ONE THOUSAND AND ONE NIGHTS.

Yen Press

www.yenpress.com

Available at bookstores near you!

One thousand and one nights 1~7

Han SeungHee · Jeon JinSeok

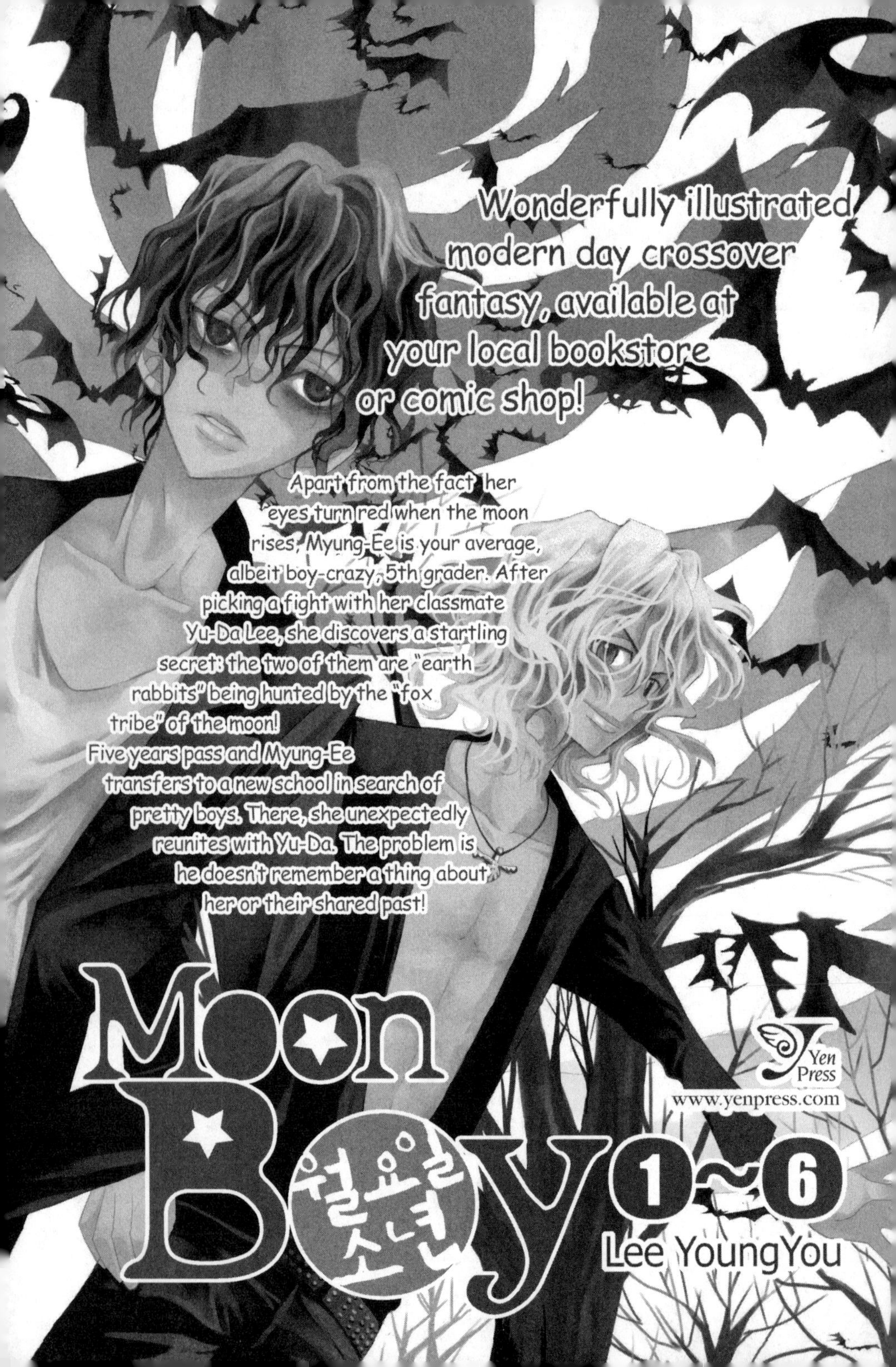
Wonderfully illustrated modern day crossover fantasy, available at your local bookstore or comic shop!
Apart from the fact her eyes turn red when the moon rises, Myung-Ee is your average, albeit boy-crazy, 5th grader. After picking a fight with her classmate Yu-Da Lee, she discovers a startling secret: the two of them are "earth rabbits" being hunted by the "fox tribe" of the moon!
Five years pass and Myung-Ee transfers to a new school in search of pretty boys. There, she unexpectedly reunites with Yu-Da. The problem is he doesn't remember a thing about her or their shared past!
Moon Boy
월요일 소년
1~6
Lee YoungYou
Yen Press
www.yenpress.com